Sleeping price codes

M000209810

L	over US$400
A	US$300-399
B	US$175-299
C	US$100-174
D	US$50-99
E	US$20-49
F	under US$20

Prices refer to the cost of a double room, not including service charge or meals unless otherwise stated.

Eating price codes

ŤŤŤ	over US$25
ŤŤ	US$15-25
Ť	under US$15

Prices refer to the cost of a two-course meal for one person, including a soft drink, beer or a glass of wine.

Footprint story

It was 1921

Ireland had just been partitioned, the British miners were striking for more pay and the federation of British industry had an idea. Exports were booming in South America – how about a handbook for businessmen trading in that far away continent? The Anglo-South American Handbook was born that year, written by W Koebel, the most prolific writer on Latin America of his day.

1924

Two editions later the book was 'privatized' and in 1924, in the hands of Royal Mail, the steamship company for South America, it became The South American Handbook, subtitled 'South America in a nutshell'. This annual publication became the 'bible' for generations of travellers to South America and remains so to this day. In the early days travel was by sea and the Handbook gave all the details needed for the long voyage from Europe. What to wear for dinner; how to arrange a cricket match with the Cable & Wireless staff on the Cape Verde Islands and a full account of the journey from Liverpool up the Amazon to Manaus: 5898 miles without changing cabin!

1939

As the continent opened up, the South American Handbook reported the new Pan Am flying boat services, and the fortnightly airship service from Rio to Europe on the Graf Zeppelin. For reasons still unclear but with extraordinary determination, the annual editions continued through the Second World War.

1970s

Many more people discovered South America and the backpacking trail started to develop. All the while the Handbook was gathering fans, including literary vagabonds such as Paul Theroux and Graham Greene (who once sent some updates addressed to "The publishers of the best travel guide in the world, Bath, England").

1990s

During the 1990s the company set about developing a new travel guide series using this legendary title as the flagship. By 1997 there were over a dozen guides in the series and the Footprint imprint was launched.

2000s

The series grew quickly and there were soon Footprint travel guides covering more than 150 countries. In 2004, Footprint launched its first thematic guide: Surfing Europe, packed with colour photographs, maps and charts. This was followed by further thematic guides such as Diving the World, Snowboarding the World, Body and Soul escapes, Travel with Kids and European City Breaks.

2010

Today we continue the traditions of the last 89 years that have served legions of travellers so well. We believe that these help to make Footprint guides different. Our policy is to use authors who are genuine experts who write for independent travellers; people possessing a spirit of adventure, looking to get off the beaten track.

Zimbabwe Handbook

Lizzie Williams

Zimbabwe began life after independence in 1980, with one of the best transport and communication infrastructures in Africa, a solid industrial base, a thriving tourism industry, and with towns and cities that were ordered, safe and well maintained.

While this is manifestly no longer the case as a result of the country's troubled political and economic woes in the last decade or so, Zimbabwe still has well-protected national parks, which are home to a full range of African animals, and a network of lodges and hotels that, even in the midst of the crisis, offer world-class standards of accommodation and service. There are also a number of museum sites and monuments, such as the ruins of Great Zimbabwe, which showcase the fractured history of the local society, while the urban arts, music and restaurant scenes have proved surprisingly resilient.

Zimbabwe's modern difficulties have never affected tourists, and now that the country's reputation for stability is improving in leaps and bounds, tourism in Zimbabwe is flourishing once again. Wherever you go in Zimbabwe, ordinary people very much welcome travellers – and their tourist dollars – to the country.

This page Makishi dancers beating drums, Victoria Falls.
Previous page Plains zebras, Hwange National Park.

Highlights

① The broad streets of Harare, Zimbabwe's capital, are lined with colonial buildings and flowering trees. ▶ page 52.

② The opportunity to walk with lions and swim with elephants in Antelope Park. ▶ page 86.

③ The rolling green hills and mountain streams full of trout in the Eastern Highlands, and are a hiker's paradise. ▶ page 93.

④ The 11th-century structures of Great Zimbabwe are the oldest in southern Africa. ▶ page 121.

⑤ Gonarezhou National Park where three rivers form a natural oasis for hundreds of species of birds and other wildlife. ▶ page 125.

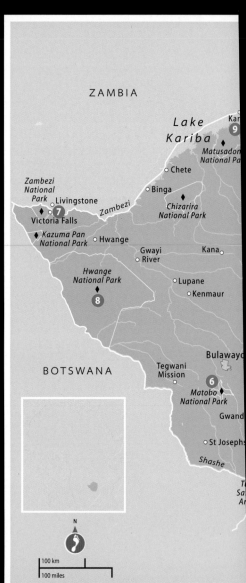

ZAMBIA

Lake Kariba

Kar

⑨

Matusadon National Par

○ Chete

● Binga

Chizarira National Park

Zambezi National Park

Livingstone

○

Zambezi

Victoria Falls

Kazuma Pan National Park ○ Hwange

Gwayi River ○

Kana ○

⑦

Hwange National Park

⑧

Lupane ○
Kenmaur ○

BOTSWANA

Tegwani Mission ○

Bulawayo

⑥

Matobo National Park

Gwand

○ St Josephs

Shashe

T Sa A

N

100 km
100 miles

⑥ Matobo National Park, an incredible landscape of balancing rocks that protects rhino, leopard and over 3000 ancient San rock paintings. ▶▶ page 144.

⑦ Victoria Falls, the 'smoke that thunders', is a UNESCO World Heritage Site and Africa's adrenalin capital. ▶▶ page 160.

⑧ Hwange National Park known for its thriving elephant population and packs of wild dog. ▶▶ page 204.

⑨ A houseboat on beautiful Lake Kariba is ideal for exploring the wildlife-laden shores or fishing for bream or tigerfish. ▶▶ page 220.

⑩ Mana Pools National Park on the banks of the Zambezi is famous for canoeing and walking safaris. ▶▶ page 222.

Map labels:

MOZAMBIQUE

Zambezi

Mana Pools National Park

⓪

kuti

Zambezi Escarpment

Muzarabani

Madadzi

Nyamapanda

Chinhoyi

Mutoko

HARARE

①

Lake Chivero

Gadzema

Chitungwisa

Nyanga National Park

Golden Valley

Juliasdale ♦

Ngwema

Kweke

Mutare

Gweru

②

Masvingo

Chimanimani National Park ♦

Zvishavane

Lake Mutirikwi National Park

④

Birchenough Bridge

West Nicholson

Hippo Valley

③

Gonarezhou National Park ♦

⑤

Mazunga

Beitbridge

Sango

Limpopo

SOUTH AFRICA

Clockwise from top

Eastern Highlands.

The structures of Great Zimbabwe.

Gonarezhou National Park.

Mana Pools National Park.

Lake Kariba.

Clockwise from top

Matobo National Park.

Harare.

Antelope Park.

Victoria Falls.

Next page Hwange National Park.

Contents

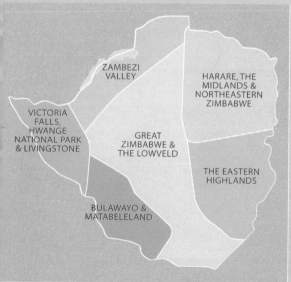

Frugal Travel Guy
Travel Treasure Trove
Today Show

Contents

Footprint features

Essentials

Planning your trip

Where to go

Though making news for all the wrong reasons in recent years, Zimbabwe was once, and will be again, among the principal tourist destinations in Southern Africa. A modest-sized, landlocked country situated between the tropic of Capricorn and the Equator, with a gorgeous climate, friendly people and a wide spectrum of landscapes and attractions, it can hardly be otherwise. The country offers one of the African continent's finest and largest concentrations of wildlife – most people visit in pursuit of the Big Five – and more than 11% of Zimbabwe's land has been set aside as parks and game reserves. Whilst the journey may be rough on the parks' bumpy and slippery roads, there is a wide range of locations in which to watch game. And you are not confined to the back of a Land Rover; walking, horse riding, canoeing and even elephant-back safaris are all on offer.

Not so well known is Zimbabwe's birdlife; the country has a huge number of species found in the savannah regions, along the rivers, and in the highlands to the east.

The Victoria Falls are the principal attraction. The mighty Zambezi spills dramatically into the Bakota Gorge, where there are endless ways to experience the river. The energy and power of an almost 2-km-wide body of water crashing into the gorge 100 m below is a spectacular sight.

Zimbabwe is also the location of the oldest stone structure south of the Sahara and Africa's largest ancient stone monument after the Pyramids: Great Zimbabwe, from which the nation takes its name.

The capital, Harare, formerly called Salisbury, is Zimbabwe's commercial and industrial centre and the location of the international airport, though flights from South Africa also arrive at Victoria Falls. There's nothing much to keep you in Harare for long, but Bulawayo, Zimbabwe's second city, is home to some interesting museums and is close to Matobo National Park. This has one of the best-protected populations of black rhino in southern Africa, and piles of balancing granite rocks conceal ancient rock paintings and the grave of Cecil John Rhodes.

Hwange National Park covers the easternmost edge of the Kalahari and is Zimbabwe's largest park; it is home to a staggering number of elephants. You can experience another aspect of the Zambezi on Lake Kariba, where the Kariba dam has halted the course of the river and formed a lake with over 2000 km of uncluttered shoreline, populated by enormous numbers of game and best enjoyed from the sunny decks of a houseboat. Alternatively, explore the river in Mana Pools National Park on a tranquil multi-day canoe safari.

Some of the game lodges and hotels are not as luxurious as in other regions of Africa, but they are improving, and some first-rate small establishments are starting to appear on the safari circuit.

Packing for Zimbabwe

A good rule of thumb is to take half the clothes you think you'll need and double the money. Laundry services are cheap and reliable in Zimbabwe and you shouldn't need to bring many clothes. A backpack or travelpack (a hybrid backpack/suitcase), rather than a rigid suitcase, is practical and survives the rigours of travel well. A lock for your luggage is strongly advised – there are cases of pilfering by airport baggage handlers the world over and Zimbabwe is no exception. Light cotton clothing is best, with a fleece or woollen jumper for evenings, and long pants to guard against mosquitoes, which are most prevalent in the early evening. However, exactly what you take will depend on the time of year: it can be sweltering before the rains (September to October) and freezing in the depths of winter (June to July). Even in summer, it may be chilly on a 0600 game drive in, say, Hwange National Park, but by 0900 it will have warmed up significantly, so bring clothes to cover all eventualities and dress in layers. Hikers and those intending to go on walking safaris will need comfortable walking boots that have been worn in, long socks (a stab by an acacia tree thorn can be very painful) and a raincoat – the latter being useful too for visiting the Victoria Falls, especially during the height of their spray (see box, page 164).

Note It is illegal to wear camouflage-patterned clothes in Zimbabwe. During the day (even in winter) you will need a hat, sunglasses and high-factor sun cream. A torch is also a good idea; although power supplies are significantly better than they were, Zimbabwe is still suffering from occasional electricity blackouts and generators cannot always be relied on. Before you leave home, send yourself an email to a web-based account with details of your passport, driver's licence, traveller's cheques, credit cards and travel insurance. Be sure that someone at home also has access to this information.

Itineraries

None of the circuits below is a complete itinerary in itself, and they are not set in stone. Rather, they are regional suggestions for travellers wishing to explore a certain part of the country. Harare or Victoria Falls are the usual arrival points into Zimbabwe for international travellers, so what you do rather depends on where you start.

One week

No visit to Zimbabwe is complete without seeing the **Victoria Falls**. They are best appreciated from the spray-drenched rainforest of the **Victoria Falls National Park**, while whitewater rafting and riverboarding are the best ways to get wet and wild in the world-renowned Grade V rapids. Or you could bungee jump 111 m off the Victoria Falls railway bridge, ride a flying fox or abseil into the gorge. You could take a scenic flight by helicopter or microlight through the 'smoke that thunders'. The area above the falls is also enticing, with an array of game to see and palm-dotted islands to enjoy. Sunset cruises and canoeing on the Upper Zambezi brings you amongst hippos and crocodiles, and you can take an elephant ride, walking safari or horse trail in the surrounding national parks and wilderness areas.

The town of Victoria Falls, affectionately abbreviated to Vic Falls by anyone who's ever been there, lies just a kilometre or so from the falls themselves and offers accommodation options to suit all budgets. The Victoria Falls are shared with Zambia, so a walk or transfer across the famous Victoria Falls Bridge brings you to the town of Livingstone, which again has facilities for tourists and various kinds of activities.

How long you stay in this region, depends on how much you want to do. There's easily four days' worth here, and you'll need at least a week to fit everything in. There is also the option of combining trips to Victoria Falls with day or overnight organized safaris to **Hwange National Park**, to witness its huge herds of elephant converging on the waterholes, or to **Chobe National Park**, not far over the border in Botswana, again famed for its large elephant population.

If arriving in **Harare**, Zimbabwe's capital and largest city, situated in the middle of the country on the highveld, there are one or two attractions to keep you occupied for a day or two (it's surprisingly sleepy for a capital city). The National Gallery houses a display of Shona soft-stone carvings, while some of the original letters and notebooks of the early explorers can be seen in the National Archives.

From Harare it's a day's drive to Bulawayo, Zimbabwe's second biggest city. The country's geographic hub, it is just as easily reached from Victoria Falls, a similar distance away. Between Harare and Bulawayo, at **Gweru**, the excellent **Antelope Park** is worth two nights to enjoy a number of activities, including walking with lions. In Bulawayo, a day is needed to visit the Natural History Museum, the National Gallery, and the Bulawayo Railway, and day or overnight safaris can be arranged to visit the rhinos and rocks in the **Matobo National Park**. From Bulawayo, there is the option of returning to Harare or continuing on to Victoria Falls, again a day's drive, or you could take the overnight train.

Two to three weeks
Lake Kariba, also a day's drive away from Harare, is an artificial inland sea of the **Zambezi Valley**. It is the continent's third largest dam, after Aswan in Egypt and Cahora Bassa on the Zambezi in neighbouring Mozambique. Probably the nicest and most relaxing way to see the lake is from a houseboat over a period of three to four days, but make sure your boat has a swimming cage, as you will need to take cooling dips. Stunning sunsets are a distinctive feature of Kariba, as are the bleached skeletal trunks and bare branches of dead trees that were drowned in the dam all those years ago. They make excellent perches for fish eagles, cormorants and other waterbirds.

There are a number of parks in this region, but the most accessible for most of the year is the **Mana Pools National Park**, where peaceful three- to nine-day canoe safaris can be arranged on the **Zambezi River**; you camp along the sandbanks and cook over open fires.

Also within a day's drive from Harare, the **Eastern Highlands** are noted for their beauty along the Zimbabwe border with Mozambique. The main gateway to the region is **Mutare**, cupped within the mountains. A short drive away is the scenic **Vumba**, an area of ancient forest and sub-tropical plants, where you can see arrays of ferns and flowers at the Vumba Botanic Gardens. Further south are the beautiful forests of **Chimanimani**, which are well worth a day's hike to visit the spectacular **Bridal Veil Falls**. To the north of Mutare is **Nyanga**, a region of mountains, waterfalls and trout streams, where visitors can walk amid magnificent scenery, play golf, fish and enjoy the mountain air. Accommodation in this region is provided at national park rest cottages and in several fine hotels.

Situated in **Masvingo**, also a day's drive from Harare, the **Great Zimbabwe Ruins** are a World Heritage Site and testimony to the region's settlement by ancient civilizations. An unfathomable ruin nearly 1000 years old, it was once home to 10,000 ancestors of the Shona people. Allow at least half a day to explore the ruins. Self-sufficient visitors with their own 4WDs may want to journey further south to the **Gonarezhou National Park**, famous for its magnificent red sandstone cliffs; due to its remoteness and the difficulties involved in getting there, it requires at least three nights, especially if you want to enjoy the solitude.

When to go

There is no bad time to visit Zimbabwe, but depending upon what you wish to see and do there are certain months that are better than others. The climate is warm without being oppressive, with a daily sunshine average of seven hours, all year round. Generally, days are bright and sunny and nights clear and cool, though nights can get very cold in July, which is in the middle of the winter. As well as hats, sunglasses and sunblock, you will need a warm fleece for when the sun starts to fade. Temperatures and rainfall are directly influenced by altitude. The highveld and Eastern Highlands are cooler and the lowveld and the Zambezi Valley hotter, with summer temperatures often soaring over 35°C, well above the highveld average of 28°C. November to April are the rainy summer months, with the dry winter running from May to July, when daytime winter temperatures range from 13-20°C, but can fall to 5°C at night. The August to October period is hot and dry throughout the country and is the best time for game viewing as the animals are concentrated around rivers and waterholes. November through to April can be difficult for game viewing, as the tracks in the parks can get muddy. The best time for birdwatching is October to April when migrant species arrive from the northern hemisphere.

The Victoria Falls are most spectacular when the volume of water is high. This

Rainfall and climate charts

	Average temperature	Average rainfall
Harare		
Jan	16-26 °C	196 mm
Feb	16-26 °C	178 mm
Mar	14-26 °C	117 mm
Apr	13-26 °C	28 mm
May	9-23 °C	13 mm
Jun	7-21 °C	3 mm
Jul	7-21 °C	0 mm
Aug	8-23 °C	3 mm
Sep	12-26 °C	5 mm
Oct	14-28 °C	28 mm
Nov	16-27 °C	97 mm
Dec	16-26 °C	163 mm
Bulawayo		
Jan	16-27 °C	142 mm
Feb	16-27 °C	109 mm
Mar	15-26 °C	84 mm
Apr	13-26 °C	18 mm
May	9-23 °C	10 mm
Jun	7-21 °C	3 mm
Jul	7-21 °C	0 mm
Aug	9-23 °C	0 mm
Sep	12-27 °C	5 mm
Oct	15-29 °C	20 mm
Nov	16-29 °C	81 mm
Dec	16-28 °C	122 mm
Victoria Falls		
Jan	18-30 °C	168 mm
Feb	18-29 °C	126 mm
Mar	17-30 °C	70 mm
Apr	14-29 °C	24 mm
May	10-27 °C	3 mm
Jun	6-25 °C	1 mm
Jul	6-25 °C	0 mm
Aug	8-28 °C	0 mm
Sep	13-32 °C	2 mm
Oct	17-33 °C	27 mm
Nov	18-32 °C	64 mm
Dec	18-30 °C	174 mm

depends not only on how much rain the falls get themselves but also on how much rain has fallen upstream in Namibia and Zambia, and also in Angola, where tributaries feed the Zambezi. By contrast, arguably the best whitewater rafting in the world occurs in low water seasons, roughly August to December, when the falls are at their lowest in terms of volume and width, for then the level of water in the Zambezi drops to expose the fun-filled rapids. The prevalence of (potentially malaria-carrying) mosquitoes is highest during the rainy season from November to April, but precautions against getting bitten should be taken all year round.

What to do

Birdwatching
ⓘ www.africanbirdclub.org.
Over 650 bird species have been recorded in Zimbabwe and birdwatching can be an added pleasure while looking for animals on safari. Serious twitchers should head for Mana Pools National Park, but anywhere along the Zambezi River, especially Lake Kariba, is a hotspot for birding. Hwange National Park has 420 species alone, including large populations of raptors, while Gonarezhou and Matobo national parks are also good for raptors and vultures. Ewanrigg Botanical Gardens near Harare draw large numbers of sunbirds, attracted to its collection of aloes and cycads. Given its leafy environs, even Harare is good for birdwatching.

Bungee jumping
The 111-m bungee jump off the Victoria Falls Bridge is hard to beat, with the falls behind and the swirling Zambezi below. Over 50,000 people to date have committed themselves to the thrill of jumping off the bridge. Ankle and body harnesses are attached to participants, who are winched back onto the bridge afterwards. Jumps are recorded with photographs and video, available to buy along with been-there done-that T-shirts.

Elephant riding
ⓘ www.wildhorizons.com, www.safpar.net, www.antelopepark.co.zw.
Lumbering through the bush on the back of an elephant is an unforgettable experience. There are three places where you can ride an elephant: at Victoria Falls, in Livingstone in Zambia, and at the Antelope Park near Gweru. As well as riding the elephants, guests are encouraged to interact with them and an interesting presentation details their lives and history. While on the ride you may see wild elephant and other plains game.

Fishing
ⓘ Details of local operators are listed in the relevant chapters.
The Zambezi River is well known for its tigerfish, bream and barbel fishing, especially in the dry season, when the water is clear and the fish can see bait clearly. If you take one of the longer canoeing options, or stay at one of the lodges on the river, fishing tackle is usually available for guests, along with boats and guides; it is also available on all Lake Kariba houseboats. A tigerfishing tournament (www.kitft.co.zw) is held annually at Lake Kariba in March and attracts some 300 teams and 500 boats. Trout fishing can be done in Nyanga National Park, but you'll need to arrange tackle with the hotels.

Golf

ⓘ www.golfzone.co.zw.

There are some 30 golf courses in Zimbabwe. Most permit temporary membership and some hire out clubs. The most popular with visitors are the 18-hole courses at the **Elephant Hills Hotel** in Victoria Falls, where you are likely to share a tee with a warthog, and the 18-hole course at the **Leopard Rock Hotel** in Vumba in the Eastern Highlands, which is the country's most scenic course. The Zimbabwe Open is held at the **Royal Harare Golf Club** in April. Prime Minister Tsvangirai is a keen golfer.

Hire-wire activities

ⓘ www.wildhorizons.com, www.thezambeziswing.com.

On both the Zimbabwean and the Zambian side of the Victoria Falls, the Bakota Gorge has been strung with a series of cables for high-wire activities such as the flying fox, zip-liner, gorge swing and abseil. Given that all the activities take place 120 m above the Zambezi, these, like the bungee jump, provide a real adrenalin buzz.

Horse riding

ⓘ Varden Safaris, www.riding-in-hwange.com.

Varden Safaris arrange multi-day horse safaris in Hwange National Park using a combination of lodges and mobile camps for accommodation. Short three-hour rides are available from Victoria Falls with Zambezi Horse Trails, which go along the river and can be booked through any of the tour operators. In Livingstone, 1½-hour rides can be arranged from the **Royal Livingstone** and **Zambezi Sun Hotels**. On horseback you can get quite close to animals as they have no fear of horses.

Safaris and game reserves

Going on safari can be a most rewarding experience in Zimbabwe. There are a number of national parks owned by the government and administered by the **Zimbabwe Parks and Wildlife Management Services**, and some in the private sector, such as local game ranches. While you can self-drive, you'll need a sturdy 4WD and be largely self-sufficient when it comes to fuel, water and food. Most people visit on an organized safari, which involves staying at a safari lodge, tented camp or, at the cheaper end of the scale, a campsite, and going out on game drives in a specially adapted vehicle. Although you'll have a guide, it's still a good idea to take along some wildlife and bird books. However, there are other safari options, including walking and canoe safaris, and in many areas wildlife can be seen outside of the national park boundaries. This is especially true for the vervet monkey and elephant, which are fairly common, especially around Victoria Falls and Kariba. The best time of day to spot animals is early in the morning and late in the afternoon, as many animals sleep through the intense midday heat. Animals are most easily seen during the dry season, when the lack of surface water forces them to congregate around rivers and waterholes. However, the animals are in the best condition after feeding on new shoots in the rainy seasons, from November to April, when you might also be lucky enough to see breeding displays. The disadvantage of the wet season is that the thicker vegetation and the wider availability of water mean that wildlife is more dispersed and more difficult to spot; driving conditions are also far harder in deep mud as none of the park roads are paved.

Driving around endlessly searching for animals is not usually the best way to view wildlife. It is better to break up drives with stops at waterholes, picnic sites and hides. Time

Game-viewing rules

- Always, keep on the roads and tracks; off-road driving is harmful because smoke, oil and destruction of the grass layer cause soil erosion.
- Do not drive through closed roads or park areas. It is mandatory to enter and exit the parks through the authorized gates.
- In the parks which feature large game species, it is forbidden to leave the vehicle except in designated places, such as picnic sites or walking trails. The exception to this is Mana Pools where you can walk.
- Stick to the parks' opening hours; it is usually forbidden to drive from dusk to dawn. At night you are requested to stay at your lodge or campsite.
- Never harass the animals. Make as little noise as possible; do not flash lights or make sudden movements to scare them away; never try to attract the animals' attention by calling out or whistling.
- Never chase the animals and remember that they always have right of way.
- Do not feed the animals; the food you provide might make them ill, and once animals such as elephants learn that humans are a source of food they can become aggressive and dangerous.
- If camping at night in the parks, ensure that the animals cannot gain access to any food you are carrying.
- Do not throw any litter, used matches or cigarette butts; this increases fire risk in the dry season, and some animals will try to eat them.
- Do not disturb other visitors; they have the same right as you to enjoy nature. If you discover a stopped vehicle and you want to check what they are looking at, never hinder their sight or stop within their photographic field. If there is no room for another car, wait patiently for your turn; the others will eventually leave and the animals will still be there. If there is a group of vehicles, most drivers will take it in turns to occupy the prime viewing spot.
- Always turn the engine off when you are watching game up close.
- Do not speed; the speed limit is usually 40 kph. Speeding damages road surfaces, increases noise and raises the risk of running over animals.
- Wild animals are dangerous; despite their beauty their reactions are unpredictable. Don't expose yourself to unnecessary risks; excessive confidence can lead to serious accidents.

spent around a waterhole with your engine switched off gives you an opportunity to listen to the sounds of the bush and experience the rhythms of nature as game moves to and from the water. It's also worth remembering that, while speed limits are often 40 kph, the optimum speed for game viewing by car is around 15 kph. Zimbabwe's game parks and reserves are well organized; following the few park rules will ensure an enjoyable stay.

Scenic flights
ⓘ *Details of local operators are listed in the relevant chapters.*

On both sides of the Victoria Falls, in Zimbabwe and Zambia, there is the option to take helicopter flights over the falls and Upper Zambezi River. The falls look incredible from the air and this is the best way to a get a grip on their immensity and power.

Walking with lions

ⓘ *www.lionencounter.com, www.antelopepark.co.zw.*

There are three places where you can walk with lions, all run by the Conolly family: Victoria Falls, Livingstone in Zambia and at the Antelope Park near Gweru. The drill is that you walk with the captive-bred juvenile lions (under 18 months) for about 1½ hours and watch them run and play; the guide tells you all you want to know about lions and the environment.

Whitewater rafting, river-boarding, kayaking and canoeing

ⓘ *www.whitewater.safpar.com.*

Considered one of the best stretches of commercially run river in the world, the Zambezi is the place to go for top-class Grade V whitewater rafting, river-boarding and kayaking. The adrenalin junkie will get a wild roller-coaster ride on a series of 23 foaming rapids stretching for 22 km. The rapids are run in large inflatable rubber rafts and launched from just below the falls. There's some striking scenery within the deep black cliffs, but remember, at almost 100 m deep, the Bakota Gorge presents a tough climb out. You'll be glad of the cold beer at the top of the gorge after a day of being thrown around in white water and the steep climb. Gentler canoe trips can be taken on the Upper Zambezi and this is an excellent way to spot game on the riverbanks.

Getting there

Air

The two international airports in Zimbabwe are **Harare International Airport** and **Victoria Falls International Airport**. International flights arrive in Harare, while regional flights from **South Africa** link Johannesburg with Victoria Falls. The airport at Harare, the only airport in Zimbabwe equipped to deal with large aircraft, was rebuilt in 2004, although many of the international airlines discontinued their services owing to Zimbabwe's economic problems (and, for a time, the lack of airline fuel). Currently only **Air Zimbabwe** flies direct from London; most other international flights arrive in and depart from Johannesburg, where there are connections with **British Airways**, **Kulula** (a no-frills South African operator) and **South African Airways** to both Harare and Victoria. The alternative is to fly into Livingstone in **Zambia** from Johannesburg with no-frills South African airline **1Time**, **British Airways** or **South African Airways**.

From Europe

Air Zimbabwe fly direct twice a week between London Gatwick and Harare on Thursday and Monday and Harare and Gatwick on Wednesday and Sunday. Both **British Airways** and **South African Airways** fly daily from Heathrow to Harare via Johannesburg; flying time is about 17 hours, but with a four-hour stop in Johannesburg – this sounds like a long time, but the OR Tambo International Airport in Johannesburg has become so vast (it's bigger than Dubai) that this is not unreasonable. Costs from London to Harare are about US$1600 return, but deals can be found if you book well in advance. Other European airlines fly to Johannesburg.

Jet lag is not an issue when flying from Europe to Zimbabwe and South Africa, as there is only a minimal time difference.

From North America

Delta has a code share (reciprocal) agreement with **South African Airways**, which run daily direct flights from Atlanta to Johannesburg, with connections to Harare.

From Australia, New Zealand and Asia

Qantas code shares with **South African Airways**, and between them they run a direct daily flight to and from Perth and Sydney and Johannesburg, with connections from other regional centres such as Brisbane and Melbourne and Auckland in New Zealand. They will ticket onward bookings for flights to Harare or Victoria Falls. Since 2010 Virgin Atlantic's Australian offshoot **Virgin Blue** has offered two flights a week between Melbourne and Johannesburg. **Air Mauritius** flies between Perth and Johannesburg once a week with a touchdown on Mauritius. Some of the Asian airlines offer cheaper alternatives for flying to South Africa, but this normally involves flying via the hub of the airline concerned. **Singapore Airlines** offers regular flights between Sydney and Johannesburg via Singapore, and has a code-sharing agreement with **Air New Zealand**, with flights linking Auckland with Johannesburg and Cape Town via Sydney and Singapore. **Malaysia Airlines** has regular flights from Perth, Melbourne, Sydney and Darwin in Australia and Auckland in New Zealand to Kuala Lumpur, connecting with a flight to Johannesburg three times a week, which continues on to Cape Town and then Buenos Aires (Argentina). **Cathay Pacific** flies daily between Johannesburg and Hong Kong, and **Emirates** flies daily between both Cape Town and Johannesburg and Dubai. With the exception of South African Airways, from Johannesburg, local connections need to be made to Harare, Victoria Falls or Livingstone.

From Africa and the Middle East

Kenya Airways flies between London and Harare via Nairobi seven days a week, **Ethiopian Airlines** six days a week between London and Harare via Addis Ababa, and **Air Namibia** flies between London and Frankfurt and Windhoek daily and has connections on to Victoria Falls on Wednesday, Friday and Sunday. Johannesburg is served by a number of regional African airlines that link all the major cities of Africa. **Emirates** connects Johannesburg with the Middle East and then ultimately with the rest of the world via Dubai.

Airlines

1Time, www.1time.co.za.
Air Mauritius, T+230-207 7070 (Mauritius), www.airmauritius.com.
Air Namibia, T061-299 6333 (Namibia), www.airnamibia.com.na.
Air New Zealand, T0800-737000 (New Zealand), www.airnewzealand.com.
Air Zimbabwe, T04-291 2875 (Zimbabwe), www.airzimbabwe.com.
British Airways, T0870-850 9850 (UK), www.britishairways.com.
Cathay Pacific, T0852-2747 1888 (Hong Kong), www.cathaypacific.com.
Delta, T1800-221 1212 (USA), www.delta.com.
Emirates, T0870-243 2222 (UK), www.emirates.com.
Ethiopian Airlines, www.ethiopianairlines.com.
Kenya Airways, T01784-888222, www.kenya-airways.com.
Kulula, www.kulula.com.
Malaysia Airlines, T0603-7843 3000 (Malaysia), www.malaysia-airlines.com.
Qantas, T131313 (from anywhere in Australia), www.qantas.com.au.
Singapore Airlines, T065-6223 8888 (Singapore), www.singaporeair.com.
South African Airways, T011-978 1111 (South Africa), www.flysaa.com.
Virgin Blue, www.virginblue.co.au.

Discount flight agents

In the UK and Ireland
Flightbookers, T0871-223 5000, www.ebookers.com.
Flight Centre, T0870-499 9931, www.flightcentre.co.uk.
STA Travel, T0871-230 0040, www.statravel.co.uk.
Trailfinders, T0845-058 5858, www.trailfinders.com.
Travelbag, T0800-804 8911, www.travelbag.co.uk.

In North America
Air Brokers International, T1800-8833273, www.airbrokers.com.
Airtech, T1212-219 7000, www.airtech.com.
STA Travel, T1800-781 4040, www.statravel.com.
Travel CUTS, T1866-246 9762 (Canada), www.travelcuts.com.

In Australia and New Zealand
Flight Centre, T133-133 (Australia), www.flightcentre.com.au.
Skylinks, T02-9223 4277, www.skylink.com.au.
STA Travel, T134-782, www.statravel.com.au (Australia), T0800 474400, www.statravel.com.nz (New Zealand).
Travel.com.au, T1300-130482, www.travel.com.au.

Rail

While National Railways of Zimbabwe runs a network of railways within the country, there were no international services for some time; the Johannesburg to Harare service was suspended some years ago. However, in 2006, a new service opened up between Francistown in Botswana and Bulawayo, departing Francistown on Tuesday, Thursday and Saturday at 0900 and arriving in Bulawayo at 1500, and departing Bulawayo on Monday, Wednesday and Friday at 0930 and arriving in Francistown at 1500. The train has standard-class coaches with reclining seats and costs about US$5 one way.

Road

Zimbabwe has a total 18,300 km of roads; some 8700 km are paved, and most are of a surprisingly good standard, with smooth tar, regular white mileage posts and clear signposts. There are a further 9600 km of unpaved roads, but again in a fairly good gravel condition, at least outside the wet seasons. Nevertheless, a 4WD is recommended for the national parks, where the roads are little more than faint tracks and some are fairly remote with very little traffic.

Most of Zimbabwe's border posts are open from 0600 to 1800, with the exception of the Beitbridge border with South Africa, which is open 24 hours, and the Victoria Falls border with Zambia, which is open 0600-2200. Its other border posts are Plumtree, southwest of Bulawayo, and Kazungula, west of Victoria Falls, both bordering Botswana; Chirundu, north of Kariba, bordering Zambia; and Nyamapanda, Mutare and Sango, all on the eastern border with Mozambique.

Bus

Most international bus services arrive and depart at Harare's Road Port Terminal (corner of Fifth Street and Robert Mugabe Road, T04-702828). There are daily direct buses between Harare and Johannesburg and Pretoria (21 hours, about US$40) with a number of economy bus companies. These leave throughout the day with such regularity that at the Road Point Terminal they queue up one behind the other and go when full. There are also numerous economy buses from the Road Port Terminal to Lusaka in Zambia (11 hours, about US$20), Francistown in Botswana (11 hours, about US$60), and Blantyre in Malawi (11 hours, about U$60). There are dozens of booking desks in the terminal building so it's best to go the day before to secure your ticket and save the hassle of carrying luggage as you trawl the desks to book a seat.

Zimbabwe from Mozambique   From Chimoio minibuses go to Manica and the Machipanda (Mozambique)–Forbes-Mutare (Zimbabwe) border. From here, onward transport is available for the 10 km to Mutare, where you can take an economy bus or night train to Harare.

Zimbabwe from South Africa   In Johannesburg, buses depart from (and arrive at) the Park City Transit Centre in the city centre, also the site of the Johannesburg Railway Station and the terminus for the new Gautrain high speed local train. (The area around the transit centre has long had a bad reputation for muggings, so be extra vigilant and don't go wandering outside with luggage.) Many of the buses depart and arrive late at night or early in the morning, so make sure you have pre-arranged a pickup with your hotel or take a metered taxi.

The best service to use for international visitors travelling between both Harare and Bulawayo and Pretoria and Johannesburg is **Greyhound** ⓘ *Harare T04-720801, Johannesburg T+27-(0)11-611 8000, www.greyhound.co.za*, a South African company which can be booked online. It runs daily overnight services between the cities, taking around 16 to 18 hours and costing about US$60 one way. These are direct routes with no stops, and the buses are much more comfortable than the economy buses, with air conditioning, reclining seats, DVDs and refreshments. The service between Johannesburg and Harare (in both directions) departs daily at 2000 and arrives at 1230. The service between Johannesburg and Bulawayo departs Johannesburg at 2030 and arrives in Bulawayo at 1200, and departs Bulawayo again at 1600 and arrives in Johannesburg at 0545.

Another luxury bus company connecting Cape Town with Livingstone, over the border from Victoria Falls, via Windhoek, the capital of Namibia, is **Intercape** ⓘ *Cape Town, T+27(0)21-380 4400, www.intercape.co.za*. The service departs from Cape Town to Windhoek at 1000 on Tuesday, Thursday, Friday and Sunday and arrives in Windhoek at 0615, then on Monday and Friday connects with the Windhoek to Livingstone service, departing at 1730 and arriving in Livingstone the next day at 1255. Buses leave Livingstone again on Wednesday and Sunday at 1200 and arrive back in Windhoek at 0525. The Windhoek to Cape Town service leaves Windhoek on Monday, Wednesday, Friday and Sunday at 1730 and arrives in Cape Town at 1330. Costs are around US$100 one way. In Livingstone, buses stop outside Barclay's Bank in the middle of town. However, this is a very long journey with two nights on the bus and a lengthy stopover in Windhoek. The best and quickest way to get between Cape Town and Livingstone or Victoria Falls is to fly, though this is a lot more expensive. For more information about crossing the border between Zambia and Namibia see page 188.

Car

Border crossings between Zimbabwe and its neighbours can be laborious or simple, depending on your preparation and the state of your vehicle's paperwork. If you are in your own vehicle you will require a Carnet de Passage issued by a body in your own country (such as the RAC) and your vehicle registration document, and you will also be required to take out third-party insurance for Zimbabwe from one of the insurance companies that have kiosks at the border posts. Most car hire companies will not allow you to take a rented vehicle out of the country in which it was hired, and only a few in South Africa will allow you to take a hired car into Zimbabwe. If they do, you will need a letter of authorization from your car hire company to drive in or out of Zimbabwe and a copy of the vehicle's registration document. In the past, if taking a Zimbabwe vehicle out of Zimbabwe, a police clearance certificate was also required (almost impossible to get) to prove that the vehicle was not stolen; this is no longer a legal requirement.

Crossing into Zimbabwe with a vehicle involves the following procedure: at immigration, you are issued with visas and a gate pass (a bit like a supermarket receipt), which gets stamped as you go along, to indicate that you've done everything properly, and is then given to the official at the boom gate after you have completed the formalities. Moving on to the customs counter, you must fill out a temporary import permit for your vehicle (valid 30 days), on which you must state chassis and engine numbers (for local cars these are on the vehicle registration document, and for international vehicles on both the vehicle registration document and the Carnet de Passage). Very roughly, and these costs can change without warning, this is what drivers in their own vehicles or in a hire car can expect to pay when entering Zimbabwe: Road Access Fee US$10; Carbon Tax

US$15-25 (depending on the size of the vehicle's engine); Third Party Insurance US$20-50 (depending on length of stay); Bridge Fees (for Beitbridge) US$15. These can be paid in US dollar cash or South African rand.

Car hire companies

For an additional fee, approximately US$250, the South African companies will permit you to take a car from South Africa (and in some cases Namibia and Botswana) into Zimbabwe. See also the Transport sections under individual towns for local operators.

Aroundabout Cars, South Africa, T+27(0) 21-422 4022, www.aroundaboutcars.com. A good South African agent which knows where to find the best deal. It also has its own fleets in Cape Town and Namibia and can organize 4WDs with camping equipment; it allows vehicles over the border into Zimbabwe.

Britz Africa, T+27-(0)11-396 1860, www.britz.co.za. Contact for camper vans and motorhomes for travel in

and beyond South Africa. Good all-inclusive deals.

Drive Africa, T+27-(0)21-447 1144, www.driveafrica.co.za. Has fully equipped 4WDs with camping equipment and provides all the necessary paperwork to take cars into Zimbabwe and Zambia with good professional back-up.

SMH Car Hire, T+27-(0)11-6083442, www.smhcarhire.co.za. Specializes in Land Rovers with roof-top tents and all equipment.

Trucks

Overland truck safaris are a popular way of exploring southern and East Africa by road. They demand a little more fortitude and adventurous spirit from the traveller, but the compensation is usually the camaraderie and life-long friendships that result from what is invariably a real adventure, going to places more pampered travellers will never visit. The standard three-week overland route most commercial trucks take through southern Africa (in either direction) is from Cape Town up to Namibia and Swakopmund via the Fish River Canyon and Sesriem for the Namib-Naukluft Park. The first weekend is usually spent in Swakopmund before heading north to the Etosha National Park via Damaraland, then into Botswana to visit the Okavango Delta and Chobe National Park and finishing in either Victoria Falls in Zimbabwe or Livingstone in Zambia to enjoy the activities around the Victoria Falls. This three-week trip can be combined with another three weeks to or from Victoria Falls or Livingstone via Zambia, Malawi, Tanzania and Zanzibar, and finishing in Kenya. Again. the circuit continues with a two-week route into Uganda to see the mountain gorillas via some of the Kenyan national parks. There are several overland companies and there are departures along the circuit almost weekly from Cape Town, Livingstone/Victoria Falls and Nairobi throughout the year.

Overland truck safari operators
In the UK
Dragoman, T01728-861133, www.dragoman.co.uk.
Exodus Travels, T020-8675 5550, www.exodus.co.uk.
Explore, T0845-013 1537, www.explore.co.uk.
Kumuka Expeditions, T0778-6201144, www.kumuka.com.

Oasis Overland, T01963-363400, www.oasisoverland.co.uk.

In South Africa
Africa Travel Co, UK, T020-8987 3305, T021-3851530, www.africatravelco.com.
Kiboko Adventures, T021-709 0094, www.kiboko.co.za.
Wildlife Adventures, T021-385 1530, www.wildlifeadventures.co.za.

Getting around

Air

The only domestic carrier is **Air Zimbabwe**, which has two daily flights from Harare to Victoria Falls (1½ hours) at 0900 and 1300, returning from Victoria Falls at 1030 and 1530, a return ticket is around US$230 and a one-way ticket US$135. They also operate two daily flights to Bulawayo (1¼ hours) at 0900 and 1900, and from Bulawayo at 0700 and 1715, US$100 one-way, around US$180 return. **Federal Air** (T0712-3959000, www.fedair.com) runs a service on Tuesday, Thursday and Sunday between Harare and Kariba, departing Harare at 0900 and arriving in Kariba at 1010, and departing Kariba again at 1100 and arriving back in Harare 1210. Costs are around US$120 one way. This company can also organize charter flights to several lodges that have airstrips, as can **Central Air Transport Services** (T04-335419, www.centralair.co.zw).

Rail

There are overnight trains between Harare and Mutare, Harare and Bulawayo and Bulawayo and Victoria Falls. Buy tickets at least a day in advance at the station (reservations are open up to 30 days prior to departure), and check the train is running on your preferred day. The booking offices at the stations are open Monday to Friday 0700-1700, 1900-2130, Saturday 0700-1130, 1800-2130, Sunday 0800-1000, 1800-2130. In theory, the Bulawayo service departs Harare Tuesday, Friday and Sunday at 2100 and arrives the next morning at 1000, and the Mutare service departs Sunday, Wednesday and Thursday at 2100 and arrives the next morning at 0600, though they often run late. The train from Bulawayo to Victoria Falls departs Bulawayo the following evening at 2000. Your ticket will not show your coach or berth number; these are posted in a glass case on the platform about an hour before the train departs. Fares are cheap (in the region of US$12 per person in Sleeper class), with children under 12 half price, children under three free. There are three classes of accommodation. Sleeper class has two-berth rooms (known as coupés) and four-berth rooms (known as compartments). These have leatherette bench seats which convert to bunks (bedding is provided) and a washbasin. The steward will come around to make up the beds. Two passengers travelling together can book a coupé, whereas a solo traveller will be booked into a four-berth compartment with passengers of the same sex. If you pay for two tickets you can have sole occupancy of a coupé. A restaurant car (though not on the Mutare train) serves basic meat-and-two-veg-type meals, plus beers and sodas. Standard class has reasonably comfortable airline-style seating that reclines. Economy class has basic seating; it is crowded and uncomfortable and you'll be sitting bolt upright all night.

Road

Bus

Local clapped-out buses, referred to in this guide as economy buses but known locally as 'chicken buses', ply all the main roads in Zimbabwe and leave when full. Expect to pay around US$10 for a city-to-city journey. The **Zimbabwe United Passenger Company**

(ZUPCO) buses seen in the cities also run on the long-distance routes. Even better for tourists, is **Citylink** (T04-772633, www.rainbowtowershotel.com), which has buses with toilets, DVDs and refreshment stops, and go from the Rainbow Towers Hotel in Harare on Tuesday, Thursday, Saturday and Sunday at 1400 and arrive at the Bulawayo Rainbow Hotel about 1930. They also stop at Kadoma, KweKwe and Gweru (see Midlands, page 91). From Bulawayo, buses to Victoria Falls depart at 1400 on Monday, Wednesday, Friday and Saturday and arrive about 1930. Costs are US$25 Harare to Bulawayo, US$50 Harare to Victoria Falls. **Pathfinder** (T09-61788, http://pathfinderlx.com) runs a daily service between Harare and Bulawayo, departing from each respectively at 0800 and 1400 and arriving at 1400 and 2000. They pick up and drop off at the Holiday Inns in each city. There are plans to extend the service and include Bulawayo to Victoria Falls, Harare to Mutare, and perhaps Harare to Johannesburg, so it's worth checking the website. Prices are similar to Citylink.

Car

If you are confident about driving in an African country, then car hire certainly gives the best flexibility when visiting Zimbabwe, and costs shared between four people are not unreasonable. However, there are very few hire companies in Zimbabwe; there are branches in airports and a couple of town offices (listed in the relevant chapters). Additionally, and awkwardly if you leave car hire until you arrive in Zimbabwe, it may be difficult to find something suitable and rates will be high.

Talk through your planned itinerary with your car hire company; they are the experts when it comes to driving in Zimbabwe and can advise on road conditions and what type of vehicle you'll need. A 2WD car is fine on the major tarred roads and will cost in the region of US$50-70 per day depending on season and length of hire; a 4WD (necessary if travelling to remote areas) will cost US$120-160 depending on the season. However, in both cases, study contracts carefully, work out your route and watch out for additional mileage costs – up to US$0.50 per kilometre. When collecting your vehicle, as well as checking it for bumps and scratches it is worth taking 10 minutes to familiarize yourself with it. Check the spare tyre (two are preferable) and how to use it. Is there a puncture repair kit and a pump? Do you know how to use them? What sort of fuel does it take? Do you have sufficient clearance for the terrain you are planning to cross? You don't want to discover a problem for the first time in an emergency in the middle of nowhere. Third-party insurance is included in the hire price but drivers are advised to take out extra insurance for 100% collision damage and loss waiver. Drivers must be at least 23 years of age (some companies stipulate 25) and need to have an international driver's licence, passport and credit card (Visa and increasingly MasterCard) to hire a car in Zimbabwe.

Driving For drivers accustomed to European roads, the traffic is virtually non-existent, but the roads are not without their dangers. In the cities you'll always need to be aware of minibus taxis (known as commuter omnibuses) stopping abruptly or pulling off the side of the road without indicating, and in the rural areas watch out for cattle and other livestock. Towards Victoria Falls and Kariba, you'll also need to look out for elephants crossing. The rural roads between the cities – the A4 Harare–Beitbridge on the South African border; the A3 Harare–Mutare; the A1 to Kariba and Chirundu on the Zambian border; the A5 Harare–Bulawayo; and the A8 Bulawayo–Victoria Falls – are all in excellent condition with relatively smooth tar and only a few patches of tarred corrugation.

After many years of fuel shortages in Zimbabwe, petrol, not a major expense, is available in the towns and cities and sporadically along the national highways (diesel less so). Nevertheless to drive a lengthy journey from, say, Bulawayo to Victoria Falls (some 440 km), fill up in the towns and don't rely on the very few service stations in between.

Driving is on the left side of the road and speed limits range from 60 kph in built-up areas to 80 km and 120 kph on the main highways (always keep an eye on the road signs for speed limits: the police tend to set up a road block a few metres before an 80 km limit changes to 120 km to catch drivers on the hop). Be careful if you find yourself on the road at night, since lighting is poor and it may be hard to spot a person or an animal crossing the road. Many vehicles don't even have tail lights or headlights, so night driving can be quite dangerous and is best avoided.

There are regular police checks; for a start, roughly 10 km outside main towns on the main arteries, there are (since 2009) road toll stops, manned by both the police and customs officials. The cost is US$1 per vehicle – keep some small change in US dollar bills – and you'll be given a ticket as you pass through. Don't be intimidated by these; they appear to be completely legitimate. The funds collected from drivers is going towards the re-tarring of roads, which in many places is visibly happening (the road out of Harare to Bulawayo, for example, has been completely refurbished). These and other police checks on the main roads will stop drivers for speeding or other offences such as not wearing seatbelts or having a broken light. If you are asked to pay a fine, always ask for a receipt on payment. If, say, the US$20 first requested by the officer is suddenly reduced to US$10, it is probably a bribe. Nevertheless, if you are polite with the police, stick to the road rules, and don't speed, you'll have few problems at police checks. If you're a tourist driving, you should experience few hassles in any case. Petrol costs about US$1.25 a litre, and diesel about US$1.05 a litre.

For emergency breakdown and road update information contact **Automobile Association of Zimbabwe** ① *T04-776760, www.aazimbabwe.co.zw.*

Hitchhiking Hitchhiking is not common in Zimbabwe. Women should never hitch, under any circumstances, even in a group. If you have to hitch, say if your vehicle has broken down, be very wary of who you are accepting a lift from; a car with a family or couple in may be fine, but avoid getting into a vehicle with a group of men.

Taxis

Metered taxis are readily available in the cities and are usually parked up in central locations such as outside the city halls or larger hotels. Restaurants will be able to organize one for you, or you can arrange with a taxi driver to come back later to pick you up.

Commuter omnibuses These are minibus taxis and the majority of Zimbabwe's population travel by them. However, the accident rate for such vehicles is notoriously high, with speeding, overcrowding and lack of maintenance being the main causes. In the cities and towns they travel along the main roads and are flagged down; you'll have to tell the driver to stop when you want to get off. Costs are cheap – about US$0.50 for a short ride, US$1 for a longer ride to the outlying suburbs and during rush hour. As there are no US$0.50 coins in existence, the method of payment is a South African R5 coin (roughly US$0.50) or three trillion old Zimbabwe dollars, which are still used on public transport as a token for bus fares. What effectively happens is that a passenger will buy two lots of three trillion Zimbabwe dollars for US$1, which allows two rides on public transport. If coming from South Africa to Zimbabwe, it is well worthwhile bringing a handful of R5 coins for use on public transport or to leave small tips. Because the US currency doesn't breakdown any smaller than a US$1 note, these coins are very much in circulation.

Maps

The best map and travel guide store in the UK is **Stanfords** ⓘ *12-14 Longacre, Covent Garden, London WC2E 9LP, T020-7836 1321, www.stanfords.co.uk*, with another branch in Bristol. There are, however, few up-to-date maps of Zimbabwe available, though South African publisher **Map Studio**, www.mapstudio.co.za, produces a wide range of maps covering much of southern Africa. The other option is to pick up a map atlas in South Africa from **Exclusive Books** (there's a branch at the OR Tambo International Airport in Johannesburg; www.exclus1ves.co.za) or from a petrol station. Most have comprehensive maps covering southern Africa. Another resource is the **Zimbabwe Tourism Authority** ⓘ *155 Samora Machel Av, T04-758712/14, www.zimbabwetourism.co.zw, Mon-Fri 0800-1630*, which produces a country map.

Sleeping price codes

L	over US$400	D	US$50-99
A	US$300-399	E	US$20-49
B	US$175-299	F	under US$20
C	US$100-174		

Prices refer to the cost of a double room, not including service charge or meals unless otherwise stated.

Sleeping

There is a wide range of accommodation on offer in Zimbabwe. At the top end are game lodges and tented camps that charge US$300-1000 per couple per day; mid-range safari lodges with self-contained double rooms with air conditioning charge around US$150-250 per room; basic national parks chalets cost about US$120, but they normally sleep four and are fully equipped for self-catering; standard and faded small town hotels used by local business people cost around US$50-100 per room; and campsites in the national parks cost about US$10 per person. Victoria Falls also has a few backpacker hostels where you can get a bed in a dorm for under US$20. At the top end, Zimbabwe now boasts some accommodation options that rival the luxurious camps in South Africa – intimate safari camps with an amazing standard of comfort and service in stunning settings, and in Harare and Victoria Falls a few upmarket hotels and lodges. Zimbabwe's hoteliers are embracing the age of the internet, and an ever-increasing number can take a reservation by email or through their websites. For the budget options, especially the smaller hotels, there is rarely any need to pre-book.

Hotels

There are some fairly luxurious hotels in Harare and Victoria Falls, but most local town and city hotels tend to be bland with poor service. Some of these may be very tired looking – which comes as a disappointment for some international visitors – but given the economic crisis in the country in the last decade it's an achievement that they stayed open at all. Many places have closed. Another quirky thing about smaller hotels is that they often have baths but no showers – a throwback to colonial times when British habits governed such things.

Lodges and tented camps

There are a few upmarket safari lodges, usually on the periphery of the national parks, in their own concession areas. These either have standard rooms or comprise permanent safari tents with their own decks and ensuite bathrooms. Rates are mostly all inclusive for meals and safari activities such as game drives and game walks, and some can also arrange transfers. Most have lounges and bars, often with excellent views or overlooking waterholes.

Backpacker hostels

Harare has a good backpacker hostel (It's a Small World, page 69), but other places which used to be popular have closed. Nevertheless, Victoria Falls still has some decent choices, and these are also excellent resources for information on the town and booking

Braai recipes

One of the first local eating terms you are likely to learn in Zimbabwe will be the braai, which translates as 'roast' in Afrikaans (from South Africa) and loosely means barbecue. It serves as a verb when describing how food is cooked and a noun when describing the cooking equipment, meaning a grill over an open fire. The braai is incredibly popular in all southern African countries, and in Zimbabwe every national park's chalet and campsite and all self-catering accommodation have a braai pit. Additionally, most types of accommodation, across all budgets, will incorporate this type of alfresco cooking in their menus.

Most Zimbabwean braais consist of a fire made in a concrete pit or a severed (cut-lengthwise), 40-gallon oil drum, both with grills; a good selection of meat (*nyama* in the Shona language), like steak, *boerewors* (a spicy local sausage), and chicken; bread rolls; *sadza* (see below); and a braai relish (see below and on page 34). A braai would normally include a good selection of salads. There is no special trick to these,

but adding some avocado to a green salad would give it a more Southern African flavour.

Learning how to cook good food on a braai is part of the fun of eating in Zimbabwe. Once you have established a core of heat using firelighters and wood or charcoal (charcoal is more eco-friendly and less smoky but wood makes for a wonderful fire), wrap up potatoes, sweet potatoes, squash, etc in heavy-duty foil and cook them in the coals for an hour or so. Set aside a good piece of meat, with a relish and a cold beer, and you will be living the Zimbabwean dream. Some people like to marinate the meat first, or simply season it with salt or curry powder and then drizzle some oil or lemon juice over it so it does not become too dry. A common indication of the ideal heat of a braai is to hold your hand over the fire and count to 10. If you have to pull your hand back before 10 it's too hot and after 10 it is not hot enough.

Zimbabwean braai recipes
Beer chicken Like roast pork and apple sauce, chicken and beer go very well

---

activities. Dorms and simple double rooms with or without bathrooms are available (bedding is supplied), and most have space in the garden for camping. While standards can obviously vary, stiff competition means that most hostels are clean and have good facilities. You can usually expect a self-catering kitchen, hot showers, a TV/DVD room and internet access. Many hostels also have bars and offer meals or nightly braais, plus a garden and a swimming pool. Most are a good source of travel information and many act as booking agents. On the whole, hostels are very safe and security is not a problem. Your fellow travellers remain the greatest threat when it comes to robbery.

Camping and national parks accommodation

Most of the national parks have campsites; many like Mana Pools and Gonarezhou have some unfenced wilderness campsites with very basic amenities, which, if you are self-sufficient, can offer a true wilderness experience. They are often most attractively sited, perhaps in the elbow of a river course but always with plenty of shade. You will need your own tent and basic equipment as these cannot be hired at the sites. You should also carry adequate supplies of fresh water, food, fuel and emergency supplies. Do not rely on local together, and this braai beer and chicken recipe not only helps keep the meat nice and moist when cooking it on the braai, but the beer, herbs and smoky flavour make for a very tasty roast chicken.

Rub oil, herbs, garlic, paprika and perhaps a bit of mustard powder into the chicken skin. Open the can of beer, drink half of it and place the half-full can into the cavity of the chicken, keeping the chicken and can upright. Push two heaps of hot charcoal on opposite sides of the braai, leaving a gap in between. Place the chicken neck end up on the grill between the two fires, with a drip tray underneath to catch any fats and juices during cooking. Then, still keeping it upright, balance the chicken on its two legs on the grill of the braai, cover it with a heavy duty pan or *potjie* pot and cook until roasted.

Sadza

You can buy mealie meal flour, the component of traditional Zimbabwean *sadza*, in all but the smallest of Zimbabwean shops. However, it is a little bit tricky to cook and requires some upper-arm strength as there is a lot of stirring involved. You will need: 2-4 cups of white mealie meal flour and water. First boil about four cups of the water in a *potjie* pot. Set aside about ¼ of your mealie meal and mix the rest with about three or four cups of water to make a thick paste. Slowly add this paste to the boiling water, stirring all the time, then slowly add the remaining mealie meal to the pot. The *sadza* should become very thick and smooth until it begins to pull away from the sides of the pot and form a large ball. Cook for a few more minutes and then serve with relish or meat. See also page 34.

Braai relish

Relish is used as a marinade or for basting the meat on a braai, as a condiment to put on your meat in a bread roll or as an accompaniment to *sadza*. To make it, fry some onions, garlic and chilli, add chopped tomatoes, brown sugar, a chopped green pepper, mixed herbs and maybe a dash of Tabasco, Worcestershire sauce or mustard (if these are available), and simmer for 30 minutes.

water supplies or rivers and streams for potable water. Any water taken from a stream should be filtered or boiled for several minutes before drinking. You should also spray the tent with mosquito repellent an hour or two before going to bed. Camping should always have minimal impact on the environment: all rubbish and waste matter should be buried, burnt, or taken away with you. Do not leave food scraps or containers that may attract and harm animals.

Formal campsites in the parks are usually near places where wildlife and birds gather, like rivers or waterholes, and they are generally well maintained with good ablution blocks and sometimes kitchen shelters with braais. Some towns have campsites, the best being the **Victoria Falls Rest Camp & Lodges** (page 173) and the **Bulawayo Municipal Caravan Park and Campsite** (page 148). The **Coronation Caravan Park** in Harare is currently being refurbished. These, and some of the national parks rest camps, also have simple self-catering chalets with a couple of bedrooms and a kitchen. Most of these are surprisingly well equipped with bed linen, towels, and cooking and eating equipment – though woe betide you if you accidentally squirrel away a fork, as items are rigidly counted when you check out. Also, electricity is not a given in the national park's rest camps.

National parks across the country are under the jurisdiction of the **Zimbabwe Parks and Wildlife Management Authority**. For pre-bookings visit the office in Harare on the corner of Borrowdale Road and Sandringham Drive in the National Herbarium and Botanic Gardens, T04-706077-8, or the office in Bulawayo on 15th Avenue between Main and Fort streets, T09-65592, www.zimparks.com. Both are open Monday to Friday 0800-1600. However you are unlikely to need to pre-book for camping, and very rarely for the chalets, but pitch up early to be sure you won't be turned away from a remote rest camp.

Eating price codes

₮₮₮ over US$25   ₮₮ US$15-25   ₮ under US$15

Prices refer to the cost of a two-course meal for one person including a soft drink, beer or a glass of wine.

Eating and drinking

Food

Traditional Zimbabwean food tends to be fairly basic, although a ubiquitous love of meat unites the country and fried chicken and beef stews served with *sadza* (mealie meal made into a paste similar to mashed potato; see boxes, page 30 and 34) are the norm. *Sadza* can also be accompanied by rape (a sort of spinach) which is mixed with a tomato and onion relish. In some of the tourist areas there is an assortment of game meat, from popular ostrich or springbok to more acquired tastes such as crocodile or warthog. Two local meat products which travellers invariably come across are biltong and boerewors. Biltong is heavily salted and spiced sun-dried meat, usually made from beef but sometimes made from game such as ostrich, kudu or impala. Boerewors is a strongly seasoned beef sausage usually grilled on a braai (see page 30). There's also a good choice of freshwater fish: kapenta from Lake Kariba, trout from the rivers in the Eastern Highlands, and bream from the Zambezi River. Common vegetables include cucumbers, beans, gem squash, butternut squash and avocados. *Dovi*, a peanut butter-like stew, is popular and may sometimes have an additional ingredient of *bowara* (pumpkin leaves), which are usually eaten raw.

Western food is well represented in Harare and there are more than 50 restaurants, though these are mostly in the suburbs. Upmarket hotel restaurants are also a good bet. Bulawayo has a few options, but Victoria Falls has few restaurants outside of the hotels. Most restaurants have menus, but it is usual to ask what is available before making a choice (this situation should improve over time). The usual form is that a restaurant waiter lists what they've got and then customers make their choice accordingly. Vegetarians will have limited choice given the country's high dependency on meat in both traditional and Western cuisine, but there should be at least one or two options on a menu. Hotel breakfasts are good value for vegetarians, for they usually comprise a buffet of yoghurt, fruit, juice, cheese, cereals, eggs, muffins and jam, as well as sausage and bacon for the carnivores.

For budget food you'll find a chain of 'inns' in the larger towns – **Pizza Inn** (pizza, whole or slices), **Creamy Inn** (for very good ice cream and milkshakes), **Bakers Inn** (pies and sandwiches) and **Chicken Inn** (chicken and chips). Effectively modern takeaways, they are hygienic and the quality of the food is reliable. Also in the towns are branches of the South African chain **Nando's** (good grilled chicken with chips or rice and coleslaw).

After many years of bare shelves during the economic crisis, supermarkets are now fairly well stocked and usually have a similar selection of groceries to that found in Europe, mostly imported from South Africa. However, check prices – there are certainly extra costs for specialist imported items. The better-stocked supermarkets are **TM** and **Spar**. The larger branches have bakery counters for pies, fried chicken, dense loaves of white bread and sugary cakes. Outside of the towns, the larger villages have very small shops. Fresh

Sadza

In the Shona language this is the name for a cooked corn or mealie meal that is the staple food in Zimbabwe and other parts of southern and eastern Africa. Other names include *isitshwala* (Ndebele), *nsima* in Malawi, *pap* in South Africa, and *ugali* in Kenya. It has the appearance of a thickened porridge, or sloppy mashed potato and is made from white maize. In Zimbabwe you'll see these tall plants being grown on small holdings on the side of the road. Despite the fact that maize started off as an imported food crop in Zimbabwe (introduced around 1890), it has become the chief source of

carbohydrate and the most popular meal for local people, who either purchase the flour in shops or grind it from their own maize. *Sadza* is usually served in a communal bowl or on separate plates and is taken with the right hand, rolled into balls, and dipped into meat, sauce, gravy or stewed vegetables. It is fairly tasteless but if properly cooked and accompanied by a flavoursome stew it is enjoyable and very filling. The standard meal for most Zimbabweans is *sadza ne nyama* – sadza and meat stew (*nyama* being the Shona word for meat). For the recipe, see page 30.

food like cheese or fruit and vegetables (other than those grown locally) can only be found in supermarkets in major towns.

Drink

Tap water in Zimbabwean towns is chemically treated and safe to drink. Bottled mineral water, which mostly comes from the springs in the mountains of the Eastern Highlands, and a good range of fruit juices are available at many outlets including petrol stations – the South African produced Ceres and Liquifruit brands are the best. A rock shandy, a mixture of lemonade, soda water and Angostura bitters, or a Malawi shandy, which replaces the lemonade with ginger beer, are very popular and superbly refreshing on a hot day. Zimbabwe produces a range of good lager-type beer, which is always served ice-cold. Major names include Zambezi and Bollengers, while Black Label, Castle and Amstel are imported. Home-brewed beer, made from sorghum or maize, is widely drunk by the African population. It has a thick head, is very potent and not very palatable to the uninitiated. It is available in large litre-sized brown plastic cartons. Wine is produced in the east of the country at the Mukuyu vineyards; it is reasonably palatable and cheap – try the white Mukuyu Bin 16. But the far superior South African wines are available at the better hotels, restaurants and supermarkets. Expect to pay in the region of US$1.50 for a local beer, US$3 for an imported can, US$1.50-2 for a tot of local spirits, US$2 for a tot of imported spirits, US$5-10 for a bottle of wine, US$1 for a coffee, and US$0.50 for a small bottle of mineral water or a soft drink like a Coke (there may be no change to give back so you may need to buy two at once from a single US$1 bill).

Entertainment

Although Harare and Victoria Falls have a few bars worth exploring, on the whole Zimbabwe is not the place to come to for nightlife. Generally, this is restricted to a few hotel bars which only really get going at weekends and on the major holidays. The few cinemas that exist are not really functioning. There are a few exceptions to this generalization; the **Book Cafe** and adjoining **Mannenburg Jazz Club** offer venues for performing arts in Harare, as does the **Reps Theatre** and **Gallery Delta** (see page 75). The Harare International Festival of Arts (HIFA; T04-300119, www.hifa.com) is a six-day annual festival and workshop programme in April/May that showcases the very best of local, regional and international arts and culture in a comprehensive festival programme of theatre, dance, music, circus, street performance, spoken word and visual arts. Venues include **The Theatre in the Park** in Harare Gardens and **Reps Theatre**. Also in May, over a weekend, the Chimanimani Arts Festival (www.chimanimani.co.zw) showcases local talent on a stage erected on the village green, with additional food and drink stalls.

Shopping

Popular African art and crafts include local fabrics, which, with their geometrical patterns and bright colours, are very appealing and can either be bought as straight bolts or fashioned into bags, cushion covers, table mats or tablecloths. A sheet of cloth, if it's in the right size, can easily be made into a duvet cover. The cloth is thick cotton and very durable. Also available are crocheted items (clothes, tablecloths, etc) which may not be so appealing to Western tastes. Woodcarvings include animals, bowls, stools and abstract pieces. When buying such items, they need to be checked carefully for flaws – cracks, dryness of the wood, etc – and it's a good idea to oil them when you get back home. Stone carvings include the famous Shona soapstone carvings, again in animal figures, human faces or abstract designs. The green-grey stone is smoothly rounded and very attractive, but while some figures are only a few centimetres tall, some are metres tall and very heavy, posing the problem of high shipping costs to get them home. Other souvenir items to buy include batiks, baskets, jewellery, home-made paper products such as notebooks and photo albums (reputedly made out of elephant dung) and metal sculptures, which are mostly birds on sticks, designed to be put in your garden.

There are several curio markets around the country. The best is probably the Falls Craft Village at Victoria Falls (page 176), which features both street vendors, their wares spread out neatly on the side of the road, and additional shops. There is also a branch of Fedex, packing services and a post office (just metres away), and there is often entertainment in the way of traditional drumming and dancing. Haggling is expected and you'll normally pay less in the market than in the more formal souvenir shops, though these too could be open to a bout of bargaining if they are short of business.

How big is your footprint?

The point of a holiday is, of course, to have a good time, but if it's relatively guilt-free as well, that's even better. Perfect ecotourism would ensure a good living for local inhabitants, while not detracting from their traditional lifestyles, encroaching on their customs or spoiling their environment. Perfect ecotourism probably doesn't exist, but everyone can play their part. Here are a few points worth bearing in mind:

- Think about where your money goes and be fair and realistic about how cheaply you travel. Try to put money into local people's hands; drink local beer or fruit juice rather than imported brands and stay in locally owned accommodation wherever possible.
- Haggle with humour and appropriately. Remember that you want a fair price, not the lowest one.
- Think about what happens to your rubbish. Take biodegradable products and a water bottle filter. Be sensitive to limited resources like water, fuel and electricity.
- Help preserve local wildlife and habitats by respecting rules and regulations, such as sticking to footpaths and not buying products made from endangered plants or animals.
- Don't treat people as part of the landscape; they may not want their picture taken. Ask first and respect their wishes.
- Learn the local language and be mindful of local customs and norms. It can enhance your travel experience and you'll earn respect and be more readily welcomed by local people.
- And finally, use your guidebook as a starting point, not the only source of information. Talk to local people, then discover your own adventure.

Responsible tourism

Sustainable or ecotourism has been described as "ethical, considerate or informed tourism where visitors can enjoy the natural, historical and social heritage of an area without causing adverse environmental, socio-economic or cultural impacts that compromise the long-term ability of that area and its people to provide a recreational resource for future generations and an income for themselves". Zimbabwe is a beautiful, wild country but also a living, working landscape and a fragile, vulnerable place. By observing certain guidelines outlined in the box above and behaving responsibly you can help to minimize your impact and protect the natural and cultural heritage of this wonderful country.

Environmental legislation plays its part in protecting tourist destinations. CITES (Convention on International Trade in Endangered Species of Wild Fauna and Flora) aims to control the trade in live specimens of endangered plants and animals and also "recognizable parts or derivatives" of protected species. International trade in elephant ivory, and the skins of wild cats is illegal. Restrictions have also been imposed on trade in reptile skins, and certain plants and wild birds. If you feel the need to purchase souvenirs derived from wildlife, it would be prudent to check whether they are protected. Importation of CITES-protected species can lead to heavy fines, confiscation of goods and even imprisonment.

Essentials A-Z

Accident and emergency

Police T995
Ambulance T994
Fire T993
All emergencies T999

Bargaining

Whilst most prices in the shops are set, the exception to this is shops selling tourist-related items such as curios, when a little good-natured bargaining is possible, especially if you are buying several items. Bargaining is very much expected in the street markets whether you are buying an apple or a soapstone souvenir. Generally traders will attempt to overcharge tourists who are unaware of local prices. Start lower than you would expect to pay, be polite and good humoured, and if the final price doesn't suit – walk away. You may be called back for more negotiation.

Children

Inform the airline in advance that you are travelling with a baby or toddler and check out the facilities when booking as these vary with each aircraft. Also useful is www.babygoes2.com.

In the towns with supermarkets, you will find plentiful supplies of all you need to feed and look after small children. Hygiene throughout the country is of a fairly good standard, especially if you are staying in the more upmarket hotels, where stomach upsets are rare and the tap water is safe to drink. Be sure to protect your children from the sun's intense rays, and be aware of the potential dangers of wild animals, snakes and insects in the bush. Most of the accommodation options welcome families; many have either specific family

rooms or adjoining rooms suitable for families, and there are plenty of family chalets or bungalows, especially in the parks. Children get significant discounts on accommodation and entry fees. Zimbabwe is very appealing to children: animals and safaris are very exciting for them (and their parents), especially when they catch their first glimpse of an elephant or lion. However, small children may get bored driving around a hot game reserve or national park all day if there is no animal activity. Many travel agencies organize family safaris that are especially designed for couples travelling with children, and there is also the option of self-drive, which is ideal for families.

Customs and duty free

The official customs allowance for visitors over 18 years includes 200 cigarettes, 50 cigars, 250 g of tobacco, 5 litres of alcohol, of which 2 litres can be spirits.

Disabled travellers

Wheelchair users will have difficulty accommodating their chairs on public road transport so will need to visit Zimbabwe on an organized tour or in a rented vehicle. With the exception of the most upmarket hotels and newer safari lodges, which have specially adapted rooms, there are few designated facilities for disabled travellers. In the national parks, most of the chalets are at ground level and are accessible, though there are no special facilities for disabled travellers and generally they are surrounded by sandy and stony ground. In the cities and towns, the pavements are fairly uneven kerbs tend to be high and most public buildings have entrance steps and no wheelchair access. However, in central Harare there are a number of 'dropped kerbs' and it shouldn't be too difficult to get around in a wheelchair. At Victoria Falls, the paths to the viewpoints in the Victoria Falls National Park are fairly flat and well surfaced so should be accessible by wheelchair.

Dress

Dress in Zimbabwe tends to be casual and most people on holiday wear shorts, sandals and a T-shirt. If you intend to do any game viewing, clothes in dark green, muted browns and khaki colours are best (but not camouflage-patterned clothes, as these are illegal). In general, bars and restaurants are casual, though some of the more upmarket establishments have dress codes where sandals, vest and shorts are not appreciated.

Electricity

Zimbabwe's supply is 220/240 volts AC and most appliances are the British square 3-pin type. However, as in most of Africa, small appliances bought locally like phones, hairdryers and razors have a round 2-pin connection. Adaptors can be bought locally, or bring an international one with you. Due to the economic situation, Zimbabwe's electricity supply has been very erratic in the last decade, and in some places still is. Some rural areas do not have electricity over long periods. Harare, Bulawayo and Victoria Falls all experience regular power cuts 2 or 3 times a week, though the larger hotels and supermarkets have back-up generators. Take advantage when there is power to recharge phones, laptops and cameras, and don't rely on regular electricity in remote regions like the national parks.

Embassies and consulates

Australia, 11 Culgoa Circuit, Canberra, T02-6286 2700, zimbabwe1@austarmetro.com.au.
Botswana, Plot 8850, Nelson Mandela Av, T039-14495.

Canada, 332 Somerst St, Ottawa, T613-421 2824, www.zimottawa.com.
France,12 rue Lord Byron, Paris 75008, T01-5688 1600, www.ambassade-zimbabwe.com.
Germany, Kommandantestr 80, T030-206 2263, www.simbabwe-botschaft.de.
Malawi, 7th floor, Gemini House, T01-733988, zimhighcomllw@malawi.net.
Mozambique, Caixa Postal 743, Maputo, T021-490699, 617 Rua Francisco Dechage Almelda, Beira, T023-327950.
South Africa, 798 Merton St, Arcadia, Pretoria, T012-342 5125.
UK, 429 Stand, London, WC2R 0SA, T0870-005 6987, www.zimbabwe.embassy-uk.co.uk.
USA,1608 New Hampshire Av, Washington DC 20009, T1202-232 4400, www.zimbabwe-embassy.us.
Zambia, 26D Cheetah Rd, Lusaka, T01-260999.

Gay and lesbian travellers

Laws passed in 2006 make any actions perceived as homosexual a criminal offence and in 2010, 2 Zimbabwean men were arrested and sentenced to prison, so gay travellers should be very discreet. Mugabe's harshest criticism of gay men and lesbians came in 1995, when he told a crowd including diplomats that such people were "lower than pig or dogs."

Health

See your doctor or travel clinic at least 6 weeks before your departure for general advice on travel risks, malaria and recommended vaccinations. Make sure you have travel insurance, get a dental check (especially if you are going to be away for more than a month), know your own blood group and if you suffer a long-term condition such as diabetes or epilepsy make sure someone knows or that you have a Medic Alert bracelet/necklace with this information on it (www.medicalert.co.uk).

Vaccinations

Confirm your primary courses and boosters are up to date. Courses or boosters usually advised: diphtheria; tetanus; poliomyelitis; hepatitis A. Vaccines sometimes advised: tuberculosis; hepatitis B; rabies; cholera; typhoid. The final decision on all vaccinations, however, should be based on a consultation with your GP or travel clinic. A yellow fever certificate is required for anyone over 1 year old and entering from an infected area.

For further information, visit www.fitfortravel.nhs.uk.

A–Z health risks
Bites and stings

These are very rare indeed for travellers, but if you are unlucky (or careless) enough to be bitten by a venomous snake, spider or scorpion sea creature, try to identify the culprit, without putting yourself in further danger. Snake bites in particular are very frightening, but in fact rarely poisonous – even venomous snakes bite without injecting venom. Victims should be taken to a hospital or a doctor without delay. Reassure and comfort the victim frequently, immobilize the limb with a bandage or a splint and get the patient to lie still. Do not slash the bite area and try to suck out the poison, as this does more harm than good. You should apply a tourniquet in these circumstances, but only if you know how to. Do not attempt this if you are not experienced.

Cholera

There was a serious cholera endemic in Zimbabwe in 2008. By December 2008 more than 10,000 people had been infected in all but one of Zimbabwe's provinces and the outbreak had spread to neighbouring countries. The Zimbabwe government declared the outbreak a national emergency. The main symptoms of cholera are profuse watery diarrhoea and vomiting, which in severe cases may lead to dehydration and death. However, most travellers are at extremely low risk of infection and the disease rarely shows symptoms in healthy well-nourished people. The new cholera vaccine, Dukoral, is only recommended for certain high-risk individuals such as health professionals or volunteers.

Dengue fever

This is a viral disease spread by mosquitoes that tend to bite during the day. The symptoms are fever and often intense joint pains; some people also develop a rash. Symptoms last about a week but it can take a few weeks to recover fully. Dengue can be difficult to distinguish from malaria as both diseases tend to occur in the same countries. There are no effective vaccines or antiviral drugs but, fortunately, travellers rarely develop the more severe forms of the disease (these can prove fatal). Rest, plenty of fluids and paracetamol (not aspirin) is the recommended treatment.

Diarrhoea

This can refer either to loose stools or an increased frequency of bowel movement, both of which can be a nuisance. Symptoms should be relatively short-lived but if they persist beyond 2 weeks specialist medical attention should be sought. Also seek medical help if there is blood in the stools and/or fever. Adults can use an anti-diarrhoea medication such as Loperamide to control the symptoms but only for up to 24 hrs. In addition, keep well hydrated by drinking plenty of fluids and eat bland foods. Oral rehydration sachets taken after each loose stool are a useful way to keep well hydrated. These should always be used when treating children and the elderly.

Bacterial traveller's diarrhoea is the most common form of diarrhoea for visitors. Ciproxin (Ciprofloxacin) is a useful antibiotic and can be obtained by private prescription in the UK. You need to take one 500 mg tablet when the diarrhoea starts. If there are so signs of improvement after 24 hrs the diarrhoea is likely to be viral and not bacterial. If it is due to other organisms such as those causing giardia or amoebic dysentery, different antibiotics will be required.

The standard advice to prevent problems is to be careful with water and ice for drinking. If you have any doubts then boil the water or filter and treat it. Food can also transmit disease. Be wary of salads (what were they washed in, who handled them), re-heated foods or food that has been left out in the sun, having been cooked earlier in the day. There is a simple adage that says wash it, peel it, boil it or forget it. Also be wary of unpasteurized dairy products as these can transmit a range of diseases.

Hepatitis

Hepatitis means inflammation of the liver. Viral causes of the disease can be acquired anywhere in the world. The most obvious symptom is a yellowing of your skin or the whites of your eyes. However, prior to this all that you may notice is itching and tiredness. Pre-travel hepatitis A vaccine is the best precaution. Hepatitis B (for which there is a vaccine) is spread through blood and unprotected sexual intercourse, both of which can be avoided.

HIV and Aids

Southern Africa has the highest rates of HIV and AIDS in the world. Efforts to stem the rate of infection have had limited success, as many of the factors that need addressing such as social change, poverty and gender inequalities are long-term processes. Visitors should be aware of the dangers of infection from unprotected sex and always use a condom. Do not inject non-prescribed drugs or share needles; avoid having a tattoo or piercing, electrolysis or acupuncture unless you're sure the equipment is sterile. If you have to have medical treatment, ensure any equipment used is taken from a sealed pack or is freshly sterilized. It may even be worth taking your own sterilized needles as part of a first-aid kit. If you have to have a blood transfusion, ask for screened blood.

Malaria

The risk of malaria exists from November until June in areas below 1200 m and year-round in the Zambezi valley. Prophylaxis are recommended for all areas, except the cities of Harare and Bulawayo. Consult with your GP or travel clinic on the best course of anti-malarials.

Malaria can cause death within 24 hrs and can start as something just resembling an attack of flu. You may feel tired, lethargic, headachy, feverish; or, more seriously, develop fits, followed by coma and then death. Have a high level of suspicion because it is very easy to write off vague symptoms, which may actually be malaria. If you have a temperature, visit a doctor as soon as you can and ask for a malaria test. On your return home, if you suffer any of these symptoms, have a test as soon as possible, even if a previous test proved negative. This could save your life.

Treatment is with drugs and may be oral or into a vein depending on the seriousness of the infection. Remember ABCD: Awareness (of whether the disease is present in the area you are travelling in), Bite avoidance, Chemoprohylaxis, Diagnosis.

To prevent mosquito bites wear clothes that cover arms and legs, use effective insect repellents in areas with known risks of insect-spread disease and use a mosquito net treated with an insecticide. Repellents containing 30-50% DEET (Di-ethyltoluamide) are recommended when visiting malaria endemic areas; lemon eucalyptus (Mosiguard) is a reasonable alternative. The key advice is to take the correct anti-malarials and finish the recommended course. If you are a popular target for insect bites or develop lumps quite soon after being bitten use antihistamine tablets and apply a cream such as hydrocortisone. Remember that it is risky to buy medicine, and in particular anti-malarials, in some developing countries. These may be sub-standard or part of a trade in counterfeit drugs.

Rabies

Rabies is endemic throughout certain parts of the world so be aware of the dangers of a bite from any animal. You may want to consider rabies vaccination before travel. If bitten, always seek urgent medical attention (whether or not you have been previously vaccinated) after first cleaning the wound and treating with an iodine-base disinfectant or alcohol.

Sun

Take good heed of advice relating to protecting yourself against the sun. Overexposure can lead to sunburn and, in the longer term, skin cancers and premature skin ageing. The best advice is simply to avoid exposure to the sun by covering exposed skin, wearing a hat and staying out of the sun if possible, particularly between late morning and early afternoon. Apply a high-factor sunscreen (greater than SPF15) and also make sure it screens against UVB. Be aware of sunburn at higher altitudes too; it might feel cool, but the sun can be strong in the rarefied air of the mountains.

A further danger in tropical climates is heat exhaustion or more seriously heat stroke. This can be avoided by good hydration, which means drinking water past the point of simply quenching thirst. Also when first exposed to tropical heat take time to acclimatize by avoiding strenuous activity in the middle of the day. If you cannot avoid heavy exercise it is also a good idea to increase salt intake.

Tuberculosis

This is most commonly transmitted via droplet infection. Ensure that you have been immunized, especially if you will be mixing closely with the local population or anyone at occupational risk, such as healthcare workers. Check with your doctor or nurse.

Other diseases

There are some other insect-borne diseases that are quite rare in travellers, but worth finding out about if going to particular destinations. Examples are sleeping sickness, river blindness and leishmaniasis. Fresh water can also be a source of diseases such as bilharzia and leptospirosis and it is worth investigating if these are a danger before bathing in lakes and streams.

Further information
Websites
British Travel Health Association (UK), www.btha.org. This is the official website of an organization of travel health professionals.

Fit for Travel (UK), www.fitfortravel.nhs.uk. This site provides a quick A-Z of vaccine and travel health advice requirements for each country.

Foreign and Commonwealth Office (FCO) (UK), www.fco.gov.uk. This is a key travel advice site, with useful information on the country, people and climate and lists of the UK embassies/consulates. The site also promotes the concept of 'Know Before You Go' and encourages travel insurance and appropriate travel health advice.

Medical Advisory Service for Travellers Abroad (MASTA) (UK), www.masta.org. Provides a quick A-Z of vaccine and travel health advice requirements for each country.

Medic Alert (UK), www.medicalert.co.uk. This is the website of the foundation that produces bracelets and necklaces for those with existing medical problems.

World Health Organization, www.who.int. The WHO site has links to the WHO Blue Book on travel advice.

Books
Lankester T *Travellers' Good Health Guide* (2nd edition, Sheldon Press, 2006).

Holidays

1 Jan New Year's Day.
2 Apr Good Friday.
5 Apr Easter Monday.
18 Apr Independence Day.
1 May Workers' Day.
25 May Africa Day.
9 Aug Heroes' Day.
10 Aug Defence Forces Day.
22 Dec Unity Day.
25 Dec Christmas Day.
26 Dec Boxing Day.

Insurance

it is vital to take out full travel insurance. There is a wide variety of policies to choose from, so shop around. At the very least, the policy should cover personal effects and medical expenses, including repatriation to your own country in the event of a medical emergency. There is no substitute for suitable precautions against petty crime, but if you do have something stolen whilst in Zimbabwe, report the incident to the nearest police station and ensure you get a police report and case number. You will need these to make any claim from your insurance company.

Internet

There are plenty of internet cafés in all major urban centres and many hotels, guesthouses or backpacker hostels offer internet access as a service. Wi-Fi internet is available at some hotels, as well as at many coffee shops in the cities, where you buy vouchers. Costs are about US$2 per 20 mins.

Language

Shona, Ndebele and English are the principal languages of Zimbabwe and although English is the official language and is widely used by everyone, about 70% of Zimbabweans are Shona speakers, while about 15%, mostly living in Bulawayo and Matabeleland, are Ndebele speakers, while about 5%, mostly white, consider English as their native language. Radio and television news is now broadcast in all 3 languages.

Media

Magazines

There are a number of publications that travellers will find useful in Zimbabwe, though these are more readily available to pick up at the airport in Johannesburg in South Africa. The monthly *Getaway* is aimed at outdoorsy South Africans, but has excellent travel features and ideas, as well as reviews of accommodation alternatives and activities throughout southern Africa. *Africa Geographical* is a glossy monthly with high-quality photographs, which publishes regular articles on southern Africa's parks, reserves and wildlife. Its sister magazine, *Africa, Birds & Birding*, also monthly, is a must for anyone with an interest in birdwatching in southern Africa. For inspiration before you leave home, pick up a copy of *Travel Africa*, www.travelafricamag.com.

Newspapers

The *Herald*, *Independent* and *Standard* are daily English-language papers with national coverage. After many years of the Zimbabwe government's Ministry of Information interfering with the press and the periodic firing of editors and journalists, in May 2010 the newly formed Zimbabwe Media Commission granted licences to 4 more newspapers: the *Daily News* (this had been shut down in 2002), *The Mail*, *Newsday*, and the *Daily Gazette*. One of the first goals of the Unity government was to reduce media restrictions, and now most newspapers run independently. Free press is expected to gain momentum as these newspapers become established.

Radio

This reaches even the most remote corners of the country. The state-owned **Zimbabwe Broadcasting Corporation (ZBC)** has 4 national stations: **Radio 1** offers news, current affairs and some staid old-fashioned music in English; **Radio 2** is the same in Shona and Ndebele, though the music seems to be a bit more up-to-date; **Radio 3** is in English and features current pop music; and **Radio 4** is largely an educational channel in all languages.

Television

ZBC, the state broadcaster, has 2 channels – ZBC TV and Channel 2. Both have news and entertainment programmes, mostly old imported shows from the US, and some movies. The paying channel M-Net offers a range of sport, sitcoms and movies, and most hotels also have satellite TV, known as DSTV which is imported from South Africa, with a range of sports, film and news channels.

Money

Currency
Exchange rates In the last few years, hyperinflation has rapidly eroded the value of the Zimbabwe dollar (Z$) until it eventually became one of the least valued currencies in the world (see Economy, page 236); the use of the Zimbabwe dollar as an official currency was effectively abandoned on 12 Apr 2009 as a result of the Reserve Bank of Zimbabwe legalizing the use of foreign currencies for transactions in Jan 2009. Now, the US dollar is the most common currency used, though the Botswana pula and South African rand are also recognized. For up-to-the-minute exchange rates, visit www.xe.com.

In Zimbabwe, The US$ comes in denominations of US$1, US$2, US$5, US$10, US$20, US$50 and US$100. Note there are no coins under US$1 in circulation

in Zimbabwe. The common form of currency under the value of the US$1 note is South African rand coins. These are a bit inconvenient if you are coming from overseas as they cannot be obtained in advance; if you are arriving from South Africa, try to pick up some (especially R5 coins, which are worth about US$0.65 cents). R5 coins can be used for short commuter omnibus journeys or to leave a tip; otherwise you are unlikely to get change from a US$1 note. When taking US dollars into Zimbabwe, remember that small denomination bills are particularly useful as the availability of small change is a constant problem. Also try and take in newer looking notes; unlike the United States (where credit cards are the norm), Zimbabwe is a cash economy and dollar notes are wearing out and becoming torn. Do not accept worn notes as change from a vendor, as the next vendor you try to pay may not accept them. There is no restriction on the amount of US dollars you can bring into the country.

At the time of writing, Harare and the surrounding area is a mainly US dollars cash economy (prices in shops are fixed in US dollars but there is still some room for using other currencies); in Bulawayo, because of its proximity to the Botswana border, Botswana pula is more frequently used; in Victoria Falls, rand is more widely accepted, probably because of the large number of South African visitors. To put this into perspective, in a supermarket, the manager will often post up the exchange rates for all 3, and supermarket staff have become adept at using calculators. If you plan on visiting neighbouring countries, note that most of their currencies can only be purchased within South Africa, and not before you leave home. However, rand can easily be exchanged in South Africa's neighbouring countries and in some cases, such as Lesotho, Swaziland, Namibia and Mozambique, is used interchangeably alongside the local currency. Probably the best way to carry your money is to take a mixture of US dollars and rand cash and a credit card (see below).

Changing money

Banking hours are Mon-Fri 0800-1500, Sat 0800-1130. All the main high street banks in Zimbabwe offer foreign exchange services to change euros and pounds sterling into US dollars, but you'll probably get a better exchange rate if you bring it with you or use an ATM to withdraw cash. Most banks have them now, though you may need to do some leg work to find one that has cash; **Barclays Bank** is the most reliable followed by **Standard Chartered Bank**. **Zimbank** does have ATMs but as yet doesn't have the facility to accept foreign credit cards, though this should change. Note that a Visa card is essential. All credit card use had ceased in Zimbabwe in 2008, but Visa is again being accepted in the cities, and although MasterCard is beginning to resurrect its services in Zimbabwe, this is not to be relied on quite yet. Also, even though some hotels and lodges take Visa, check that their machines are working when you check in, as they could be down. Be sure to let your bank know that you are intending to use a credit card in Zimbabwe before you leave home; otherwise they might block it once you are there. You should also clarify the charges they make for using ATMs abroad. Traveller's cheques can be cashed in banks and larger denomination ones can be used to pay for activities at Victoria Falls.

Cost of travelling

Since dollarization in 2009, Zimbabwe is fairly good value for money for tourists spending US dollars, pounds sterling or euros. For a while prices were very high in US dollars, mainly because of the surge of imported goods after many years of shortages and lack of buying power, but prices seem to have stabilized and are not that much higher than in the neighbouring countries. Accommodation will represent your principal daily expense. In first-rate luxury lodges, expect to pay in excess of US$400 per night for a double, while a dorm in a Victoria Falls hostel will cost less than US$20. Meals out average about US$15 for a main course and US$3 for a beer. For the budget traveller, there are fast-food outlets, and almost every supermarket has a deli counter serving hot and cold meals. For independent travellers, transport is fairly cheap; the long-distance buses and overnight trains charge as little as US$12 per person. After accommodation, probably the biggest expense in Zimbabwe is activities. Adventurous visitors may have researched which of the adrenalin-pumping adventures on offer at Victoria Falls they want to do, but when they get there, and see the whitewater rafts bobbing on the foaming Zambezi, the bungee jump from the Victoria Falls Bridge, or the high-wire activities over the Bakota Gorge, the list is invariably extended (or modified). The problem is you need cash to pay for them, so be prepared. It's not unusual to spend US$500 or more on activities over just a couple of days at Victoria Falls.

Opening hours

Banks Mon-Fri 0900-1530, Sat 0830/0900-1030/1100.
Businesses Mon-Fri 0830-1700, Sat 0830-1400.
Post offices Mon-Fri 0830-1600, Sat 0800-1200; minor branches have slightly shorter hours.
Shops and supermarkets Mon-Fri 0800-1800, Sat 0800-1300, Sun 0900-1300.

Post

Both internal and international mail is generally reliable. If you are sending home souvenirs, surface mail to Europe is normally the cheapest method but will take at least 6 weeks. However, surface mail from Zimbabwe at the time of writing had been suspended. It is probably best to use registered mail for more valuable items so that you can track their progress. Letters to Europe and the US should take no more than a few days, although can take longer over the busy Christmas season. There is a 'speed service', known as EMS, but this costs significantly more. Parcels can be sent by normal airmail post; expect to pay in the region of US$14 per kg to Europe and about US$16 per kg to the rest of the world; maximum weight is 20 kg.

Courier services are useful for sending valuable items. **DHL** (www.dhl.co.zw) has branches in Harare, Mutate, Bulawayo and Victoria Falls, and **Fedex** (www.fedex.com/zw) has a branch in Victoria Falls.

Safety

Zimbabwe has had more than its fair share of well-publicized political problems throughout the 1990s; its tragic political situation caused a rapid descent into chaos, often turning violent. Civil unrest occurred in Harare and the large urban areas and also in some rural areas when white-owned farms were forcibly taken over. But that violence was all politically related and motivated and, despite Zimbabwe's bad press, tourists were never in any danger. The main tourist areas, including Victoria Falls and the national parks, were unaffected, simply because they are not in regions of farmland.

As for crime, by taking sensible precautions visitors need not worry about their safety any more than they would in any foreign country. Petty crime and muggings are almost unheard of in Zimbabwe, but nevertheless the best advice for avoiding any incidents is to remember not to flash your valuables, to avoid insalubrious areas, to refrain from walking around in urban centres at night, and to avoid driving after dark. If you are travelling alone in a car, it's a good idea to have a mobile phone; useful in any case if you break down. Most visitors are carrying a fair wad of cash to

Zimbabwe, though this is likely to change as ATMs become more prolific and the credit card companies reinstate their services in hotels, shops, etc (increasing all the time). Carry your cash in a slim money belt under clothes, but keep enough ready cash in your pockets for use during the day, and whenever possible utilize a hotel safe. Finally, with the odd exception, compared to people in some of the crime-ridden countries in Africa, where tourists are targeted because it's assumed they have huge amounts of wealth, the people in Zimbabwe are naturally helpful and friendly, and euphoric that tourists should return to support the economy and many jobs. Visitors are unlikely to have any safety issues. For specific advice for women travellers, see page 48.

Telephone

Country code: +263.
The telephone service used to be very efficient in Zimbabwe but many people lost their landlines in recent years, mostly due to lack of maintenance. Numbers remain a bit hit and miss, but this is being addressed and the system is rapidly being repaired. After lagging behind the rest of the world by having only dial-up internet, Zimbabwe now has broadband, so communication is just about on track again (though it can be interrupted by power cuts). Cell phones have fairly good coverage (though not in extreme rural areas) and local sim cards can be bought at the airports on arrival for about US$20, which includes US$5 air time. Airtime vouchers can be bought from street vendors at traffic lights for about US$5. Overseas visitors should be able to use their mobiles on roaming.

Time

Zimbabwe has one time zone: GMT +2 hrs (+1 during UK Summer Time Mar-Oct), 8 hrs ahead of USA Eastern Standard Time,

1 hr ahead of Europe; 8 hrs behind Australian Eastern Standard Time. There is no daylight saving.

Tipping

Waiters, hotel porters, stewards, chambermaids and tour guides should be tipped 10-15%, according to the service. When leaving tips make sure it goes to the intended person. It is common practice to tip petrol pump attendants, depending on their service, up to (US$0.50 or a R5 coin) for a fill up, oil and water check and comprehensive windscreen clean.

Tour operators

UK
Abercrombie & Kent, T0845-070 0600, www.abercrombiekent.co.uk.
Acacia Adventure Holidays, T020-7706 4700, www.acacia-africa.com.
Africa Explorer, T020-8987 8742, www.africa-explorer.co.uk.
Africa Travel Resource, T01306-880770, www.africatravelresource.com.
Bailey Robinson, T01488-689777, www.baileyrobinson.com.
Expert Africa, T020-8232 9777, www.expertafrica.com.
Explore, T0870-333 4001, www.explore.co.uk.
Global Village, T0844-844 2541, www.globalvillage-travel.com.
Ngoko Safaris, T01676-535165, www.ngoko.com.
Okavango Tours and Safaris, T020-8347 4030, www.okavango.com.
Safari Consultants Ltd, T01285-880980, 01787-888590, www.safari-consultants.co.uk.
Steppes Africa, T01285-880980, www.steppestravel.co.uk.
Tim Best Travel, T020-7591 0300, www.timbesttravel.com.
Zambezi Safari & Travel Co, T01548-830059, www.zambezi.co.uk.

North America
Adventure Center, T1800-228 8747, www.adventure-center.com.
Africa Adventure Company, T1800-882 9453, T1954-491 8877, www.africa-adventure.com.
Bushtracks, T1707-433 0258, www.bushtracks.com.

Australia and New Zealand
The Africa Safari Co, T+61-(0)2-9541 4199, www.africasafarico.com.au.
African Wildlife Safaris, T+61-(0)3-9249 3777, www.africanwildlifesafaris.com.au.
Classic Safari Company, T+61-(0)2-9327 0666, www.classicsafaricompany.com.au.
Peregrine Adventure, T+61-(0)3-9662 2700, www.peregrine.net.au.

South Africa
Africa Travel Co, T+27-(0)21-385 1530, www.africatravelco.com.
Go2Africa, T+27-(0)21-481 4900, www.go2africa.com.

Zimbabwe
African Encounter, T04-702814, www.africanencounter.org.
Classic Africa Safaris, T04-884226, www.classic.co.zw.
Experience Africa Safaris, T04-369185, www.xafricasafaris.com.
Limbe Safaris, T04-300335, shamba@mweb.co.zw.
Natureways Safaris, T04-745458, www.natureways.com.
Nyati Travel, T04-495804, www.nyati-travel.com.
Travel AfriKa, T09-67449, trvlafr@netconnect.co.zw.
United Touring Company (UTC), T04-770623, www.utc.co.zw.

Tourist information

The Zimbabwe Tourism Authority (ZTA), 55 Samora Machel Av, Harare, T04-780651, www.zimbabwetourism.co.za, has a website but only with limited information, though their offices produce a number of leaflets and maps. ZTA also has offices around the world (see below), which are useful for pre-travel information. There are very few local tourist offices once in the country and those that are there are listed under individual towns.

Tourist offices overseas

Germany Hochstrasse 17, 60313 Frankfurt, T069 9207730, info@zimbabwe-tourism.de.
South Africa 4th floor, Office Tower, Bradford Rd, Bedfordview, Johannesburg, T011-616 9534, zta@telkomsa.net.
UK 429 Strand, London WC2, T020-7240 6169, zta.london@btclick.com.
USA 128 East 56 St, New York, NY 10022, T1212-4863444.

Useful websites

www.africaguide.com Everything you need to know about African travel. Also sells holidays and reviews guidebooks.
www.afrizim.com South African website with good comprehensive information about Zimbabwe. Acts as a booking agent for hotels and activities in Zimbabwe.
www.fco.gov.uk UK Foreign Office, for the official advice on latest political situations.
www.go2africa.com Accommodation and holiday booking service, with useful practical information and links to overland companies.
www.overlandafrica.com A variety of overland tours offered throughout Africa.

Vaccinations

See Health, page 38.

Visas and immigration

Most nationalities including EU nationals and citizens from the USA, Canada, Australia and New Zealand need visas to enter Zimbabwe and they are available on arrival at the airports and land borders. Visitors from these countries are granted temporary visitors' permits lasting up to 90 days. When arriving, ensure you put a date on the visa form that is for 90 days, even if you are staying a much shorter time, to cover all eventualities. If you put the date of your flight out, for example, and the flight gets cancelled or delayed, effectively you will have overstayed your visa.

You must have a valid return ticket or voucher for onward travel, at least 1 completely empty page in your passport, which must be valid for at least 6 months from date of entry into Zimbabwe. It is possible to apply for a visa extension for a maximum of 6 months at one of the offices of the immigration offices: Linquenda House, corner Nelson Mandela Av and First St, in Harare, T04-791912; corner of Herbert Chitepo St and Eleventh Av, in Bulawayo, T09-65621; or you could go to the border post at Victoria Falls.

Visa requirements and fees can change without notice so it's always a good idea to check with your local embassy or high consulate. Single/double-entry visas are US$30/45 for most nationalities, but the exceptions are US$55/70 for UK passport holders and US$75/150 for Canadians. Currencies accepted are US dollars, pounds sterling, South African rand and euros, but if paying in anything other than US dollars you may not be able to rely on the correct amount of change, so keep it simple and take US dollars in cash.

Zambia

Most nationalities including EU nationals and citizens from the USA, Canada, Australia and New Zealand need visas to enter Zambia; the exception are Irish passport holders, who don't need one. Visas are available on arrival at the airports and land borders, and requirements are identical to Zimbabwe. Single/double entry visas cost US$50/80. At the border with Victoria Falls, there is also an additional 'day-trippers' visa for US$20; this allows visitors to Zimbabwe to go across to the Zambian side of the falls for activities. This is valid for only one day and you have to return to Zimbabwe across the same border ie the Victoria Falls Bridge.

Botswana

Very few nationalities need visas for Botswana. However, remember if you don't have a double-entry visa back into Zimbabwe, you'll have to get another one on return.

Weights and measures

The metric system is used in Zimbabwe, Zambia and Botswana.

Women travellers

Very refreshingly, Zimbabwe is a secure and safe country for women to travel in, even on their own, and walking around the towns and cities, and even driving should present no problems. However, the usual rules of not travelling alone after dark, never hitchhiking, avoiding quiet areas and carrying a cell phone in a car in case of an emergency always apply. It is also a good idea to cover up in more conservative or rural areas; avoiding tight, revealing tops and short skirts should help. On the whole, sexual crime in Zimbabwe is almost unheard of, and Zimbabwean men are very respectful of women and will do their utmost to assist you.

Working in Zimbabwe

There are no opportunities for travellers to obtain casual paid employment in Zimbabwe and it is illegal for a foreigner to work without an official work permit. Most foreign workers in the country are employed through embassies, development or volunteer agencies or through foreign companies. For the most part, these people will have been recruited in their countries of origin. A number of NGOs and voluntary organizations can arrange placements for volunteers, usually for periods ranging from 6 months to 2 years; visit www.volunteerafrica.org, or www.africanimpact.com.

Contents

At a glance

⊖ Getting around On foot in the city centre; organized tours, bus or self-drive to the outlying attractions.

⏱ Time required A minimum of 2 days to see the sights in the city centre and suburbs.

☀ Weather Moderate temperatures of around 20-25°C year round, but often cloudy.

✗ When not to go Nov-Apr are the wettest months when it can also be hot and humid.

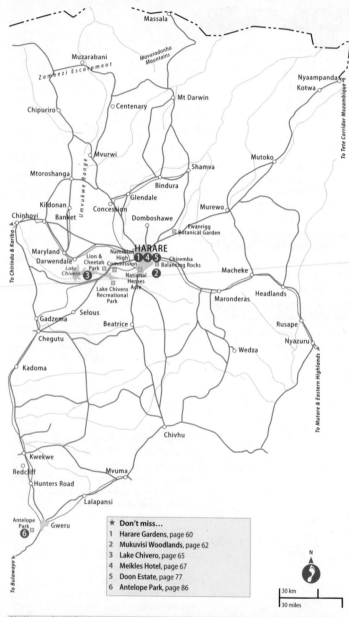

★ **Don't miss...**

1 Harare Gardens, page 60
2 Mukuvisi Woodlands, page 62
3 Lake Chivero, page 65
4 Meikles Hotel, page 67
5 Doon Estate, page 77
6 Antelope Park, page 86

30 km
30 miles

Zimbabwe's capital, Harare, is set on an elevated plateau 1470 m above sea level and above the sweltering river lowlands of the Zambezi River in the north and the Limpopo River in the south. It's a small capital city by international standards, though the wider metropolitan area has a population of around 1.6 million.

The main road from Harare to Bulawayo, the A5, passes through the towns of the Midlands Province. Founded in colonial times as service towns for the surrounding gold and ore mines, none are remarkable and there's little to see or do, but the drive to Bulawayo affords the opportunity to experience the populated middle belt of Zimbabwe, away from the remote bush regions. The exception and the highlight along this route is the Antelope Park near Gweru, where there are a number of game activities on offer.

Harare and around

Harare, Zimbabwe's capital, grew from a colonial town called Salisbury, founded in 1890. Today it is the largest city and the country's administrative, commercial and communications centre. It has year-round good weather. The central business district is a neat grid of modern office blocks, intercepted by some older colonial buildings, with broad streets lined with flowering trees. The suburbs, too, are colourful in spring, when the jacaranda and flame trees are in bloom. Although the once-excellent infrastructure suffered during Zimbabwe's economic meltdown and the subsequent bankruptcy of the city council, improvements are finally being made; there are visible signs of pot holes being repaired and public gardens being tended. ▸▸ *For listings, see pages 67-82.*

Ins and outs → *Phone code: 04. Population: 1.6 million. Colour map 2, B1.*

Getting there

Air **Harare International Airport** ⓘ *12 km southeast of the city in Harare South on Airport Rd, T04-575 164/8, www.caaz.co.zw,* is the major gateway for flights into the country. For more information about getting to Zimbabwe by plane, see Essentials, page 20. There is a US$30 international departure tax and a US$5 domestic departure tax from Harare, but these are usually included in the price of an air ticket.

There are two terminal buildings at Harare International Airport. The fairly new 36,000 sq m international terminal opened in 2000 for a much larger number of flights than it currently handles. Its distinctive feature is the control tower built to resemble the conical ruins at Great Zimbabwe (see page 121). Facilities include banks, ATMs (Visa only), bureaux de change (generally open 0600-2200), post office, restaurants and, beyond customs, duty free shops. There are car hire desks in international arrivals (see Transport, page 81) and taxis meet incoming flights. A ride into the city centre should cost in the region of US$20-30, but check with someone inside the airport first. Alternatively pre-arrange an airport pickup with your hotel. The original building was built in 1951 and now houses the domestic terminal.

Rent a Fone ⓘ *T04-585041/2/3, www.tradefone.co.zw,* has a desk in the arrivals section of the international terminal, which rents out cell phones for US$10 per day and sim cards for US$10 per day if you have your own hand set. Much better value is to buy a new sim pack for US$20, which includes US$5 air time.

Bus and train Most international buses arrive at and depart from the **Road Port Terminal** on the corner of Robert Mugabe and Fifth streets (see Getting there, page 22). Economy buses to and from Zimbabwe's other towns leave from the **Mbare Musika** bus terminal south of the market in Mbare. The only option from here into the city centre is to catch a commuter omnibus. The luxury **Citylink** buses, which link Harare with Bulawayo and then Victoria Falls arrive at and depart from the **Rainbow Towers Hotel** and the **Pathfinder** buses to and from Bulawayo arrive and depart from the **Holiday Inn**.

The **railway station** is centrally located off Kenneth Kaunda Avenue. Trains connect Harare with Bulawayo and then Victoria Falls, and there's another service to Mutare. Taxis are available at the station. See Essentials, page 25, for details about travelling by train.
▸▸ *For further details, see Transport, page 81.*

Getting around

Orientation In the **Central Business District (CBD)**, Samora Machel Avenue runs from west to east through the financial and administrative district. South of here and bordered by Julius Nyerere Way and Sam Nujoma Street, and Robert Mugabe Road in the south, is the **commercial district** where most of the shops are located. North of here is **Avenues**, a leafy area of large houses, embassies and private hospitals and schools, while to the southwest of the CBD around **Mbare** is the more informal and rougher part of the city where there are markets, roadside businesses and teaming commuter omnibus stands. To the north of the city are numerous suburbs, once the enclaves for wealthy white residents; they have retained the names given to them by the colonial administrators, such as Borrowdale, Mount Pleasant, Avondale and Marlborough. To the southwest of the city, sprawling and highly populated **Highfield** incorporates a number of chronically poor townships.

Buses and taxis The CBD is small enough to walk around. To get to the suburbs, both government-run buses operated by the **Zimbabwe United Passenger Company (ZUPCO)** and **commuter omnibuses** ply the main roads. The larger buses stop at clearly marked bus stops while the commuter omnibuses need to be flagged down and stop when a passenger wants to get off. Because of overcrowding and the danger of petty crime, neither is particularly recommended for visitors, and the commuter omnibus drivers are notoriously bad. But costs for both are cheap – about US$0.50 for a short ride, US$1 for a longer ride to the outlying suburbs and during rush hour. As there are no US$0.50 coins in circulation, fares are paid with South African R5 coins (roughly US$0.50) or three trillion old Zimbabwe dollars. A passenger will buy two lots of three trillion Zimbabwe dollars for US$1, which will provide two rides on public transport. If you are going to Zimbabwe from South Africa, it is well worthwhile bringing a handful of R5 coins for such purposes, as well as for leaving small tips.

Taxis are metered and can be found outside most hotels and at stands throughout the city. You can also hire a car for a day or two to explore on your own; apart from the odd pothole and non-working traffic lights. The traffic is fairly orderly. However, drive slowly and do watch for commuter omnibuses that often stop sharply to pick up passengers and pull away from the side of the road without indicating. ▶▶ *For further details, see Transport, page 81.*

Maps Street maps of Harare are very scarce; ask at the tourist office to see if any new ones have been published. However, the grid pattern of the CBD is fairly easy to navigate.

Best time to visit

Harare sits at an altitude of 1472 m, so temperatures are modest. During the warm and wet season from November until April, days are sunny with temperatures averaging 25°C during the day. The rains, usually short afternoon electrical showers, begin in November and the wettest month is January. May through August are the coolest and driest months, and daytime temperatures average 20°C but drop significantly at night to around 7°C; in July there are even occasional frosts. The hottest months are October and November, when daytime temperatures climb into the 30s°C; before the onset of the rains is when it is at its most humid. Flowering trees with vivid colours line many streets at different times of the year. The jacarandas in September and October are spectacular.

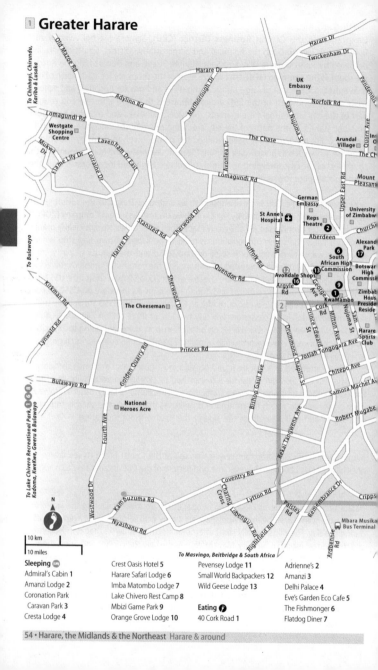

1 Greater Harare

Sleeping 🛏

Admiral's Cabin **1**
Amanzi Lodge **2**
Coronation Park
Caravan Park **3**
Cresta Lodge **4**

Crest Oasis Hotel **5**
Harare Safari Lodge **6**
Imba Matombo Lodge **7**
Lake Chivero Rest Camp **8**
Mbizi Game Park **9**
Orange Grove Lodge **10**

Pevensey Lodge **11**
Small World Backpackers **12**
Wild Geese Lodge **13**

Eating 🍴

40 Cork Road **1**

Adrienne's **2**
Amanzi **3**
Delhi Palace **4**
Eve's Garden Eco Cafe **5**
The Fishmonger **6**
Flatdog Diner **7**

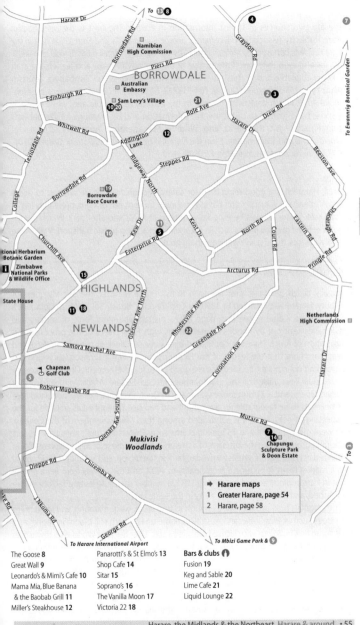

The Goose **8**
Great Wall **9**
Leonardo's & Mimi's Cafe **10**
Mama Mia, Blue Banana
  & the Baobab Grill **11**
Miller's Steakhouse **12**

Panarotti's & St Elmo's **13**
Shop Cafe **14**
Sitar **15**
Soprano's **16**
The Vanilla Moon **17**
Victoria 22 **18**

Bars & clubs 🍷
Fusion **19**
Keg and Sable **20**
Lime Cafe **21**
Liquid Lounge **22**

Tourist information

There are two sources of tourist information in Harare. The best is the very helpful **Harare Publicity Association** ① *corner of George Silundika Av and Sam Nujoma St in the Harare Gardens opposite the Meikles Hotel, T04-705085/6/7, Mon-Fri 0800-1600, Sat 0800-1200*, for although they have little to give out in the way of maps and leaflets the staff are knowledgeable and enthusiastic. The second resource is the **Zimbabwe Tourism Authority** ① *155 Samora Machel Av, T04-758712/14, www.zimbabwetourism.co.zw, Mon-Fri 0800-1630*, which deals with tourism in the country as a whole and, when in stock, has some basic leaflets to distribute. For information and reservations for Zimbabwe's national parks, visit the **Parks and Wildlife Management Authority** ① *corner of Borrowdale Rd and Sandringham Dr in the National Herbarium and Botanic Gardens, T04-706077-8, www.zimparks.com, Mon-Fri 0800-1600*.

Safety

Overall, Harare has a good reputation for safety, though tourists are advised to avoid displays of wealth. Valuables and passports should be kept out of sight, preferably left in a hotel safe. Visitors should be especially cautious at ATMs and after dark. Watch out for pickpockets in crowded places such as Mbare Market and on public transport. If you have a car always lock it and never leave anything on display.

Background

Originally called Salisbury after the then British Prime Minister, the 3rd Marquess of Salisbury, Harare was founded in 1890 by Cecil Rhodes' British South Africa Company's (BSAC) Pioneer Column (see box, page 87), a military volunteer force of settlers and missionaries sent out by Rhodes to make deals with local chiefs, in the process of his colonization of Africa. Harare is dominated by a *kopje* (a hillock or pile of boulders), and it was from here that the leader of the Pioneer Column, Frank Johnson, surveying the surrounding open plains, decided it was a good place for a settlement. On 13 September, the Union Jack was raised on the spot that became Cecil Square (Africa Unity Square after independence), and a 21-gun salute was made to Queen Victoria. The Mashonaland area was believed to be favourable for agriculture and had been identified as suitable for the prospecting of gold. Land was subdivided among the civilian members of the Column, who were given 1250 ha and 15 mining claims each. The settlers built an earthwork fort on sloping ground along the left bank of a stream, now the course of Julius Nyerere Way in modern-day Harare. More settlers arrived to farm in the region, and Salisbury quickly grew into a market town; it became a municipality in 1897, and the railway from Beira on the coast in Mozambique arrived in 1899. By 1935, a number of industries and factories were established, and it officially became a city in the same year.

The colonials built avenues wide enough to turn an ox-wagon around, and lined them with trees such as jacarandas and Australian flame trees, which still bloom in spring, and built some fine buildings with lattice balconies. Later, after the First World War, townships of simple houses were built for returning black soldiers, but standards of accommodation contrasted sharply with the spacious gardens and houses of the European suburbs. Later, in the 1950s during a prosperous period of tobacco farming, some 80 office blocks went up in the city centre. During the second anniversary of Zimbabwean independence in 1982, the city's name was changed to Harare. This was derived from the Shona chieftain Neharawa, which had lived in the area before the colonials arrived. The chief was called

Haarare, meaning 'one who does not sleep'. It was said that no enemy could ever launch a sneak attack on him.

Sights

Although sights in Harare are limited, there is a clutch of good museums that exhibit the country's history, flora and fauna, some attractive parks, and the best shops and restaurants in the country. The National Gallery showcases Zimbabwe's unique and splendid Shona sculptures, and Heroes Acre is a monument to those who fell during the grim guerrilla war that finally ended with independence in 1980. Outside Harare are a number of outdoors attractions including the Ewanrigg Botanical Gardens, which are famed for their aloes, and Lake Chivero, a popular venue for boating, fishing and game-viewing.

Central Business District (CBD)
Harare's skyline boasts a mixture of architecture that reflects the city's history. A number of colonial buildings have survived, including the shops around Robert Mugabe Avenue, which date to the turn of the 20th century. They feature wrought-iron pillars and Cape Dutch gables, and some have pillared canopies over the pavement under which shoppers can walk. The imposing **Town House** on Julius Nyerere Way was built in 1933 and has a white-pillared facade with some art deco and Florentine features. Today it is home to the Harare City Council. From here, walk four blocks east along Jason Moyo Avenue to **Africa Unity Square**. Formerly Cecil Square and named after Cecil Rhodes, this was established on the spot where the Pioneer Column first raised the Union Jack in 1890. A bronze flagstaff marks the spot. The impressive fountain was built to commemorate the colony's Diamond Jubilee in 1950; its name was changed in 1988 to celebrate the joining of the two main political parties, ZANU and ZAPU, to form ZANU-PF. Today it's an attractive little park of established trees and flowering plants, some of which originally came from Rhodes' own garden at his cottage in Muizenberg in Cape Town. Flower and souvenir sellers can be found on the Jason Moyo Avenue side.

Across Nelson Mandela Avenue to the northwest is the **Saint Mary and All Saints Anglican Cathedral** ① *daily 0645-1845*, which stands on the site of the first church built in 1890 from mud and poles. The original altar cross, made of cigar boxes, is now in the cathedral's St George's Chapel. The cathedral was designed by the acclaimed architect Herbert Baker, who built many prominent buildings in South Africa, including Union Buildings, Pretoria's seat of government. Construction began in 1913 but it was only fully completed in 1964. The 10 bells in the tower were cast in London; each bears an English rose and an African flame lily in its casting. The cathedral's stark interior of granite columns is softened a little by some pastel-coloured murals of the Stations of the Cross.

To the east of the cathedral, on the corner of Nelson Mandela Avenue and Third Street, the **Parliament Buildings** date to 1895 but have been considerably expanded and amended since then. Today the building is considered too small and the government is seeking funding (possibly from China) for a new parliament. Nearby, the sandstone **Supreme Court** on the corner of Union Avenue and Third Street dates to 1927, and was built on the site of Cecil Rhodes' headquarters for the British South Africa Company (BSAC), originally built in 1895.

With one notable exception – the monstrously ugly 19-floor **Monomotapa Hotel** (see Sleeping, page 67) on the edge of Harare Gardens – there is little evidence of 1970s architecture, as the Bush War halted any development during this period. The 1980s

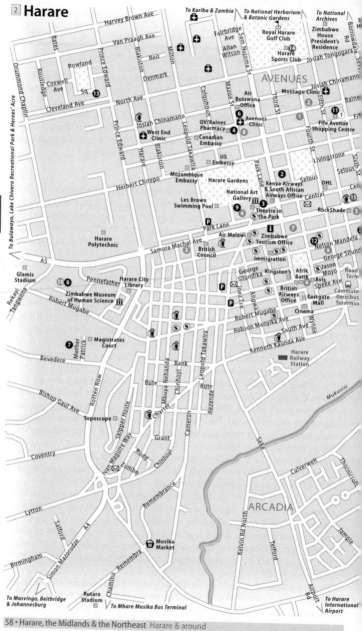

To Kariba & Zambia

To National Herbarium & Botanic Gardens

To National Archives

Harvey Brown Ave

Van Praagh Ave

Fairbridge Ave

Royal Harare Golf Club

Zimbabwe House President's Residence

Milton

Allan Wilson

Harare Sports Club

Beit

Denmark

AVENUES

Montagu Clinic

Coxwell Ave

Rowland Sq

Cleveland Ave

North Ave

Josiah Chinamano

Air Botswana Office

Avenues Clinic

Fife Avenue Shopping Centre

West End Clinic

QV/Baines Pharmacy

Canadian Embassy

US Embassy

Livingstone

Herbert Chitepo

Mozambique Embassy

Harare Gardens

Park Lane

Kenya Airways & South African Airways Office

DHL

Les Brown Swimming Pool

National Art Gallery

Theatre in the Park

RockShade

Harare Polytechnic

Park Lane

Air Malawi

Zimbabwe Tourism Office

Nelson Mandela

Samora Machal Ave

British Council

Immigration

George Silundika

Glamis Stadium

Harare City Library

Pennefather

George Silundika

Kingston's

Afrik Batik

Jason Moyo

Road Term

Zimbabwe Museum of Human Science

British Airways Office

Avis Speke Ave

Commute Omnibus Terminus

Robert Mugabe

Eastgate Mall

Inez Tce

Magistrates Court

Robson Manyika Ave

Cinema

Bevedere

Mother Patrick

South Ave

Wynne

Kenneth Kaunda Ave

Harare Railway Station

Bishop Gaul Ave

Rotten Row

Bute

Mbuya Nehanda

Bank

Chinhoyi

Bute

Rezende

Mukuvisi

Toposcope

Charter

Coventry

Skipper Hoste

Grant

Rudd

Cameron

Chinhoyi

Remembrance

ARCADIA

Lytton

Ivan Maguire Way

Zumbo

Culverwell

Birmingham

Simon Mazorodze

A4

Chaminu Remembra

Musika Market

To Masvingo, Beitbridge & Johannesburg

Rutaro Stadium

To Mbare Musika Bus Terminal

To Harare International Airport

Airport Rd

To Bulawayo, Lake Chivero Recreational Park & Heroes' Acre

➡ **Harare maps**
1 Greater Harare, page 54
2 Harare, page 58

300 metres
300 yards

Sleeping ⊜
Baines Hotel 1
Bronte Hotel 2
Cresta Jameson Hotel 3
Crowne Plaza Monomotapa 4
Holiday Inn 5
Meikles Hotel 6
New Ambassador Hotel 7
Palm Lodge 8
Quality International Hotel 9
Rainbow Towers 10

Eating 🍴
Alo Alo 1
Alexander's 2
Bannie's 3
The Bottom Drawer 4
Coimbra 5
Gaby's 6
Jaipur 7
La Patisserie & Harvest Garden 8
Le Français 9
L'Escargot 10
Lucullus Cafe & Book Cafe 11
Mokador 12
The Wild Cherry 13

Bars & clubs 🍸
Maiden Public House 14
Symphony 15

Entertainment 🎵
Mannenberg Jazz Club 1

were a little more prosperous, though, and today the CBD is dominated by a clutch of modern skyscrapers built in the wake of post-independence confidence. The city's most striking modern building is the **Eastgate Centre** (see Shopping, page 78), south of Africa Unity Square and hemmed in by Sam Nujoma Street and Robert Mugabe Road. Opened in 1996, it is Zimbabwe's largest shopping and office complex. With its distinctive row of pink cooling chimneys, it was thought at the time to be the first modern building in the world to use natural methods of ventilation. It has no conventional air conditioning or heating, yet its temperature stays regulated year-round using design methods inspired by self-cooling mounds of African termites. Inside their mounds, termites farm a fungus, their primary food source, which must be kept at a moderate temperature; the termites achieve this by constantly opening and closing air vents in their mound. The Eastgate Centre's ventilation system operates in a similar way; it is estimated that it uses around 10% less energy than a conventional building of its size would use – just as well given the 1990s fuel shortages.

To the southwest of the CBD, the **Kopje**, a granite hill rising above central Harare, is a great place to go for views of the city. To get here, walk or drive up Skipper Hoste from Robert Mugabe Road or Rotten Row. The first commercial area of the city was built at its foot; it is now called Mbare. A toposcope indicates the direction and distances of various points of interest.

National Gallery of Zimbabwe
ⓘ *20 Julius Nyerere Way, T04-704666/7, www.nationalgallery.co.za, Mon-Sat 0900-1630, US$1, children under 12 US$0.50.*
Located in an airy glass-panelled building with plenty of light, this houses a valuable and interesting collection of paintings and has a permanent display of outstanding Shona soapstone carvings. Opened in

1957, it displays a significant number of European old masters, including a selection of 19th-century pre-Raphaelite and Impressionist work, as well as contemporary art from across the African continent. Upstairs is a display of traditional artefacts such as head rests, beadwork, baskets and weapons. The gallery hosts frequent temporary exhibitions; portraits of independence heroes or HIV/AIDs prevention posters from around the world are recent examples. Formerly known as the Rhodes National Gallery, it was for a time under the directorship of Frank McEwen, who is credited with bringing the Shona sculpture into the spotlight. In the late 1960s, McEwan ran a workshop for sculptors at the gallery, and in the 1970s went on to take their work overseas, to the Museum of Modern Art in New York and Musée Rodin in Paris, among others. The exhbitions met with critical acclaim, and Shona sculpture is now popular worldwide. The gardens at the rear and front of the gallery contain some fine examples. Most have abstract designs and represent images from folklore and the spirit world of the Shona people. In 2007, the gallery celebrated its 50th anniversary. There's a cafe with Wi-Fi access and a curio shop.

Harare Gardens

Behind the National Gallery, the Harare Gardens is the city's largest and oldest park. Standing on a portion of land set aside for public use by Cecil Rhodes when he planned the city, it has an island-like stand of rainforest that contains a miniature model of Victoria Falls, the Zambezi Gorge and the famous railway bridge. These were made to scale by a former superintendent of the park – even a rainbow can be seen over the falls in the morning sun. Also in the park is a rather plain, sandstone obelisk dedicated to those who lost their lives in the First World War, and a lily-covered pond, built in 1937 to celebrate the coronation of George VI. The park is a popular picnic spot with established trees, manicured lawns and tended flower beds, and an open-air public swimming pool popular with school children. It is also a venue for the Harare International Festival of the Arts (HIFA). See page 35.

Zimbabwe Museum of Human Science

ⓘ *Civic Centre, Rotten Row, T04-771797, 0900-1700, US$5, children (5-12), US$3, under 5 free.*
Formerly known as Queen Victoria Museum, this dusty little museum opened in 1903 and shifted three times before settling in the Civic Centre in 1964. It has displays on natural history, including some mock-up recreations of the various landscapes found in Zimbabwe, with a collection of stuffed mammals, birds and amphibians, and some fossil and palaeontology displays. There are illustrations of early stone-walled cities such as Great Zimbabwe, and also a life-size 19th-century homestead demonstrating typical traditional village life of the Shona people. It's mildly diverting but is eclipsed by the far superior Natural History Museum in Bulawayo (see page 140).

Mbare

Mbare is a poor, high-density suburb off Cripps Road, 3 km to the south of the CBD. Under Rhodesian racial law (see page 238), the urban areas were no-go areas for Africans, and so the township was established in 1907. It was supposed to be a temporary arrangement and the dwellings reflected that intention, with all kinds of shacks with poor amenities. Africans of whatever status lived in Mbare in line with the dictates of the Land Apportionment Act, and unsurprisingly it became a hotbed of nationalist organization against minority rule during the colonial times. Significant parts of Mbare were destroyed in 2005 during the government's Operation Murambatsvina. In Shona, the word *murambatsvina* roughly translates as 'drive out rubbish', but in English it was also known as Operation Restore

Order. It was an ostensible move to get rid of illegal structures, illegal businesses and criminal activities in urban areas. Today it's home to a frenetic and vibrant market, known as *Musika*, selling just about everything imaginable from fruit and vegetables and second-hand clothes, to traditional medicine and curios. There are plenty of commuter omnibuses running here from town, or you can get here by walking down Rotten Row or Cameron Street. It's very crowded so beware of pickpockets. Mbare is also the home of the Rufaro Stadium, which hosted Bob Marley during independence celebrations in 1980 and the 6th All-Africa Games in 1995. It's also the home ground of Dynamos Football Club, considered to be Zimbabwe's best team.

Around the city → *For listings, see pages 67-82.*

National Archives
ⓘ *Borrowdale Rd, Gun Hill, take Seventh St 3 km north of the CBD, T04-792741, Mon-Fri 0830-1600, free.*

Founded in 1935, the archives hold a priceless collection of Rhodesiana and Africana documentation. It is the custodian of all the records of central government and local authorities and also holds the papers, diaries and notebooks of private individuals who have contributed to the history and development of the country. Some of these date back to the mid-16th century and document the first Portuguese adventurers. Original works of some of the greatest names in African exploration and missionary can be viewed, including Livingstone's diaries and paintings of the pioneering days by Thomas Baines. Not to be missed is his painting of the Victoria Falls; he was the first artist to paint them. Additionally it is home to the national reference library, which has pictorial, audio-visual and map collections, and special deposits, such as coins, medals and postage stamps. Although much is off limits, the parts of the collection open to visitors are very interesting, and it is a major source for the history of not only of the colonial period but of the Shona and Ndebele peoples. At the entrance you can buy some good prints of early sepia photographs of Victoria Falls and other turn-of-the-20th-century historical scenes.

National Herbarium and Botanic Gardens
ⓘ *Corner of Fifth St Extension and Downie Av, Alexandra Park, follow Fifth St from the CBD for 4 km, T04-708938, www.nationalherbarium.org.zw, 0600-1800, US$2, children (under 12) US$1, car US$1.*

The 68-ha National Herbarium and Botanic Gardens was started in 1909 by a Mr MG Mundy, who was appointed as the Government Agriculturist and Botanist. Today they are home to more than 900 species of wild trees and shrubs and about 500,000 plant specimens. The greater part of the garden is dedicated to Zimbabwean flora, and approximately 80% of the indigenous woody plant species found in the country are grown here. They are arranged to depict the main vegetation landscapes such as the semi-arid Zambezi Valley or the high-altitude forested slopes of the Eastern Highlands. It also serves as the main reference centre in southern Africa for identifying and naming plants of the Flora Zambesiaca region. This comprises Zimbabwe, Zambia, Malawi, Mozambique, Botswana and the Caprivi Strip in Namibia. There are some non-indigenous species from Australia and Asia, like eucalyptus and Burma teak, which also thrive in Zimbabwe's climate. There are paths to follow, the trees are well labelled, and there's an attractive artificial lake, which is covered in water lilies and Okavango water figs. There used to be a tea garden here; it may reopen in the future.

Mukuvisi Woodlands

ⓘ *5 km from the CBD, follow Samora Machel Av for 4 km, turn right into Glenara Av, the entrance is on the left on the corner of Hillside Rd, T04-757111, 0800-1700, US$1 adults and children, tea garden, Wildlife & Environment Zimbabwe (WEZ) shop, T04-747859, Mon-Fri 0800-1700, Sat 0900-1700, Sun 0900-1300.*

The Mukuvisi Woodlands is a 275-ha area of preserved woodland on the banks of the small Mukuvisi stream. It is home to a variety of birdlife and some animal species, including giraffe, zebra, impala, tsessebe, wildebeest, bushbuck, steenbuck, reed buck and eland. As it's so close to the city, it's popular with familes at weekends, who come to enjoy a braai, and groups of local schoolchildren, some of whom are seeing such animals for the first time, as they are generally found only in the larger game parks. You can take a self-guided walk along the network of trails or hire a braai stand (US$1) and buy a bundle of firewood (US$2). However, the best options are to join the one-hour guided walk (US$5; daily at 0830 and 1430), or a one-hour horse ride (US$5; suitable for complete novices; daily at 0830, 1100, 1500), to learn more about the trees and animals. There are also shorter pony rides (US$2) for young children. With a recorded list of over 270 bird species, the woodlands are an ideal spot for birdwatching and birdwatching safaris for up to four people can be arranged with Daniel, the resident ornithologist, for US$40. The Prinsilla's tea garden serves scones, pies, milkshakes and ice cream. In the car park, the shop run by the voluntary Wildlife & Environment Zimbabwe (WEZ) is quite a treasure trove. As well as selling curios, paintings and prints, its shelves are stacked high with new and second-hand books, with a strong emphasis on wildlife, nature, local history and local writers.

National Heroes Acre

ⓘ *Warren Park, 7 km from the CBD off the A5/Bulawayo road, US$10, children (under 12) US$5, 0800-1630.*

Covering 57 acres on a hill overlooking Harare, this has been a favourite spot for President Mugabe to deliver bombastic speeches denouncing his foes; the amphitheatre on the opposite hill seats 5000 people. Built in 1981 as a memorial and burial ground to the heroes who lost their lives while fighting for independence in the Bush War, the complex includes 80 tombs which curve away in rows. These include tombs of some of the main leaders in the fight for independence including Jason Moyo, Joshua Nkomo, and Leopold Takawira. One of the tombs contains the remains of Mugabe's mother; it is not yet known if he intends to be buried alongside her when he dies. There is also a 40-m-high soaring black granite obelisk topped with an eternal flame (an electric light), a bronze statue of the Unknown Soldier, comprising a male soldier with a flag, a male soldier with a bazooka, and a female soldier carrying an AK47. A series of bronze bas reliefs show scenes from the dark days of the struggle, including one scene of white Rhodesian soldiers bearing down on a black woman with a baby strapped to her back. The architects were from North Korea and from the air the mausoleum is meant to resemble an AK47 rifle, the most potent weapon in the guerrilla war for independence; the central stairway is the barrel, the obelisk is the bayonet and the graves are the bullets in their chambers. Parts of the monument are also meant to denote aspects of Great Zimbabwe. It is worth enlisting the services of a guide (free) at the visitor centre to explain the full significance of each part of the complex. The visitor centre also has a very interesting gallery of photographs from the liberation struggle, including grainy shots of Mugabe and Joshua Nkomo from the 1960s (when they were detained with others by Ian Smith's government), and some very gruesome photographs of detention camps and mass graves. Despite all misgivings about modern Zimbabwe today, it's a fascinating look at the liberation struggle. An added advantage is the great view from the top of the monument, across the skyline of Harare and as far at the airport control tower.

Chapungu Sculpture Park

ⓘ *1 Harrow Rd, Msasa, 8 km from the CBD off the A3/Mutare road, next to the shops at Doon Estate (see Shopping, page 77), T04-486 648 or 486 656, www.chapungusculpturepark.com, Mon-Fri 0800-1700, Sat-Sun 0900-1700.*

Founded in 1970, Chapungu Sculpture Park has been instrumental in the promotion of Zimbabwe Shona stone sculpture all over the world; indeed, there is now a sister sculpture park in Colorado in the US. Some fine sculptures are showcased in the gardens of this 6-ha park, which has an attractive dam, shady trees and rocky outcrops. It comprises 80 pieces altogether, covering eight sections: Nature and the Environment, The Family, Custom and Legend, Village Life, The Role of Women, The Spirit World, The Role of the Elders and Social Comment. Many are human and animal figures, while others are completely abstract. Some of the outside sculptures reach heights of 2-3 m, while smaller ones are displayed in the indoor gallery. Dotted around the park are informal thatched shelters where you can watch and chat to the sculptors while they work. To buy sculptures, either negotiate with the sculptors directly or with one of managers, who will soon find you if you are wandering around. Statues made here are also displayed in the Chicago Botanical Gardens and the Kirstenbosch Botanical Gardens in Cape Town.

Chiremba Balancing Rocks

ⓘ *Epworth, off Chiremba Rd, 13 km from the CBD.*

These unusual and large granite rock formations are quite striking, and years of erosion have left a series of boulders scattered around the bush; these literally balance on top of each other. Pictures of them once graced some Zimbabwe banknotes. You can drive out here or take a taxi, but you'll see similar balancing rock formations in Matobo National Park near Bulawayo (see page 144) and other places around the country.

Ewanrigg Botanical Garden

ⓘ *36 km from the CBD; follow Enterprise Rd, after 29 km take the left-hand fork, the A13 Shamva road, and after 4 km turn right for 3 km on gravel to the entrance, daily 0800-1700, US$10, children 6-12 US$5, under 6 free, car US$5.*

This 100-ha garden is known for its collection of aloes and cycads, best seen in the winter months, which attract large numbers of nectar-eating birds, particularly sunbirds. There is also a further 200 ha of miombo woodland, also excellent birdwatching territory, where some 275 species have been recorded. The garden was established by Harold Christian, who came to Rhodesia to farm in 1914. He turned his attention to botany and planted his garden with aloes, cycads and many species of small succulents. He named the garden after his brother Ewan, who was killed in the First World War, and added 'rigg', the Welsh word for 'ridge'. In 1950, he gave his garden to the government, after which it was extended with plants that hold interest throughout the year, spacious lawns and a water feature, and it was opened to the public. The many sunbirds are a main attraction, particularly during June, July and August when the aloes are in flower. Species of sunbird to look for include the white-bellied, variable, scarlet-chested, amethyst and miombo double-collared, all of which are common. Other birds include the grey-rumped swallow, cattle egret and Abdim's stork and, in the miombo woodland, Whyte's barbet and the greater blue-eared starling. There are picnic sites but no other facilities.

Mbizi Game Park

ⓘ *22 km south of the CBD; follow Seke Rd south, turn left into Dieppe Rd, right on to Airport Rd, left on to Harare Drive, then right on to Twentydales Rd and follow it to the end, reservations T04-700676-8, park 04-291 5737, www.mbizi.co.zw, daily 0800-1700, tea garden 0930-1700, US$5, children (under 12) US$3, canoe hire US$10 per person, mountain bike hire US$10, game drive US$10, game walk US$5, horse riding US$10, children's pony rides US$2.*

This is a privately run 1000-sq-km game park which is well stocked with zebra, giraffe, impala, steenbok, eland, kudu and warthog. It can be explored on guided game drives, walks and horse trails or you can hire mountain bikes. *Mbizi* means zebra in Shona. The landscape is typical savannah bush and the animals are easily seen. An 11-km stretch of the Manyame River is also navigable by canoe. There is some good overnight accommodation (see Sleeping, page 69), but day visitors are welcome for activities and to visit the pretty tea room, which has tables on the lawns and serves organically produced beef, chicken, dairy products and vegetables grown in the park. All visitors can also use the swimming pool which is built 30 m above ground on a *kopje*, with a waterfall slide and great views of the park.

Bally Vaughan Animal Sanctuary

ⓘ *40 km from the CBD; follow Enterprise Rd, after 20 km take the left-hand fork, the A13 Shamva road for 20 km; T04-497588, 303518, www.ballyvaughan.co.zw, Tue-Sun 0900-1700, US$3, children 2-12 US$2, under 2s free, optional tours 0930-1230 and 1400-1700, US$5; restaurant.*

This sanctuary for sick and abandoned animals was established in 1992. It was put under increased pressure during Zimbabwe's economic crisis, as many wild and farm animals were abandoned in the region. Nevertheless it managed to find the funding to remain open and it welcomes visitors' donations. Antelope, zebra and giraffe roam the 12-ha area of bush and woodland that surround a pretty lake. A half-day visit, which must be pre-booked, includes a guided tour of the enclosures to see, among other species, lion, leopard, blue duiker, caracal, serval, civet and crocodile. There's the opportunity to feed and see baby vervet monkeys and baboons, owls being prepared for rehabilitation into the wild and farm animals such as sheep and donkeys. Most unusually, the sanctuary is home to both a *zorse*, a cross between a zebra and a horse, and a *zonkey*, a cross between a zebra and a donkey. Additionally, on afternoon tours, visitors can watch the cats and the crocodiles being fed at 1600. Morning or afternoon tea and cakes are included and lunch in the restaurant is available on request.

Lion and Cheetah Park

ⓘ *23 km from Harare on the Bulawayo road, T062-27567, Mon-Fri 0830-1630, Sat-Sun 0830-1730, US$5, children (2-12) US$3, entry to cub enclosure US$3 (no children under 12), snake park US$4, children (2-12) US$2.*

Just a 15-minute drive from the city centre, this park offers the opportunity to see some great wildlife up close, and not all in cages and behind fences. There are three parts to the park: the lion enclosure, which you can drive through, and as it's not so big you are almost guaranteed to get just metres from the eight lions that live there; the main zoo section, laid out in pretty gardens among giant boulders, which has lots of animal enclosures including more lion, one pair of cheetah, hyena, baboon, crocodile, ostrich and a giant 300-year-old Galapagos tortoise; and a large game-drive area with free-roaming wildebeest, zebra, impala, nyala and lots of birds, which takes about 30 minutes to drive around. In the zoo section, a guide will meet you in the car park and then take you around; information boards at each enclosure also give details about the animals. While the park has only two cheetah at present, it is home to over 40 lion, so there are usually cubs. These live in the cubs' enclosure until they are three months old, and for an extra fee visitors can enter the enclosure to pet and play with them. The lions are fed most afternoons between 1400 and 1700. There's a tea and curio shop, and at the main entrance on the Bulawayo road there's a small snake park with some local snakes behind glass.

Lake Chivero → *For listings, see pages 67-82. Colour map 2, B1.*

Lake Chivero, about 10 km south of the Bulawayo road, was created out of the Hunyani River, which was dammed in 1952 to create a reservoir to supply Salisbury with drinking water. The dam wall is 400 m long. The northern shore is reached by two roads: one turns off 16 km from the city centre, and the other 13 km further on (the lake is about 10 km from both roads). The lake is very much a weekend day-trip destination for Harare residents, who braai, mountain bike and mess about in boats here, and there are a number of private yacht clubs on the northern shore. It is also popular with fishermen after tigerfish, carp and bream, so there are some fenced private fishing camps and jetties. Even if you are here for the day, a stop at the **Harare Safari Lodge** (see Sleeping, page 69) on the northern shore is worthwhile, to have tea on the veranda and stroll across the rolling green lawns to the lake for a view of the dam wall. In contrast, the southern shore is the location of a game park, the Lake Chivero Recreational Park (see below), which is accessed from a road further south along the Bulawayo road. **Note** The presence of bilharzia and the odd crocodile means you can't swim in the lake.

Kuimba Shiri Bird Garden
① *Take the turn-off from the Bulawayo road 16 km from the city centre, T062-2309, birdpark@ mweb.co.zw, Mon-Fri 1000-1700, Sat-Sun 0900-1700, US$7, restaurant.*
The name of this bird park means 'the birds are singing' in Shona. It is located under msasa trees on the shores of Lake Chivero, and perhaps provides the best public facilities at the lake. It is popular at weekends with locals, who come to picnic, swim in the pool, use the children's playground and eat in the open-air restaurant; there are also campsite and chalets (see Sleeping, page 70). Some 450 species of birds are housed in spacious enclosures and a walk-through aviary with trees, shrubs and little pools, and there's a flamingo pool and parrot house. Most birds common in Zimbabwe can be seen here, including the hornbill, black eagle, barn owl and ostrich, while the peregrine falcon, umbrella cockatoo, Indian mynah, Saker falcon and Cape vulture, to mention just a few, constitute the exotic brands. Every afternoon at 1500, the garden hosts a free-flying bird of prey display. Some of the birds have been hand-reared from eggs, while others are brought to the aviary because they have been wounded or abandoned, often by flying into power lines.

Lake Chivero Recreational Park
① *T062-3337, www.zimparks.com, 0600-1800, US$10, children (6-12) US$5, (under 6) free, car US$5.*
Lake Chivero Recreational Park covers 6100 ha, of which 2632 ha is taken up by the irregularly shaped Lake Chivero, which has a total shoreline of 48 km and is 8 km across at its widest point. The park, which features open savannah and clutches of woodland, was

inaugurated in 1962, and was formerly known as Lake McIlwaine Recreational Park, after Sir Robert McIlwaine, a former high court judge.

Ins and outs The game area is accessed along a different road from the one used to access facilities on the north shore of the lake. Entry to the park is only permitted in a vehicle, and is accessed 32 km from Harare, on the A5/Bulawayo road. Turn left just after Manyame River Bridge which leads to the dam wall and the spillway on the lake. Before reaching the wall, take the right-hand fork to the entrance, office and rest camp. In the wet season, parts of the access road can become muddy but is still accessible in a normal car. There is a network of gravel roads in the park, of which Ostrich Loop and Impala Drive may require 4WDs in the wet. Guided 1½-hour horse rides around the park can be arranged at the office at 0800 and 1530 every day except Monday, US$15. Experienced riders can get very close to the rhino. There is accommodation in the way of ZPWMA chalets and campsites (see Sleeping, page 69).

Sights The park is home to a number of species of game, most of which were relocated from Hwange, but additional animals were brought in from Lake Kariba during the game rescue operation better known as Operation Noah (see page 218) in 1961. Animals present include white rhino, giraffe, zebra, wildebeest, warthog, ostrich, a variety of antelope including impala, eland and tsessebe, and shyer smaller mammals such as spring hare and rock hyrax. With a bird list of over 400 species, this is one of Zimbabwe's premier birdwatching destinations. The lake not only attracts waterfowl but many raptors, including African marsh-harrier, peregrine falcon, red-footed falcon and Wahlberg's eagle, and many pairs of African fish eagle breed around the lakeshore.

Hotel prices

L over US$400   A US$300-399   B US$175-299
C US$100-174   D US$50-99   E US$20-49
F under US$20

Restaurant prices

♔♔♔ over US$25   ♔♔ US$15-25   ♔ under US$15

See pages 29-34 for further information.

◉ Sleeping

Central Business District (CBD) p57, map p58

A Meikles Hotel, corner Jason Moyo Av and Third St, T04-251705/707 721, www.meikleshotel.com. Operating since 1915, this, the city's best hotel, has succeeded in retaining its 5-star grandeur. It has 317 a/c rooms, a good terrace restaurant overlooking Africa Unity Square, rooftop pool, gym, sauna, beauty parlour, business centre, tea lounge and the popular **Explorer's Club** (see Bars and clubs, page 74). The lobby and the foyer convey tranquil old-world opulence, complete with smartly dressed doormen, lush, deep-pile carpets and huge bowls of fresh flowers on polished wooden tables.

B Holiday Inn, Samora Machal Av, T04-795611, www.ichotelsgroup.com. Standard chain hotel offering 201 rooms in a white block, with satellite TV and a/c. Good mid-range standards and centrally located with secure parking. The **Vumba** restaurant serves buffets, plus Mongolian-style build-your-own stir fries and braais at the weekend, while the **Spur** is a steakhouse franchise. There's also a swimming pool, Wi-Fi and 2 bars.

B Rainbow Towers, Pennefather Av, T04-772633-9, www.rainbowtowershotel.com. This glass and concrete tower with 304 rooms was once a Sheraton. It was built in the early 1980s and hasn't had a refurbishment since then, so think brown/

beige decor, lumpy beds and old-fashioned atmosphere. On the plus side though, there are good city views from the higher floors, a reasonable buffet restaurant, experienced staff and a large well-maintained pool.

C Bronte Hotel, 132 Baines Av, T04-707522, www.brontehotel.com. Set in established subtropical gardens dotted with ponds and Shona sculptures in the peaceful Avenues area. It centres on the original Cape Dutch homestead built in 1911 for the director of the Rhodesia Mining Company. It has an 18-m swimming pool, and there are 102 plain but comfortable rooms, **Palms Restaurant** and **Wild Date Bar**. There are 32 slightly cheaper rooms in the **Queensgate Hotel** across the road, which shares the same facilities.

C Cresta Jameson Hotel, corner Samora Machal Av and Park St, T04-774106, www.cresta-hospitality.com. This is a neat modern block with 122 good standard rooms with a/c and satellite TV, terrace and cocktail bars, pool, parking, gift shop, business centre and 24-hr room service. Lunch and dinner are served at **Tiffany's Restaurant**; buffet breakfasts are at the **Sandawana Coffee shop**.

C Cresta Oasis Hotel, 124 Nelson Mandela Av, T04-704217-9, www.cresta-hospitality.com. Not quite as nice as the other Cresta properties and in an older building, but cheaper. Given the professional management, it represents good value, with 110 rooms with a/c and satellite TV, a neat pool with umbrellas and sun loungers, restaurant and bar, and gift shop.

C Crowne Plaza Monomotapa, 54 Park Lane, T04-704501, www.ichotelsgroup.com. This enormous 19-storey, 180-room hotel may not be aesthetically pleasing but it offers great views over Harare Gardens, and although a little dated is comfortable, with all mod cons including Wi-Fi, a/c, and minibars in the rooms. Facilities include 2 restaurants, gym, pool, massage parlour and 24-hr room service.

C New Ambassador Hotel, 88 Kwame Nkrumah Av, T04-708121/3/4, www.hararehotelnewambassador.com. A neat 3-star option with 72 simple but adequate rooms with TV and tea- and coffee-making facilities. The **Bird and Bottle** restaurant serves buffet and à la carte meals, and other facilities include a cocktail bar, pool and tennis court. Centrally located but no parking. Can be a little noisy.

D Baines Hotel, 121 Baines Av, Avenues, T04-707522/7. Situated diagonally across from the **Bronte** (see above), this is a slightly cheaper option with 35 comfortable rooms with TV, writing desks and spotless bathrooms. Breakfast is included and guests can use the restaurant, pool and other facilities at the **Bronte**. The hotel and avenue are named after Thomas Baines, renowned for his meticulous pictures of Victoria Falls painted on his travels in Zimbabwe during the late 19th century. Prints of these hang in the breakfast room.

D Palm Lodge, 11 Mazoe St, T04-708 419, www.palmlodge.co.zw. 32 simple but reasonably comfortable en suite rooms with TV and spotless bathrooms, some with balconies and additional bunk-beds for children. Located in a dated brick block in a quiet area of the Avenues, with parking and close to restaurants. A decent full English breakfast is included.

D Quality International Hotel, corner Nelson Mandela Av and Fourth St, T04-794460-9, www.qualityhotel.co.zw. A standard business hotel with 121 a/c rooms, in a boring square block with 4 floors. Centrally located with a fairly good range of facilities including room service, laundry, conference rooms, business centre, reasonable restaurant, coffee shop (selling cappuccino) and bar.

Around Harare *p51, map p54*
L Imba Matombo Lodge, 3 Albert Glen Close, Glen Lorne, T09-499071. Sitting high

on a hill in Harare's tranquil suburb of Glen Lorne, a 15-min drive from the CBD, is a luxury boutique hotel built of stone and thatch, with beautiful gardens. The spacious accommodation, either rooms in the main house or garden suites, is of a good standard, with satellite TV and African decor. There's a large pool set on sweeping lawns, a gym, tennis court and well-regarded **Conservatory Restaurant** with silverware and antique furnishings.

A Orange Grove Lodge, 22 Orange Grove Drive, Highlands, T04-496088, www.amanzi.co.za. Run by the same operation as the **Amanzi** property (see below), this is a beautifully restored 1940s Portuguese-style double-storey house with antiques and pine floors, and with an attractive water feature at the entrance. It sleeps 2-5 in 2 bedrooms, with 2 bathrooms, one with a claw-foot bath. Breakfast is included, and there's a kitchen for self-catering. There's also a pool in the tropical gardens.

A Pevensey Lodge, 6 Pevensey Rd, Highlands, T04-480880, www.amanzi.co.za. Another upmarket offering from the Amanzi stable, this house, in the style of a Tuscan villa, is set in woodland, with 6 spacious rooms, 2 with lofts for children, decorated in earthy tones and with Moroccan touches, stone showers, verandas, satellite TV, and Wi-Fi. There's a swimming pool, and dinner is available on request.

B Amanzi Lodge, 1 Masasa Lane, Kambanji, T04-499257, www.amanzi.co.za. Comprises 12 beautifully decorated thatched suites named after African countries, with relevant themed decor, colours and textiles. Mozambique has a seashell/driftwood style while Kenya, which has antiques and old leather suitcases, has a colonial feel. Some have free-standing baths, stone showers and private verandas overlooking superb landscaped tropical gardens. Facilities include Wi-Fi, pool and beauty treatments. Free transfers are provided to their restaurant on Enterprise Rd (see Eating, page 72).

C Cresta Lodge, Samora Machel Av, 6 km from the CBD towards Mutare, T04-477154, www.cresta-hospitality.com. Some way out of town towards Greendale, this was built in the late 1990s and still retains its freshness with 158 modern a/c rooms with satellite TV, large pool in spacious gardens, secure parking, Wi-Fi, **Chatters Restaurant** and **Continental bar** serving pub lunches.

C Wild Geese Lodge, 2 Buckland Lane, off Alps Rd, Borrowdale, T04-2930379, www.wildgeese.co.zw. Set in 12 ha of private wildlife sanctuary that is home to zebra and numerous antelope, this has 10 elegant safari-style rooms in thatched garden cottages, with bright touches of colour and modern art, satellite TV and verandas. The very attractive **Goose Restaurant** with drapes and nicely decorated tables serves good-quality set meals (see Eating, page 72). **Wild Geese Lodge** was originally owned by Sally Carney, wife to Daniel Carney who wrote the best seller *The Wild Geese*, which was turned into a movie in 1978 starring Roger Moore, Richard Burton and Richard Harris.

C-D Mbizi Game Park, 22 km south of the CBD, follow Seke Rd south, turn left into Dieppe Rd, right on to Airport Rd, left on to Harare Drive, then right on to Twentydales Rd and follow it to the end, reservations T04-700676-8, park 04-291 5737, www.mbizi.co.zw. The main thatched lodge has 14 comfortable en suite rooms decorated with Zimbabwean teak railway sleeper furniture. Rates are for dinner, bed and breakfast, and meals are taken socially with the hosts around a long 5-m dining table. Good farm cooking, swimming pool and plenty of activities (see page 64) make for an enjoyable stay. There are also 6 rustic 2-bed self-catering family cottages dotted around the bush, with stove, fridge and braai.

E-F It's a Small World Backpackers Lodge, 25 Ridge Rd, Avondale, T04-335176, www.backpackerslodge.com. A neat well-run set up and the only one of the many former Harare backpacker hostels that survived the economic meltdown. It has spotlessly clean rooms, some with en suite, 2 dorm rooms, hot showers, bar with pool table and DSTV, thatched elevated deck, shared kitchen, breakfast and laundry service and friendly staff.

F Coronation Park Caravan Park, 6 km east of the CBD on the Mutare road, T04-486398. At the time of writing this municipal caravan and camping park was barely functioning, with smelly broken toilets and showers and grass a metre high. However, it is being fully refurbished with new ablution blocks, landscaped camping and caravan sites with power points, braais and laundry areas, and 21 smart thatched 2-bed fully equipped self-catering chalets are being built, which should cost in the region of US$40 per night.

Lake Chivero Recreational Park *p65, map p54*

C-D Harare Safari Lodge, take the turn-off 16 km from Harare on the Bulawayo road, signposted to the left, T04-746302. With a good location on the shores of Lake Chivero, Harare Safari Lodge has managed to keep up reasonable standards with 18 rooms, all set on rolling lawns in a clutch of indigenous trees. The best are the 6 thatched double-storey chalets overlooking the lake. Facilities include country-style restaurant, a bar with fireplace, and activities like guided birdwatching and sunset pontoon rides on the lake.

D-E Lake Chivero Rest Camp, reservations Zimbabwe Parks and Wildlife Management office, corner Sandringham and Borrowdale roads, T04-706077/8, www.zimparks.com. The basic rest camp here offers 1- to 3-bed rustic self-catering chalets with cutlery and crockery. The electricity is from generators, and drinking water is from a borehole. Fish Eagle and Kingfisher, located 1.5 km from the office, have the best views of the lake. Cheaper chalets share an ablution block. There are 2 swimming pools and a clay tennis court (rackets and balls can be hired). **Bushman's Point** and **Public Mooring** are undeveloped campsites (**F**) on the south shore; campers need to be fully equipped. The **Msasa caravan and camping site** (**F**) on the north bank, 29 km from Harare and reached by using a separate entrance, has braais, ablution block and firewood. Camping is US$10 per person.

E-F Admiral's Cabin, at the Kuimba Shiri Bird Garden, take the turn-off from the Bulawayo road 16 km from the city centre, T062-2309, birdpark@mweb.co.zw. In a shady spot on the lakeshore there are some campsites with braai pits, concrete tables and a simple ablution block with cold water, plus basic 1- to 2-bed chalets with bare rooms. The restaurant is popular at weekends.

Eating

For cheap eats, there are several branches of the combined takeaway chain **Pizza Inn**, **Baker's Inn** (pies and cakes), **Chicken Inn** (chicken and chips) and **Creamy Inn** (ice cream) around the city. Most centrally located is the food court at the (now defunct) Ster-Kinekor cinema opposite Eastgate Mall on Robert Mugabe Rd. Other than that, Harare has more than 100 restaurants, some surprisingly good, but they are mostly in the more affluent suburbs, so you will need to drive or organize a taxi from your hotel.

Central Business District (CBD) *p57, map p58*

Alexander's, 7 Livingstone Av, T04-700340, 744336. Daily 1200-1500, 1830-late. Tired decor but reasonable food with a variety of salads, and a range of beef, chicken and fish dishes, although the vegetarian options of quiche or omelette are uninspiring. No wine list, but the selection on offer is displayed near the bar and comprises an acceptable choice of both local and imported wines.

Harvest Garden, Rainbow Towers Hotel, Pennefather Av, T04-704501.

Open 1200-1400, 1800-2200. The Rainbow Towers' formal though barn-like restaurant decorated with large canvases of artwork and clay pots of dried flowers, is known for its buffet dinners. There's a walk-up counter of hot and cold starters, cheese and biscuits, mains like chicken stew, oxtail and braised beef accompanied by *sadza*, rice and sweet potato, and international wines.

La Fontaine, Meikles Hotel, corner Jason Moyo Av and Third St, T04-251705, 707721, www.meikleshotel.com. Open 1230-1400, 1900-2200. Run by one of Zimbabwe's award-winning chefs, this opulent dining room in the city's best hotel holds a dinner-dance with a live band every evening. Delicately presented dishes include pan-fried kingklip or flambéd steak, and there's a good choice for vegetarians and a long wine-list, including some wines that are available by the glass – unusual in Zim. Special touches include fresh flowers and white linen on the tables.

Le Français, Crowne Plaza Monomotapa Hotel, 54 Park Lane, T04-704501, 0700-1000, 1200-1500. Open 1800-2200. Good food, depending on the availability of the French-style ingredients (snails for example) but limited wine-list. The hotel's coffee lounge has a snack menu, which is also available on the pool deck. Convenient parking in the basement of this large hotel.

Alo Alo, Alliance Française, 328 Herbert Chitepo Av, T04-734974/7. Tue-Sat 1800-2230. Despite the fact that it is located at Alliance Française, this is not particularly French. The menu is quite broad with a big selection of meat, chicken and fish dishes, as well as a few vegetarian options. For vegans there are some soups, salads and pastas. Unusual and tasty breads made with courgettes and butternut squash, and good choice of South African wine.

Coimbra, 61 Selous Av, T04-700237. Mon-Sat 1100-2230. This place has been around for decades, and although housed in a scruffy house made of breeze blocks with virtually no decor to talk about, is justifiably famous for its Portuguese peri-peri chicken, which falls off the bone, accompanied by great chips. Also offers Portuguese *caldo verde* (green soup with chorizo sausage) and fresh calamari from Mozambique, and there's plenty of cold beer. A good, simple place to have an easy meal.

Jaipur, Sunrise Sports Club, Hurstview Rd, near the Magistrates Court, T04-740714. Tue-Sun 1230-1500, Tue-Sat 1830-2200. Located at a sports club with views over the cricket oval and city lights at night, this is a well-priced Indian restaurant with good service, beer and soft drinks but no wine, so BYO. There's an extensive well-explained menu with plenty of vegetarian dishes. Affordable platters to share, and home-made Indian ice cream with almonds for dessert.

L'Escargot, corner of Selous Av and Eighth St, 04-706411. Daily 1200-1430, 1800-2200. A faded restaurant with old wobbly leather chairs and dim lighting but with a good standard of food including, as the name suggests, snails, as well as steaks with unusual toppings like asparagus and hollandaise sauce. There's a limited selection of local Mikuyu wines but otherwise a well-stocked bar.

Mokador, Michael House, 62 Nelson Mandela Av, T04-705038. Mon-Sat 0900-2200. On the 1st floor with an old fashioned elevator, this was the hang-out for the international press corps during the Bush War in the 1970s, where newspaper, TV and radio hacks would gather to enjoy alcoholic suppers and return for a fry-up in the morning. It has since had a refurbishment of sorts with black and orange decor. The menu features soup or chicken livers to start, steak, fish or chicken with chips, rice or *sadza*, and a few Greek dishes such as moussaka for mains, and chocolate cake and ice cream for pudding.

Cafés

Bannie's, Shop 6, ground floor NSSA Building, Julius Nyerere Way, T04-251450.

Open 24 hrs. Modern restaurant next to the National Gallery with outside tables surrounded by pot plants. Basic but cheap menu featuring beef or chicken stews and curries, pork chops and steak served with rice, *sadza* or chips, and chocolate cake or gateaux for dessert. Also does full cooked breakfasts (available all day), milkshakes, pies and toasted sandwiches.

Gaby's, Travel Plaza, 29 Mazowe St, T04-700094. Mon-Sat 0800-1700. An attractive restaurant, with rag-washed terracotta walls and lovely pictures of Mediterranean-looking coastlines. Serves breakfasts and light lunches such as sandwiches and pies and more substantial dishes like fillet of bream, home-made hamburgers or vegetarian pasta and good cappuccinos.

La Patisserie, Rainbow Towers Hotel, Pennefather Av, T04-704501. 0700-1800. Set in the gleaming marble lobby of the **Rainbow Towers** with refreshing a/c and a shoeshine man, this offers good frothy coffees, fresh juice, club sandwiches, filled croissants, cream cakes and scones.

Lucullus Cafe, Spar Supermarket, Fife Av Shopping Centre, T041-250771. Open 0800-1800, lunch 1230-1400. Supermarket café with good-value 'weigh-and-pay' lunchtime buffet to eat in at black granite tables and aluminium chairs or take away. Salads, pasta, rice dishes, stews, curries, potato wedges, trifle and fruit salad for dessert, and coffee and cake in the afternoon.

Meikles Lounge, at the **Meikles Hotel**, corner Jason Moyo Av and Third St, T04-251705/707721, www.meikleshotel.com. Open 0800-1800. In the lobby of the hotel, the lounge area is open all day for light meals and snacks. You can order a good and substantial afternoon tea for US$12 with a 3-tiered cake stand piled high with sandwiches and fancies. The service, however, is very slow. Also has Wi-Fi access for laptops. In former times tea at Meikles was popular with the tobacco farmers who came into town for the tobacco sales.

The Wild Cherry, 1 Roland Sq, Milton Park, T04-727870. Mon-Fri 0900-1600, Sat 0900-1200. Pleasant garden café and Wi-Fi spot with shady tables for coffee, home-made lemonade, breakfasts and a decent selection of salads, crêpes, sandwiches and light lunches such as rosemary chicken with potato wedges or lasagne, and cakes, plus strawberries and cream in season.

Around Harare p61, map p54

Amanzi, 158 Enterprise Rd, Highlands, T04-497 768, www.amanzi.co.zw. Mon-Sat 1200-1500, 1900-2130. One of the best restaurants in the city, with a long menu of creative gourmet dishes of African, Mediterranean Mexican and Thai origin in a stunning interior decorated with African antiquities and contemporary art. The outside water feature is stocked with koi carp and is floodlit at night. There's a good selection of tapas from US$8, and main dishes of lamb, duck or steak are around US$20. Wines are imported from South Africa, with a few from Australia.

Delhi Palace, Greystone park Shopping Centre, Graydon Rd, Greystone Park, T04-885358. Tue-Sat 1200-1500, 1800-2200. Indian restaurant with a good local reputation and wide choice of traditional curries. Generous portions, plenty of choice for vegetarians, and special touches like hot scented hand towels at the tables; peruse the menu at the bar with popadoms and dips. Limited winelist, so BYO.

The Goose, Wild Geese Lodge, Buckland Lane off Alpes Rd, Borrowdale, T04-860466. Sun 1200-1600. Popular for set Sun lunches with great views of the lodge's game park; try to get a table on the lawn on a nice day. The menu features soup and starter platters followed by a buffet of roasts and sticky puddings. Efficient service.

Leonardo's, Sam Levy's Village, Borrowdale, T041-883158. Mon-Sat 1200-2200. Popular family restaurant in a shopping centre, with good service, a mixed menu of meat, chicken and fish,

some interesting starters such as Greek dips and crumbed goat's cheese and home-made fresh pasta. There are only a handful of desserts, but the likes of chocolate mousse, pecan pie, brandy snaps or crème brûlée please most customers.

Miller's Steakhouse, Ballantyne Park Shopping Centre, Ballantyne Park, T04-860466. Mon-Sat 1200-1500, 1800-late. This restaurant is best known for its excellent steaks and gourmet burgers with a variety of sauces like creamy pepper or garlic and the Mozambique prawns to start. Has a saloon-style bar and leather high-back chairs, and a good choice of South African and Australian wines (available by the glass) plus sparkling wine and port.

Sitar, 2 Cecil Rhodes Drive, off Enterprise Rd, Newlands, T04-2906169. Wed-Mon 1200-1430, 1800-2200. Considered the best Indian restaurant in Harare with very authentic dishes served in copper bowls to share, a full range of tikka, vindaloo, korma and vegetarian options, freshly baked Indian breads, and unusual desserts like semolina balls dripping in syrup. Recently relocated, this has been run by 3 generations of the Patel family for almost 30 years.

Victoria 22, 22 Victoria Drive, Highlands, T04-776429. Mon-Fri 1200-1345, Mon-Sat 1900-2030. Set in an attractive thatched building in leafy gardens, this offers pre-dinner drinks in the bar or garden terrace accompanied by snacks and dips, and a short uncomplicated menu of starters and mains with an Italian twist, including a good choice of pastas. Good atmosphere and service and an impressively long list of South African wines.

Blue Banana and Baobab Grill, Newlands Shopping Centre, Old Enterprise Rd, Newlands, T04-252269. Mon-Fri 1230-1400, Mon-Sat 1800-2130. Situated next door to each other, these 2 restaurants are managed together. The **Blue Banana** specializes in Asian cuisine with the likes of spring rolls, chicken satay, hot and sour soup, lamb curry and chicken and cashew nuts, while the **Baobab Grill** offers Zimbabwe favourites such as chicken livers, steak and pork ribs.

The Fishmonger, 50 East Rd, Avondale, T04-308164. Tue-Sat 1200-1500, 1830-2200, Sun 1200-1500. With its oceanic decor this place specializes in seafood, including several dishes with a Mediterranean slant. There's a good variety of prawns, calamari and fish, such as hake or kingklip, all in generous portions, and there's a sizeable selection of local and imported wine.

Great Wall, 94 East Rd, Avondale, T04-334149. Tue-Sat 1130-1430, 1800-2200. Chinese restaurant which also sells ingredients from a small shop during the day. Has an unremarkable barn-like interior but offers a good choice of soups, starters, beef, pork, chicken and vegetarian mains, rice and noodle dishes, large portions, rapid service and good value. Some imported wines or BYO.

Flatdog Diner, 5 Harrow Rd, Msasa, next to Doon Estate (see Shopping, page 77), T04-498408. Mon-Sat 1130-1500, 1800-late. Affordable and unfussy restaurant with an outside gazebo bar and a blackboard with daily specials, occasional live music, best known for its 12 king-size prawns for about US$12 and peri-peri chicken for US$7. In Harare's industrial area so mostly virtually empty.

Mama Mia, Newlands Shopping Centre, Old Enterprise Rd, Newlands, T04-252276. Mon-Fri 1230-1500, Mon-Sat 1830-2200. Friendly and bustling family-run Italian restaurant offering starters such as Caprese salad and beef carpaccio, good thin-crust pizzas, pasta with a variety of traditional sauces, steaks and calamari, and tiramisu for dessert. Good choice for vegetarians, and lunchtime specials of a starter, pasta and ice cream for US$10.

Panorotti's, Avondale Shops, King George Av, Avondale, T04-307089. Open 0800-2200. Popular family-run South African/Italian chain with a children's menu, play area and garden seating. Serves good-value pizza and pasta in generous portions. Prompt service, specials on Tue and Fri evening of 'eat as much pizza as you like' for

US$10. Cartons and bottles of many of the ingredients used are displayed in cabinets and on shelves.

Sopranos, Argyle Rd, Avondale, T04-333833. Open 0830-2200. With minimalist steel and blue decor, this modern restaurant serves good coffees, breakfasts (though it's halal so no bacon), salads, pasta and grills, and is well known for its generous portions of cheesecake and chocolate cake. It's a good option for children, with a kiddie's menu and jungle gym in the garden. Also a Wi-Fi hotspot.

Adrienne's, Shop 2B Fairways Building, Sam Nujoma St, Shopping Centre, Belgravia, T04-335602. Daily 1200-1500, 1800-2230. Near the Reps Theatre and a popular pre-theatre venue, with open and airy decor thanks to the glass walls, and a menu of fish, including Kariba bream, steaks, chops and chicken. Not much for dessert except fruit salad and ice cream. Good value for money and good service, though limited selection of wine.

St Elmo's, Avondale Shops, King George Av, Avondale, T04-334982. Open 1100-2200. Standard South African pizza chain which also delivers. A broad range of dependable wood-fired thick- and thin-crust pizzas, also available in slices. Good for kids, play area.

Cafés

There are many coffee shops in the wealthier suburbs which cater for local business meetings and work-time lunches, and for mothers with young children meeting up. Many are in private houses, often with spacious gardens for outside tables, while others can be found in the local shopping centres.

40 Cork Road, 40 Cork Rd, Avondale, T04-253585-6. Mon-Sat 0800-1600. Smart house with shady garden and Wi-Fi access serving breakfasts, unusual crêpes like spinach and scrambled eggs, and desserts such as apple strudel and muffins. The attached shop sells linen, ceramics and modern paintings.

The Bottom Draw, 14 Maasdorp Av, Belgravia, T04-745679. Mon-Fri 0830-1700, Sat 0830-1200. A rambling house with a children's jungle gym and outside tables under a veranda in the garden. Serves good cappuccinos and a choice of teas, salads, quiches, home-made pot pies, and gooey desserts. The decor shop in the house has a range of imported kitchen items and some food from **Woolworths** in South Africa (similar to the UK's Marks & Spencer), as the owners go to Johannesburg regularly.

Eve's Garden Eco Cafe, 5 Hurworth Rd, Highlands, T04-497888. Mon-Fri 0730-1530, Sat 0730-1200. A health food café which also has an on-site beauty therapist for aromatherapy massages and pilates and yoga classes, with a peaceful garden and fat sofas inside. There are smoothies and freshly squeezed juices, hot and cold soups with home-made bread, whole grain pasta, couscous dishes, and desserts made with Greek yogurt. Good cappuccinos.

Mimi's Cafe, Sam Levy's Village, Borrowdale Rd, Borrowdale, T04-870576. Mon-Fri 0800-1700, Sat-Sun 0800-1500. Best known for its magnificent cakes and freshly baked muffins, this offers a welcome break from shopping in the Sam Levy's mall. They serve a selection of breakfasts, sandwiches and light lunches such as quiche or fish and chips, pavement tables surrounded by plants.

Shop Cafe, Doon Estate, Mutare Rd, Msasa, T 04-446684. Tue-Sat 0800-1630, Sat 0800-1300. Lovely setting among the shops at Doon Estate (see Shopping, page 77) for the excellent breakfasts and light lunches with home-made olive or beetroot bread, lemonade, freshly squeezed juice, savoury pastries, salads and specials such as vegetarian pasta or rhubarb ice cream.

The Vanilla Moon, Seagrove Rd, Alexander Park, T04-333394. Mon-Sat 0800-1700. Attractive house with neat pine tables, serving freshly baked cakes and muffins, breakfasts, light lunches such as filled wraps and gourmet burgers. There's an attached hairdresser and beauty salon for manicures and pedicures (about US$20 each) and it's a Wi-Fi hotspot.

♠ Bars and clubs

Harare *p52, maps p54 and p58*
Harare offers little in the way of nightlife and places open and close regularly. Check with the Publicity Association for recommendations or simply settle for a late night drink in one of the hotel bars.

Explorers Club, Meikles Hotel, corner Jason Moyo and Third St, T04-792291, www.meikleshotel.com. Popular hotel bar decorated with pictures of David Livingstone and other early explorers, animal trophies, hunting guns and brass lamps. Serves bar snacks such as chicken drumsticks and meatballs and set lunches like roast beef and Yorkshire pudding aimed at businessmen between 1200-1430.

Fusion, Gate 1, Grandstand side, Borrowdale Racecourse, Borrowdale Rd, Borrowdale, T04-480248. Tue-Sat 1130-2330. Well-stocked bar overlooking the racecourse, with tall tables and stools and some sofas, green and white decor with large pots of flowers, and TVs for music videos and sport. Serves snacks including sushi (rare in Zimbabwe) and popular with Harare's white youth at weekends.

Keg and Sable, Sam Levy's Village, Borrowdale Rd, Borrowdale, T04-884455. 1100-2300. English-style pub with teak bar, Guinness on tap, and hearty good-value meals like pies, bangers and mash, and fish and chips, or 'munchie' baskets of chicken wings, samoosas, onion rings with dips.

Lime Cafe, Rolfe Valley Shopping Centre, Borrowdale, T04-851045. Mon-Fri 1100-late, Sat-Sun 0900-late. A late-night bar with a restaurant deck overlooking the cricket pitch of the neighbouring school. Serves seafood, steaks and burgers. The bar is a popular watering hole among locals and has flat-screen TVs with DSTV for rugby and other sports.

Liquid Lounge, Rhodesville Shopping centre, 3 Cecil Rd, Greendale, T011-405601. Open 1000-late. Wine bar and grill serving steak and fish and chips and snack platters with chicken and pork strips and meatballs, couch or tall table and stool seating, TVs for sports, sociable atmosphere, holds regular wine-tasting or karaoke nights.

Maiden Public House, Harare Sports Club, Josiah Tongogara Av, T04-700037. Mon-Sat 1200-2300, Sun 1200-2100. Cavernous and mostly empty pub at the Harare Sports Club overlooking the cricket oval, with pool tables, long bar, outside tables, TVs showing sport, and short menu offering pub grub such as sausages and mash, *eisbein* (pork hock) or oxtail, depending on availability.

Symphony, 144 Samora Machel Av, T091-2611210. Mon-Thu 0800-2200, Fri 0800-0200, Sat 0800-2400. A centrally located lounge bar and restaurant open from breakfast until late, with a good selection of imported spirits and wine. Popular with the after-work crowd, and well known for its Sympathy gourmet burgers. Wi-Fi and dance floor with DJ, which gets going at the weekends.

✪ Entertainment

Harare *p52, maps p54 and p58*

Arts centres

Gallery Delta, 110 Livingstone Av, T04-792135, www.gallerydelta.com. Mon-Fri 0830-1700, Sat 0900-1200. Established in 1975, this is an important venue for changing exhibitions of Zimbabwean paintings, graphics, mixed-media sculptures and ceramics. The gallery is situated in the former home (built in 1894) of Robert Paul (1906-1980), now regarded as Zimbabwe's finest landscape painter. There are some fine examples of Zimbabwe contemporary art for sale.

Cinemas

The Elite 100 Cinema, at the Avondale Shops on King George Av in Avondale,

T04-339995. Shows Hollywood releases. Expect to pay around US$6 for a ticket.

Sterkinekor, www.sterkinekor.co.zw. A South African chain, runs multi-screen cinemas at Westgate Shopping Centre, Bluff Hill, on the Kariba road to the northwest of the city, T04-332 212, and in the city centre at 105 Robert Mugabe Rd opposite the Eastgate Shopping Mall, T04-701 933. At the time of writing both had been closed for some time, though they may reopen.

Music

Book Cafe, Fife Av Shopping Centre, corner Fife Av and Sixth St, T04-253239, www.zimbabwearts.org. Open 0800-2300. Friendly bar and restaurant. Few books for sale, but a venue for the arts with regular open mic nights for live music, poetry and occasional public discussions organized by the Pamberi Trust, a local arts promotion organization. As you may imagine, it attracts a fairly highbrow crowd.

Mannenberg Jazz Club, Fife Av Shopping Centre, corner Fife Av and Sixth St, T04-253239, 730902, www.zimbabwearts.org. Tue-Sun 1800-0200. The later night version of the **Book Cafe**, which is on the opposite side of the upper floor of the Fife Av Shopping Centre. Has regular live jazz, a fully stocked bar, stage, small dance floor, and a dark but traditional jazz club atmosphere.

Theatre

The Reps Theatre, Second St Extension Shopping Centre, T04-308159, www.reps.co.zw. This was established in 1931 and is an amateur society which performs plays, music and comedy. Around Christmas they stage pantomimes and the venue occasionally hosts comedians and musicians from South Africa. Tickets are around US$10 and are for sale from the box office in the foyer, which is open 1 hr before shows begin and on Tue-Fri 0900-1600, Sat-Sun 0900-1200.

The Theatre in the Park, next to the National Gallery in Harare Gardens, is run by Rooftop Promotions, T04-797233, www.rooftopaudio.co.zw. It stages contemporary plays, some with a political slant, and is a venue for the Harare International Festival of Arts (HIFA) (see below), in Apr. This is a pleasant open air theatre with a small round stage under thatch, modelled on an African hut. Tickets are around US$10.

⊕ Festivals and events

Harare *p52, maps p54 and p58*
Apr-May Harare International Festival of the Arts (HIFA), T04-300119, www.hifa.co.zw, is a 6-day annual festival and workshop programme that showcases the best of local and regional arts and culture in a comprehensive festival programme of theatre, dance, music, circus, street performance, spoken word and visual arts. Since its inauguration in 1999, this has become hugely successful and is staged at a number of venues including the Theatre in the Park in Harare Gardens and the Reps Theatre in Avondale.

⊙ Shopping

Harare *p52, maps p54 and p58*
Books
Book Cafe, Fife Av Shopping Centre, corner Fife Av and Sixth St, T04-253239, www.zimbabwearts.org. 0800-2300. Has a few local arty books for sale, but is predominantly a venue for the arts (see above).
Kingston's, with several branches around the city including Sam Levy's Village at Borrowdale, Westgate Shopping Centre, and the corner of Sam Nujoma St and Jason Moyo Av in the CBD. Mon-Fri 0900-1700, Sat 0900-1300. They sell novels and educational books, plus magazines, cards, stationery and CDs, but there isn't a great choice. Does do photocopying though.

Clothing
Feredays, Sam Levy's Village, Borrowdale, T04-882156. Mon-Fri 0830-1700, Sat-Sun 0900-1300. A well-stocked shop for good-quality safari clothing, tents, sleeping bags, mosquito nets, fishing gear, cooler boxes, camp beds and chairs and gas cookers. It sells just about everything for the great outdoors and is a useful stop if you are intending to undertake self-drive trips and camping safaris.

Food
There are supermarkets in both the larger and suburban shopping centres in Harare. TM is the most prolific, with **Spar** and **OK** (South African franchises) in others. Most are now fully stocked with products (unlike a few years ago when they had empty shelves), with bakeries, and sometimes cafés. Check prices before buying. You may find some items – a can of tuna, say, or a jar of Nescafé – are outrageously expensive, because they are imported (usually from South Africa). Nevertheless, most common groceries are available.
The Cheese Man, 101 Richwell Av, off Sherwood Dr, Meyrick Park, T04-2915499, www.cheeseman1.com. Mon-Fri 0830-1630, Sat 0830-1200. Popular deli that supplies restaurants and hotels with a good range of cheese, yoghurt, butter, ice cream, fish, coffee and fruit juice, most of which is sourced from all over Zimbabwe. They also organize the **Zimbabwe on a Plate**, an annual competition for restaurants, with reviews, ratings and prizes, so the website is worth checking out.
Veldemeers Handcrafted Belgian Chocolates, Doon Estate, 1 Harrow Rd, Msasa, T04-486169. Tue-Sat 0800-1630, Sat 0800-1300. Beautifully located chocolate shop in the **Shop Cafe** (see Eating, page 74) set in the gardens of Doon Estate (see Shopping, page 77), where the aroma of the finely crafted home-made chocolates fills the shop and café. They are decorated with hazelnuts, walnuts and pistachios and there's a range of sugar-free chocolates. The boxes are wrapped in ribbons.

Handicrafts and souvenirs

Given that it's a tourist-driven town, Victoria Falls is probably the best place in Zimbabwe to buy handicrafts and souvenirs, but Harare also has a few spots worth checking out. If you only go to one place in Harare, than make it **Doon Estate** (see below), which has a number of shops in one place, as well as the **Chapungu Sculpture Park** (see page 63) for Shona soapstone sculptures.

Afrik Batik, Intermarket Life Tower, corner Jason Moyo Av and Sam Nujoma St, T04-708935. Mon-Fri 0900-1700, Sat 0900-1400. Batiks, jewellery, stuffed animals and mounted animal heads, safari clothes, wooden and soapstone sculptures, ostrich leather products like belts and bags, and (fake) carved ivory. They also have a small outlet at Harare International Airport.

Doon Estate, Harrow Rd, Msasa, 8 km from the CBD, off the A3/Mutare road. Mon-Fri 0900-1630, Sat 0900-1300. This is a delightful collection of shops located in restored railway workers' houses (next to the railway line to Mutare) in Msasa's industrial area. Has a wide selection of quality crafts, jewellery, pottery and artwork, plus hand-crafted clothes and shoes. The attractive and pleasant garden setting is a nice place in which to wander around, have coffee, and buy unhurriedly in the upmarket gift, homeware and souvenir shops. The shops include **The Works**, a Fair Trade shop, **Ros Byrne** (www.rosbyrne.co.zw), which specializes in Zimbabwe fabrics, ceramics and furniture made from teak railway sleepers, and **Emma French** (www.emmafrenchcollection.com), run by designer Emma, producing some uniquely Zimbabwe crafts using sustainable materials and made by locals artists (only dead wood is used for carvings, tins and plastic bottles are used to make lamps and ornaments, and local vines are used to make baskets). Emma is best known for her hand-painted textiles, which are made into bedding, cushions and table linen. Also here are **House of Sabrina** for women's clothes; **Savannah Wood** for more teak railway sleeper furniture and home accessories; art galleries selling local artists landscape and animal paintings; and the **Shop Cafe** (see Cafés, page 74), among other establishments. A book fair is held at Doon Estate on the last Sat morning of the month.

Inside Out, 50 Quorn Av, opposite Arundal Village, Mt Pleasant, T0912-262767. Mon-Fri 0900-1700, Sat 0900-1300. In this small house in Arundal, each room is themed with different craft work and you can pick up quality fabrics, candles, wine glasses, hard wood games, metal bird sculptures, batiks, pewter, home-made paper products, beaded items and ceramics, among many other things. It carries a similar range of curios and decor accessories to Doon Estate (above) and everything is made in Zimbabwe.

KwaMambo, in the 40 Cork Rd coffee shop (see Eating, page 73), 40 Cork Rd, Avondale, T04-253585-6. Mon-Sat 0800-1600. Sells quality linen such as tablecloths and cushions, plus Zimbabwe ceramics, imported homeware, glass, art and sculptures.

Markets

Avondale Market, at the Avondale Shops (see below) on King George Rd, is well worth a browse (open daily), for the good-quality second-hand and new clothes, and excellent range of second-hand books (actually a better choice than any bookshop in Harare and with the largest collection of books for sale in Zimbabwe), mostly brought up from South Africa, DVDs and CDs, and some souvenirs. Wandering around the lanes of stalls here is hassle-free; the traders are very good natured and will negotiate on prices. This is the preferred shopping destination for Harare's wealthier residents.

Mbare (see page 60) is home to a frenetic and vibrant market known as **Musika**, which sells just about everything imaginable, from fruit and vegetables and second-hand clothes to traditional medicine and some curios. However, this is a busy area so watch for pickpockets and don't take anything of value with you. A market porter (usually with a wheelbarrow) may trail after you and will expect a tip if you make use of his services.

Shopping malls

There are shops all around the CBD and pedestrianized First St, between Kwame Nkrumah Av and Robert Mugabe Rd, features the larger (mostly South African) chain stores, as does **Eastgate Mall** on Robert Mugabe Rd, though shopping in the city centre is far from exotic and there's nothing very special to buy. Around the suburbs are small regional shopping centres which serve the local communities, usually with a supermarket or grocers, perhaps a coffee shop, petrol station and butcher's.

The main modern shopping malls are **Sam Levy's Village** on the Borrowdale Rd in Borrowdale, which has more (South African) chain stores, a DHL office, banks with ATMs, a flea market on Sun 0900-1500, a basic Kingston's bookshop, a Clicks pharmacy and beauty store, and cafés and restaurants; the once-prosperous **Westgate Shopping Centre** on the Lomagundi Rd in Bluff Hill on the way out to Chinhoyi, which has a TM Supermarket, post office, cheap clothes shops and little else, as most units now stand empty; the **Arundal Village** on Quorn Rd in Mount Pleasant, which has a particularly well-stocked Spar supermarket, coffee shops and some more unusual shops, including a second-hand clothes shop for ladies' designer clothes; and **Avondale Shops**, on King George Rd in Avondale, to the north of the city, where there are a couple of restaurants and the Avondale Market, best known for its second-hand clothes (some of which are quite high quality), Chinese-produced fashion, second-hand book-stalls, DVDs (4 for US$10) and some snacky food-stalls. There's a large car park here and banks with ATMs.

▲▲ Activities and tours

Harare p52, maps p54 and p58
There used to be a number of tour operators based in Harare that ran city tours and trips to the outlying sights. There are virtually no reliable operators today, though check with the Publicity Association (page 56) to see if they can at least recommend a good taxi driver. Alternatively 1- to 2-days' car hire will get you out to attractions like Lake Chivero or the Lion and Cheetah Park, and the city centre (CBD) is compact enough to walk around.

Cricket

Harare Sports Club, Fifth St Extension. Initially known as Salisbury Sports Club in the colonial days, this is Harare's only cricket oval. It gained notoriety in 1992 when it became a test venue for Zimbabwe's inaugural test against India (they drew). Surrounded by jacaranda trees and a beautiful gabled pavilion, it is bordered by the heavily guarded presidential palace on one side and the prestigious **Royal Harare Golf Club** on another. With the appearance of some quality players in the late 1990s, including Andy Flower, and his brother, Grant (see box, page 79), the Zimbabwe national team had some successes, including a series of wins against Pakistan in test cricket; but the political situation in Zimbabwe after that had a detrimental effect on the team's quality of players and performances. Most of the players are currently contracted overseas, but the International Cricket Council (ICC) is planning to reinstate Zimbabwe back into test cricket.

Golf

Chapman Golf Club, Eastlea off Samora Machel Av, turn right after the Enterprise Rd junction, T04-747487, www.chapman golfclub.co.zw. This 18-hole, 6582-m course is in a well-kept park-like setting

Andy Flower

Born in 1968 and the elder of two cricket-playing brothers, Andy Flower, was for a long time Zimbabwe's only batsman of true test quality. For a period of about two years, from the start of 2000, he was so phenomenally consistent that he was deemed to have no rival in Zimbabwe's cricket history. From his high school days at Vainona High School, Harare, Flower played alongside his younger brother Grant, who also went on to play test cricket. He made his international debut in a one-day international against Sri Lanka during the 1992 Cricket World Cup in New Zealand. Zimbabwe's wicket-keeper for more than 10 years, he was considered to be one of the world's best wicket-keeper

batsmen. In 2003, nearing the end of his career, Flower achieved international recognition (along with team mate Henry Olonga) by wearing a black armband in a Cricket World Cup match to protest against the policies of Zimbabwe's Mugabe-led government. He and Olonga released a statement on 10 February 2003, stating that they were "mourning the death of democracy in our beloved Zimbabwe". This act led to pressure from Zimbabwe's government and Flower's retirement from Zimbabwean cricket. He is the only Zimbabwean in the ICC's 'Top 100 All-time Test Batting' rankings. At the time of writing he was the England's team coach.

and hosts the annual Zimbabwe Open. Clubs can be hired.
Royal Harare Golf Club, Fifth St Extension, T04-702927. Established in 1898, this 6467-m 18-hole course is set in attractive wooded parkland. The course was re-seeded and the clubhouse refurbished in early 2010. Clubs can be hired.

Horse racing

Borrowdale Racecourse, Borrowdale Rd, Borrowdale, T04-480248, www.mashturf. co.zw. Horse racing in Harare had its beginning in 1894, with the formation of the Mashonaland Turf Club. Cecil Rhodes originally set aside land for a racecourse. There are race meetings most weekends. **Fusion** (see page 74), a popular bar, is also here.

Swimming

Les Brown Swimming Pool, Harare Gardens, near the Monomotapa Hotel, May-Aug 1000-1600, Sep-Apr 1000-1800, US$2. Public Olympic-sized outdoor pool. It's been surprisingly well maintained and hosts local swimming galas and school groups.

⊖ Transport

Harare *p52, maps p54 and p58*
Air
Harare International Airport is 12 km southeast of the city on Airport Rd in Harare South, T04-575 164/8, www.caaz.co.zw. The only domestic carrier is **Air Zimbabwe**, which has 2 daily flights to **Victoria Falls** (1½ hrs) at 0900 and 1300, returning from Victoria Falls at 1030 and 1530, around US$230 return, US$135 one-way. It also operates 2 daily flights to **Bulawayo** (1 hr 15 mins) at 0900 and 1900, and from Bulawayo flights depart at 0700 and 1715, US$180 return, US$100 one-way. There are also a number of regional flights with **Air Zimbabwe** to **Lusaka**, **Lilongwe** and **Johannesburg**, and **Air Malawi** connects Harare with **Blantyre** and **Lilongwe** and **Air Botswana** connects Harare with **Gaborone**.

Airline offices Most airline offices are open Mon-Fri 0800-1630, Sat 0800-1200. **Air Botswana**, Travel Plaza, corner Josiah Chinamano Av and Mazowe St, T04-793 228/9, www.airbotswana.co.bw. **Air Malawi**,

Throgmorton House, corner of Samora Machel Av and Julius Nyerere Way, T04-752563, www.airmalawi.com. **Air Zimbabwe**, airport T04-575 1111, town office, Third Speke Av, T04-253752, www.airzimbabwe.aero. **British Airways**, 5th floor, Intermarket Life Tower, 77 Jason Moyo Av, T04-747400, www.britishairways. com. **Kenya Airways**, 1st floor, SCC (Social Security Centre), corner Sam Nujoma Av and Julius Nyerere Way, T04-720015, www. kenya-airways.com. **South African Airways**, 1st floor, SCC (Social Security Centre), corner Sam Nujoma Av and Julius Nyerere Way, T04-738922, www.flysaa.com.

Bus

Local Zimbabwe United Passenger Company (ZUPCO), T0800 4041, www.zupco. co.zw, runs full-size buses along the major routes from the city to the suburbs. Bus stops are clearly denoted on the side of the road and destinations are displayed at the front of the buses; short distance shouldn't cost more than US$2. These are complemented by the hundreds of commuter omnibuses, which follow the same main routes but are flagged down, with most journeys generated from the frenetic commuter omnibus terminus on Robert Mugabe Rd and Fifth St, but they also collect at various places on the side of the road in the CBD. They are not especially recommended as they are overcrowded and driven recklessly. Additionally, as they are cheaper than US$1, old Zimbabwe bank notes are still used (see page 43).

Long distance Local clapped-out buses, ('chicken buses'), depart when full from the **Mbare Musika Bus Terminal** a few kilometres south of town off Arbennie Rd. However, this is in the suburb of Mbare, part of which was famously demolished in 2005 in Operation Murambatsvina (see box, page 246), and which is a rough and potentially unsafe area. The overcrowded and poorly maintained buses are not recommended in any case.

The better option is to take the ZUPCO (see above) buses from the **Road Port Terminal** on the corner of Robert Mugabe Rd and Fifth St. These link Harare with daily services to regional towns including **Bulawayo**, **Mutare**, **Victoria Falls** and **Masvingo**. Expect to pay around US$10 for a city-to-city journey. However, due to financial restraints for maintenance, few ZUPCO buses are running on long-distance routes these days.

Even better for tourists is **Citylink** (T04-772633, www.rainbowtowershotel.com), whose buses have toilets, DVDs and make refreshment stops. They leave from the Rainbow Towers Hotel in Harare Tue, Thu, Sat and Sun at 1400 and arrive at the Bulawayo Rainbow Hotel about 1930. They also stop at **Kadoma**, **Kwekwe** and **Gweru** (see Midlands, page 91). From Bulawayo to **Victoria Falls** they depart at 1400 on Mon, Wed, Fri and Sat and arrive at about 1930 (US$25 Harare–Bulawayo, US$50 Harare–Victoria Falls), and will drop off in **Hwange** town for US$5 less (US$45), though you still have to arrange local transport from there to the gate of Hwange National Park (and then there is a very poor chance of hitching a lift into the park). **Pathfinder** (T09-61788, http://pathfinderlx.com) runs a daily service between Harare and **Bulawayo**, departing from each respectively at 0800 and 1400 and arriving at 1400 and 2000. They pick up and drop off at the Holiday Inns in each city. They may extend the service soon to include Bulawayo–Victoria Falls, Harare–Mutare and perhaps Harare–Johannesburg, so it's worth checking the website. Prices are similar to Citylink. Again it is essential to confirm schedules.

Car

Driving in central Harare can be a little challenging because of the traffic and the confusing one-way system, but roads are clearly marked and laid out in a grid system and most places are signposted. Watch for commuter omnibuses as they can brake very suddenly to pick up passengers. Away from the CBD where there is less traffic, driving is very straightforward. For information about car hire rates, see Getting around, page 26.

Car hire companies Avis, airport T04-575431/3, town office, next to the Meikles Hotel, corner Third St and Jason Moyo Av, T04-796409/10, www.avis.com. **Budget**, airport, T04-575421, www.budget. com. **Easy Go**, corner Kwame Nkrumah Av and Third St, T04-795294, www.cmed. co.zw. **Europcar**, airport T04-575592, town office, corner Patricks and Airport rds 4 km from the airport, T04581411-20, www. europcar.com. **Led Car Rental**, 6 Fereday Dr, Eastlea, T04-747669, www.ledcarrental. co.zw. **RockShade**, 113 Samora Machel, T04-701803, www.rockshade.co.zw.

Taxi
There are metered taxi ranks around the CBD, mostly outside shopping centres and hotels. Restaurants and hotels can order one for you. A short journey within the CBD should cost in the region of US$5-7 and a taxi from the airport about US$20-30. **City Cab**, T09-338322.

Train
Harare Railway Station is south of Kenneth Kaunda Av, booking office Mon-Fri 0700-1700, 1900-2130, Sat 0700-1130, 1800-2130, Sun 0800-1000, 1800-2130. Overnight trains to **Bulawayo** and **Mutare** are run by the **National Railways of Zimbabwe (NRZ)**, T04-733901, www.nrz.co.zw. Buy tickets at the station at least a day before you intend to travel, although reservations are open 30 days prior to departure, and check the train is running on your preferred day. In theory, the **Bulawayo** service departs Harare Tue, Fri and Sun at 2100 and arrives the next morning at 1000, and the **Mutare** service departs Sun, Wed and Thu at 2100 and arrives the next morning at 0600, though they often run late. The train from Bulawayo to **Victoria Falls** departs Bulawayo the following evening at 2000 (see page 154). Your ticket will not show your coach or berth number; these are posted in a glass case on the platform about 1 hr before the train departs. Fares are cheap; in the region of US$12 per person for Harare–Bulawayo and Bulawayo–Victoria Falls in Sleeper class, children under 12 half price, children under 3 free. There are 3 classes of accommodation. Sleeper class has 2-berth rooms (known as coupés) and 4-berth rooms (known as compartments). These have leatherette bench seats which convert to bunks (bedding is provided) and a washbasin. The steward will come around to make up the beds. 2 passengers travelling together can book a coupé, whereas a solo traveller will be booked into a 4-berth compartment with passengers of the same sex. If you pay for 2 tickets you can have sole occupancy of a coupé. A restaurant car (though not on the Mutare train) serves basic meat-and-2-veg-type meals, plus beers and sodas. Standard class has reasonably comfortable airline-style seating that reclines. Economy class has basic seating but is not recommended as it's crowded and uncomfortable.

ⓘ Directory

Harare *p52, maps p54 and p58*
Banks
There are banks all over the CBD and in the shopping centres in the suburbs. Most have ATMs for Visa cards. They include **Zimbank**, corner of First St and Speke Av; **Barclay's** on the corner of First St and Jason Moyo Av; **Standard Chartered** on Sam Nujoma St near Africa Unity Sq.

Cultural centres
Alliance Française, 328 Herbert Chitepo Av, T04-704795, www.afzim.org, Mon, Wed, Thu, Fri 1000-1900, Sat 1000-1600, has a library and art exhibition space, offers language courses and is an occasional venue for

music and drama. The **British Council**, 6th floor, Corner House, Samora Machel Av, T04-775 313, www.britishcouncil.org.zw, Mon-Fri 0900-1700, Sat 0900-1300, has a library and language school.

Embassies and consulates
Australia, 1 Green Close, Borrowdale, T04-852471, www.zimbabwe.embassy. gov.au. **Botswana**, 22 Phillips Av, Belgravia, T041-729551. **Canada**, 45 Baines Av, T04-252181-5, www.zimbabwe.gc.ca. **Germany**, 30 Ceres Rd, Avondale, T04-308655, www. harare.diplo.de. **Mozambique**, 152 Herbert Chitepo St, T04-790837. **Namibia**, Grasmere Lane, Borrowdale, T04-885841. **Netherlands**, 2 Arden Rd, Highlands, T04-776701. **South Africa**, 7 Elcombe Rd, Belgravia, T04-750 3147. **UK**, 3 Norfolk Rd, Mount Pleasant, T04-338800, http://ukinzimbabwe.fco.gov.uk. **US**, 172 Herbert Chitepo Av, T04-250 593/4, http://harare.usembassy.gov. **Zambia**, 48 Kwame Nkrumah Av, T04-773777.

Immigration
Linquenda House, corner Nelson Mandela Av and First St, T04-791912.

Internet
There are internet cafés all around the CBD and post offices offer access. Most hotels have Wi-Fi in the rooms or public areas, where you can buy a token (about US$3 for 30 mins).

Medical services
Hospitals At all costs, avoid the public hospitals, which are poorly staffed and equipped. Harare's largest and best private hospital is **Avenues Clinic**, corner of Mazowe St and Baines Av, Avenues, T04-251180. Also in Avenues, **Montagu Clinic**, 135 Josiah Chinamano Av, T04-700216, and **West End Clinic**, 13 Baines Av, T04-706257, are also

good. In Avondale, **St Anne's Hospital** is on King George Rd, T04-339933, www. stannes.co.zw.

Pharmacies The range of medication available in pharmacies varies widely. The ones in Avondale are reasonably well-stocked. **Avondale Pharmacy**, Avondale Shops, T04-336642; **Lemon Pharmacy**, Avondale Shops, T04-302755; and **Shamrock Pharmacy**, Avondale Shops, T04-336 730. **QV/Baines Pharmacy**, 60 Baines Av, T04-704020, is close to the private clinics in Avenues, and has a medical laboratory for malaria tests, T04-727131. Late night pharmacies are listed in the **Herald** newspaper.

Police
Harare Central Police Station, on the corner of Kenneth Kaunda Av and Inez Terrace, T04-733033. **Emergencies** T999.

Post
The main post office is on Jason Moyo Av, and there's another large one on Samora Machel Av. Both are open Mon-Fri 0830-1600 and Sat 0800-1130. There are others in the suburbs, usually in the shopping centres.

Courier companies DHL, corner of Central Av and Fourth St, T04-700120, www.dhl.co.zw. **Federal Express**, 101 Nelson Mandela Av, T04-705588, www.fedex.co.zw.

Telephone
There are telephone booths all over the CBD but most are unreliable given that there are no longer any coins used in Zimbabwe. Some take phone cards, which are available at the post office. Cell phone start-up packs and sim cards are sold at the airport, supermarkets and from street vendors for about US$20, including US$5 air time. Local service providers include **Telecel**, **Econet** and **Net One**.

The Midlands and Northeastern Zimbabwe

Beyond Lake Chivero, the A5 heads southwest for 439 km to Bulawayo. It goes through Mashonaland East and then into the Midlands Province. Unlike the Bulawayo to Victoria Falls road – the A8, which is almost devoid of habitation – there are a number of small towns along the A5, though few will distract tourists for too long. It's a region that is rich in gold, asbestos, nickel and chrome, so the towns support these industries, as well as agriculture; there have been many white-owned farm invasions in the area over the last decade.

The alternative to the A5 from Harare to Gweru is the A4, en route to Masvingo, which is a mere 6 km shorter than the A5 to Gweru, and goes via the small and unremarkable settlements of Beatrice and Chivhu.

The two major tarred roads that leave Harare to the north, are the A1, which goes northwest via Chinhoyi to the border with Zambia at Chirundu and the Zambezi Valley (namely Lake Kariba and the Mana Pools National Park: see Zambezi Valley chapter, page 211), and the A2 that goes northeast to the Mozambique border at Nyamapanda (see box, page 89). There is little in between the two roads except for remote, arid settlements which drop away to the Zambezi Escarpment and the border with Mozambique. This 'triangle' of land in northeast Zimbabwe is rarely visited and is, in the most part, only accessible by 4WD on basic gravel roads. It is also a region that has little interest to tourists and has also been hard hit by farm invasions. Nevertheless, despite a lack of facilities, this region leading up to the Zambezi Valley is where the (mostly defunct) farmland peters out to give way to pristine African bush, and it may become ripe for 4WD exploration in the future (if fully prepared with fuel and provisions). Some wildlife can be spotted, including many herds of elephant. » For listings, see pages 90-92.

Southwest of Harare → For listings, see pages 90-92.

Ins and outs
If you intend to pick up provisions or break your journey to Bulawayo with a night in a hotel, then the A5 via Chegutu, Kwekwe and Gweru is the better bet. This is the route that most of the buses take. It is a fairly busy, good tarred road, and there are facilities for drivers and bus passengers, such as petrol stations in the towns and takeaways selling pies and fried chicken. Signposts and mileage marks (white stones at the side of the road) are also good. » For transport, see page 91.

Norton → Colour map 2, C1. Phone code: 062.
The small industrial township of Norton is 40 km southwest of Harare on the A5, and was founded in 1914 when a siding on the railway was constructed. It was named after a local farmer. It has a large pulp and paper mill and tobacco, maize and wheat are grown on the surrounding farms.

Darwendale Recreational Park
ⓘ 76 km southwest of Harare. The best route to the park is to take the right turn-off in Norton towards Chinhoyi and, after approximately 23 km, take the right turn-off to the park, which is a further 11 km, www.zimparks.com, US$10, children (6-12) US$5, car US$5.
This little-visited park surrounds Lake Manyame, formed when the Manyame River was damned in 1973, and covers 11,200 ha. It is is principally a spot for angling for bass, blue bream and tigerfish. The largest bass caught here was during the Bass Masters Tournament

fishing competition in 2004; it weighed in at 8.2 kg. A small area is reserved for game, mostly herbivores including sable, waterbuck, reedbuck, duiker and warthog, as well as baboon and vervet monkey. More than 450 bird species have been recorded including large numbers of waterfowl. There are picnic sites under thatch on the northwestern shore, with braai pits, campsites and two self-catering units (see Sleeping, page 90).

Chegutu → *Colour map 1, C6. Phone code: 053.*

Formerly known as Hartley, this sleepy small town in Mashonaland West province is on the A5, 110 km southwest of Harare but has little more than a Zim Bank, petrol stations, some cheap and basic takeaways, and supermarkets, the best of which is the Town and Country on the right as you pass through the town. The only mildly interesting thing to see is the rusting and dilapidated shells of two Viscount aircraft on the southern outskirts of town. In better days, these served as an imaginative restaurant. There's a turn-off here to Chinhoyi, 94 km north of Chegutu.

Kadoma → *Colour map 1, C6. Phone code: 068.*

From Chegutu, the road passes through a flat savannah of maize, cotton and cattle country. The next town of note is Kadoma, 144 km southwest of Harare. Originally called Gatooma until 1982, it was founded in the 1890s as a gold mining camp. The Specks Hotel was opened in 1907, and Jameson High School started the same year when Mrs Amelia Fitt, wife of the first mayor of Kadoma, started to give classes to the town children in her house. A public electricity supply was introduced in Kadoma in 1922. The town is at the centre of a mining area, and the **Cam and Motor gold mine** is in Eiffel Flats, 7 km outside Kadoma. Although pretty dilapidated and defunct, the only notable building in town is the colonial **Grand Hotel**, which opened in 1925 and had a sprung floor for dancing, the first such floor in Zimbabwe. Its faded elegant façade, hints at the gold rush days, when it hosted prospectors and hunters. These days, the **Kadoma Hotel** on the approach to town from Harare offers the best option for accommodation (see Sleeping, page 90). Outside, on the main road, is a small collection of rusting steam locomotives which used to be in service with Rhodesia Railways. The Citylink buses stop here for a break and to pick up and drop off passengers. ▸▸ *See Transport, page 91.*

Kwekwe → *Colour map 1, C6. Phone code: 055.*

From Kadoma, it's 80 km to Kwekwe, or Kwe Kwe, and formerly Que Que, which is centred pretty much in the middle of Zimbabwe in the Midlands Province. It's a centre for steel and fertilizer production. It was founded in 1898 and named after a nearby river 16 km to the south of town and the theory goes is that the name is derived from the noise frogs make in the river. Again, like Kadoma, it was an early a gold mining town. More recently Kwekwe has become known for its steel production and there is a large steel works not far away at Redcliff, though this is run by the government and has been dogged with problems of corruption and under production in recent years. This has severely affected the local economy as the steels works used to employ a lot of people. There are a spattering of banks and supermarkets along the main road, but there is little other reason to stop, except perhaps for the souvenir stalls on the approach to town from Harare and the **Wimpy** at the petrol station on the first roundabout. Again like Kadoma, there's an established hotel, the **Golden Mile**, 2 km on the road out towards Bulawayo, where the buses stop.

The principal centre of the Midlands Province and 62 km south of Kwekwe, this sprawling unappealing town was founded in 1894 and was named after the (dry) river that passes through the centre of town. In its first year six hotels were established as it became a popular settlement for gold prospectors, and the first bank opened its doors in 1896. A year later saw the launch of one of the country's pioneer newspapers, the *Northern Optimist*, later known as the *Gweru Times*, and the arrival of the railway in 1902 triggered Gweru's development. It remains an important railway hub in the middle the country. Gweru is also the birthplace of one of the best known multinational shoe manufacturers, **Bata**, which opened its manufacturing plant in the town in 1939. These days, Gweru's only notable constructions are a couple of faded colonial buildings, the gracefully curved Municipal Offices set in a delightful rose garden, the (strangely named) Boggie Clock Tower at the

Gweru

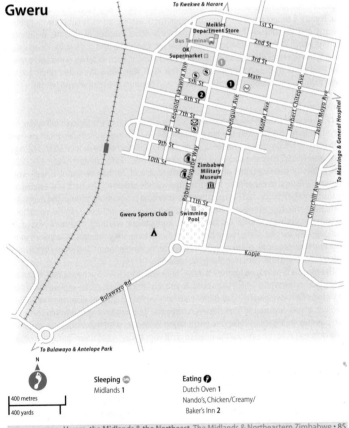

Sleeping 😴
Midlands **1**

Eating 🍴
Dutch Oven **1**
Nando's, Chicken/Creamy/
Baker's Inn **2**

400 metres
400 yards

junction of Robert Mugabe Way and Main Street – erected in 1928 by a Mrs Jean Boggie in memory of her late husband – and the Zimbabwe Military Museum (see below), which has a neat public park next to it. Of much more interest is the town's proximity to the excellent Antelope Park (see below).

Ins and outs

The Citylink buses stop at the **Regency Chevron Hotel** (see Sleeping, page 90). The desk of the poorly manned **Gweru Publicity** ① *inside the door of the Municipal Offices on the corner of Eighth St and Robert Mugabe Way, T054-28606, Mon-Fri 0800-1600.* In town, there are a couple of basic hotels, a Meikles department store, supermarkets and banks.

Zimbabwe Military Museum
① *Lobengula Av, 0900-1700, US$2.*

Gweru is home to the Thornhill Air Base, which is the country's largest air-force base, as well as the Zimbabwe Military Academy. As such it makes sense for Zimbabwe's Military Museum, documenting the history of the army, air force and police, to be located here too. There's a collection of uniforms and equipment associated with Zimbabwe's military history, and the outside hangar houses an impressive number of aircraft, including a Spitfire, North American Harvard, English Electric Canberra, and a Vampire FB amongst others. The open-air displays also feature ground armour, such as tanks, personnel carriers and field guns, from both world wars and the Bush War, while the faded photographic gallery details the struggle for independence and honours the martyrs and heroes.

Antelope Park
① *11.5 km southwest of Gweru; turn right 5.5 km from Gweru at the Dabuka rail siding, and the main gate is 6 km from the main road, T054-251949, www.antelopepark.co.zw; walk with lions US$75 (no children under 12), cub viewing US$25, children (under 12) US$12, night encounter US$95, children (under 12) US$48, elephant ride US$45, children (under 12) US$22.* This is one of the highlights of the Midlands region of Zimbabwe and it is well worth coming to Gweru to experience the incredible wildlife activities. The park was established by the Conolly family in 1987 as a captive lion-breeding programme, though the park is also naturally home to a number of free-ranging game species, including giraffe, wildebeest, tsessebe, waterbuck, impala, red hartebeest, kudu, zebra, warthog, bushbuck and jackal, and over 150 species of bird have been identified. There are a number of activities in the park and there's a rustic camp with permanent tents, simple rooms and plenty of camping space next to a scenic dam (see Sleeping, page 90).

The place is best known for the 1½-hour 'Walk with the Lions'. For a long time it was the only place in the world where you could do this, but the park has since moved some lions to Victoria Falls (see page 171) and there are now similar operations elsewhere in Africa. It involves a walk with young lions between three and 15 months of age to watch them play and possibly stalk game. Visitors are encouraged to interact with them (they can become a little boisterous at time, hence the need to walk with sticks to bat them gently away) and, if there are very young cubs, you can pick them up. There are also night-time safaris by vehicle to track some of the older lions who are released into the bush after dark in order for them to practice their stalking and hunting skills. The park also has two tame elephants that you can ride, orphaned from mothers that died in a severe drought some years ago. If you don a swimsuit, you can even ride on their backs as they swim in the dam – this may be the only place in the world where you can do this. Boating and canoeing is also on offer

The Pioneer Column

The Pioneer Column was a force raised by Cecil Rhodes and his British South Africa Company in 1890 and used in his efforts to annex the territory of Mashonaland, the northern region of Zimbabwe running up to the Mozambique border and including what has become Harare. Rhodes was anxious to secure Mashonaland before the Germans, Portuguese or Boers did, and his first step was to persuade the Matabele King Lobengula, in 1888, to sign a treaty giving him rights to mining and administration in the region (but not settlement as such). Using what was to become known as the Rudd Concession (so called because Rhodes' business partner, Charles Rudd, was instrumental in securing the signature), this treaty was drawn up between Rhodes' British South Africa Company (allegedly on behalf of Queen Victoria though without her official knowledge or authority) and Lobengula; Rhodes then sought and obtained a charter from the British government allowing him to act. The next step was to occupy the territory. Rhodes' military advisers estimated that it would take 2500 men and about £1 million to win the war that would, they thought, inevitably result when Lobengula realized that Rhodes was intent on occupying his land.

However, Frank Johnson, a 23-year-old adventurer, undertook to deliver the territory in nine months with a lot fewer men and for just £87,500. Frederick Selous, a hunter with close knowledge of Mashonaland, agreed to join the effort as a guide. Johnson posted recruitment notices in Kimberley (now in South Africa), offering each volunteer 3000 acres of land and 15 mining claims. On the advice of Rhodes, Johnson recruited mostly sons from wealthy families, so that if they were imperilled by Lobengula, their families would be more likely to enlist British government support for their rescue. Johnson's column eventually consisted of 180 civilian colonists, 62 wagons and 200 volunteers (who ultimately formed the nucleus of what later became the British South African Police). A further party of 110 men, 16 wagons, 250 cattle and 130 spare horses later attached itself to the column. The troopers were equipped with Martini-Henry rifles, revolvers, seven-pound field guns and Maxim machine guns, as well as an electric searchlight, which they later used to good effect to intimidate Matabele warriors shadowing the column.

The pioneers' route began in Bechuanaland (now Botswana) in June 1890. It proceeded northeast and then north over a distance of about 650 km, intending to terminate at an open place about 15 km northwest of present-day Harare, an area that Selous had explored a few years earlier and called Mount Hampden. However, the column halted before that, at a naturally flat and marshy meadow bounded by a steep rocky hill, today's Harare Kopje. The British Union Flag was hoisted on 12 September (later celebrated as a Rhodesian public holiday). The Pioneer Column was officially disbanded on 1 October 1890 and each member was granted land on which to farm.

and fishing tackle can be hired from reception (for bass, bream and catfish). There are also options for game-viewing by vehicle, horseback or on foot in the surrounding bush. All activities can be arranged on arrival but you really need at least two nights to get the most out of it.

South of Harare → For listings, see pages 90-92.

Beatrice → Colour map 2, C1. Phone code: 065.

This small agricultural settlement 54 km south of Harare on the the A4 (the alternative road to the A5) was named after Beatrice Borrow, a sister of a Mr HJ Borrow who had mining claims in the area in the early 20th century, though there are no mines operating today. It was near Beatrice that Morgan Tsvangirai's vehicle was involved in an accident with a truck in March 2009, resulting in the death of his wife Susan (see box, page 244), often described as a 'mother figure' during the Movement of Democratic Change (MDC) campaign trail, and a vital support to her husband. They had been married for 31 years and had six children. Her funeral in the rural village of Buhera, 160 km south of Beatrice, where she was born, and the memorial service in Harare (which Robert Mugabe attended) drew thousands of mourners.

Chivhu → Colour map 2, C1. Phone code: 057.

Another small agricultural settlement, Chivhu is 146 km south of Harare on the A4/ Masvingo road. It was known as Enkeldoorn before independence, after the acacia tree, which is known as *enkeldoorn* in Afrikaans. It was founded by Afrikaans-speaking Boer farmers and Voortrekker settlers in around 1850 and later became an Afrikaner stronghold in predominately English-speaking white Rhodesia. It developed as an agricultural region, based on poultry and dairy cattle; many white farmers have been expelled from this area in recent years and the settlement is now mostly surviving on subsistence farming.

Mvuma → Colour map 2, C1. Phone code: 032.

Mvuma is the next non-descript village on the A4, 51 km south of Chivhu; the only significance here is the turn-off on the A14 to Gweru (see page 85), 84 km to the west; otherwise the A4 continues 100 km to Masvingo (page 120).

Northeast of Harare → For listings, see pages 90-92.

Harare to the Mavuradonha Mountains

The drive north from Harare on the A11 passes through some richly fertile land. The first settlement, 40 km north of Harare, is **Mazowe**, which lies in a deep bushy valley of citrus farms. Mazowe orange juice is manufactured here. The Mazowe Dam on the Mazowe River ('the river of elephants') was completed in 1920 and irrigates a large area, including the 21,000-ha Mazowe Citrus Estate. It is well known for the size of the carp caught in its waters. The citrus trees are in full bearing during May and June. About 1 km north of Mazowe the A11 swings east to **Bindura**, 46 km away, another agricultural centre where there is also a nickel mine, and then on to **Mount Darwin**. This 1509 m high mountain is known locally as Pfuru, meaning 'the one that surpasses' and was named in 1889 by hunter Fredrick Selous (see box, page 87) in honour, rather inexplicably, of Charles Darwin. On the summit are the remains of some stone walls built here at an unspecified period and for some unknown reason. The country around the village of the same name remains wild and undeveloped.

In the other direction, some 15 km north of Mazowe, is the village of **Concession**, named when an American, Henry Clay Moore, secured a concession to establish mining stakes here prior to the arrival of Cecil Rhodes in 1893. Beyond here is the village of **Centenary**.

Border crossings: Zimbabwe–Mozambique

Nyamapanda–Zobué (via the Tete Corridor)

Zimbabwe's Nyamapanda border is 238 km northeast of Harare on the A2 and is open from 0600-1800. Beyond the border drivers travel on a tarred 263-km road running from Nyamapanda through the Mozambique town of **Tete** to **Zobué** on the **Malawi** border, from where it is a short drive to Blantyre. Both Mozambique and Zimbabwe visas are available at the border. Most nationalities do not require a visa for Malawi. If you are in a hire car, you must have a letter of permission from the hire car company to allow you to take a vehicle over the border and a copy of the car's registration document to obtain a temporary import permit at the border (see Essentials, page 23, for more details on taking cars in and out of Zimbabwe). In Mozambique, it is essential to have a sticker on the vehicle indicating where the car has come from – ZW or SA, for example – and carry a set of two red warning triangles. Police in Mozambique can fine drivers for not having these. The **Tete Corridor** road is featureless and straight, passing through a largely empty region of flat low-lying bush dotted with baobab trees. The town of Tete is equally unremarkable, though it is divided by the mighty Zambezi River, crossed by the impressive 1-km-long Ponte Presidente Samora Machel suspension bridge, built in the 1960s.

The Mavuradonha Mountains → *Colour map 2, A2.*

Sometimes referred to as the Mavuradonha Wilderness Area, this is approximately 190 km north of Harare, beyond the village of Centenary – continue on from there to the settlement of Muzarabini and ask there for the best access road. The mountains are virtually uninhabited by humans, though sable antelope, zebra and elephant may be spotted, and the escarpments and gorges are very scenic. The first thing a visitor new to this area notices is that while some of the hills look almost bare, with only grass and sparse scrubby-looking bushes, others are covered in thick vegetation, trees and granite boulders. This is because the properties of the soil and geology differ drastically from one hill to the next. The reason for this is that the Mavuradonha Mountains are at the northern end of the Great Dyke, a 500-km-long fault line through which magma rose through the earth's crust to form hills of a completely different chemical composition from their neighbours. It was the highly valuable minerals and metals in this rock - among them platinum, gold and silver - that led to the country's prosperity many millennia later.

Except for a few barely accessible tracks running north, east and west of Muzarabani, there are few access points into the mountains these days. Be prepared for bush camping too, and perhaps carry extra jerry cans of fuel and water; a 4WD is essential. There is also the option from here to go cross country to Mana Pools National Park (see page 222), but a detailed map (rare in Zimbabwe) and a GPS are essential and it is advisable to travel in at least a two-vehicle convoy in case of a breakdown. Travel is best done during the dry season between April and November. Hiking is not out of the question, but hikers need to be completely self-sufficient and experienced, with equipment such as compasses; ideally they should enlist the help of a guide in Muzarabani. Most tracks within the region follow feint trails made by animals.

For Sleeping and Eating price codes and other relevant information, see Essentials pages 29-34.

⊜ Sleeping

Darwendale Recreational Park *p83*

D Rest camp, for information and reservations visit the Parks and Wildlife Management Authority office on the corner of Borrowdale Rd and Sandringham Drive in the National Herbarium and Botanic Gardens (see page 61) in Harare, T04-706077-8, Mon-Fri 0800-1600, or the Bulawayo office on 15th Av between Main St and Fort St, T09-65592, Mon-Fri 0800-1600, www.zimparks.com. There are 2 basic lodges in the park about 2 km from the main entrance and office, each with 4 beds in 2 rooms, fully equipped kitchen with utensils, stove and fridge, and outside braai pits (firewood is available to buy). The campsite (US$10 per person) is close to the launching site for boats on the lake, with ablution block with hot water, braai pits and electric points.

Kadoma *p84*

C Kadoma Hotel, on the right hand side of the road as you enter Kadoma from Harare, T068-22106/22199, www. rainbowkadomahotel.com. A surprisingly large hotel with 147 spacious rooms with DSTV, fans, and nicely tiled bathrooms, in hacienda-style low blocks with parking outside. Recently refurbished, this is a vast property dotted with palms and with the odd peacock strutting around. There's Wi-Fi in the restaurant, where a band plays most evenings.

Kwekwe *p84*

D Golden Mile Hotel, 2 km from town on the Bulawayo Rd, T055-23711. A typical small-town hotel with 28 reasonable rooms with floral bedspreads, TV, fan, clean bathrooms with showers, garden, outside bar, pool, slot machines in a semi-operating casino and restaurant with nicely dressed tables. English breakfast is included in the rates. Citylink and Pathfinders buses stop here.

Gweru *p85, map p85*

There's not much choice in town and most budget travellers head out to the Antelope Park.

D Regency Chevron Hotel, 1.6 km from town on the Bulawayo road, T039-253085, www.regencyafrica.com. Another small town hotel built in 1971, with 50 reasonable and airy if not plain rooms with DSTV, a decent restaurant offering room service, packed lunches and a weekend braai popular with locals, pool, fairly well-stocked bar, well-tended gardens, and large secure car park. Citylink and Pathfinder buses stop here.

D The Village Lodge, 5 km before Gweru if coming from Harare, T054-231671/2, www.thevillagezim.com. Pleasant rural retreat in brick and thatched chalets in grounds dotted with acacia trees. Rooms have 2 double beds, teak furnishings, DSTV, coffee stations, minibars; the honeymoon suite has a jacuzzi, good restaurant serving buffets for breakfast and dinner, room service, bar and motel-style parking.

D-F Antelope Park, see page 86. There is a mixture of rustic accommodation here, including brick-and-thatch twin-bed en suite A-frame lodges with fridges and heaters, and permanent en suite tents on decks under thatch, all are furnished with indigenous teak furniture and with spacious wooden decks overlooking the dam. Basic but cheaper rooms are available for backpackers and there's a spacious campsite with braais and good ablutions. Facilities include a pool, dining boma, laundry, fire pit and gardens. With notice, all meals are available, though there is no bar so BYO.

D-F Jabulani Safaris, Bon Accord Farm, Shangani, 64 km south of Gweru and 100 km north of Bulawayo, 22 km off the main road,

T050-3306, www.jabulanisafaris.co.za.
A game farm off the Harare–Bulawayo road
with 8 comfortable thatched rooms, offering
hearty farm cooking at a table where you
eat with the hosts and other guests. Game
drives – there are 40 animal species on the
farm – pool and fishing for bass and bream
are on offer, and there's a campsite.

E Midlands Hotel, Main St, T054-708121.
Opened in 1927 by the Meikles brothers (also
known for their chain of department stores
in Zimbabwe), this has a beautiful colonial
façade and the 52 rooms are spread over
2 floors. However, they are very dated, only
have baths (as befits most colonial hotels
given that they were built by the British) and
there's a dark and seedy bar and restaurant,
where the menu is very unreliable.

Camping

F You can camp at the deserted and dull
municipal campsite at the Gweru Sports
Club south of town on the Bulawayo road,
but the overwhelmingly superior option is
at the lovely campsite next to the dam at
the **Antelope Park**, which has good, clean
ablution blocks and braai pits. Shop for
provisions in Gweru.

⊖ Eating

Kadoma *p84*

🍴 **Kadoma Hotel** (see Sleeping). This is
the best place to eat and the restaurant is
open 0630-0930 for breakfast, 1230-1400
for lunch and 1900-2130 for dinner. Light
meals on the veranda bar next to the pool
are available 1000-2200. The menu features
whatever is locally available but expect steak
and chicken main and toasted sandwiches
for snacks.

KweKwe *p84*

There's a **Wimpy** on the main street and
takeaways at the petrol stations. A meal at
the **Regency Fairmile Hotel** is probably the
best option.

Gweru *p85, map p85*

There are Chicken and Creamy inns at the
Total service station as you approach town
from Harare, and another crop – Nando's,
and Bakers, Creamy and Chicken Inn – on
Sixth St.

🍴 **Dutch Oven**, Fifth St. Mon-Sat 0745-
2000. A basic cafeteria selling the likes
of omelettes for breakfast, doughnuts,
pancakes, chicken pies, hamburgers and
chips. Nothing special, and greasy.

O Shopping

KweKwe *p84*

There is an **OK** and a **TM** supermarket in
town, both just off the main street. A few
curios are for sale from a stall just before
going into town from the Harare road.

Gweru *p85, map p85*

There's an **OK** supermarket just to the
northwest of the Boggie's Clock Tower off
Robert Mugabe Way, and on the opposite
corner of this junction and to the south
of the Boggie's Clock Tower, a **Meikles**
department store.

▲ Activities and tours

Gweru *p85, map p85*
Swimming

The public pool on the corner of Eleventh
Av and Robert Mugabe Way used to be a
good place to swim – check that there is
water in it!

⊖ Transport

KweKwe *p84*
Bus

Citylink and **Pathfinder** buses stop at the
Golden Mile Hotel, while local economy
buses stop on the side of the road at the
Harare end of the main drag.

Train
The railway station is east of town at the end of Second St.

Gweru *p85, map p85*
Bus
Citylink buses stop at the Regency Fairmile Hotel, 1.6 km south of the town centre towards Bulawayo. Local economy buses stop at the town terminal on Robert Mugabe Way to the north of the Midlands Hotel.

Taxi
Taxis line up outside of the Midlands Hotel.

Train
The railway station is at the end of Tenth St.

Directory

KweKwe *p84*
Banks There are a couple of banks along the main street, Robert Mugabe Way, including **Zimbank**, but don't rely on them having US$ cash in the ATMs.

Gweru *p85, map p85*
Banks There are a number of banks around town. The best bet to get US$ cash from the ATMs is probably **Barclays** on the corner of Robert Mugabe Way and Main St. **Zim Bank** is near the post office further south on Robert Mugabe Way and **Standard Chartered** is on Fifth St.
Medical services The general hospital is on Shurugwi Rd to the east of town, T054-51301, but this is very poor so for medical emergencies head for Harare or Bulawayo.

Contents

Footprint features

Border crossings

Eastern Highlands

At a glance

◒ **Getting around** On foot in Mutare; self-drive to the outlying attractions or, at a push, local economy buses linking the small towns.

⏱ **Time required** 2 hrs to wander around Mutare; 2 days to enjoy the mountains and perhaps go hiking.

☼ **Weather** Moderate temperatures, 20-25°C, all year, but often cloudy, and in the higher mountains misty with frosts May-Oct.

✘ **When not to go** Nov-Mar are the wettest months. Annual rainfall 2000 mm in the Eastern Highlands (higher than London).

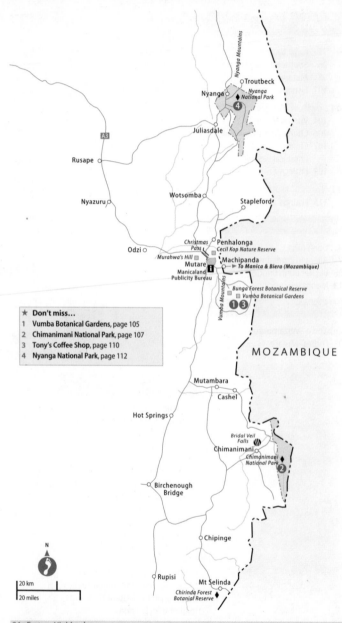

★ **Don't miss...**

MOZAMBIQUE

N

20 km
20 miles

Running for roughly 300 km from north to south, the Eastern Highlands are a rugged range of mountains that form the natural border with Mozambique. The region has a very different landscape and climate from the rest of the relatively flat and arid Zimbabwe, and the green hillsides, deeply dissected gorges, mountain streams and cool mists come as a surprise to most visitors. For the early settlers, who likened the region to the moors of Scotland, the Eastern Highlands long served as respite from the dry interior. They built dams for fishing and country hotels, and utilized the fertile climate by establishing pine plantations.

However, the region has been little visited by foreign tourists, and few know about this verdant strip of misty mountains on the edge of Zimbabwe. The region offers a breath of fresh air after the heat of a safari in the bush, it is easily accessible from Harare, and has some of the country's best country hotels and an outstanding golf course (at Leopard Rock). Other activities include trout fishing, horse riding and unlimited mountain hiking. Scenic highlights include the Botanical Gardens in Vumba, the tea plantations around Nyanga, Mount Inyangani – at 2593 m the highest mountain in Zimbabwe – and the jagged fairytale peaks of Chimanimani.

The principal town in the region is Mutare, which lies at the end of the A3, 263 km southeast of Harare. A bit like Bulawayo, it has the atmosphere of a sleepy backwater town, but is commercially bolstered by being the border town with Mozambique. From here it is 290 km to the busy port of Beira, a major trade point for exports coming in and out of Zimbabwe and the other landlocked countries in the interior.

The road to Mutare

The A3 passes through the small centre of Ruwa and then begins to climb to a rural plateau dotted with impressive granite domes covered in bright green lichens. This is rich farmland, though sadly neglected of late, as many previously white-owned farms were confiscated in this region. However, it does support Zimbabwe's only reasonably successful wine-producing venture. Mutare is the principal city of the Eastern Highlands and is also a border town with Mozambique. It has a pleasant laid-back country atmosphere but there is nothing to detain visitors for very long; it's the nearby mountains that are the real attraction in this region.
➤➤ *For listings, see pages 101-102.*

Southeast from Harare → *For listings, see pages 101-102.*

Ins and outs
The journey to the Eastern Highlands is a straightforward drive along the A3 from Harare. Mutare is 263 km southeast of Harare. There are regular buses from Harare's Mbare Musika bus terminal south of the market in Mbare; these go when full and cost about US$4. An overnight train costs about US$12. ➤➤ *For further details, see page 102.*

Ruwa → *Colour map 2, C1. Phone code: 073.*
Just 28 km east of Harare on the A3, Ruwa is a small town on the railway line, which has a group of shops on the main road serving passing traffic and the local farming community. Although it has grown fairly rapidly as a commuter destination for Harare and supports a number of manufacturing industries, it's an unremarkable town; but it does have an extraordinary UFO story to tell (see box, page 97).

Marondera → *Colour map 2, C2. Phone code: 079.*
Another ramshackle farming town, Marondera is 72 km southeast of Harare, and at 1640 m above sea level is one of Zimbabwe's highest towns. Named after a local chief, it was one of the earliest centres of white settlement in Rhodesia and a successful producer of tobacco, maize, beef and dairy products until the seizure of white-owned farms began in 2000. During the South African (Boer) War it was used by the British as a staging point for military operations into the Transvaal, and after the Second World War became home to many Polish refugees. Thanks to its high elevation and good climate, Marondera is known for its wine production; the Mukuyu label, named after a wild fig tree that grows in this region, has vineyards in the Ruzawi River Valley south of town (their wine can be bought in supermarkets but it's not as well regarded as South African wine). Also here, is one of the best boarding schools in Zimbabwe, **Peterhouse**, which was established in 1955; it can be seen from the main road 9 km east of town. From Marondera the road continues through gum and pine plantations, and after about 40 km, just beyond Macheke, it tops a rise known as **Eagle's Nest**, which has the first good view of the Eastern Highlands. Then, 92 km after Marondera, the road crosses the Lesapi River to Rusape.

Imire Safari Ranch
ⓘ *Near the village of Hwedza; from Harare turn right on a minor road 3 km before Marondera and follow signs for 40 km, T0912-522201, www.imiresafariranch.co; day trips are US$50, children (3-12) US$40, or you can stay overnight (see Sleeping, page 101).*

Aliens in Zimbabwe

On the morning of 16 September 1994, teachers and school officials at Ruwa's Ariel School were amazed when the school's students, aged between five and 12, reported that a flying object had landed in the school grounds. The teachers were in a meeting at the time, so the 62 children were unsupervised while in the playground on their morning break. The children claimed they had seen three objects in the sky, which disappeared and then reappeared in a different location. Then, they said, one object moved closer and closer to the ground and finally landed in a patch of bush about 100 m from the playground, where a small man, about 1 m high, got out. Described as having a scrawny neck, long black hair and huge eyes, the man walked towards the children. But, when he noticed them, he vanished and then reappeared back at the object, which then took off and disappeared. The smaller children were very frightened and were said to have been distressed. The incident attracted interest from many international UFO experts, who went to Zimbabwe to interview the children, asking them to draw pictures of what they had seen. Astonishingly, most of the pictures were almost identical, and the headmaster of the school said he thought the children were telling the truth. Those who believe in UFO sightings considered the incident to be one of the most significant close encounter cases in UFO history, and even today the story circulates on the internet.

Situated 105 km east of Harare, this safari ranch is situated in a farming area where indigenous wildlife species were hunted out to make way for cattle and cropping. In 1972 farm owner Norman Travers decided to restore some of the wildlife and established Imire Safari Ranch and a black rhino breeding programme. To date, this has released 13 black rhinos in Matusadona National Park (see page 221), in spite of a tragic setback in 2007 when poachers killed three black rhino on the Imire property. Today the ranch is home to four rhino and four elephant, one of which, Nzou, a 35-year-old female, has rather unusually become a matriarch figure to a herd of buffalo. Short elephant rides can be arranged for US$40. Other game includes sable, hyena, giraffe and wildebeest. The day programme begins at 0930 with coffee and biscuits followed by a morning game drive, lunch and an afternoon game drive ending about 1600.

Rusape → Colour map 2, C2. Phone code: 025.

Another quiet, nondescript agricultural town, Rusape takes its name from the Lesapi River; it means 'sparing of the waters' and refers to the river's erratic flow. The town was established in 1894 as a supply post for the British South Africa Company. Its population today is around 20,000, a figure that has risen sharply in recent years, as former farm workers have settled here, many in crowded townships. Surrounding the town are *kopjes*, msasa trees, occasional tobacco farms and densely crowded villages. Oddly, Rusape has a substantial community of African Jews. Judaism is thought to have been introduced by a Jewish former slave who visited in the late 19th or early 20th century, though another, older theory suggests they are the descendants of Jewish tribes from Yemen who crossed to Africa.

Of interest locally, though not easy to reach, is the inexplicably named **Diana's Vow**, an unusual rock formation with a Bushman painting about 28 km northeast of town. Ask locally for directions to a narrow and hopelessly pot-holed road which starts in the

Juliasdale area of town, just after the church. Follow the road for 28 km, and then take a sandy farm track on the right for about 500 m to clusters of balancing rocks and one huge base rock with a wide overhang. The whole face of the overhang is covered with a 2000-year-old Bushman painting, though the parts exposed to the elements are being weathered away. It depicts a sable antelope dance, a traditional ceremony that induces trance and invokes potency, centring on a huge reclining male figure, probably in a trance, and a smaller female figure below, both wearing sable antelope headdresses. Lower down are at least 17 dancing male figures, also wearing sable costumes. The whole scene seems to take place in a camp, as there are gourds, baskets, dogs and children just above the figures.

From Rusape, the main road heads into the foothills of the mountains and increasingly shrubs, trees and wild flowers appear. About 85 km from Rusape it climbs the **Christmas Pass**, named by its surveyor, FW Bruce, who camped here at Christmas. The summit of the pass has great views of the valley sheltering Mutare, and of the granite mountains to the east and south. From there it's a steady 6-km descent through forest to Mutare. There's an alternative road from Rusape, the A14, that goes to Nyanga (see page 114), a distance of 120 km.

Mutare → *For listings, see pages 101-102. Colour map 2, C3.*

Sitting in a broad mountain-rimmed valley at an altitude of 1220 m above sea level and 8 km from the Mozambique border, Mutare is the capital of the province of Manicaland. Its name is derived from the Manyika people, a Shona sub-tribal group who traditionally live in the region. (Over the border in Mozambique, the first town after Mutare is called Manica, after the same people.) Mutare itself means, perhaps rather oddly, 'a piece of metal', and probably derives from the fact that small deposits of gold were discovered in the Mutare River in the early settler days. Pre-independence it was known as Umtali, meaning the same thing, but in 1982 the name was changed to the more accurate (in local spelling) Mutare. This is the largest town in the Eastern Highlands, with a population of around 300,000, though there is little to indicate this in its semi-deserted streets. With hardly a high-rise building in sight, its 'provincialness' is perhaps its strongest feature. There's very little to see or do, but it does serve as a springboard for the Eastern Highlands, and, circled by high granite mountains, has one of the most beautiful locations in Zimbabwe. The valley in which the town lies forms a natural gateway between the coastal lowlands of Mozambique and the interior of Zimbabwe. For this reason, it's long been considered Zimbabwe's gateway to the Indian Ocean.

Ins and outs → *Phone code: 020. Population: 300,000.*

Getting there and around Mutare is situated 263 km southeast of Harare and 290 km west of the port of Beira in Mozambique. It is linked to Harare by local buses and trains (see Transport, page 102). Buses from Harare's bus terminal pull into Mutare's central bus terminal on the corner of First Avenue and Herbert Chitepo Street; the journey takes three to fours hours. The railway station is on Railway Street, about 500 m south of the bus terminal. The final descent by road from Christmas Pass into town is spectacular, with the whole panorama of the valley spreading out below and the Vumba Mountains to the southeast. For information about getting to Mutare from Mozambique and vice versa, see page 22. In town, urban commuter omnibuses ply the main roads during daylight hours, and taxis are lined up at major intersections along Herbert Chitepo Way.

Best time to visit Being in a relatively low valley, in contrast to the surrounding (and significantly more chilly) high mountains, Mutare has a moderate mean daytime temperature of about 20°C. The coldest month, as elsewhere in Zimbabwe, is July, when there's a minimum of 8°C at night, but daytime highs of about 20°C. The hottest month is January, with warm nights from 17°C and days creeping up to 26°C. The rainy season is from December to February, although heavy showers are possible before and after this in the mountains, where temperatures are a few degrees lower than in Mutare throughout the year. In the mountains, May to October are the cooler winter months, when mists and frosts are common, and fleeces/sweaters, long trousers, closed shoes, etc are definitely required. Strangely, it doesn't snow, despite the high altitude. In Mutare, December is the best time to see the flame trees in flower, while September and October are the time for blooming jacarandas, bougainvillea and flamboyants.

Tourist information The **Manicaland Publicity Association** ① *corner of Herbert Chitepo St and Robert Mugabe Way, T020-64711, www.manicalandpublicity.co.zw, Mon-Fri 0830-1600*, covers the whole of the Eastern Highlands and can make reservations for hotels in the region.

Background

Mutare, then called Umtali, was founded on the railway in 1896 (see box, page 146), which linked landlocked Rhodesia with Beira on the Mozambique coast, 285 km away. However, the first Umtali started life as a rough and ready gold-mining camp in 1891 at another site on the banks of the Mutare River. When the railway was being constructed, Cecil Rhodes visited the old Umtali and informed the residents that the engineers wanted the railway to go through the easiest possible pass through the mountains, namely the valley of the Sakubva Stream, 17 km to the south and separated from old Umtali by a high granite ridge. Rhodes bought old Umtali and distributed £50,000 to the residents, enabling them to move to the new site on the railway (a much cheaper solution than re-routing the railway). The new Umtali was born and the old one abandoned to the bush. Rhodes and his surveyors laid out a fine new town with wide, flamboyant-lined streets, parks and a racetrack. It achieved city status in 1971.

Despite suffering tremendous economic setbacks over the past few years, Mutare is today home to a large sawmill that provides much of the country with timber, and Tanganda Tea, the largest tea producer in Zimbabwe. Off the Nyanga road, about 17 km north of the city, is the Methodist-run Africa University, which opened in 1992 and teaches bachelor's degrees in mostly agriculture and theology to around 1300 students from about a dozen African countries.

Like most cities in Zimbabwe, residential suburbs in Mutare are split by economic class and population density. The upscale neighbourhoods of **Fairbridge Park**, **Murambi** and **Tiger's Kloof** are on the north end of the city along the foothills of the mountains. South of the railway track lies the high-density suburb of **Sakubva**, which contains nearly half the city's population despite being just a little over 4 sq km. Sakubva's economy centres on a large outdoor food and flea market. Like high-density areas in other cities, such as Mbare in Harare, Sakubva was hit hard in 2005 during Operation Murambatsvina, a move by the Mugabe government to get rid of illegal structures, illegal businesses and criminal activities in urban areas (see page 246). An estimated 60,000-70,000 people lost their homes to bulldozers and were displaced.

Sights

The **Mutare Museum** ① *Victory Av, off Aerodrome Rd, T020-63630/005, daily 0900-1700, US$10, children (4-12), US$4, under 5 free,* was established in 1945 and in 1959 was taken over by Zimbabwe's National Museums and Monuments. It was moved from its original home in a wooden and corrugated-iron building to the present 1960s brick structure. There are displays on rock formations and minerals found in the Eastern Highlands, a collection of pistols and firearms that belonged to the museum's first curator, a Captain EF Bloutbee, other edged weapons like swords and bayonets from various places around the world, and transport, including some vintage cars. There is also a small collection of early tractors, which includes a 1903 Ivel, the first motorized tractor imported into Zimbabwe and, apparently, the second-oldest tractor in existence anywhere. Outside the museum is a massive Bow McLachlan engine dating from 1896. There is also a collection of faded-looking stuffed animals, some of which are poised in hunting scenes (eagles sinking their talons into hares and owls preying on rats), traditional Shona headrests (used as 'pillows' for sleeping, and also as an item for chiefs and medicine men to rest their heads for contemplation), snuff boxes, axes and musical instruments in the ethnographical section. Attached to the museum is a large walk-in aviary which used to house some birds indigenous to Zimbabwe. However, some pesky vervet monkeys damaged the fences of the aviary and most of the birds flew out, so it is temporarily closed.

The **National Gallery of Zimbabwe** ① *122 3rd St, corner of 11th Av, Tue-Sun 0800-1630, US$4, children (4-12) US$2,* opened in 1999 at Kopje House, a historical building that dates from 1897 and was Mutare's first hospital. It was declared a Monument in the late 1970s under the custody of National Museums and Monuments of Zimbabwe. The gallery runs an annual programme of exhibitions showing work from the Harare National Gallery (page 59), while offering local artists the much-needed opportunity to display their work.

Mutare Main Park, a short stroll to the east of the Publicity Association, is shaded by exotic trees, with plenty of park benches, and a palm-lined stream running down the centre. The result of many years of hard work, the **Aloe Gardens** contain about 10,000 aloes and numerous indigenous shrubs and cycads. The 243 species of aloe were collected from all over Africa and Malagassey.

The **Cecil Kop Nature Reserve** ① *Arcadia Rd, 2.5 km north of the city centre, follow Herbert Chitepo St, T020-61537, 0700-1800, US$2,* was set up in 1977 as an educational facility for local schoolchildren. This 1750-ha wildlife reserve consists of three distinct areas: **Tiger's Kloof**, the forested northeastern mountain face, which has numerous springs rolling down to the dam and surrounding msasa woodland; **Thomson's Vlei** with its undulating grasslands; and the **Wilderness Area** of heavily wooded forest, gullies and springs. It is home to giraffe, zebra, ostrich, a wide range of antelope, vervet and samango monkeys, and baboons. A variety of birdlife can be seen around the dam, including Egyptian goose, grey heron and cormorant. There are picnic sites, a refreshment kiosk and braai facilities, and visitors can game- and birdwatch from two elevated thatched viewing platforms.

On the eastern boundary of the city, the **Cross Kopje** dominates the Mutare skyline with its 10-m-high cross, erected by a Colonel Methuen as a memorial to African soldiers who fell in the First World War. It's a short but energetic walk to the summit and the path leads off Rekayi Tangwena Drive.

Murahwa's Hill ① *4 km west from the town centre, open sunrise to sunset, admission free,* is accessed on a steep path from the Christmas Pass road, or from a gentler path near Mutare's old showgrounds off Robert Mugabe Drive. This 5-ha patch of woodland surrounds the most obvious *kopjie* in the Mutare valley as you look from town towards the

Christmas Pass. It is a lovely place for a hike, but it's isolated and is at least an hour's walk from town. Near the summit of the *kopjie* are the stone walls of an ancient iron-age village (though they are not remarkable), parts of which can be seen in the Mutare Museum. The spot has a good diversity of tree species – 132 have been identified – harbouring birds, butterflies and wild orchids.

◉ The road to Mutare listings

For Sleeping and Eating price codes and other relevant information, see Essentials pages 29-34.

◉ Sleeping

Southeast from Harare *p96*

C Imire Safari Ranch (see above), T0912-522201, www.imiresafariranch.com. Bush setting with 6 comfortable thatched en suite rondavels, pleasant outside thatched *boma* with bar and restaurant serving farm-style breakfasts and dinners. Picnic lunches are taken next to the ranch's dam as part of the day trip (see page 96). Large swimming pool; rates include game drives. There are also 4 empty thatched huts in a bush camp (bring sleeping bags and mats) with hot showers and a central open kitchen area.

C Musangano Lodge, Champion Mile Rd, Odzi, 25 km before Mutare off the A3, T020-442267, www.musangano.com. A useful stopover en route to, or as a base to visit the Eastern Highlands, with 5 doubles and 4 self-catering lodges sleeping 4-6, exquisitely furnished with fireplaces and large showers. There's a restaurant and an attractive swimming pool. A number of hikes and mountain-bike trails have been marked out on the 140-ha property, one of which goes up to a beacon with a stunning 360° view.

D Christmas Pass Hotel, 10 km before Mutare on the Christmas Pass on the A3, T020-63857, 63883, xmasspass@mweb. co.zw. Colonial hotel at the top of the pass as the road descends to town. Has 17 rooms with old-fashioned and neglected furnishings, but also a decent pool and friendly staff (your car is washed), bar and a restaurant serving mostly Zimbabwean food.

D Marondera Hotel, corner Ash Rd and Fourth St, Marondera, T079-24005/24006. A faded small-town hotel in a series of red-brick blocks, with 41 average en suite rooms, a reasonably pleasant pool and terrace area, restaurant, bar and conference facilities.

D Wise Owl Motel, 2 km before town on the A3, T020-64643, wiseowl@mweb.co.za. Passable but featureless motel with 69 well-maintained rooms with DSTV, reasonable restaurant, 2 bars, pool and pleasant gardens.

F Mutare Municipal Campsite, 5 km before Mutare on the A3, no phone. Like other municipal campsites in Zimbabwe, this has received hardly any visitors in recent years, but it's still staffed, the grounds are neat, and the ablution blocks are kept clean.

Mutare *p98*

C Holiday Inn, corner Aerodrome Rd and Third St, T020-64431, www.ichotelsgroup. com. A boring brick block, but with 98 comfortable, modern rooms and a lovely palm-shaded swimming pool. Generous buffet breakfasts, a branch of the steak chain restaurant **Spur**, and the **Forester's Pub**, a popular watering hole.

D Christmas Pass Hotel, 8 km out of town on the Christmas Pass on the A3 coming from Harare, T020-63818. Fairly basic country hotel on the brow of the hill as you approach Mutare, with good views but tired rooms set in gardens in 3-storey blocks. Has a pool, restaurant and bar and the 'casino' still sometimes functions.

D Mountview Hotel, corner Second St and Seventh Av, T020-66101/5. A dull old-fashioned block predominantly aimed at business people, or at least that was the intention when it was built. 27 single bedrooms and 24 doubles with TV and dated furnishings, restaurant, gazebo bar in the quiet garden and pool.

F Mutare Municipal Caravan Park and Campsite, about 6 km from town on the Christmas Pass, T020-60823. This is little utilized and barely functional, with basic ablution blocks and unkempt grassy sites, but like other council-owned caravan parks in Zimbabwe it is still staffed. There are fine views down into the valley over Mutare and the trees provide good shade.

❼ Eating

Mutare *p98*

Mutare is not one of Zimbabwe's liveliest places, and there are hardly any places to eat out at night.

❦Green Coucal, 111 Second St, T023-897871, freencoucal@zol.co.zw. Open 0800-1600. One of Mutare's favourite local eateries, with an art gallery and outside seating. Open for breakfast and lunch until mid-afternoon, with occasional private functions on Fri evening. Has a small but inventive chalkboard menu offering dishes such as fishcakes and salad or barbecued chicken and savoury rice, and chocolate cake and iced coffee.

❦-❦Stax, 2 First Mutual Centre, Herbert Chipito St, T020-62653. Open 0730-2000. Popular during the day for milkshakes, smoothies, waffles and pizza, light meals such as fish or steak and chips, and free Wi-Fi. The food is plain but good service and cheap; the decor is cottagey pastels. No wine but beer and spirits and good coffees.

❦Portuguese Club, 5 Hosgood Av, take the first road right opposite the fire station on the way into town from Harare. Mon-Sat 1000-2300, Sun-1000-1400. Excellent value and famous for its peri-peri chicken with chips, salad and bread (US$8 for half a chicken). Also does good steaks and steak rolls.

❍ Shopping

Mutare *p98*

Jairos Jiri Craftshop, 41 First St, T020-63970. Mon-Fri 0745-1645, Sat 0800-1400. Sells items made by mostly local disabled artists, including batiks, wood and stone carvings, musical instruments, leather bags, wall hangings, beadwork and tie-dye cloth, as well as many other craft products. There are other branches at Victoria Falls and Bulawayo.

❒ Transport

Mutare *p98*

Bus

In town, commuter omnibuses ply the streets and pick up and drop off when flagged down. Local economy buses arrive at the town terminus on Herbert Chitepo St more or less opposite the park. Expect to pay around US$4-5 from **Harare** (about 5 hrs). Buses and commuter omnibus taxis also go to the regional towns and villages; **Cloudlands** for **Vumba** (1 hr), **Chimanimani** (4-5 hrs), **Chipinge** (4-5 hrs), **Nyanga** (3½ hrs).

Train

The railway station is on Railway St to the south of town which runs parallel to Herbert Chitepo St. In theory the Mutare service to Harare departs Mon, Thu and Sat at 2100 and arrives the next morning at 0600, though they often run late. Expect to pay around US$8 for a sleeper compartment (see page 25 for more information about the train services). In the other direction, trains run from **Harare** to Mutare on Sun, Wed and Fri, also departing at 2100. Note that there is no dining car on the Harare to Mutare train, so bring food and drinks, and there's no bedding, so you will need a sleeping bag.

Border crossings: Zimbabwe–Mozambique

Forbes-Mutare—Machipanda

The border is 10 km east of the city centre and is open 0600-1800. Follow signs along Robert Mugabe Avenue, on which there are commuter omnibus taxis, although a regular taxi is the safer bet if you have luggage. Mozambique visas, US$25 or the equivalent in South African rand if you have them, are available at the border. If you are coming from Mozambique, Zimbabwe visas can also be obtained at the border. On the Mozambique side there are minibus taxis for the 290-km journey to **Beira**; commonly known as the **Beira Corridor**. For information on the documentation necessary for taking a car in or out of Zimbabwe, see page 23. In Mozambique, it is essential to have a sticker on the vehicle indicating where the car has come from (ZW or SA for example), and carry a set of two red warning triangles. Police in Mozambique can fine drivers for not having these.

The road to Beira is in good condition. About 60 km from the border, the first main town on the Mozambique side is **Chimoio**, which has petrol stations, banks and a Shoprite supermarket. After another 87 km there is a turn-off south along the coast road to Maputo, while Beira is another 131 km straight on. If you are crossing the border late in the day, the first decent place to stay is 44 km into Mozambique and is well signposted: **Casa Msika Lodge** (www.casamsika.com) sits in a gloriously scenic location on Lake Chicamba, and offers affordable rondavels sleeping up to six, camping and good Portuguese food. It accepts Mozambique metical, South African rand and US dollars.

South of Mutare

An enormous ridge of granite, the steep and green Vumba Mountains clothed in indigenous forest, lie southeast of Mutare. Although often covered in cloud, they offer breathtaking views north towards Mutare and into neighbouring Mozambique, east over coffee plantations and south towards the Burma Valley and the Chimanimani Mountains. The mountains are dominated by savannah miombo woodland, as well as extensive sub-montane grasslands, local mist-belts with mosses, ferns and evergreen forest in the deeper ravines. The higher levels are sparsely vegetated, with shrubs such as aloes and proteas, the latter grown for export. Although it is not easy to define the boundaries of the Vumba (also known as Bvumba, which is the Shona word for 'mist'), it more or less covers 200 sq km and straddles the border with Mozambique; the Chicamba Dam can be seen from the mountains.

From Mutare, the road climbs into the mountains through msasa woodland, which abruptly changes into evergreen mist forest. To the south lie the Zimunya and Chigodora communal lands and further on the Burma Valley, which has banana and other tropical fruit plantations. This valley separates the Vumba from the Tsetsera range, also known as the Himalayas. To the north is Essex Valley, which is used for commercial forestry, where the Wattle Company has eucalyptus plantations.

The resemblance to the English countryside is superficial, and on closer examination the proliferation of tropical birdlife, the striking colour infusions of wildflowers, blue skies and verdant green all speak undeniably of the tropics. This is one of the most scenic quarters of southern Africa, and justly deserves its reputation as the most beautiful and best-kept secret in the region. The highlight is the 30-ha Vumba Botanical Gardens with its colourful variety of indigenous and exotic plants such as azaleas, fuchsias and hydrangeas, while the Bunga Forest Botanical Reserve has footpaths, natural streams and varied plant life. The Vumba is a hotspot for birding enthusiasts and there are a number of endemic species including the Swynnerton's robin, Robert's warbler, bronzy sunbird, and the Gurney's sugarbird. The forests are also home to the noisy samango monkey and shy blue duiker, and the flora is well known for attracting a host of butterflies.

The Vumba is also famous for its hotels. These range from the Leopard Rock Resort, featuring what is reputed to be Tiger Woods' favourite golf course, to the deeply traditional White Horse Inn offering haute cuisine and a sense of old-world colonial charm. ▶▶ *For listings, see pages 109-110.*

Vumba Mountains → *Colour map 4, A6.*

Ins and outs

Getting there The best way to visit is by car, and the road that reaches the mountains from Mutare provides one of the most spectacular drives in Zimbabwe, climbing steeply to 1585 m above sea level within 10 km of the city. The Botanical Gardens in the heart of the Vumba are only 32 km from Mutare. Stay on the Vumba Road, which climbs first to the Bunga Forest Botanical Reserve then the Vumba Botanical Gardens and ends at Leopard Rock Hotel, all overlooked by the highest peak in the Vumba, the granite-domed Castle Beacon (1910 m). The road twists around the slopes of this dome and tunnels its way through attractive patches of forest, farmland and pine plantations, snatching views of the lowlands of Mozambique. There are a number of lay-bys on this road, with concrete seats for picnicking and good views. At the 11-km road marker, another road goes north: the

Introduction

A large proportion of people who visit Zimbabwe do so to see its spectacular wildlife. This colour section is a quick photographic guide to some of the more fascinating mammals you may encounter. We give you pictures and information about habitat, habits and characteristic appearance to help you when you are on safari. It is by no means a comprehensive survey and some of the animals listed may not be found throughout the whole country. For further information about Zimbabwe's mammals, birds, reptiles and other wildlife, see the Land and environment section of the Background chapter.

Above: Leopard with a kill. **Opposite page left:** Black rhinoceros. **Right:** White rhinoceros.

The Big Nine

It is fortunate that many of the large and spectacular animals of Africa are also, on the whole, fairly common. They are often known as the 'Big Five'. This term was originally coined by hunters who wanted to take home trophies of their safari. Thus it was, that, in hunting parlance, the Big Five were elephant, black rhino, buffalo, lion and leopard. Nowadays the hippopotamus is usually considered one of the Big Five for those who shoot with their cameras, whereas the buffalo is far less of a 'trophy'. Equally photogenic and worthy of being included are the zebra, giraffe and cheetah. But whether they are the Big Five or the Big Nine, these are the animals that most people come to Africa to see and, with the possible exception of the leopard and the black rhino, you have an excellent chance of seeing them all.

■ **Hippopotamus** *Hippopotamus amphibius*. Prefers shallow water, grazes on land over a wide area at night, so can be found quite a distance from water, and has a strong sense of territory, which it protects aggressively. Lives in large family groups known as 'schools'.

■ **Black rhinoceros** *Diceros bicornis*. Long, hooked upper lip distinguishes it from white rhino rather than colour. Prefers dry bush and thorn scrub habitat and in the past was found in mountain uplands. Males usually solitary. Females seen in small groups with their calves (very rarely more than four), sometimes with two generations. Mother always walks in front of offspring, unlike the white rhino, where the mother walks behind, guiding calf with her horn. Their distribution has been massively reduced by poaching and work continues to save both the black and the white rhino from extinction. You might be lucky and see the black rhino in Matobo and Matuadona national parks.

■ **White rhinoceros** *Diceros simus*. Square muzzle and bulkier than the black rhino, they are grazers rather than browsers, hence the different lip. Found in open grassland, they are more sociable and can be seen in groups of five or more. More common in Zimbabwe due to successful breeding programmes, which have been most successful in Matobo National Park.

■ **Common/Masai giraffe** *Giraffa camelopardis*. Yellowish-buff with patch-work of brownish marks and jagged edges, usually two different horns, sometimes three. Found throughout Africa in several differing subspecies.

■ **Common/Burchell's zebra** *Equus burchelli*. Generally has broad stripes (some with lighter shadow stripes next to the dark ones) which cross the top of the hind leg in unbroken lines.

■ **Leopard** *Panthera pardus*. Found in varied habitats ranging from forest to open savannah. They are generally nocturnal, hunting at night or before the sun comes up to avoid the heat. You may see them resting during the day in the lower branches of trees.

■ **Cheetah** *Acinonyx jubatus*. Often seen in family groups walking across plains or resting in the shade. The black 'tear' mark is usually obvious through binoculars. Can reach speeds of 90 kph over short distances. Found in open, semi-arid savannah, never in forested country. Although endangered in some parts of Africa, they are more commonly seen than the leopard but not as widespread as the lion (*Panthera leo*).

■ **Lion** *Panthera leo* (see page i). The largest (adult males can weigh up to 450 pounds) of the big cats in Africa and also the most common, lions are found on open savannah all over the continent. They are often not at all disturbed by the presence of humans and so it is possible to get quite close to them. They are sociable animals living in prides or permanent family groups of up to around 30 animals and are the only felid to do so. The females do most of the hunting (usually ungulates like zebra and antelopes).

Left: Common giraffe. **Right:** Burchell's zebra.
Opposite page top: Cheetah.
Opposite page middle: Leopard.
Opposite page bottom: Hippopotamus.

v

■ **Buffalo** *Syncerus caffer*. Considered by hunters to be the most dangerous of the big game and the most difficult to track and, therefore, the biggest trophy. Generally found on open plains but also at home in dense forest, they are fairly common in most African national parks but they need a large area to roam in, so they are not usually found in the smaller parks.

■ **Elephant** *Loxodonta africana*. Commonly seen; even on short safaris and at the side of the road in the northwest of the country. Despite having suffered from the activities of ivory poachers, today they thrive in Zimbabwe and there is an estimated population of about 88,000; 50,000 in Hwange National Park, many of which migrate seasonally between there and Chobe National Park in Botswana. There are also healthy populations in Gonarezhou National Park.

■ **Gemsbok** *Oryx gazella*, 122 cm. Unmistakable, with black line down spine and black stripe between coloured body and white underparts. Horns (both sexes) straight, long and look v-shaped (seen face-on). Found in arid, semi-desert country to the west of Zimbabwe in the Kalahari Desert, but they often stray into Hwange National Park. ■ **Nyala** *Tragelaphus angasi*, 110 cm. Slender frame, shaggy, dark brown coat with mauve tinge (males). Horns (male only) single open curve. The female is a different chestnut colour. They like dense bush and are often found close to water. Gather in herds of up to 30 but smaller groups more likely. Found across Zimbabwe. ■ **Common waterbuck** *Kobus ellipsiprymnus* and **Defassa waterbuck** *Kobus defassa*, 122-137 cm. Very similar with shaggy coats and white marking on buttocks. On the common variety, this is a clear half ring on rump and around tails; on Defassa, the ring is a filled-in solid white area. Both species occur in small herds in grassy areas, often near water.

Top: Gemsbok. Bottom left: Nyala. Bottom right: Common waterbuck.

■ **Sable antelope** *Hippotragus niger*, 140-145 cm and **Roan antelope** *Hippotragus equinus*, 127-137 cm. Both are similar in shape, with ringed horns curving backwards (both sexes), longer in the sable. Female sables are reddish brown and can be mistaken for the roan. Males are very dark with a white underbelly. The roan has distinct tufts of hair at the tips of its long ears. Sable prefers wooded areas and the roan is generally only seen near water. Both species live in herds.

■ **Greater kudu** *Tragelaphus strepsiceros*, 140-153 cm. Colour varies from greyish to fawn with several vertical white stripes down the sides of the body. Horns long and spreading, with two or three twists (male only). Distinctive thick fringe of hair running from the chin down the neck. Found in fairly thick bush, sometimes in quite dry areas. Usually live in family groups of up to six, but occasionally larger herds of up to about 30.

■ **Topi** *Damaliscus korrigum*, 122-127 cm. Very rich dark rufous, with dark patches on the tops of the legs and more ordinary looking, lyre-shaped horns.

Top: Greater kudu. **Middle:** Sable antelope. **Bottom:** Topi.

■ **Hartebeest** In the hartebeest the horns arise from a bony protuberance on the top of the head and curve outwards and backwards. There are three sub-species: **Coke's hartebeest** *Alcephalus buselaphus*, 122 cm, is a drab pale brown with a paler rump; **Lichtenstein's hartebeest** *Alcephalus lichtensteinii*, 127-132 cm, is also fawn in colour, with a rufous wash over the back and dark marks on the front of the legs and often a dark patch near shoulder; and the **red hartebeest** *Alcephalus caama*. All are found in herds, sometimes they mix with other plain dwellers such as zebra.

Top: Blue wildebeest. **Middle**: Red hartebeest.
Bottom: Eland.

■ **Brindled** or **blue wildebeest** or **gnu** *Connochaetes taurinus*, 132 cm. Found only in southern Africa and is often seen grazing with zebra.

■ **Eland** *Taurotragus oryx*, 175-183 cm. The largest of the antelope, it has a noticeable dewlap and shortish spiral horns (both sexes). Greyish to fawn, sometimes with rufous tinge and narrow white stripes down side of body. Occurs in groups of up to 30 in grassy habitats.

■ **Bushbuck** *Tragelaphus scriptus*, 76-92 cm. Shaggy coat with white spots and stripes on the side and back and two white, crescent-shaped marks on front of neck. Short horns (male only) slightly spiral. High rump gives characteristic crouch. White underside of tail noticeable when running. Occurs in thick bush, near water. Either seen in pairs or singly.

■ **Klipspringer** *Oreotragus oreotragus*, 56 cm. Brownish-yellow with grey speckles and white chin and underparts with a short tail. Has distinctive, blunt hoof tips and short horns (male only). Likes dry, stony hills and mountains.

■ **Bohor reedbuck** *Redunca redunca*, 71-76 cm. Horns (males only) sharply hooked forwards at the tip, distinguishing them from the oribi (see page xiii). It is reddish fawn with white underparts and has a short bushy tail. They usually live in pairs or otherwise in small family groups. Often seen with Oribi, in bushed grassland and always near water.

■ **Steenbok** *Raphicerus campestris*, 58 cm. An even, rufous brown colour with clean white underside and white ring around eye. Small dark patch at the tip of the nose and long broad ears. The horns (male only) are slightly longer than the ears: they are sharp, have a smooth surface and curve slightly forward. Generally seen alone, prefers open plains, often found in arid regions. Usually runs off very quickly on being spotted.

■ **Common (Grimm's) duiker** *Sylvicapra grimmia*, 58 cm. Grey-fawn colour with darker rump and pale colour on the underside. Its dark muzzle and prominent ears are divided by straight, upright, narrow pointed horns. This particular species is the only duiker found in open grasslands. Usually the duiker is associated with a forested environment. It's difficult to see because it is shy and will quickly disappear into the bush.

■ **Oribi** *Ourebia ourebi*, 61 cm. Slender and delicate looking with a longish neck and a sandy to brownish-fawn coat. It has oval-shaped ears and short, straight horns with a few rings at their base (male only). Like the reedbuck it has a patch of bare skin just below each ear. They live in small groups or as a pair and are never far from water.

Common (Grimm's) duiker.   Klipspringer.

Top left: Oribi. **Bottom left**: Bohor reedbuck. **Top right**: Suni. **Bottom**: Steenbok

■ **Suni** *Nesotragus moschatus*, 37 cm Dark chestnut to grey-fawn in colour with slight speckles along the back, its head and neck are slightly paler and the throat is white. It has a distinct bushy tail with a white tip. Its longish horns (male only) are thick, ribbed and slope backwards. This, one of the smallest antelope, lives alone and prefers dense bush cover and reed beds.

Top: Bushbuck. Bottom: Impala.

■ **Impala** *Aepyceros melampus*, 92-107 cm. One of the largest of the smaller antelope, the impala is a bright rufous colour on its back and has a white abdomen, a white 'eyebrow' and chin and white hair inside its ears. From behind, the white rump with black stripes on each side is characteristic and makes it easy to identify. It has long lyre-shaped horns (male only). Above the heels of the hind legs is a tuft of thick black bristles (unique to impala) which are easy to see when the animal runs. There's also a black mark on the side of abdomen, just in front of the back leg. Found in herds of 15 to 20, it likes open grassland or sometimes the cover of partially wooded areas and is usually close to water.

There are many other fascinating mammals worth keeping an eye out for. This is a selection of some of the more interesting or particularly common ones.

■ **African wild dog** or **hunting dog** *Lycacon pictus*. Easy to identify since they have all the features of a large mongrel dog: a large head and slender body. Their coat is a mixed pattern of dark shapes and white and yellow patches and no two dogs are quite alike. They are very rarely seen and are seriously threatened with extinction (there may be as few as 6000 left). Found on the open plains around dead animals, they are not in fact scavengers but effective pack hunters.

■ **Brown hyena** *Hyaena brunnea*.
High shoulders and low back give the hyena its characteristic appearance. The spotted variety, larger and brownish with dark spots, has a large head and rounded ears. The brown hyena, slightly smaller, has pointed ears and a shaggy coat, and is more noctural. Although sometimes shy animals, they have been know to wander around campsites stealing food from humans.

■ **Warthog** *Phacochoerus aethiopicus*.
The warthog is almost hairless and grey with a very large head, tusks and wart-like growths on its face. It frequently occurs in family parties and when startled will run away at speed with its tail held straight up in the air. They are often seen near water caking themselves in thick mud which helps to keep them both cool and free of ticks and flies.

Top: African wild dog. **Bottom:** Caracal.

Chacma baboon *Papio ursinus*. An adult male baboon is slender and weighs about 40 kg. Their general colour is a brownish grey, with lighter undersides. Usually seen in trees, but rocks can also provide sufficient protection, they occur in large family troops and have a reputation for being aggressive where they have become used to the presence of humans.

Rock hyrax *procavia capensis*. The nocturnal rock hyrax lives in colonies amongst boulders and on rocky hillsides, protecting themselves from predators like eagle, caracal and leopard by darting into the rock crevices.

Caracal *felis caracal*. Also known as the African lynx, it is twice the weight of a domestic cat, with reddish sandy colour fur and paler underparts. Distinctive black stripe from eye to nose and tufts on ears. Generally nocturnal and with similar habits to the leopard. They are not commonly seen, but are found in hilly country.

Vervet monkey *Chlorocebus pygerythrus*, 39-43 cm. A smallish primate and one of the most recognized monkeys in Africa. Brown bodies with a white underbelly and black face ringed by white fur, and males have blue abdominal regions. Spends the day foraging on the ground and sleeps at night in trees.

Opposite page top: Rock hyrax.
Opposite page middle: Warthog.
Opposite page bottom: vervet monkey.
Above: Chacma baboon.
Below: Brown hyena.

Vumba North Road, which leads to the **White Horse Inn**, another 2 km away. Alternatively you can drive along the Burma Valley Road, which is a 75-km circuitous route that branches off the Vumba Road about 9 km from Mutare and rejoins the Vumba Road at Cloudlands, 3 km south of the turn-off to the Vumba North Road and about 17 km from Mutare.

There is a daily bus that leaves Mutare about 1000 and returns about 1700, but it goes only as far as Cloudlands. From there it is a 17-km walk uphill to the gardens. Nevertheless, for keen hikers it's a rewarding walk through flower-dotted pastures and forest. In this area any trip should end with a visit to **Tony's Coffee Shop** (page 110) for outstanding cakes and teas.

Best time to visit With an average annual rainfall of 1800 mm a year (higher than London), the Vumba can be pretty wet, especially during the rainy season between November and March, and throughout the year there are occasional showers on a cloudy day. Most mornings are misty, but this usually lifts by early afternoon. Visibility is best just after the main rains, when there are clear skies and excellent views. July and August are the coldest months and temperatures may drop to below zero at night.

Vumba Botanical Gardens → Colour map 4, A6.

ⓘ The road from Mutare is tarred as far as Cloudlands, 17.7 km from Mutare, then turn right on to a gravel road and drive for about 15 km; open 0600-1800, US$10, children (6-12) US$5, (under 6) free.

The 184-ha gardens were established in 1917 by a retired miner called Edger Evans on what was then called Manchester Farm, as the previous owner was from Manchester. It was taken over in 1923 by a Fredrick John Taylor, a former mayor of Umtali (now Mutare), who worked on the gardens in his retirement. The gardens were opened to the public in 1940 and were proclaimed a national park in 1958; the present name of Vumba Botanical Gardens was adopted in 1975. The well-wooded reserve has landscaped gardens built around perennial streams which form a small lake. Sheltered walks between indigenous fern trees lead to displays of banked hydrangeas, proteas and azaleas, begonias, lilies, aloes, fuchsias, cycads and many other species. The birdlife is abundant and there are large numbers of samango monkey, which is endemic to the Eastern Highlands. There's a campsite within the reserve.

Bunga Forest Botanical Reserve → Colour map 4, A6.

More or less adjoining the Botanical Gardens (the two entrances are about 4 km apart but the reserves are effectively joined in area), this 24-ha rainforest reserve is moist, cool and lush, even on a hot day in October. The forest floors, trees and rocks are covered in ferns, mosses and orchids, and it is a fine representation of the flora found in the Vumba; the ferns alone number a reputed 250 species. In patches of prehistoric-looking spiny tree ferns one could almost imagine a dinosaur around the next corner, and a miniature look-a-like in the form of the endemic Marshall's dwarf chameleon may even cross your path. A path leads into the deep heart of the forest, eventually ending at the Bunga Views, an area of cliffs overlooking the lower parts of the forest and the Burma Valley. The forest is probably at its best in spring when the whole area is a pallet of colours as the msasa trees unfold their new red and orange leaves. At other times of the year, flowering epiphytic orchids provide a beautiful contrast against the trees they grow in. The path, which leads you back to the main road, winds through montane grassland and wild proteas, which in turn attract sunbirds and sugarbirds.

Back on the main road, another path takes you to **Chinyakwaremba (Leopard's Rock)**, one of the main peaks in the Vumba. It takes about 20 minutes to hike to the top where there is a sheer drop on the other side. On a clear day the views are superb. Lake Chicamba, in neighbouring Mozambique, stretches into the distance, clear blue and seemingly endless; the tall buildings in Beira on the Mozambique coast can often be seen. Far below the cliffs, you can look down on miniature people playing golf or zebras grazing at the **Leopard Rock Hotel**.

Chimanimani Mountains

This mountainous region south of Vumba is regarded as the southern end of the Eastern Highlands. Like the Vumba, the Chimanimanis ('squeezed together'), which stretch for around 50 km and are about 20 km wide, share the border with Mozambique. They form an important link between the Drakensberg Mountains in South Africa through to Nyanga and the mountains in Malawi and East Africa. The region is distinguished by large peaks of rifted quartzite; the highest, reaching 2436 m, is Mount Binga on the Mozambique side. The foothills feature gentler and more rounded forested hills which are ideal hiking territory. Deeply dissecting the northern part of the mountains is the Mussapa River, which flows eastwards into Mozambique through the Mussapa Gap. The Haroni and Bundi rivers run north–south, joining with the Rusitu River before turning east to Mozambique. The Chimanimani National Park (see below) is one of the highlights of the Eastern Highlands and is 150 km from Mutare; if you are properly equipped and self-sufficient, it offers beautiful paths through the mountains. During the war for independence, the mountain passes in the Chimanimani area were frequently used by guerrilla fighters, as they were well placed between Zimbabwe and their training camps in Mozambique.

Ins and outs
Getting there Chimanimani is 148 km south of Mutare, about a 2½-hour drive, and is clearly signposted off the A9 road about 70 km from the city. After the turn-off the road climbs on an increasingly scenic route into the mountains. Buses from Mutare and Masvingo arrive at the market in Chimanimani village.

Best time to visit The climate of the Chimanimani Mountains fluctuates between dry winters and wet summers; most rain falls between November and March. The high precipitation combined with low temperatures causes a typical tropical mountain climate. The temperatures range between 12° and 15°C during the cold season and between 18° and 26°C during summer. Frost is not uncommon between May and October.

Chimanimani village → *Colour map 4, A6.*
The village of Chimanimani was founded by Thomas Moodie in 1892 and was moved to its current site in 1895. It was originally called Melsetter after Moodie's family home on the Orkney Islands in Scotland, but the name was changed in 1982, after Zimbabwean independence (1980), first to Mandidzudzure and then, after consultation with local residents, to Chimanimani. The village has a bank (but no ATM), grocery and curio shops and the faded colonial-style **Chimanimani Hotel** (see page 109). As well as having good views of the Chimanimani Mountains, the village is dominated to the north by a large 1992-m hill called **Nyamzune** (also known as Pork Pie, on account of its domed, rounded shape). In theory, this is the home of Chimanimani's Eland Sanctuary, but the gracious antelope has

long been poached out. Nevertheless, the 5-km drive or walk is worthwhile for the good mountain and village views. Turn left in the village after the post office, then first right and follow the road up to the top of the hill. A more notable sight near Chimanimani are the **Bridal Veil Falls**, 4 km northwest (ask for directions to the dirt track); the round trip from the village should take around three hours. The water cascades down a 50-m rock face into a pool, and when the wind lifts the froth it resembles a floating bride's train; hence the name. You can swim here but the water is very cold. On either walk, look out for birds, particularly the malachite sunbird and Gurney's sugarbird, which are attracted to the bottle brush trees. The starred robin, Cape robin, and Livingstone's lourie are also often seen at Bridal Veil Falls.

Chimanimani National Park → *Colour map 4, A6.*
ⓘ *Dec-Mar park office 0600-1200, 1400-1700, Apr-Nov 0700-1200, 1400-1600, US$10, children (6-12) US$5, (under 6) free.*

Development in the 17,110-ha park has been limited in order to preserve the natural pristine beauty and wild landscapes of this mountainous area. At present the park provides only basic facilities, catering for the self-sufficient explorer. Activities include hiking and birding in the thick evergreen forest, and camping in caves among the sparkling waterfalls and natural swimming pools. Orchids and hibiscus grow on the tangled slopes, while lobelia heather and many species of meadowland wild flowers carpet the intermittent savannah plains. Wildlife species found in the park include eland, sable, bushbuck, blue duiker, klipspringer and an occasional leopard, but animals are rarely seen in the thick forest. The birds and butterflies, though, are easily spotted from the tranquil paths through the forest of cedar and yellowwood trees. Forest bird species include Gurney's sugarbird and malachite sunbird, while grassland species include the secretary bird and Shelley's francolin. On a marked track off the approach road lies **Tessa's Pool**, where you'll find a classic swimming hole and a rope swing, along with a shelter with braai pits. It's actually one in a series of three pools on government land outside the national park, used by Zimbabwe's Outward Bound School. Most visitors stop on their way to the mountains, but it's even more welcome after a long hike.

A fairly good 19-km gravel road leads from Chimanimani village to the **Mutekeswane Base Camp**, where there is the park office, a car park and ablutions; it should take about an hour to drive, and about four hours to walk. From Chimanimani set out along the Tilbury road for 9 km to Charles Wood, turn left at the coffee plantation and then fork immediately right; after 5 km you'll reach the Outward Bound/Tessa's Pool turn-off. From there, it's a further 5 km to the Mutekeswane Base Camp. There are no roads in the park beyond this point, just footpaths, and the ranger on duty will advise visitors on the best route to take into the mountains. Paths climb from the base camp at 1250 m above sea level to the refuge hut, situated on the west bank of the Bundi River about 1630 m above sea level (two or three hours should be allowed for this walk by anyone unused to mountain walking). Fully equipped hikers can stay in the hut (see Sleeping, page 109); several paths radiate from it, including one which goes down into the valley below and then up the other side to the lower slopes of **Binga Mountain** on the border with Mozambique.

Chirinda Forest Botanical Reserve → *Colour map 4, B6.*

Taking a packed lunch, you can drive (on tar) to the Chirinda Forest, 32 km south of the village of **Chipinge**, and 183 km south of Mutare. The forest is on the border of Mozambique at an elevation of 1200 m, near the settlement of **Mount Selinda** in Zimbabwe and

Birchenough Bridge

Birchenough Bridge spans the Save River 126 km southwest of Mutare, on the A9 en route to Masvingo. It was planned by Sir Henry Birchenough and completed in 1935. At a length of 329 m, it was then the third-longest single-arch suspension bridge in the world.

Ralph Freeman, the bridge's designer, was also the structural designer on the Sydney Harbour Bridge and the two bridges bear a close resemblance, although Birchenough is only two-thirds of the length of the Australian bridge. This design of bridge was tried out in Zimbabwe and when it proved to be successful the Sydney Harbour Bridge was built. The Birchenough Bridge is widely considered to be one of the country's finest pieces of architecture and, as such, appeared on the now defunct 20 cent coin. Ralph Freeman also designed the bridge over the Zambezi at Victoria Falls on the Zimbabwe/Zambian border, built in 1905 (see page 167).

Birchenough was a British civil servant appointed by the British South Africa Company, and chairman of the Beit Railway Trust from 1931 until 1937, the organization that funded the building of the Birchenough Bridge. The Beit Trust was established under the will of Mr Alfred Beit, a mining magnet, who died in 1906. A close associate of Cecil Rhodes, Beit thought that Southern and Northern Rhodesia (Zimbabwe and Zambia) and the adjacent territories would be too poor to fund their own development and be unlikely to attract private capital. In his will he therefore created the Beit Railway Trust, the primary purpose of which was to promote the development of communications in the region. The trust provided funds to build most of the region's great bridges: over the Save in Zimbabwe; over the Limpopo at Beitbridge on the border of Zimbabwe and South Africa; over the Kafue in Zambia; over the Luangwa on the Great East Road from Zambia to Malawi; and over the Zambezi at Chirundu, between Zambia and Zimbabwe. More than 400 smaller or low-level bridges were also built, providing much-needed communication in rural areas. Assistance was also given to the railways, with the provision of rolling stock and the laying of tracks. In 1932 a large grant was authorized to help establish civil aviation, paying for air surveys, landing grounds and certain airport buildings. After Birchenough's death, his ashes were interred in a pillar of the Birchenough Bridge.

Espungabera in Mozambique. It is a 949-ha primeval subtropical forest containing what is reputed to be the oldest tree in Zimbabwe: the 'Big Tree', a 1000-year-old red mahogany (Khaya nyasica), which is nearly 16 m in circumference and is almost 60 m high. The paths to the tree are reasonably clear. Again it's a good destination for birdwatching and there are an estimated 100 tree species, plus an array of ferns, creepers and orchids. The odd samango monkey may be spotted, and butterflies, insects and squirrels are numerous. The forest is quite beautiful and, although similar to the Vumba forest, the canopy is higher and the trees bigger and older. The forest surrounds an old hilltop mission station and village known as Mount Selinda. The mission station was established in 1892 by the East Central Africa Mission, and in 1919 became a centre to teach Western farming and irrigation methods to the local people. Today, it comprises a small school, basic hospital, orphanage and church (now run by the United Church of Christ in Zimbabwe). The track leading to the Big Tree and picnic site is signposted just before the settlement.

For Sleeping and Eating price codes and other relevant information, see Essentials pages 29-34.

◉ Sleeping

Vumba Botanical Gardens *p105*

B Leopard Rock Hotel, at the top of the Vumba road beyond the Botanical Gardens, T020-60115, www.theleopardrockhotel.com. The most luxurious option in the Eastern Highlands with 58 elegant and recently refurbished rooms, some with balconies. Has a full-blown casino, pool, restaurants and a game park that is home to antelope, zebra and giraffe, with nature trails and picnic sites. The highlight is the hotel's incredible mountain views, especially from the beautifully maintained 18-hole golf course, reputedly a favourite of Tiger Woods.

C Inn on the Vumba, 8 km from Mutare on the Vumba road, T020-60722, www. innsofzimbabwe.co.zw. Pleasant country hotel with 18 rooms and 2 cottages with floral furnishings, set in manicured gardens with swimming pool. Good views over the lower Vumba Mountains. The central area has a cocktail bar and restaurant. Rates are for dinner, bed and breakfast. Friendly staff and professionally run.

D White Horse Inn, Laurenceville Rd, off the Vumba Rd, 18 km from Mutare, T020-60318, www.whitehorseinn.co.zw. Well regarded country hotel that has been family run for more than 30 years, with 14 individually decorated comfortable rooms. Extensive gardens that attract many birds and monkeys, plus a pool, pub with roaring fire in winter and an excellent restaurant.

F National Parks Camping and Caravan Site, Vumba Botanical Gardens, T020-67592 (there's little need to book, but you can do so through the Parks and Wildlife Management Authority office, see page 61, T04-706077-8, www.zimparks.com). Pleasant campsite set among established trees, with shaded lawns, good ablutions

with water heated on a wood boiler and outstanding views over Mozambique, some 1000 m below. Bring all provisions with you.

Chimanimani *p106*

D Chimanimani Hotel, T026-2850, www.chimanimanihotel.co.zw. Right in the middle of the village on the main street, this white block built in 1961 is dated and dull, but the 35 rooms are adequate and clean, there's a half-decent restaurant and bar, and a pool in the neat gardens. Pay a little more for mountain views. They will consider taking campers and the large grounds appear secure.

D Frog & Fern Cottages, turn left at the petrol station in Chimanimani village and the turn-off is about 1.5 km on a fairly steep dirt road after the turn-off to Bridal Veil Falls, the cottages are about 3 km from this junction, T026-2294, www.thefrogandfern. com. Set in a scenic location, this is a good base for a hike into the mountains, with 3 stone and thatch fully equipped self-catering chalets, 1 sleeping 6 with 2 bathrooms with showers, baths and fireplaces, 1 with shower and fireplace, and 1 sleeping 3 with bath only.

F Chimanimani National Park (see page 107). Dec-Mar office open 0600-1200, 1400-1700, Apr-Nov 0700-1200, 1400-1600. There's little need to book, but you can do so through the Parks and Wildlife Management Authority office in Harare (see page 61), T04-706077-8, www.zimparks.com. There are a few very basic dorm beds with thin mattresses at both the **Mutekeswane Base Camp** and the **refuge hut** which cost US$10, and basic braai facilities, but you need to bring everything with you, including a sleeping bag. You can camp anywhere in the park for free, except at the Mutekeswane Base Camp, which also costs US$10 and has braai facilities and an ablution block. Daring visitors have the option of spending the night in either Terry's or Peter's caves (disused mine shafts). These are padded with grass to put your sleeping bag on but you'll need to bring everything else, including cooking equipment, though there are fireplaces. The mountain stream water is safe to drink anywhere in the park.

🍴 Eating

The hotels are the best bet for eating in the Eastern Highlands. Most are English-style dining rooms, a little old fashioned, but nevertheless offer a fairly reliable choice of meals.

Vumba *p104*

¶¶ **White Horse Inn** (see Sleeping, above). Open 0700-0900, 1230-1400, 1900-2100. Hotel restaurant open to all, with a fine local reputation, and adjoining pub with roaring fire. There's a good choice of dishes such as braised impala in red wine sauce, home-made steak and kidney pie, or roast duck, good-sized portions and fresh heaped vegetables. For Zimbabwe, a staggering range of imported port, brandy and single malt whiskies on offer.

¶ **Tony's Coffee Shop**, 24 km from Mutare on the Vumba road, T020-62536. Tue-Sun 0800-1700. A legendary spot run by the affable Tony (as the name suggests), serving unusual refreshments like hot chocolate with a shot of chilli, almost 100 types of tea, including black, green, rooibos, fruit and herbal combinations, liqueur coffees (soothing in the mountains on a cold day), accompanied by delicious home-made delicacies like orange and coconut cake or whiskey and chocolate cake. Definitely worth a stop.

🔺 Activities and tours

Vumba *p104*
Golf
Leopard Rock Hotel (see Sleeping, above). Sweeping around the hotel is a magnificent, award-winning 18-hole championship course – the best in Zimbabwe, and some say in Africa – planted with hundreds of trees and plants endemic to the Vumba ecosystem. Players enjoy breathtaking views into the valley below the course. Non-resident golfers can play on a casual basis. Costs are in the region of US$80 for 18 holes.

🚌 Transport

South of Mutare *p104*
Bus
Economy buses and commuter omnibuses link the regional towns and villages in the Eastern Highlands with Mutare. Most leave Mutare in the mornings before noon. (See Transport for Mutare, page 102).

North of Mutare

The principal attraction to the north of Mutare is the Nyanga National Park, which features part of the Nyanga Mountains stretching some 300 km along the Mozambique border to the north of Mutare and including Zimbabwe's highest mountain, Mount Nyangani. The main tarred road branches off the Harare–Mutare road 9 km west of Mutare from the Christmas Pass. This climbs to the settlement of Juliasdale, 81 km from Mutare and, 9 km beyond, enters Nyanga National Park. An alternative route leaves the Harare–Mutare road 1 km before the main road and goes via Penhalonga. This is a fairly rough gravel road, but it passes through a beautiful wooded area of wild fig and acacia trees. ▸▸ For listings, see pages 115-115.

Penhalonga → *Colour map 2, C3.*

Penhalonga is a village 17 km north of Mutare on the scenic route to Nyanga in a valley where the Sambi and Imbeza rivers meet the Mutare River. This region is where the first colonists began mining for gold (and was the site of old Umtali before it moved nearer the railway, see page 99), though the mines closed in 1943. The two earliest gold claims in the Umtali district were laid out in 1888 by British mining engineer James Henry Jeffreys. The district was then considered to be part of the province of Manica in the Portuguese colony of Mozambique. Politically astute, Jeffreys decided to name the mining claims after officials from the Companhia de Moçambique, the company which possessed the trade concessions for Manica province (and other areas of the colony). The first gold claim was named Penhalonga, after Count Penhalonga, chairman of the Mozambique Company, and the second after Baron de Rezende, the Mozambique Company's Director of Operations in Africa. Then in 1890 the area was annexed by Cecil Rhodes' British South Africa Company (BSAC), which effectively took control of the mining tracts in the name of Britain. Jeffreys, however, remained at the mine, and played a major role in its development (in fact, he even served as Mayor of Umtali before his death in 1926). Penhalonga grew up as the centre for the mines, and some colonial buildings, severely dilapidated, still line the main street. From Penhalonga, the road climbs up the Mutare River Valley and eventually joins the main Mutare–Nyanga road at Watsomba.

Honde Valley

Beyond Penhalonga on the scenic road to Nyanga is the Honde Valley. The road into the valley is tarred and it twists and turns steeply as it drops 800 m in about 20 km. The average altitude of Honde Valley is around 900 m above sea level while its immediate surroundings rise above 1800 m. This abrupt drop in topography creates an ideal environment for growing tea, and the first estates were established in the 1950s. The spectacular **Mtarazi Falls** (also spelt Mutarazi Falls) is a 761-m, free-leaping waterfall of two delicate tiers; it is the tallest waterfall in Zimbabwe and the second tallest waterfall in Africa. The upper tier is typically hidden from view by forest at the top of the falls. On the road to Mtarazi is the **Honde View**, a sunning vista from an escarpment that drops 762 m into the fertile valley and beyond into Mozambique. Closer to Nyanga there's another viewpoint overlooking the **Pungwe Gorge** and the 240-m-high **Pungwe Falls**, though the view of this is mostly obscured by trees. Both these viewpoints can also be reached from within the Nyanga National Park.

Juliasdale → *Colour map 2, C3.*

Straggling the main road to Nyanga, the last settlement before the Nyanga National Park consists of little more than a couple of shops, a post office and a petrol station. It is the location of an upmarket resort, the **Montclair Hotel and Casino**, see page 115, which is also open to passing trade for tea and drinks.

Nyanga National Park → *Colour map 2, C3.*
① *Sunrise to sunset, US$10, children (6-12) US$5, car US$5.*

Lying at an altitude of 1800-2593 m, the 470-sq-km Nyanga National Park contains the highest land in Zimbabwe. It features green hills, sometimes slightly wooded, and perennial rivers, and is best known for its stunning mountain views. In the centre of the park Mount Nyangani is the highest point. The vegetation is mostly moorland with rainforest on the higher slopes. Although there's no big game, there are a variety of mammals in the park, including antelope species like kudu, reedbuck, duiker, waterbuck, sable and klipspringer, wildebeest and the occasional buffalo, although these are usually infrequent visitors from Mozambique. The park also hosts at least 246 bird species, including the rare taita falcon, wattled crane, pallied harrier and blue swallow. Small dams have been built on a few of the rivers and streams in the park and they host a number of aquatic wildlife such as fish, reptiles and waterfowl. Lake Gulliver and the Mare, Udu, Purdon and Rhodes dams have been stocked with trout, and fly-fishing permits are included in the entry fee. There is a fantastic range of wild flowers such as flame lilies (Zimbabwe's national flower), orchids, gladioli and many species of heather. The core areas of the park were once the private estate of Cecil Rhodes. He acquired it with the aim of growing apples and raising sheep,

Nyanga National Park

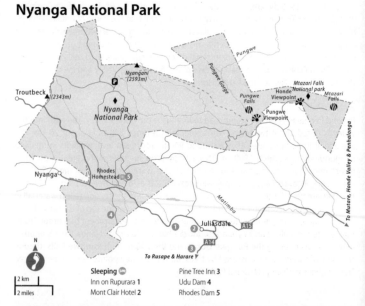

Sleeping 🛌
Inn on Rupurara **1**
Mont Clair Hotel **2**

Pine Tree Inn **3**
Udu Dam **4**
Rhodes Dam **5**

Mount Nyangani

Mount Nyangani is the highest mountain in Zimbabwe at 2593 m. The mountain vegetation is largely composed of heath around the summit plateau, with evergereen forest along the wetter eastern slopes and grassland to the western side. Annual rainfall totals are high (around 2200 mm) but long spells of dry weather occur during the winter period between May and August. Due to its relatively low altitude and tropical location, snow hardly ever falls, and has not been recorded since 1935. The mountain is composed of an upper sill of dolerite and sandstone, with the harder dolerite forming cliffs and ridges. Nyangani is unusual in that the summit lies atop a small outcrop of rock around 40 m above the surrounding area. The remainder of the peak is a broad moor of mainly rolling hills and plateau which covers an area of about 8 sq km. The edges of this plateau then fall steeply to the east and west sides and on a clear day you can get a view into Mozambique. The mountain can be accessed from four base points within Nyanga National Park, and hikers of average fitness can reach the peak within one to three hours. The ascent brings you to an altitude of about 2200 m and the remainder is mostly walking across the gentler gradients of the summit plateau. The hazards here are produced by bewilderingly fast-changing weather, which can switch from sunny skies to thick fog that reduces visibility to less than 50 m, so hikers need to be fully prepared. Go up in fine weather and take something warm to wear in case the mist comes in. The main access to the mountain is the 'tourist path' from the west, which ascends along the edge of the upper Nyamuziwa River and crosses onto the main plateau north of the summit. The hike starts at the car park off the 'circular drive' and is marked out by white cairns.

and spent the last years of his life at his homestead near Rhodes Dam. This now serves as a small museum.

Ins and outs Nyanga National Park is located 260 km east of Harare. From Harare take the Harare–Mutare road (A3) east for 170 km to Rusape and turn left, then follow the Nyanga road for 90 km through Juliasdale and on to the park entrance, which lies 13 km southeast of Nyanga village itself. From Mutare there are two routes: on a rough gravel road via Penhalonga and the Honde Valley (above), or take the Harare–Mutare road (A3) west for 11 km and turn right at the Juliasdale road and continue as above.

The roads in the western side of the park are good gravel (the most common drive is the 'circular drive') and there are numerous footpaths from the rest camps. The north and eastern reaches of the park are less developed and a 4WD is required.

Sights The park is dominated by **Mount Nyangani** (see box, above), which lies in the centre and is the highest mountain in Zimbabwe. The park is well watered by numerous streams and rivers and there are some spectacular waterfalls on the higher slopes. The Nyangombe River (whose tributaries include the Mare River and the Nyamuziwa River) and the Kayirezi River both flow north out of the park, ultimately to join the Mazowe River, which then flows into the Zambezi Basin. The **Nyangombe Falls** are about a 15-minute walk from the car park just north of the 'circular drive'. The Pungwe River rises at the foot of Nyangani and flows southwards through the park before dropping into the densely wooded Pungwe Gorge. There are a few scattered ruins in the park, referred to as 'pit structures' or 'forts' and thought to have been used as cattle pens in the 15th to 17th centuries. The central and western areas of the park, stretching from the park office at Rhodes Dam to Mount Nyangani, are the most developed. This area includes the three rest camps and five dams.

Nyanga → *Colour map 2, C3.*

On the good main tarred road as it goes through the Nyanga National Park roughly 20 km north of Juliasdale, Nyanga village nestles in a valley surrounded by mountains and grasslands. It serves as a small regional service centre with shops, and buses arrive here from Mutare.

Troutbeck → *Colour map 2, C3.*

High in the mountains on the northern side of Nyanga National Park, Troutbeck is a steep 10-km drive or walk from Nyanga Village. It lies on a 2100-m plateau where the weather can be cool and drizzly when the rest of the country swelters. It is best known for the **Troutbeck Resort** (see Sleeping, page 115) and 'World's View', the name given to the western edge of Troutbeck's plateau on account of the wide vista from the edge of the escarpment. The view encompasses the plains and hills rolling away from the range to the far west. Rusape and even (it is claimed) Harare can be seen on clear days. To get there, follow the dirt road to **Troutbeck Inn** and veer off 6 km from Nyanga village and then 4 km to the World's View car park.

For Sleeping and Eating price codes and other relevant information, see Essentials pages 29-34.

ⓢ Sleeping

Juliasdale *p112, map p112*

C Inn on Rupurara, 10 km from Juliasdale on the Nyanga road, T029-3021, www. innsofzimbabwe.co.zw. Quality country retreat with 17 individual rooms widely spaced and overlooking a dam or the Nyanga Mountains, with neat modern furnishings and spacious verandas. The restaurant is well regarded (see Eating, below), horse riding and trout fishing can be arranged, and there is a splash pool. It's also a good base for scenic walks. Rates are full board.

C Montclair Hotel, T029-2441/6, www. montclair.co.zw. Another country retreat with 84 spacious rooms, pool, tennis courts, casino, crazy golf, spacious grounds and good mountain views. The **Topside** restaurant specializes in Nyanga trout. A little faded these days and primarily a conference venue.

C Pine Tree Inn, 6 km from Juiasdale on the Rusape road, T029-2388, www. innsofzimbabwe.co.zw. Similar set up to the Montclair with 14 rooms, floral, cottagey decor, wing-back chairs and frilly standard lamps. Most rooms have mountain views, and there's a cosy bar, good restaurant and nice gardens. Rates include breakfast and dinner; the latter is a rather impressive 5-course affair.

Nyanga National Park *p112, map p112*

C-F Rest camps. There is little need to book, but you can do so through the Parks and Wildlife Management Authority office in Harare (see page 61), T04-706077-8, www.zimparks.com. There are 3 large rest camps, all of which consist of fully equipped, self-catering stone- and thatched-lodges sleeping up to 8, each with fridge, stove and

cooking utensils. **Rhodes Dam**, which is also the park headquarters, is located near the main entrance in a pine forest overlooking the dam, while **Mare Dam** is some 8 km east of Rhodes Dam, in the centre of the park and overlooking the dam, and **Udu Dam** is in the northwest of the park, again overlooking the dam and a stand of acacia trees. There are well-sheltered campsites and caravan stands (some with electricity) at each, with braais and ablution blocks.

Nyanga *p114*

B Troutbeck Resort, 17 km north of Nyanga village, T029-8487, www.africansunhotels. com. With its own 9-hole golf course and private trout lake, this 73-room resort offers some of the most pleasant accommodation in the Eastern Highlands. There are good views and attractive grounds with ornamental lakes. Facilities include stables for horse riding, pool, tennis courts, restaurants, **Horse & Hound** pub. Non-guests can drop in for afternoon tea.

ⓔ Eating

Juliasdale *p112*

₥ Inn on Rupurara (see Sleeping, above). Open 0700-1000, 1130-1400, 1800-2100. A good-quality hotel restaurant with an inventive 4-course set menu in the evening. Dishes featured in the past include fish cakes with saffron sauce and coconut and spinach soup. Pre-dinner drinks are taken in **Trevor's Bar** where the waiter brings the night's menu. Crème caramel or crêpes suzette for dessert.

Nyanga *p114*

₥ The Beck, Troutbeck Resort (see Sleeping, above). Open 0700-1000, 1200-1600, 1830-2200. Hotel dining room which overlooks the hotel gardens and lake, with buffet and à la carte meals like steak or Nyanga trout served with potatoes, rice or *sadza*, plus mixed vegetables. Desserts include old-fashioned delights such as jam swiss-roll and lemon meringue pie. Also does cream teas on the lawn and has a well-stocked bar. Passing guests are welcomed.

Contents

Footprint features

Border crossings

At a glance

◉ **Getting around** Local economy buses or self-drive.

◉ **Time required** Masvingo will take only 2 hrs to walk around and to pick up provisions; allow half a day at Great Zimbabwe; maybe a night in and around the Mutirikwi Recreational Area; for self-drivers at least 2 nights in Gonarezhou National Park.

☀ **Weather** Hot and dry Apr-Oct, hot and wet Nov-Mar.

✖ **When not to go** Summer (Nov-Mar) is wet, but this shouldn't hamper a trip to Masvingo and Great Zimbabwe, though 4WD would definitely be needed in the Gonarezhou National Park.

Great Zimbabwe & Lowveld

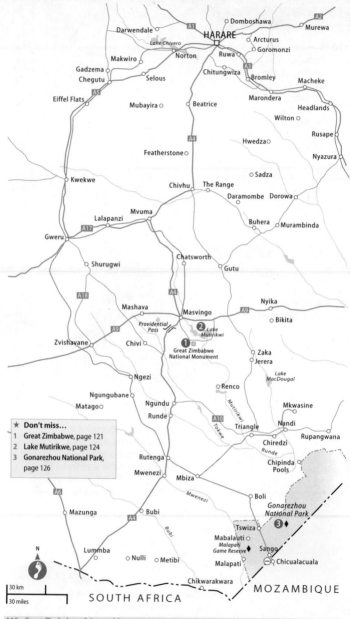

★ Don't miss...
1 Great Zimbabwe, page 121
2 Lake Mutirikwe, page 124
3 Gonarezhou National Park,
   page 126

Masvingo Province is in the southeast of Zimbabwe and borders Mozambique on its eastern side, the provinces of Matabeleland to the south, the Midlands to the north and Manicaland to the northeast. Its provincial capital, the town of Masvingo, was founded in 1890 and was the first large settlement to be established by the British South Africa Company, making it the oldest town in Zimbabwe.

Masvingo province is in the lowveld, a term used to describe low-lying arid regions of the country, particularly in the southeast, where rainfall is minimal and uncertain, and a large area of the southern part of the province is prone to drought. Most parts of the province are therefore unfit for agriculture, but suited to cattle ranching. *Kopjies*, grey and bald in the hot sun, dot the countryside and mopane trees, drought-tolerant and sturdy, are common.

The busy A4 highway connects the major centres of Masvingo and Beitbridge, the latter being the only border post between Zimbabwe and South Africa. The principal attractions in the region are the world-famous stone ruins of Great Zimbabwe, after which the country is named, the nearby Lake Mutirikwi (formerly Lake Kyle) and the little-visited but spectacular Gonarezhou National Park, famed for its large herds of elephant.

Masvingo, Great Zimbabwe and around

Masvingo is a dry and dusty mining and farming town for most of the year, but in September its purple jacarandas and scarlet poinsettias set the streets alight. The first white settlement in the country, it was originally called Fort Victoria, after the British queen, but post-independence Masvingo acknowledges a more relevant royalty. Its current name refers to the walled enclosures of Great Zimbabwe nearby, a name derived from a Shona expression meaning 'stone walls' and used for some 150 walled ruins that are scattered throughout the countryside. ▶ *For listings, see pages 132-134.*

Masvingo

Ins and outs → *Colour map 4, A4. Phone code: 039. Population: 100,000.*

Getting there Masvingo is 192 km south of Harare, on the A4. The road is good tar, although between Chivhu and Harare the edges of the road have started to crumble a little

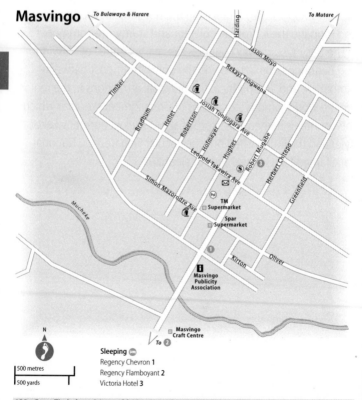

Masvingo

Sleeping 🛏
Regency Chevron **1**
Regency Flamboyant **2**
Victoria Hotel **3**

due to the heavy traffic – trucks and buses coming up from South Africa. Local economy buses ply this road all day, taking Zimbabwe residents to and from Johannesburg. Other buses link Masvingo and Bulawayo.

Getting around Masvingo itself is small enough to walk around. It is a springboard for visiting Great Zimbabwe and Lake Mutirikwi, 28 km east of town. You can get to these under your own steam by using minibus taxis. Gonarezhou National Park is really only accessible on 4WD self-drive trips.

Best time to visit A temperate climate typifies the region of Masvingo Province, with daytime temperatures averaging between 15°C and 30°C throughout the year. It's generally dry and hot from April to October, with a wet (but still hot) season from November to March.

Tourist information The **Masvingo Publicity Association** ⓘ *1001 Robert Mugabe St, T039-62643, Mon-Fri 0830-1600*, has only a few dated leaflets to pick up, although the attendant can supply basic local information.

Sights
The first large settlement to be established by the Pioneer Column of the British South Africa Company, Masvingo is laid out in an orderly grid system, as befits early colonial planning. There's nothing much to see, though there are plenty of petrol stations, a TM and Spar supermarket, banks and the Chevron Hotel on the main road in the middle of town, which makes a decent stopover for lunch on the way to Great Zimbabwe.

Great Zimbabwe → *Colour map 4, B4.*

ⓘ *28 km southeast of Masvingo, 0600-1800, US$10.*
The Great Zimbabwe ruins are beautifully set in a lush and flourishing valley at the head of the Mutirikwi River. In a Shona dialect 'Zimbabwe' means 'large houses of stone', and is the name given to the stone ruins spread out over a 722-ha area. Construction started in the 11th century and continued for over 300 years, making the ruins at Great Zimbabwe some of the oldest and largest structures in southern Africa. They are a UNESCO World Heritage Site, recognized for the amazing effort and skill that went into cutting the stone and assembling it in what are mostly geometrical forms, using only simple tools and technology.

Ins and outs The turn-off to the ruins is 4 km from Masvingo on the Beitbridge road. Local minibuses run around Lake Mutirikwi and will drop off at the turn-off to the site, which is 1 km from the road. You can walk around the whole complex, and there's a museum where you can pick up a guide – no charge but a small tip, roughly US$2, is appreciated. There's also a campsite/picnic area, and the **Great Zimbabwe Hotel** is a short walk away.

Background It is estimated that, at its peak, Great Zimbabwe had as many as 25,000 Shona inhabitants. The ruins can be broken down into three distinct architectural groups: the Hill Complex, the Valley Complex and the Great Enclosure. The Hill Complex was used as a temple, the Valley Complex was used by the citizens, and the Great Enclosure was for the king. The Great Enclosure is the most formidable structure, with 11-m-high walls extending for 250 m, making it the largest ancient structure south of the Sahara Desert. It is built out of granite using dry-stone walling, demanding a high level of masonry expertise.

What little evidence exists suggests that Great Zimbabwe was a centre for trade, with finds suggesting that the city formed part of a trade network extending as far as China. Chinese pottery shards, coins from Arabia, glass beads and other non-local items have been excavated there.

By 1500 the site was abandoned. There are several theories about the decline of Great Zimbabwe. One is environmental, that as a result of the soil on the plateau became exhausted of overgrazing and drought, firewood supplies were depleted and game was hunted out; a decline in land productivity would easily have led to famine. The other explanation is that the people of Great Zimbabwe moved on in order to maximize their exploitation of the gold trade network.

Portuguese traders were the first Europeans to visit in the early 16th century, though the ruins were rediscovered during a hunting trip by Adam Renders, an American-born German, in 1867. He found structures built with granite slabs that fit so tightly together that there was no need for mortar. Many 19th-century archaeologists found it difficult to admit that Africans had the know-how to build such an intricate set of structures. Adam Renders stated that Great Zimbabwe "could never have been built by blacks", and Cecil Rhodes, when he visited the site in the 1890s, told the local chiefs in the area that he had come to see "the ancient temple that once upon a time belonged to white men". White explorers and archaeologists continued to believe and promote this theory, even though there was no evidence of whites building or living at the complex. Artefacts that were found, such as bronze and copper spearheads, axes and tools for working with gold, all pointed to the Shona people. But in their attempt to exploit the African land and stamp their colonial seal on the territory, the colonials didn't want anyone to believe that Africans were capable of building such a complex social system.

Great Zimbabwe Region

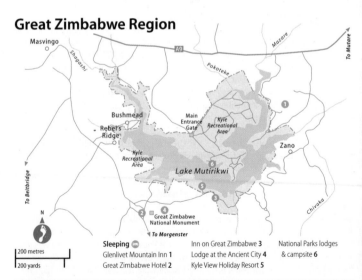

Sleeping
Glenlivet Mountain Inn **1**
Great Zimbabwe Hotel **2**
Inn on Great Zimbabwe **3**
Lodge at the Ancient City **4**
Kyle View Holiday Resort **5**
National Parks lodges & campsite **6**

Soapstone birds

In addition to the architecture, Great Zimbabwe's most famous feature are the eight birds carved out of soapstone that were found in its ruins. The sculptures combine both human and avian elements, substituting human features such as lips for a beak and five-toed feet for claws; the bird itself resembles the bateleur eagle. This mix of characteristics suggests they are not birds at all but some kind of mythical figures. It is known that six of the sculptures came from the Hill Complex, but their precise arrangement can only be surmised.

Archaeologists have suggested that the birds served as emblems of royal authority, perhaps representing the ancestors of Great Zimbabwe's rulers.

Five of the birds were taken by Cecil Rhodes to South Africa, where they were put in the South African Museum in Cape Town. They were returned to Zimbabwe in 1981 and are now on display in the museum at Great Zimbabwe. At the time, the return of the birds was a matter of considerable importance for the Zimbabwe people, symbolizing their independence from colonial rule.

In 1902, the British continued with their falsification agenda when British archaeologist Richard Hall was hired to investigate the Great Zimbabwe site. Hall asserted in his work *The Ancient Ruins of Rhodesia* (1902) that the structures were built by "more civilized races" than the Africans. Hall went out of his way to eliminate archaeological evidence that would have proved an indigenous African origin of Great Zimbabwe. He removed a 2-m layer of archaeological remains, effectively destroying the evidence that would have established an indigenous African origin of the site. He condescendingly stated that his goal was to "remove the filth and decadence of Kaffir occupation". In 1906, British archaeologist David Randall MacIver challenged this and stated the complex was "unquestionably African in every detail". However, his findings did not sit well with Cecil Rhodes, who banned any further independent archaeological study of the site for approximately 25 years.

In 1928, Gertrude Caton-Thompson, another British archaeologist, identified Chinese and Persian artefacts on site dating from the 1300s to the 1500s. She also agreed that Great Zimbabwe was wholly built by Africans and published her findings in her 1931 book *The Zimbabwe Culture: Ruins & Reactions*. Once myths take hold, however, they are hard to eradicate, and the falsification of Great Zimbabwe continued, with visitors being led to believe Great Zimbabwe was built by Europeans. To black anti-colonialist groups, Great Zimbabwe became an important symbol of achievement by black Africans. Reclaiming its history was an important aim of those seeking independence. In 1980 the newly independent country was renamed after the site, and its famous soapstone bird carvings became a national symbol, depicted in the country's flag. Great Zimbabwe was declared a UNESCO World Heritage Site in 1986.

The site

The **Hill Complex** is thought to be the oldest part of the ruins. It is a steep walk up to a granite hilltop, with views over the whole complex and of Lake Mutirikwe. Rather than build from granite blocks in free-standing walls, its builders molded the structures around existing granite outcrops and balancing boulders. It's been suggested that this area was used as a temple for spirit-mediums who conducted healing ceremonies and communed with the ancestors (most of the bird carvings were found here). The **Great Enclosure**, at the bottom of the hill to the south (which you are most likely to come to first) has a massive conical tower and parallel passage around it. This is thought to be where the royal family was ensconced. Though the tower itself is solid, the enclosing 11-m wall gives an indication of how the royal family achieved privacy from their subjects' wood and reed huts, which would have surrounded the complex. The **Valley Complex** is thought to have been used by the mass of the population; the few stone remains may have been entrances to houses built by the wealthier citizens. The **museum** has a small collection of items unearthed at Great Zimbabwe, including the soapstone birds (see box, page 123), metal tools, fragments of Chinese and Persian crockery and other odds and ends.

Lake Mutirikwe (Kyle Recreational Park)

ⓘ *31 km from Masvingo off the Mutare road (A9), which is the game park area; the southern shores can be reached from the lakeside road 6 km from Great Zimbabwe; 0700-1800, US$10, children (under 12) US$5, car US$5.*

Kyle Recreational Park surrounds Lake Mutirikwe, and the two names are basically interchangeable. It covers 16,900 ha, of which the Y-shaped lake covers 9300 ha, and has a varied shoreline of rocky beaches, sheer granite boulders, balancing rocks and patches of thick woodland. The dam in the south of the park was constructed in 1960, the same

Great Zimbabwe National Monument

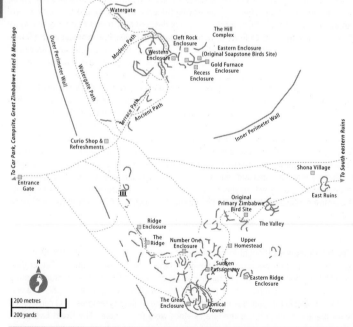

year the park was established. The dam wall, 62 m high and 311 m long, was built on the confluence of the Mutirikwe and Mshangashi rivers to provide water to the farming regions further south in the lowveld around Triangle and Chiredzi, where there are considerable sugarcane plantations. In the 1980s, drought drastically lowered the water levels in the lake and the sugarcane plantations effectively withered to the point where, for a time, Zimbabwe had to import sugar; during the 1990s the water levels recovered significantly. The game park section, which is set on the northern shoreline, is home to more than 25 species of mammal, including buffalo, duiker, eland, impala, kudu, reedbuck, warthog, waterbuck, white rhino, wildebeest, zebra and giraffe. Some 270 species of bird have been recorded around the lake in the miombo woodland, including marsh owl and African marsh harrier. Ducks, egrets and herons are common on the lake, as is the majestic African fish eagle. There's a 64-km network of roads around the park for game viewing, although not all are passable in the wet; alternatively, you can walk around the lodges and campsite and get to the lakeside.

Masvingo to Beitbridge → For listings, see pages 132-134. Colour map 4, A4-C3.

About 11 km south of Masvingo on the A4, the road reaches a small monument marking the top of **Providential Pass**, named in 1890 by Fredrick Selous, leader of the Pioneer Column (see box, page 87), a natural pass from the lowveld to the highlands. Sixty kilometres south of Masvingo at Ngundu, the A6 leads off to the east for 82 km to the oddly named small town of **Triangle**. This is a major sugarcane-growing region and the name derives from early experimental plantations of sugarcane, which were planted in the shape of a triangle. A large-scale irrigation system was built in the 1930s, and today there are some 13,000 ha of tall wavy sugarcane plants in the region, bringing a startling greenness to the dry lowveld. About 12 km beyond Triangle is the regional hub **Chiredzi**, which has a good hotel, the **Nesbitt Arms** (see Sleeping, page 133), petrol stations and supermarkets. Neither place warrants much time, but they are en route to the Gonarezhou National Park (see below) and useful for picking up provisions.

Back on the A4, the road heads south through a hot and arid region of baobab and mopane trees. Rainfall in the far south of Zimbabwe is a scant 200 mm a year. After 213 km from the turn-off to Triangle and Chiredzi (308 km south of Masvingo), the road reaches **Beitbridge**, on the border with South Africa (see box, page 127). The name also refers to the border post and bridge spanning the Limpopo River. This has often been described as the busiest border in southern Africa, partly due to the number of Zimbabwean migrants crossing into South Africa in the wake of Zimbabwe's political and economic troubles. It is also the only border between Zimbabwe and South Africa and, as such, is a major artery for supply trucks coming north. It's a fairly unappealing impoverished town with sprawling makeshift townships, although the drop in the number of people fleeing Zimbabwe in the last couple of years has improved the economics of the town. The 475-m-long bridge over the Limpopo opened in 1929 and is named after Alfred Beit, a founder of the De Beers diamond mining company and associate of Cecil Rhodes. The bridge was partially washed away in heavy floods and a new one was built in 1995. The old bridge is still there and is used for the railway between Zimbabwe and South Africa, though no passengers services have run on this route for many years.

Mapungubwe National Park

Mapungubwe is South Africa's youngest and northernmost national park. It developed across from Zimbabwe, on the South African side of the confluence of the Shashe and Limpopo rivers. At the confluence itself is a picnic site with a view over the point where South Africa, Zimbabwe and Botswana meet. The park forms part of what has become the **Greater Mapungubwe Transfrontier Conservation Area**, covering the corner of South Africa's Limpopo Province, Botswana's Tuli Block, and communal land in Zimbabwe. It protects important San rock art sites, but is best known for Mapungubwe Hill, which researchers believe was the site of the first capital of the ancient kingdom of Great Zimbabwe between AD 900 and 1300. It is believed to be the earliest evidence of Africa's Iron Age and was awarded World Heritage status in 2003. The park now covers 28,000 ha of arid bush and tufted grassveld dotted with acacia thorn and giant baobab trees. It's home to a variety of wildlife, including black and white rhino, elephant, kudu, zebra, eland, waterbuck, gemsbok, giraffe and baboon. Although predators such as lion, cheetah, hyena and leopard are present, they are rarely sighted. Pythons and black mambas, on the other hand, are common. Birders can tick off 400 species, including kori bustard, tropical boubou and Pel's fishing owl. There are four camps within the park, all accessible by normal car. The access point for the park is in South Africa, 68 km from Musina on the R572. For more information visit www.sanparks.org.

Gonarezhou National Park

① *0700-1800, US$10, children (under 12) US$5, car US$5.*

The A9 goes east from Masvingo towards the Eastern Highlands. The Chimanimani National Park (see page 107) is 280 km away via the Birchenough Bridge (see box, page 108) over the Save River. As elevation drops into the lowveld temperatures rise and baobab trees and rocky boulders are a common sight, but then the road climbs again into the mountains on the Mozambique border.

This park, covering 5023 sq km on the Mozambique border, is second in size to Hwange National Park and is one of Zimbabwe's best-kept secrets, located in the lowveld region of baobabs, scrublands and spectacular sandstone cliffs. If you have a 4WD (essential even for the approach roads to the park) and are self-sufficient in the way of food and camping equipment, this is possibly one of the wildest, most remote and rewarding wildlife experiences in southern Africa; you are unlikely to see any other visitors.

Ins and outs

Getting there The park is split into two main areas, namely the Chipinda Pools (Runde and Save rivers sub-region) in the east and the Mabalauta (Mwenezi River sub-region) in the west, which are accessed by different routes and are some distance from one another. Effectively, you will have two choices to enter the park, and to visit the other section it is a fairly long drive around the northern reaches, outside the park, to get to the other gate (we would recommend a night at the Nesbitt Arms in Chiredzi).

For **Chipinda Pools** (where there is a camp, see Sleeping, page 133), follow the main tarred road from the Chirediz turn-off to Mutare for 18 km. Turn off south at the Chipinda

Border crossings: Zimbabwe–South Africa

Beitbridge

Border opening hours The Beitbridge border is very busy and is now open 24 hours. In peak seasons – December, for example, when Zimbabweans are returning from South Africa for Christmas and New Year – it can process up to 12,000 people and 5000 cars daily. Formalities can be very slow. It also gets very hot here during summer, and freezing very early in the morning in winter (when the international buses from Johannesburg pull into the border).

Customs and immigration No visas are required for South Africa, but visas for Zimbabwe vary from US$30 to US$55 depending on nationality; they are issued at the border and are valid for 90 days. Fees can be paid in US dollars or South African rand. South Africans do not require visas for Zimbabwe. There is a duty-free shop on the South African side, selling a limited range of cigarettes and spirits, and a VAT-refund office to claim back tax on goods exported from South Africa; expect a long wait to process this.

Vehicle formalities See page 23 for regulations on taking a car into or out of Zimbabwe. In addition to the documents listed in Essentials, you will need to pay a carbon tax, a road tax and a toll fee to drive over the bridge. All payments can be made in rand or US dollars cash.

Safety Be wary of petty thieves, especially on the Zimbabwe side. Lock everything up and make sure anything on the outside of the vehicle is tied down. Do not accept help from touts in the car park who offer to sell relevant forms or 'look after' your car; all forms are available free of charge inside the border control building, and official uniformed security guards patrol the car park.

Facilities The nearest town on the South African side is **Musina**, which is 12 km south of the border post, at the end of the N1 highway, which has been expanded to a double-lane highway on this short stretch. From Musina, the N1 leads 463 km to Pretoria and 521 km to Johannesburg. Musina's main street is lined with shops, banks, petrol stations and fast-food outlets, all catering to the steady stream of traffic to and from the border. It's not an especially attractive town, and is increasingly being dwarfed by large, hastily built townships that are home to Zimbabweans who have managed to cross the border. Although there's little of interest in town, you will pass through Musina en route to Mapungubwe National Park (see box, page 126) to the west and the northern camps of Kruger National Park to the east. There is very little choice of accommodation in town, but try the (B) **Musina Lodge** 9-13 Limpopo Avenue, T015-534 3352, www.musina-lodge.co.za, which has 13 spacious rooms set in tropical gardens with an enormous baobab tree and swimming pool; campers can head to the (D-F) **Baobab Caravan Park**, on the right as you head out of town, T015-534 3504. For Beitbridge listings, see pages 132-134.

Public transport There is a through bus service with Greyhound (www.greyhound.co.za) between Johannesburg or Pretoria and Bulawayo (12 hours) or Harare (14½ hours). There are often long delays at the border as all Zimbabwean bus passengers are searched thoroughly and there can be lengthy vehicle queues on both sides of the border.

Pools signpost. Follow the gravel road for approximately 34 km to the entrance of the park, which in total is 59 km from Chiredzi. Further into the park from Chipinda Pools Camp are a series of undeveloped campsites (see Sleeping, page 133) which afford the best views of the Chilojo Cliffs.

For **Mabalautu**, turn east off the Masvingo–Beitbridge road (A4) at the turn-off to the Mwenezi police station, about 20 km south of Rutenga, and proceed down the dirt road for about 3 km. Turn left at the entrance to the police station – you may need to ask for directions from here, but do not turn off this road, which follows the Mwenezi River southeast to Chikombedzi (the river will not be visible from the road). The only intersection you will encounter is 20 km from the Mwenezi police station but head straight through to Chikombedzi. After entering Chikombedzi, where a national parks sign indicates the route to Gonarezhou, turn right. The total distance from the Masvingo–Beitbridge road to Mabalauta (where there is a park office and the Shimuwini Rest Camp) is about 105 km. Note that this latter route is very unpredictable: the roads are terrible, so allow lots of time and ask locals the way. The Mabalauta region can also be accessed from Mozambique through the Sango border post (see page 130), and on an another rough track outside the park from Chipinda Pools.

Getting around A 4WD is essential. Some of the gravel roads in and out of the park are fairly passable in the dry season, but if you want to go off the beaten track and follow the

Gonarezhou National Park

Sleeping
Chipinda Pools 1
Pamushana Lodge 2
Swimuwini 3

Africa's Rio Grande

The Limpopo River marks the 300-km border between South Africa and Zimbabwe, and Beitbridge is the only border post. For a decade now, the river has been likened to the Rio Grande, the river marking the border between the US and Mexico, over which thousands of Mexicans try to cross illegally in search of a better life in the US. When the recent political and economic problems in Zimbabwe were at their height, several thousand Zimbabweans attempted to cross this border every week, in the hope of a better future in South Africa. Some crossed legally and legitimately through Beitbridge to shop in South Africa, and then returned with much-needed provisions (supermarkets shelves were bare in Zimbabwe). For the most part, though, they crossed the crocodile-infested Limpopo illegally, and then had to get through three walls of fortified fencing on the South African side. If they didn't get stopped and sent back to Zimbabwe, they headed down to Gauteng to live in relative anonymity in the townships (though these are routinely raided for illegal immigrants). In early 2009, the situation was eased when South Africa relented and scrapped visas for Zimbabweans. Their policy now is to accept mass migration into South Africa from Zimbabwe rather than prevent it. The view of the South African government is that the people from Zimbabwe are economic migrants rather than political asylum seekers (a distinction that had been a confusing issue between the two countries) and will return to Zimbabwe once they have earned enough money to do so. It is also hoped that the increased flow of foreign currency going into Zimbabwe from returning migrant workers (and also from remittances home) will boost Zimbabwe's economy.

fainter tracks only 4WDs will do, and you might want to consider a GPS. Tracks can peter out and you may be forced to follow your own tyre tracks back. Always ask the wardens at the entrance gates which tracks are navigable.

Best time to visit Gonarezhou experiences mild, dry winters and warm, wet summers with temperatures that can exceed 40°C. The Mabalauta and Chipinda Pools areas are open throughout the year, but during the rainy season (November to April), access to certain parts of the park is restricted; visitors should consult with the wardens before undertaking game drives.

Sights

Gonarezhou is now part of the 35,000-sq-km **Great Limpopo Transfrontier Park** (www. greatlimpopopark.com) that links the **Kruger National Park** in South Africa and the **Parque Nacional do Limpopo** in Mozambique. Animals can move freely between the three sanctuaries. Gonarezhou was formed in 1975 by uniting former hunting areas and tsetse fly control corridors, though the park was closed to the public during the Rhodesian Bush War and again during much of the Mozambique Civil War due to movements of troops over the remote borders. Gonarezhou means 'place of many elephants' in Shona and as the name implies is well known for its large herds of elephant with unusually large tusks. During the park's closures in the war years, elephants were hunted by guerrillas and poachers after ivory. However, when the park re-opened in 1994, it was found that

Border crossings: Zimbabwe–Mozambique

Sango–Chicualacuala

Border opening hours In the extreme south of the Mabalauta region of Gonarezhou National Park is this remote border post with Mozambique (open 0800-1800).

Customs and immigration Visas for both Mozambique (US$25) and Zimbabwe (US$30-55 depending on nationality) are available at the border.

Vehicle formalities For Mozambique, a vehicle import permit, border tax, and third-party insurance must be acquired, and again like the other borders carnet de passages must be stamped in and out of each country (for information on taking vehicles across the border, see page 22).

Beyond the border

The road is poor: corrugated sand in the dry season and slippery mud in the wet. Localized flooding when rivers rise is also a problem. The road is currently being improved but it is best to check on conditions locally if planning to travel after heavy rains. This part of Mozambique is really just a huge network of pans and vleis and the road follows the course of the Limpopo River. It's approximately 400 km from the border to the main tarred coastal road (the EN1) at Macia and then another 180 km south to Maputo.

The other option is to explore the Parque Nacional do Limpopo, the Mozambique section of the **Great Limpopo Transfrontier Park** (www.greatlimpopopark.com). During the wet season, this involves heading south of the border as far as Chokwe, about 320 km from the border, where a bridge crosses the Limpopo, and then turning back on yourself on the EN205 towards the entrance to the park at Massinger, approximately 125 km. Quite remarkably, here the road crosses an incredibly long (4.6 km) and high (46 m) dam over the Elephants River, a tributary of the Limpopo. The 103-sq-km lake is now a significant breeding place for crocodile and tigerfish, and the tourist potential around the lake is starting to be recognized. During the dry season it is also possible to cross the Limpopo at the Mapai entrance gate and enter the park from the north, but again 4WD is essential for this route.

Just beyond the dam is the Massingir entrance gate to the Parque Nacional do Limpopo (0800-1800, entry about US$10 per person and US$10 per vehicle). Facilities in the park are still being developed, and you will need to be self-sufficient as there are only basic campsites and no hotels or fuel stations in the park, though the new entrance gate and office are very impressive. A more luxurious option is to stay at the private Machampane Tented Camp (www.dolimpopo.com, www.mozaictravel. com), situated in the solitude of a pristine wilderness area in the Lebombo Mountains, with five luxury ensuite tents on raised decks, set into the riverbank overlooking the Machampane River, a firm favourite with elephant. Rates are inclusive and there's a pleasant deck for game viewing; guides take guests out on morning and evening game walks. **Note** To explore both Gonarezhou National Park and the Parque Nacional do Limpopo, you will need to carry extra jerry cans of both fuel and water.

the elephant numbers had not declined as expected; in fact, an excess 750 had to be relocated that same year. Nevertheless the Gonarezhou elephants are understandably shyer (and more aggressive) than elephant elsewhere the country, and are certainly not fond of humans or vehicles. They are well known for charging, or conversely, running away. In addition to elephant perishing through poaching, the park has lost a number of other species, including both black and white rhino, which have been extinct since 1990, and a drought in 1991-1992 resulted in the local extinction of Lichtenstein's hartebeest. Nevertheless, in recent years the private Malilangwe Trust concession area in the northeast of the park, where the **Pamushana Lodge** (see Sleeping, page 133) is located, has introduced rhino from KwaZulu Natal in South Africa.

Gonarezhou is an exceptionally scenic park full of rugged and beautiful landscapes, and three major rivers – the Save, Runde and Mwenzezi – cut their course through the park. The river flood plains are interspersed with lagoons and riverine forest, notable species being the nyala berry tree, ebony and Natal mahogany. The arid hinterland comprises mopane woodland and ironwood forest as well as the sabi star that grows on rocky outcrops and has a lovely pink flower during flowering season. One of the most prominent and enduring natural features of Gonarezhou are the beautiful Chilojo Cliffs. These magnificent red sandstone cliffs, formed through aeons of erosion, overlook the scenic Runde River Valley. Sunrise and sunset intensify the deep colours of the rocks, which are made even more dramatic by the silhouettes of baobabs; this is possibly one of Zimbabwe's best and most memorable vistas.

As well as the many elephant in Gonarezhou, other animals present include lion, leopard, cheetah (including the rare king cheetah), buffalo, giraffe, zebra and many species of large antelope. The rare nyala and smaller suni, two of the park's smaller antelopes, are highlights. Game viewing is best along the riverine regions and close to the many perennial pools and springs. The park has the widest variety of birds in Zimbabwe, with the annual count often reaching over 400 species. Specials include bateleur, tawny, brown-snake and Martial eagle, which are all breeding residents, several species of vulture, including Lappet-faced vulture, peregrine falcon, which breed on the spectacular Chilojo Cliffs, and Dickinson's kestrel, which is common in the groves of ilala palms.

For Sleeping and Eating price codes and other relevant information, see Essentials pages 29-34.

⊜ **Sleeping**

Masvingo *p120, map p120*
There's not much choice in Masvingo but there's also little reason to stay; most people head directly to the accommodation around Great Zimbabwe and Lake Mutirikwe.
C-D Regency Chevron Hotel, Robert Mugabe St, in the centre of town opposite the Publicity Association, T039-253085, www.regencyhotels.co.zw. Old-fashioned concrete block built in the 1960s but offering good service, a decent roadside restaurant serving the likes of steak or fish and chips, secure parking, and 49 reasonable rooms with satellite TV and phone. There's also a small gym and a popular bar, which is probably the only option in the centre of town for a drink in comfortable surroundings.
C-D Regency Hotel Flamboyant, 2 km south of town on the A4, T039-253085, www.regencyhotels.co.zw. 106 rooms in neat and tidy double-storey blocks with balconies or patios. Has spacious lobby, bar with satellite TV for watching sport, restaurant and pool, and full English breakfast is included. Flamboyant trees in the garden (hence the name), motel-style parking; the best option in town.
E Victoria Hotel, Robert Mugabe St, T039-263074. Basic lodgings in an old whitewashed colonial building. The rooms are en suite, but bare; don't expect much more than a bed and a bath (no showers). Clean, though, and an option if arriving late. Street parking only.

Great Zimbabwe *p121, map p122*
B Lodge at the Ancient City, a few metres past the entrance gate overlooking the Great Enclosure; central reservations in Harare, T04-722588, www.rtg.co.zw. Excellent standards in what can only be described as a Great

Zimbabwe-themed lodge, with granite stone walls and soaring ceilings, and incorporating giant boulders into the design. 19 rooms with lovely African-inspired decor, restaurant, bar, pool and wooden deck where a fire is lit in the evening.
C Great Zimbabwe Hotel, just before the entrance gate, T039-262274, www.africansunhotels.com. Located close to the ruins, which are a short 700-m walk away, this well-run hotel has 38 neat rooms, with satellite TV and tea and coffee stations, laid out in a half-moon shape around a leafy garden courtyard. Restaurant, well-stocked bar and large and exceptionally deep pool.

Lake Mutirikwe (Kyle Recreational Park) *p124*
B Inn on Great Zimbabwe, on the south lakeshore road overlooking Lake Mutirikwe, T039-261766, www.innsofzimbabwe.co.zw. Well-regarded country-style lodge set on a hill with great views of the lake from the verandas of the 8 comfortable rooms and 4 self-catering units. Excellent food (homely dinners and full English breakfasts), lounge with fireplace, library and lovely manicured gardens. A relaxing place to stay, with superb service.
C-F National Parks Lodges and Campsite, on the north shore of the lake at the HQ for the game park section of the Lake Kyle Recreational Park, T039-62913 (pre-booking is unnecessary but you can do so through the Zimbabwe Parks and Wildlife Management Authority office in Harare, (see page 56), or Bulawayo (see page 138), www.zimparks.com. There are 10 basic but fully equipped 1- or 2-bedroomed self-catering thatched chalets, and 11 camping sites (US$10 per person) with 2 ablution blocks with hot showers, and kitchen shelters with braais. There are good views of the lake and a giant boulder is the perfect vantage point to watch the sun go down. Guided walks can be arranged with the office.

D Glenlivet Mountain Inn, 37 km from Masvingo on the northeast shore; follow the A9 towards Chipinge and after 26 km follow a gravel road for 11 km (well signposted), T039-66041, glenlivethotel@sdzim.com. Set among hills on the northeast lakeshore, this is a faded but adequate hotel with 18 rooms, restaurant, English pub-style bar, big terrace with great view of the lake, pool, children's playground and tennis court. Friendly owners.

E-F Kyle View Holiday Resort, off the southern lakeshore road, T039-264878. Simple resort with a small restaurant and 12 bare and basic chalets, but lots of grassy space for camping on the lakeshore and fairly decent ablution blocks.

Masvingo to Beitbridge p125

D Holiday Inn Express, Beitbridge, just after the junction with the A6 road from Bulawayo and the A4 from Masvingo, about 3 km before the town, T086-23001, www.africansunhotels.com. Boxy block with 106 rooms. Nothing special but the only decent place to stay in Beitbridge, with restaurant and pool, but very faded these days.

D Lion and Elephant Motel, 75 km before Beitbridge on the Bubi River, phone coverage is patchy here, www.lionandelephant.com. This is primarily a stop for motorists between South Africa and Harare with 38 thatched, well-equipped rooms including some family rooms with extra bunk beds sleeping up to 5, and a campsite (**F**), in a nice riverside setting with a pool. There's a restaurant and bar and an additional café open from 0600-2200, offering pies, burgers, steak sandwiches, chips and drinks, and clean rest rooms to drivers stopping for a break.

D Nesbitt Arms, 238 Marula Dr, Chiredzi (turn left along Impala Drive before the petrol station), T031-5071, 5162, www.nesbittarms.co.zw. A large old colonial hotel with mock-Tudor and stone design, with 28 good mid-range a/c rooms with DSTV, shady gardens, pool, friendly pub, restaurant, large

car park, where you can negotiate to get your car washed, and good service. A decent and welcome alternative stop when driving between each side of Gonarezhou.

D Sika Lodge, up a steep hill behind the Nesbitt Arms, Chiredzi, T031-2978, 3053. This is the former home of Ian Smith (ex-Rhodesian Prime Minister) with 5 basic rooms, some with en suite bathrooms. A big rambling unkempt house rather than a hotel, but there is a decent reception area, a restaurant and bar, and it is situated on a very high *kopjie*. It's simple budget accommodation in a historic house.

Gonerzhou National Park p126, map p128

L Pamushana Lodge, reservations, T+27-(0)21-6833424 (South Africa), www.singita.com. This super-luxury lodge lies in the Malilangwe Trust concession area to the northeast of Gonarezhou, and is run by Singita, who have the best safari lodges across southern and eastern Africa. It has 6 a/c suites and 1 5-bed villa, with indoor and outdoor showers, private plunge pools, fireplaces and game-viewing decks with telescopes. The main lodge area has dining areas, bar, library, open-air lounge, wine cellar, 2 heated swimming pools and a jacuzzi, all set in an attractive tract of forest overlooking a dam. Rates start from US$800 per person. Michael Douglas and Catherine Zeta-Jones booked this camp exclusively in 2003.

National Parks Accommodation, T031-397, there is unlikely any reason to pre-book but you can do so through the Parks and Wildlife Management Authority office in Harare (see page 56) or Bulawayo (see page 138), www.zimparks.com.

There are 19 sites at the beautiful **Chipinda Pools Camp** (US$15), each with basic shelter, braai area and ablution facilities. To the southeast is a series of undeveloped campsites (US$25) along the Runde River with minimum facilities (concrete table and long-drop toilet); they are located at **Nyahungwe**, **Madumbini**, **Bopomela**, **Lisoda**, **Gota**, **Chitove**, **Chamaluvati** and **Chilojo** (the last being the best for views of the cliffs). Dead wood in the vicinity may be collected for firewood but you need to bring your own water. The campsites are wonderfully remote and camping in the depths of the wild is quite an experience. In the Mabalauta region, the **Swimuwini Rest Camp** has 5 simple but well-maintained 2-bed chalets (US$115) overlooking the Mwenzi River, with fully equipped kitchens and braais (but don't rely on electricity). You can also camp (US$15) here and there are good ablutions and an open kitchen area.

🍴 Eating

Masvingo *p120, map p120*
Eating is effectively restricted to the few hotels in the region. The **Flamboyant** and the **Chevron** hotels in Masvingo are the best bets for lunch or dinner; neither is expensive and both offer good service but don't expect more than a plate of chicken or steak and chips and a beer. You'll need to be fully equipped for self-catering in Gonarezhou National Park. There are supermarkets in Masvingo and Chiredzi. TM is the best stocked and has takeaway counters for pies, fried chicken, etc. A cool box is necessary to take food and drink into the park for more than 1-2 days.

🛍 Shopping

Masvingo *p120, map p120*
Handicraft and souvenirs
The **Masvingo Craft Centre** is a row of thatched stalls to the south of town en route to the turn-off to Great Zimbabwe. It sells wooden carvings, crocheted tablecloths and the like, and soapstone figures. Due to the lack of visitors, a few bargains many be negotiated here, but remember the curio sellers have suffered a long period of hardship, so accept a fair price.

Supermarkets
In town, both **TM Supermarket** and **Spar Supermarket** are just off the main road, Robert Mugabe St, on Simon Mazorodze Av. They are fairly well stocked and open all week, including Sun mornings.

Masvingo to Beitbridge *p125*
Cheredzi
Everything is clustered along or off the main street, including a petrol station. You can get fuel from Carlines in the industrial area (turn left before the shops), which is open 7 days a week from 0800-1800. There are a few supermarkets in town; ignore the **Spar** with its limited stock and head for the **TM**, which has more choice.

🚌 Transport

Masvingo *p120, map p120*
Bus
During the day several international buses an hour ply the route between Harare and Johannesburg.

Masvingo to Beitbridge *p125*
Cheredzi
Local minibuses go from Robert Mugabe Av.

ℹ Directory

Masvingo *p120, map p120*
Banks Branches of Barclay's, Standard Chartered and Zimbank (all with ATMs) can be located along Robert Mugabe St and are open Mon-Fri 0800-1500, Sat 0800-1130.
Police Hughes St, T039-262986.

Masvingo to Beitbridge *p125*
Cheredzi
Banks There is a branch of **Standard Chartered Bank** near the petrol station but don't rely on withdrawing cash from the ATM.

Contents

Matabeleland

At a glance

⊖ **Getting around** The centre of Bulawayo is compact enough to walk around. Day tours or overnight self-drive trips to Matobo National Park.

✪ **Time required** 1 day to walk around Bulawayo and visit the museums; at least 1 day for Matobo National Park.

☀ **Weather** Bulawayo enjoys a moderate climate all year.

✖ **When not to go** The heaviest rains fall between Dec and Feb, but apart from filling up potholes in the roads these shouldn't hamper travel.

20 km
20 miles

Bulawayo is located 439 km southwest of Harare in Matabeleland, which comprises the whole of western Zimbabwe from the South African border in the south to Victoria Falls in the north. It is Zimbabwe's second largest city and is located on the confluence of the country's major roads: the A5, from Harare in the northeast; the A7 to the Plumtree border with Botswana in the southwest; and the A8 to Victoria Falls in the northwest.

As such, most visitors will pass through Bulawayo en route to these destinations by road. There is very good reason to stop off. This attractive city has wide streets lined with colonial buildings, good facilities such as hotels, restaurants and shops, and is an excellent base from which to explore the regional attractions of Chipangali Wildlife Orphanage, Khami Ruins and Matobo National Park, well known for its large rhino population and rock paintings, as well as being the site of the grave of British imperialist Cecil Rhodes.

Bulawayo and around

Despite being the largest city after Harare, Bulawayo is reminiscent of a sleepy English town, with wide tree-lined and largely traffic-free streets, leafy parks, Victorian buildings and a slow-paced atmosphere. It is home to the country's main museum, the Natural History Museum, a railway museum, the Bulawayo Art Gallery, which is housed in an attractive turn-of-the-20th century building, theatres, the Mzilikmzi Art and Craft Centre, good hotels and one of the finest caravan and camping parks in Zimbabwe. ▶▶ *For listings, see pages 148-156.*

Ins and outs → *Colour map 4, A1. Phone code: 09. Population 1.3 million.*

Getting there

Air **Joshua Mqabuko Nkomo International Airport** ① *T064-226491-3*, lies 21 km north of Bulawayo. Follow Robert Mugabe Way out of the city. **Air Zimbabwe** operates daily flights between Bulawayo and Harare. Taxis meet the flights.

Citylink and **Pathfinder** luxury bus companies link Bulawayo with Victoria Falls, and Harare, via Gweru, Kwekwe and Kadoma, and the regular slower economy buses ply the same routes. The **railway station** ① *Lobengula St, T09-322284*, is a short taxi ride from the city centre. There are overnight services from both Harare and Victoria Falls. Buy tickets at the station at least a day before you travel and check the train is running on your preferred day. ▶▶ *See also Getting there, page 22, and Transport, page 153.*

Getting around

The centre of Bulawayo is compact and easy to get around on foot and most of the limited sights are close to one another. **ZUPCO** buses and commuter omnibuses follow the major arteries and link the city centre with the suburbs. Most start their journeys at the **City Hall Terminus**. Regular taxis are readily available and can be found around the City Hall area or outside the larger hotels.

Tourist information

The **Bulawayo and District Publicity Association** ① *municipal car park on Robert Mugabe Way between Leopold Takawira Av and Eighth Av, T09-60867, Mon-Fri 0830-1645, Sat 0830-1200*, is the most helpful and organized tourist information office in the whole country. There are plenty of brochures to pick up, and a big noticeboard displays train and bus information. Additionally there is nothing about the area that the staff don't know, and they are happy to answer questions.

The **Zimbabwe Parks and Wildlife Management Authority office** ① *15th Av between Main St and Fort St, T09-65592, www.zimparks.com, Mon-Fri 0800-1600*, will book accommodation in the Maleme Rest Camp in Motobo National Park.

Best time to visit

Due to its relatively high altitude of 1358 m above sea level, Bulawayo has a subtropical climate and moderate daytime temperatures averaging 15-20°C. It has dry, cool winter from May to August, a hot dry period in spring from late August to early November, and a warm wet period in summer from early November to April. The heaviest rains fall between December and February but due to the city's proximity to the Kalahari Desert over the border in Botswana, it does suffer from long rainless months, which can bring on drought.

The hottest and driest month is October when daytime temperatures can reach 30°C. Nights are always relatively cool, ranging from 8°C in July to 16°C in January.

Background

The history of the region dates back over 2000 years when the San (Bushmen) created their unique rock art in the caves of the Matobo Hills (see page 144). By the 15th century the Rozvi kings had built a stone city at Khami (see page 143). The first settlement of Bulawayo was founded by a Ndebele king, Mzilikazi ka Matshobana around 1870 after the Ndebele people arrived from Zululand, now in South Africa. The name is derived from the Ndebele word *KwaBulawayo*, which means 'a place where he is being killed', a reference, it is thought, to Mzilikazi's son and heir, Lobengula, who was attacked and forced to flee the site during the Ndebele Wars in 1893 when the British ransacked and destroyed the royal homestead. Cecil Rhodes' British South Africa Company took control of the area and built a new settlement for white settlers on the ruins. The town was laid out in a classic grid with streets wide enough for a team of oxen to turn around comfortably. Within four months 4000 licenses had been issued to gold prospectors and a branch of the Standard Bank of South Africa had been established.

In March 1896, the Ndebele people revolted against the authority of the British South Africa Company in what became known as the Matabeleland Rebellion. The Ndebele believed the white settlers were responsible for the drought, locust plagues and the cattle disease rinderpest, all of which were ravaging the region at the time. The battle lasted until October 1897, during which Bulawayo was under siege for many months. Many settler homes, ranches and mines were burned and there were a large number of deaths and casualties on both sides. However, the Ndebele made the fatal mistake of not disconnecting the telegraph line from Bulawayo to other British bases, such as Mafikeng in South Africa, enabling the Bulawayo Field Force to summon the help of a British relief force. In May 1986, the British broke the siege on Bulawayo and some 50,000 Ndebele retreated to the Matobo Hills; they finally laid down arms in October after negotiations with Cecil Rhodes.

With the termination of the rebellion, Bulawayo resumed its development. By 1897, the new town acquired the status of a municipality, and in 1898 electricity and water supplies were connected to the town, despite the enormous problems involved in transporting machinery and equipment by ox wagon, a journey that usually took about three months from Mafikeng. Bulawayo actually acquired electricity before London.

The railway reached Bulawayo from South Africa in 1898, from where it was extended east to Salisbury (Harare) and north to the coalfields around Hwange and on to the Zambezi River at Victoria Falls (see box, page 167). In 1943, Bulawayo became a city, and was in its colonial hey-day. While government matters were retained in Salisbury (Harare), Bulawaya was considered the capital for agriculture and industry and was the centre for the railways. Close to Botswana and South Africa, it was ideally placed for the export and import of commodities.

In more recent years, Zimbabwe's economic crisis has taken its toll on the city and it's far from the prosperous place it once was. It is traditionally a stronghold for opposition to the Mugabe government and as such has received little, if any, investment from central government. Industry and formal employment have all but collapsed. The Bulawayo residents that do work, do so in informal trades, in unregulated transport or working as street hawkers. The provision of basic amenities has been hit particularly harshly. In 2008 the city's water was deemed unfit to drink and an outbreak of cholera occurred.

The centre of Bulawayo is fairly spacious and leafy, and dominated by the Centenary Park and Central Park, next to each other across Leopald Takawira Avenue and together making 45 ha of green space in the city centre. Central Park boasts Zimbabwe's largest ornamental fountain, erected to commemorate the city's 75th birthday in 1968. Along with a miniature railway, an aviary, a botanical garden and the municipal campsite, Bulawayo's theatre and Natural History Museum are in Centenary Park.

Natural History Museum

ⓘ *Centenary Park, corner of Leopold Takawira and Park Lane, T09-230045, www.nmmz. co.zw, 0900-1700, US$5, café.*

This was first established as the Rhodesian Museum in 1901, and moved to its present location in a four-storey circular building in Centenary Park in in 1964. Renamed the Natural History Museum in 1981, it's the biggest and best museum in the country, showcasing a large display of stuffed mammals (look out for the enormous elephant), birds, insects and fish, totalling around 75,000 specimens in all. There are also exhibits on prehistoric man, a geology display and a replica of a gold mine shaft. The ethnographic collection covers all aspects of Zimbabwe's history from the various early Ndebele and Shona chiefs to colonial figures such as Cecil Rhodes.

National Gallery

ⓘ *Corner Main St and Leopold Takawira Av, T09-70721, www.nationalgallerybyo.com, Tue-Sun 0900-1700, US$1, children (under 12) US$0.50.*

Established in 1980, this is the Bulawayo branch of the National Gallery in Harare (see page 59). Of most interest, perhaps, is the superbly restored building dating from 1901 in which the museum is set. The double-storey house with its ornate wrap-around balconies is presently known as Douslin House, after its architect William Douslin, but started life as the Willoughby's Building after Sir John Willoughby, an early surveyor of the town appointed by Cecil Rhodes. Erected at a cost of £22,000, the building has two wings with a central courtyard, and at the time it was built had 46 offices let to local business people. On the north side of the courtyard is a block of 12 offices; astonishingly, these offices remained locked for 50 years. It is thought that they may have been used as quarters by men who fought in the Anglo-Boer War and never returned (possibly employees of Willoughby). When the rooms were eventually unlocked in 1952, a variety of weapons dating from the Anglo-Boer period were found inside, but the identity of the men who owned them has never been established.

The building has an imposing entrance on Main Street with a portico decorated with cornices and pillars. Inside, a sweeping Burma teak and walnut staircase leads to the upper floor. The gallery's exhibits are well presented in the grand rooms, and there are some artists' studios lining the courtyard; if any are in residence you may be able to watch them work. Refreshingly, unlike the National Gallery in Harare, the collection here is not dominated by Shona stone sculptures; there is a spectrum of media, including paintings, basketry, ceramics, mosaics, and wood and clay sculptures, plus some ethnological items such as traditional wooden headrests and woven sitting mats. There's also a pleasant coffee shop, with tables in the courtyard, and an excellent souvenir shop selling some high quality crafts.

Bulawayo City

Sleeping
- Bulawayo City Lodge 1
- Bulawayo Club 2
- Bulawayo Rainbow Hotel 3
- Cresta Churchill Hotel 4
- Holiday Inn 5
- Hornung Park Lodge 6
- Municipal Caravan & Campsite 7
- Nesbitt Castle 8

Selborne Hotel 9
Southern Comfort Lodge 10

Eating
- Art Groove 1
- Cape to Cairo 2
- Cattleman 3
- Coffee Shoppe 4
- Golden Spur 5

Grillo's 6
Indaba Book Cafe & Sandwich Shop 7
Le Piazza Deli & Bistro 8
Mary's Corner 9
Roasted Berry 10

Bars & clubs
Safari Bar & Grill Shop 11

Rhodesia Railways

The railways in Zimbabwe were developed at the turn of the 20th century to serve its towns, mines and farms, and to link the landlocked country with sea ports in Mozambique and South Africa. Line construction began from Fontesvilla, 56 km inland from Beira on the Mozambique coast, to Umtali (now Mutare) in September 1892, and from Vryburg in the Cape Province to Bulawayo in May 1893. The Bulawayo line was completed in October 1897 and the Mutare line in February 1898. The link between Salisbury (Harare) and Bulawayo was finally completed in October 1902 after initial construction was brought to a halt by the outbreak of the Anglo-Boer War in 1899. The next stage was the line north from Bulawayo, which began in 1903, crossed the Zambezi River on the Victoria Falls Bridge (see box, page 167) in September 1905 and reached the Congo border in December 1909. For several years this whole system was operated by the Beira and Mashonaland and Rhodesia Railways Company, but by 1936 Rhodesia Railways Limited became the owners of the whole railway system in Zimbabwe and Zambia, as well as the Vryburg–Bulawayo section. In 1967, the system was divided at the Victoria Falls Bridge, with Zambia Railways operating in the north and Rhodesia Railways in the south. Rhodesia Railways was renamed the National Railways of Zimbabwe after independence in 1980.

Railway Museum
① *First St, Mon-Fri 0800-1700, Sat-Sun 0800-1600, US$2.*
Located in a maze of tracks behind the main railway station, this museum houses a collection of railway memorabilia large and small, including steam locomotives, rolling stock and a variety of other exhibits dating back to 1897 when the first steam engine rolled into the country. The main building is the original station from Shamva, complete with fire buckets, signals and timetables, which was dismantled and rebuilt at the museum when it opened in 1972. Pride of place is Cecil Rhodes' well-preserved private carriage, with its teak panelling and leather seats, fully laid-out dining table and monogrammed linen in his sleeper. It's easy to imagine Rhodes standing on the observation deck as he steamed through Matabeleland; the carriage was used on many trips including the one that carried his body from the Cape to Bulawayo for his burial in the Matobo Hills. Other exhibits include a gold-crested dinner service from the 1947 royal train and interesting photographs of the building of the Victoria Falls Bridge (see box, page 167).

Around Bulawayo

Chipangali Wildlife Orphanage → *Colour map 4, A2.*
① *23 km from Bulawayo on the Gwanda/Johannesburg road, T09-287739, 287740, www. chipangali.com, Tue-Sun, 1000-1700, US$20, children under 12 US$10.*
Opened in 1973 by ex-game ranger Viv Wilson, Chipangali has been instrumental in caring for sick, injured and abandoned wild animals and birds as well as being a refuge for confiscated game pets. Although zoo-like, with a series of cages, it claims not be a zoo, as whenever possible the animals are returned to the wild. This is true of birds, monkeys and antelope, though it is not possible with the large cats, as once these have been in captivity they lose their skills to survive in the wild. The word Chipangali comes from

the Chinyanja language in eastern Zambia, where Viv Wilson originally began his career as a tsetse-fly control operator with the Zambia Government; it means 'open friendly country'. The animals come from across Zimbabwe, including the national parks; there's an interesting variety of some 250 animals to see close up (good photo opportunities if you've not been lucky enough to see everything in the parks), and it's particularly popular with school groups learning about the protection of wildlife in Zimbabwe. Nevertheless, it has struggled to stay open in economic hard times – getting food for the animals has been a particular challenge – and deservedly needs all the financial support it can get. As well as the entrance fee, visitors are encouraged to adopt an animal or sponsor an enclosure. There's also a tea room and some curios for sale.

Khami Ruins → *Colour map 4, A1.*
ⓘ *22 km west of Bulawayo on a minor road, follow Eleventh Av out of the city to Old Khami Rd, 0800-1630, US$10.*

Khami is a late Iron Age city, which is probably second in significance to Great Zimbabwe (see page 121) and is also a UNESCO World Heritage Site (since 1986). The dry-stone architectural style is similar to that at Great Zimbabwe, though only the pavements and foundations survive and it is not as impressive. Unfortunately, the site has received little attention in recent years, and vegetation damage has occurred, with trespassers foraging for firewood and building stones further destabilizing the site. The town is thought to have been founded at the time of the disappearance of the state at Great Zimbabwe, and to have developed between 1450 and 1650. It has been identified as the capital of the Torwa state, which appears to have inherited much of the power of Great Zimbabwe, but was abandoned during the Ndebele incursions of the 19th century. Among the ruins, archaeologists have found Ming porcelain, Portuguese imitations of 17th-century Chinese porcelain, and Spanish silver, which suggests the dynasty traded with the Portuguese on the Mozambique and East Africa coasts. It appears to have once had seven built-up areas known as the royal enclosure or hill complex, which were occupied by the royal family. Remains of huts in the open areas in the valley were probably occupied by commoners. It seems the royal enclosure had to be on higher ground than other buildings. There are also low stone walls, which are thought to be cattle kraals.

The walls at Khami have more decoration than those at Great Zimbabwe; the most common forms being a check pattern and lines of darker dolerite stones. Despite architectural differences, Khami clearly belongs to the same cultural tradition as Great Zimbabwe; at both sites the stone structures were associated with status and prestige while the majority of the population lived in huts outside the stone walls. There are no facilities other than picnic sites next to Khami Dam.

Tshabalala Wildlife Sanctuary
ⓘ *8 km from Bulawayo on the road to Matobo National Park, daily 0600-1800, US$10, children 6-12 US$5, under 6 free.*

In the late 1800s this was the home of a British sailor and his Ndebele wife, who was one of the daughters of the last Ndebele king, Lobengula. This thorn-studded area of savannah is home to some of the less dangerous wildlife, including antelope, giraffe, zebra and warthog, which can be viewed on foot on a series of trails. It used to be a popular place to cycle, so if ever there's the opportunity to hire bikes in Bulawayo this would make a pleasant excursion from the city.

Matobo National Park → *Colour map 4, B1.*

ⓘ *T08-38257/338, www.zimparks.com, 0600-1800, US$15, children (6-12) US$7.50, under 6 free, car US$5.*

As you leave Bulawayo on the road south, you'll notice granite outcrops increase in number and size, and by the time you're through the main gate of the 434,000-ha park you will be surrounded by dramatic and enveloping scenery that is quite extraordinary. The Matobo National Park is located in the magnificent 80-km-long Matobo Hills, a 200-million-year-old range of domes, spires and balancing rock formations hewn out of a solid granite plateau through years of erosion. The hills cover an area of about 3100 sq km, of which 424 sq km comprise the national park, the remainder being largely communal land and a small area of commercial farmland. The highest point in the hills is the promontory named **Gulati** (1549 m) just outside the northeastern corner of the park. The park was established in 1953, and in 2003 the Matobo Hills were proclaimed a UNESCO World Heritage Site for having one of the largest concentrations of rock art in southern Africa. The rugged terrain is interspersed with wooded valleys, and the diverse vegetation supports a wide range of wildlife, including a large population of black and white rhino that are successfully breeding here. Matobo was named by Ndebele King Mzilikazi, and refers to the balancing rocks, which he compared to an assembly of elders from his tribe – *amaTobo*m means 'bald heads'. On his death in 1868, Mzilikazi was buried in the Matobo Hills just a short distance from the park. The Matobo area has great spiritual and cultural significance for the local people and there are many sites where important ceremonies still take place.

Matobo National Park

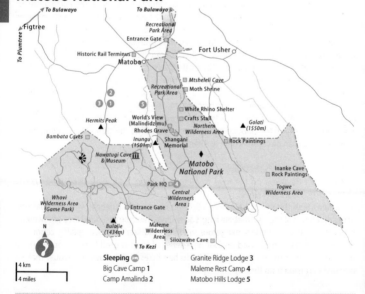

Sleeping 🛏
Big Cave Camp 1
Camp Amalinda 2
Granite Ridge Lodge 3
Maleme Rest Camp 4
Matobo Hills Lodge 5

Ins and outs

The park is located 34 km south of Bulawayo along the Kezi/Maphisa road. From Bulawayo follow Robert Mugabe Avenue out of the city. There is no public transport, but the park can be explored on an organized tour from Bulawayo (see page 153). Beyond the entrance gate of the park, the main road to Maleme Rest Camp is tarred; all other park roads are gravel but mostly in good condition. It's easy to drive around and there are car parks at the major sites, which are well signposted. Accommodation is in National Parks chalets and campsites at the Maleme Rest Camp near the Maleme Dam (see Sleeping, page 149), from where there are short walks to some of the rock art. Alternatively there are a number of private camps just outside the border of the park, or it can be easily visited on a day trip from Bulawayo.

Sights

Administratively, Matobo National Park is divided into a number of wilderness areas including the **Recreational Park Area** in the north around **Hazelside**, **Sandy Spruit** and **Lake Matopos**, and in the south a 100-sq-km game park known as **Whovi Wilderness Area**, which is where the black and white rhino are. The white rhino where transferred here in the 1960s from KwaZulu Natal in South Africa and the black rhinos in the 1990s from the Zambezi Valley. The park has some beautiful scenery, including the spectacular balancing rocks, and there are impressive views in the Thuli, Mtshele, Maleme and Mpopoma river valleys. It is an area of high botanic diversity, with over 200 species of trees, including the mountain acacia, wild pear and the paperbark tree; there are also many aloes, wild herbs and grass species. As well as the sizeable populations of rhino, it is home to zebra, wildebeest, giraffe, kudu, eland, sable, klipspringer, hyena, cheetah, hippo, warthog, waterbuck, common duiker, crocodiles, baboons and vervet monkeys. Although still fairly elusive, there is an exceptionally high concentration of leopard here thanks to the abundance of rock hyrax (or dassies), a small rodent that is a favourite food of leopard. Missing from the park are elephant and lion, but this does mean that visitors can walk in the parts of the park that don't contain the rhino and go on game drives in the parts that do. The birdlife is rich, too, and the park is famous for its large concentration of black eagles, which can be seen perched on or soaring off the rock formations and cliffs. Other species include fish eagle, martial eagle, francolin, secretary bird, weavers, pied crow and Egyptian geese. Matobo is also home to a large number of multi-coloured lizards (the ones in the car park at World's View are practically tame), and some snakes, including the black mamba, though these are rarely encountered.

Additionally the park is well known for more than 3000 exceptionally fine rock paintings, and there are numerous sites that were once occupied by the San (Bushman) hunter-gatherers. The main periods of painting were between AD 320 and 500; in some of the caves and crevices, clay ovens, knife-like tools and crude scrapers have been found. The paintings at **Nswatugi Cave** are some of the finest in the country and include beautiful renditions of giraffe, eland and kudu. Other areas with fine rock paintings are **Bambata Cave**, **Inanke Cave** and **Silozwane Cave**, which is just outside the park. The faint but distinct outline of a rhinoceros at the White Rhino Shelter was the impetus for the reintroduction of the species to the park in the 1960s. All the caves are easily accessible and each has a unique setting in the granite wilderness.

Also around the park are some historic sites relating to the Ndebele wars with the white settlers at the end of the 19th century. The grave of imperialist Cecil John Rhodes (see box, page 146) is at the summit of Malindizimu (Ndebele for 'hill of benevolent spirits'),

Cecil John Rhodes

Known as perhaps the greatest African imperialist, and founder of the state of Rhodesia, which was named after him, Cecil John Rhodes played a major political and economic role in southern Africa. A financier, statesman and empire builder, he had an ambitious dream to paint the map red for Britain with his Cape to Cairo railroad. (On geopolitical maps, British dominions were always denoted in red or pink.) Although successful in some regards, he never achieved this dream and ended up with many personal and political disappointments in his later years.

Rhodes was born in Bishop's Stortford, Hertfordshire, England in 1853. He was a sickly child, and as a young man in 1870 was sent to Natal in South Africa to stay on his brother's cotton farm. The pair soon became involved in the rush to exploit South Africa's newly discovered diamond deposits and set up fruitful claims in Kimberley, which went on to become the richest diamond pipe in the world. Rhodes bought up more claims and by 1888 he owned all the small-scale mining operations at Kimberley and consolidated them under the banner of the De Beers Mining Company. By

this time he was today's equivalent of a billionaire; by 1891 his company owned 90% of the world's diamond mines.

As befits a grand imperialist, Rhodes combined his hugely successful business ventures with a career in politics. He was first elected to the Cape parliament in 1880, and soon gained a reputation as an ardent supporter of British interests in South Africa. In 1890 he became the Cape Colony's Prime Minister and advocated the expansion of British rule to the whole of southern Africa. Despite his economic success with diamonds, bad advice led him to miss out on making a fortune in gold when it was discovered on the Witwatersrand in South Africa. Frustrated by this, he began to look towards lands north of the Limpopo River, where local people were involved in small-scale mining for gold. In 1888, Rhodes sent his Kimberley business partner, Charles Rudd, across the Limpopo to secure mining rights with Lobengula, the head of the Ndebele people. This granted Rhodes gold-mining rights in part of the territory in exchange for 1000 rifles, an armed steamship for use on the Zambezi and a monthly rent of £100. With these arrangements satisfactorily

also known as **World's View** after Rhodes' own reference to it. The tomb is carved out of solid granite and is surrounded by a natural amphitheatre of massive boulders. His right-hand man and leader of the Jameson Raid (the 1895 revolt against South Africa's President Kruger), Leander Starr Jameson, who died in 1917, and the first Prime Minister of Rhodesia Charles Coghlan, who died in 1930, are buried a short distance away.

in place, Rhodes sent the first party of colonists across the Limpopo in 1890; they settled on the site that later became the town of Salisbury (today Harare) and began prospecting for gold. In support of Rhodes' scheme, the government declared the area a British protectorate in 1891. Rhodes received a charter from Queen Victoria authorizing the British South Africa Company to develop new territory, and as the charter had no northern limit, Rhodes annexed Nyasaland (now Malawi) and Northern Rhodesia (now Zambia). Meanwhile, Rhodes' railway from South Africa's Cape reached Bulawayo in 1896, though he failed to achieve his dream of connecting the Cape with Cairo. The railway reached Victoria Falls in 1904, after Rhodes' death, and while the Victoria Falls Bridge was completed in 1905 the line wasn't extended north through Zambia and on to Tanzania until 1976.

Rhodes' dreams of finding great gold reserves in the new territories proved illusory and he failed to find another Witwatersrand. He turned his attention back to his investments in the Transvaal, but his annoyance with President Kruger's constraints on non-Boer residents led him to make his greatest political mistake by backing the ill-fated Jameson Raid in 1895. This failed attempt to overthrow Kruger's government led to a serious breach in relations between Rhodes and Afrikaners in the Cape and he was forced to resign as Prime Minister. He took a less public role in the Charter Company of Rhodesia and spent the Anglo-Boer War in Kimberley, including the siege of Kimberley (15 October 1899-16 February 1900). His health was poor throughout much of his life, and the harsh conditions during the siege did not help. Rhodes died of a heart attack in 1902 at his cottage in Muizenberg, Cape Town. He was only 49. Although his political visions never came to be, his business endeavours made him very prosperous. He bequeathed most of his wealth to Oxford University; nearly £3 million was used in the creation of the famed Rhodes Scholarships. Rhodes decreed in his will that he was to be buried at World's View in the Matobo Hills, and his body was transported from Cape Town by train to Bulawayo. His burial was attended by Ndebele chiefs, who asked that the firing party should not discharge their rifles as this would disturb the spirits.

For Sleeping and Eating price codes and other relevant information, see Essentials pages 29-34.

⏺ Sleeping

Bulawayo *p138, map p141*

B Holiday Inn, Milnerton Dr, Ascot, T09-252460, www.ichotelsgroup.com. In a quiet location with some rooms overlooking Ascot Racecourse, this is a standard mid-range option with 157 rooms in a boring white block. But there are adequate facilities and fairly good food in the buffet restaurant and **Spur** chain steak franchise, plus a well-stocked pub, pool and Wi-Fi.

B Hornung Park Lodge, 79 Burnside Rd, Burnside, 7 km south of the city centre, follow Hillside and then Burnside roads, T09-246868, www.hornung-park-lodge.com. Swiss-run lodge in established gardens in the suburbs with 5 spacious thatched self-catering chalets with stone floors, patios, fireplaces and TV. Swimming pool and bar, and meals can be arranged on request. Friendly hosts. Rates include airport transfers and temporary membership to a nearby sports club to play tennis, squash or a round of 9-hole golf.

B The Nesbitt Castle, 6 Percy Av, Hillside, follow Twelfth Av out of the city centre and turn right on to Percy Av, T09-282726, www.nesbittcastle.co.zw. Bizarrely in Zimbabwe, this is actually a castle with circular towers and ramparts. It was built in the 1940s by a Mr Holdengarde, a former Mayor of Bulawayo, who had an interest in castles and medieval history. No plans were ever drawn up and he built it with his mind's eye. It was restored and opened as a hotel in 1990. The 9 rather stuffy rooms are decorated with antiques, and have a/c and satellite TV. Some have 4-poster beds, and in the public areas are mounted animal heads and weapons. Facilities include a pool, billiards room, the **Coach House** restaurant. Afternoon cream teas can be taken in the beautiful garden (see Eating, page 150).

C Bulawayo Club, corner of Eighth Av and Fort St, T09-64868, www.bulawayoclub.com. An imposing white colonial club with a red-tiled roof, wide verandas and teak-panelled rooms, this was built in 1895 and was fully restored as a boutique hotel in 2009. Features include high ceilings, chandeliers, sweeping staircases, heavy drapes and old prints and paintings on the wall. It still functions as a club and members still use the fine restaurant, bar and billiards room, but some of the splendid bedrooms are now open to non-members.

C Cresta Churchill Hotel, Matobo Rd, Hillside, T09-244243/8, www.cresta-hospitality.com. A similar mid-range but old-fashioned set up to the Cresta hotels in Harare with 50 a/c rooms with satellite TV in a mock-Tudor building. Inglenook restaurant, small pool, tropical gardens with palms. It is predominantly a local conference venue but very professionally run.

C Southern Comfort Lodge, 22 Jaywick Rd, Matsheumhlope, follow Twelfth Av out of the city centre, which turns into Esigodini Rd, T09-281340, www.zimtours.com. A peaceful retreat in the suburbs with 6 thatched en suite chalets with rustic furniture and decorated with African prints, all overlooking a small dam that is home to ducks and geese and attracts a wealth of other birds. Breakfast is included and a 3-course dinner is available on request in the central dining room/bar. Airport transfers can be arranged, and the personable owners can organize tours (see page 153).

D Bulawayo City Lodge, corner of 14th Av and Fife St, T09-76487, www.byocitylodge.com. Decent budget hotel with 12 neat rooms with TV for in-house movies, Wi-Fi and tea- and coffee-making facilities. Also includes a popular pub and Friar Tuck's steak restaurant. A cooked breakfast is US$10.

D Bulawayo Rainbow Hotel, corner Josiah Tongogara and Tenth Av, T09-881273, www.bulawayorainbowhotel.com. The largest hotel in town in a 1950s-built block, with 171 spacious a/c rooms with dated but adequate bathrooms. Also offers a palatial reception area, professional service, decent restaurant and 2 bars, though these can get quite rowdy/noisy in the evening.

D Municipal Caravan Park and Campsite, Caravan Way, in Central Park, T09-233851. Just a short stroll through the park from town (but don't walk at night). Camping is under shady jacaranda and palm trees. Outside the dry season it's gloriously green and flowering. There is also a clutch of very basic brick chalets with beds, a kettle and nothing else.

D Selborne Hotel, corner of Leopold Takawira Av and George Silundika St, T09-65741, www.selborne.co.zw. Built in 1930, this is an old-fashioned town hotel opposite the city hall with 36 simple en suite rooms with overhead fans, TV and dark furnishings set in a rambling corner block with wide arches and lattice balconies. The restaurant has a good choice of dishes; some of the friendly staff have been there for decades.

Matobo National Park *p144, map p144*
In and around Matobo National Park are a number of recommended private lodges that offer reasonable accommodation with good views of the granite skyline. They can all provide pre-arranged transfers from Bulawayo city centre or from the airport, as well as game drives to see the rhino and other animals, visits to rock-art sites and to World's View to see the grave of Cecil Rhodes. Most take only a few guests at a time so expect to interact – and possibly share meals – with your hosts and guides.

The lodges are situated on private concession areas on the edge of the park. To get to them in your own car, follow Robert Mugabe St/Matobo Rd out of Bulawayo, passing the turn-off to Matobo National Park after 30 km, and continue along the road to Kezi and Maphisa. The distance to each lodge off this road is indicated below.

L Camp Amalinda, 44 km, T09-243954, www.campamalinda.co.zw. A well-run luxury safari lodge with friendly hosts, this has 9 unusual thatched rooms built among the balancing rocks, with sweeping views of the Matobo Hills and a delightful swimming pool set in boulders. Home-cooked food is taken sociably around a long teak table, and you can hire the services of a masseur. Rates are exclusive of meals and park entry fees.

L Matobo Hills Lodge, 50 km from Bulawayo, T09-881273, www.matobohillslodge.com. 17 comfortable stone-and-thatch en suite chalets with bright Zim batik bedding and curtains, rock swimming pool, glass-fronted bar and lounge with views of the hills, and outdoor dining area around a bonfire, all linked by raised walkways. The guides are very knowledgeable, and rates are inclusive of meals and 2 activities. There are good deals for families.

C Big Cave Camp, 46 km, turn left at the sign on a gravel road for 2 km until you reach the car park where you will be collected by a 4WD vehicle, T082-579 8811, www.bigcave.co.za. In the Matobo Hills, 7 granite-and-thatch ensuite A-frame units, some sleeping families. Facilities include 'Leopard's Lair', which is the lounge, a bar and dining room, with impressive walls of giant boulders, atmospherically lit by lanterns at night. As well as game drives and rock-art viewing, visits to local villages and schools can be arranged.

C-D Maleme Rest Camp, in the park, approx 17 km south of the entrance gate, reservations, T04-706077/8 (Harare), or T09-65592 (Bulawayo), www.zimparks. com. Electrified accommodation is found at **Maleme Rest Camp** where the main park offices are located. There are 12 simple 5-, 4- and 2-bed lodges with a kitchen with fridge, stove, cutlery and crockery, a dining table, heaters, and bathroom with hot water. The best are **Fish Eagle**, **Black Eagle** and **Imbila**, which have additional gardens and verandas with views over the Maleme

Gorge. There are 5 cheaper 1-bed chalets (US$30) that share an ablution block and kitchen facilities with basic 2-plate stoves, plus an attractive campsite (US$10 per person) with ablution block and braai sites next to the Maleme Dam.

D Granite Ridge Lodge, 48 km from Bulawayo, T09-230215, www.graniteridge matobo.com. Simple lodge with 12 self-catering tin-roofed or thatched chalets. You can also eat meals at the farmhouse, where there is a bar and pool. The Granite Ridge itself, a bluff some 2 km from the lodge, makes for a good hike to enjoy the views of the hills; it also has a campsite with ablution block and hot water.

❼ Eating

Bulawayo *p138, map p141*
Eating out in Bulawayo is not terribly inspiring and the hotels will remain your best bet. Nevertheless there are a couple of good daytime cafés that are worth seeking out, and there are a number of the takeaway chains around town – Chicken Inn, Creamy Inn, Bakers Inn, Pizza Inn (chicken, ice cream, pies and pizzas, respectively), are on Fort St, between Sixth Av and Leopold Takaiwira Av, where there is also a **Nando's** (grilled chicken) and **Steers** (burgers). There is another crop of these near the City Hall around Eighth Av and Jason Moyo St, plus a branch of **Wimpy**. There are also a couple of oriental takeaways near the Publicity Association on Eighth Av.

♈♈♈ The Coach House, Nesbitt Castle, 6 Percy Av, Hillside, T09-282726, www.nesbittcastle. co.zw. Lunch 1200-1500, high tea, 1600-1800, dinner 1900-2100. Set in a mock castle in this boutique hotel. The 3-course meals are well regarded; expect the likes of cream of cauliflower soup or bacon and feta cheese tartlets to start, mains such as fillet steak with pepper sauce or oven-baked bream, followed by crème caramel and chocolate cheesecake. With Persian carpets and artefacts, military pictures, weapons and memorabilia of a bygone age, there is plenty to gaze at whilst enjoying the first glass of wine.

♈♈♈ Loziba, Bulawayo Rainbow Hotel, see Sleeping, T09-881273, www.bulawayo rainbowhotel.com. Open 0700-1000, 1130-1400, 1800-2200. Large hotel restaurant decorated with bright ethnic prints, serving buffets and an à la carte menu. Dishes include casseroles and roast dinners, with vegetables such as sweet potatoes and butternut pumpkin, and there's a reasonable salad bar. Varied wine list and good value for money.

♈♈ Arizona Spur, Holiday Inn Bulawayo, see Sleeping, T09-256871, www.ichotelsgroup. com. Family steakhouse chain with a Wild West theme, this isn't for romantic couples but it's good for kids, with a play area and crayons. The salad bar can be a bit hit and miss depending on availability, but generally the steaks and the Mexican dishes are dependable and generous in size.

♈♈ Cape to Cairo, corner of Leopold Takawira Av and Robert Mugabe Way, T09-72387. Mon-Sat 1200-2200. Well-established restaurant serving a long menu of steaks and various sauces, some Zimbabwe fish and good vegetarian options. A fully stocked bar including South African wine.

♈♈ The Cattleman, corner 12th Av and Joshia Tongogara, T09-76086. Tue-Fri 1200-1350, 1800-2145, Sat 1800-2145, Sun 1200-1350, 1800-2130. A popular steak restaurant specializing in cuts of rump, sirloin and fillet with a range of sauces, including monkey-gland (see box, page 151), mushroom or garlic, plus filled baked potatoes, pizza and a fairly good range of salads.

♈♈ Golden Spur, Robert Mugabe Way, T09-70318. Open 1200-2100. Wild West-themed restaurant with checked tablecloths and tilly lamps, mock log walls and horse tack. Serves a good choice of steaks with sauces, and, unusually for a steak restaurant, bream and chicken curry. Chocolate desserts and a good choice of wine.

Monkey-gland sauce

A perennial favourite of the southern African steakhouse is monkey-gland sauce. There are several recipes but they usually include most of the following ingredients: fruit chutney, red wine, port, tomato ketchup, curry powder, Tabasco, Worcester sauce, pepper, mustard powder, garlic, onion, chillies, brown sugar and vinegar. The sauce was invented by French chefs who'd been lured to Johannesburg to cook at the old Carlton Hotel in the early 1950s. The rich white clients of the hotel dining room had plenty of money but lacked sophistication, and try as they might the chefs could not please their customers with their finely nuanced haute cuisine sauces. One day, in desperation and with a certain amount of venom, they threw every commercial sauce preparation they could lay their hands on into the pot and called the concoction monkey-gland sauce. Lo and behold, the customers enjoyed the sauce on their steaks, the chefs enjoyed the joke, and a legend was born. No monkeys were actually harmed in its making.

Grillo's, Zonke Iziswe Shopping Centre, off Hillside Rd, T09-880494. Tue-Sat 1200-2200. Restaurant with jungle murals and outside deck, offering a mixed menu of pizza, lasagne, chicken schnitzel, steaks, fish and chips and sometimes prawns, but as in most Bulawayo restaurants, what's available can be hit and miss.

Inglenook, Cresta Churchill Hotel, see Sleeping, www.cresta-hospitality.com. A mock-Tudor-style interior with imitation oak beams and leaded windows, pub benches, a decent wine list and prompt and professional service. A lot of thought has gone into the imaginative menu, but as with many restaurants the choice of food depends on what is available.

Cafés

Art Groove, National Gallery, corner of Main St and Leopold Takawira Av, T09-70721, www.nationalgallerybyo.com. Tue-Sun 0900-1700. Situated in the lovely red sandstone building of the National Gallery, this coffee shop has a courtyard and an indoor area, with old wooden floors and painted terracotta walls. It serves light meals such as pasta or chicken burgers, plus toasted sandwiches, salads, muffins and scones, 2 choices of breakfast and good cappuccinos.

Coffee Shoppe, Ascot Race Track, off Ascot Way, Suburbs, T09-250728. Open 0900-1500. Although horse racing stopped at the racetrack several years ago, some of the buildings are being used for other businesses such as this café. Situated in the original Members' Club, it has a view over the racetrack from the balcony, and 2 African wildlife murals on the walls. Serves a variety of toasted sandwiches and wraps with a good selection of fillings, cakes and teas, coffees and soft drinks.

Indaba Book Cafe & Sandwich Shop, corner of Ninth Av and Josiah Tongogara St, T09-67068. Mon-Fri 0800-1600, 0800-1400. A smart café with Wi-Fi selling a small but well chosen selection of international novels and an excellent range of locally written books – local publishers often hold book launches here. Breakfasts, gourmet sandwiches with tasty fillings (roast beef, roast peppers and caramelized onions, for example), light meals, scones and cakes.

La Piazza Deli & Bistro, Twelvth Av. Tue-Fri 0900-1500, Sat 0900-1400. Pretty garden venue with established trees, green lawns, water features and children's playground, and tables on a shaded outside terrace. Serves breakfasts, toasted sandwiches, salads, filled omelettes and specials, which are chalked up on the blackboard. The adjoining **Afrodizziac** shop (see page 152) is well worth a browse.

Mary's Corner, 88 Josiah Tongogara St, between Eighth Av and Ninth Av, T09-76721. Mon-Fri 0730-1600, Sat 0800-1200. An inexpensive, old-fashioned local café and takeaway serving breakfast, fried snacks, a meat and 2-veg lunch, cold drinks and tea and sugary cakes. An easy stroll from the campsite.

The Roasted Berry, 26 Park Rd, Suburbs, T09-237325. Open 0900-2100. Located in an old colonial house with a large garden dotted with tables on leafy Park Rd, this has a good local reputation and is known as **The Berry**. Although it's not licensed, it stays open in the evening for full meals, and serves wraps, stir-fries and coffees during the day. The most intriguing items on the menu are the 'mini wrap platter' with a variety of inventive fillings such as chicken and pineapple or strips of beef with roast vegetables, and the 'Affrogato' – espresso with ice cream and honey.

Bars and clubs

Bulawayo *p138, map p141*
There's very little nightlife in town, so the hotel bars are the best bet. Try the **Sethule Bar** in the **Bulawayo Rainbow Hotel** (see Sleeping). There also used to be a smoky and poky jazz club under the hotel but it's been closed (supposedly for refurbishment) for some time.

Safari Bar and Grill Shop, corner of Tenth Av and Josiah Tongogara St, T09-882030. 1600-late. A modern, if a little rough and ready, bar with blacked-out windows and leopard-print decor.

Entertainment

Bulawayo *p138, map p141*
There are 3 cinemas in the centre of Bulawayo but they are no longer operating and now function as churches.

Shopping

Bulawayo *p138, map p141*
There are shopping centres at the Bulawayo Centre on Main St between Eighth Av and Ninth Av, and **Zonke Iziswe Shopping Centre** on Hillside Rd.

Arts and crafts

Afrodizziac, at La Piazza Deli & Bistro (see Eating, page 151), T0911-413474. Mon-Fri 0900-1600, Sat 0900-1200. A treasure trove of top-quality African crafts and home decor items. A great deal of thought has gone into their presentation, with good lighting and inventive displays. One room has tribal items from southern and West Africa, including textiles and sculptures, while another has locally made and brightly coloured pottery. There's a particularly good choice of pewter pieces (both decorative and practical) and jewellery.

Fazak Gift Centre, 79 Main St, opposite the post office, T09-61108. Mon-Fri 0830-1630, Sat 0900-1200. A good selection of Zimbabwe products, including carvings, baskets, brass and copperware, traditional safari wear and leather products. A distributor for Courteney boots, leather safari boots handmade in Bulawayo.

Induna Arts, next to **The Cattleman** restaurant, see Eating, T09-69175. Mon-Fri 0900-1600, Sat 0930-1230. A converted house crammed with locally produced gifts and curios, including carvings, cloth, baskets, pewter, pottery, decorative ostrich eggs, leather shoes, T-shirts and an excellent selection of fiction and non-fiction books produced in Zimbabwe. Look out for wildlife paintings by acclaimed local artist Linda Lemon.

Jairos Jiri Craftshop, corner of Robert Mugabe Way and Leopold Takawira Av, next door to the Publicity Association (see page 138), T09-74331/2. Mon-Fri 0745-1645, Sat-Sun 0800-1400. Sells items made mainly by local disabled artists. The shed-like building is crammed with batiks, wood and stone carvings, musical instruments, leather bags, wall hangings, beadwork, and tie and dye cloth, among many other craft products. There's another branch at the Victoria Falls curio market.

Mthwakazi Crafts, 81 Samuel Parirenyatwa St, T09-72729. Mon-Fri 0830-1700, Sat 0830-1400. Local crafts, mostly made by women's groups and female school leavers (those that cannot afford to continue their education but are too young for formal employment), including embroidery, mohair jerseys, ceramics, batiks, cushions and glass beadwork. This is an initiative started by Bulawayo's City Council in colonial times.

Mzilikazi Art and Craft Centre, situated just out of town off the Old Falls road, follow Masotsha Ndlovu Av north from town, T09-207245. Mon-Fri 0830-1600. Located in a poor but well-established and friendly township on the periphery of town, this centre is worth a visit. Choose from a wide selection of skilfully crafted sculptures, basketry, pottery, beadwork and woodwork – all done by local residents. Like **Mthwakazi Crafts**, above, it was originally set up as a community project by the City Council in the 1960s; unfortunately, few tourists have visited in recent years.

▲ Activities and tours

Bulawayo *p138, map p141*
Tour operators
The following companies can arrange day trips from Bulawayo to Matobo, but to get up-to-date details about the operators book through the Publicity Association (see page 138). **African Wanderer**, T09-72736; **Black Rhino**, T09-241662; **Travel AfriKa**, T09-67449; **UTC**, corner of George Silundika

St and Fourteenth Av, T09-61402, www.utc.co.zw; **Zim Tours** based at Southern Comfort Lodge, T09-28130, www.zimtours.com.

⊕ Transport

Bulawayo *p138, map p141*
Air
Air Zimbabwe operate 2 daily flights from Harare to Bulawayo (1¼ hrs) at 0900 and 1900, and from Bulawayo flights depart at 0700 and 1715, around US$180 return, US$100 one-way. Flights between Bulawayo and Victoria Falls go via Harare (3¾ hrs) including the 45-min connection time in Harare. **South African Airways** (SAA) has a daily flight between **Johannesburg** and Bulawayo (1 hr 25 mins) at 1145, which departs again from Bulawayo at 1325. Fares are around US$590 return and US$310 one-way.

Airline offices Air Zimbabwe, airport T09-226 491-3, town office, Treger Gouse, Jason Moyo St, T09-72051, www.airzimbabwe.aero. **South African Airways**, Johannesburg OR Tambo International Airport, T+27-11-978 1111, www.flysaa.com.

Bus
Local The main city terminus for ZUPCO buses and commuter omnibuses is the **City Hall Terminus** on Eighth Av between Fife St and Robert Mugabe Way for vehicles going to the northern, eastern and southern suburbs. Buses to the low-income western suburbs go from the **Lobengula St Terminus** at the west end of Sixth Av.

Long distance Local economy buses for **Harare**, **Victoria Falls**, **Mutare**, **Masvingo** and **Beitbridge** arrive and depart from the **Renkini Bus Terminus** on Sixth Av extension. **Citylink** (T09-881273) www.rainbowtowershotel.com), go between the Rainbow Towers Hotel in Harare Tue, Thu, Sat, Sun at 1400 and arrive at the Bulawayo Rainbow Hotel about 1930. The buses go back from the Bulawayo Rainbow Hotel

Border crossings: Zimbabwe–Botswana

Plumtree–Ramokawebane

From Bulawayo it's 100 km on the A7 to the small town of Plumtree with its cluster of shops and railway buildings, and 2 km beyond here to the Plumtree/Ramokawebane border post with Botswana (0600-2000). Francistown, the first major centre in Botswana, is 87 km south of this border.

Facilities Like the Beitbridge/Musina border with South Africa (see page 127), there is a large reception facility here to deal with migrants between Zimbabwe and Botswana. Since 2008 it has provided humanitarian assistance to returning migrants to Zimbabwe in the form of food, basic health care and transport. Funded partly by the UK's Department for International Development (DFID), it also provides training to border officials, police, social service providers and relevant local authorities on migrant rights, human trafficking, irregular migration and smuggling.

Customs and immigration Visas for Zimbabwe are available at the border (see Essentials, page 47); they can be paid for with US dollars, Botswana pula or South African rand. Very few nationalities require a visa to enter Botswana (information on the Botowana Tourism Board's website: www.botswanatourism.co.bw). Remember that if you don't have a double-entry visa for Zimbabwe you'll need to get a new visa when you come back into the country.

Vehicle formalities If you are going into Zimbabwe from Botswana in a car hired from and registered in South Africa, you'll need a cross-border permit and ZA stickers. These must be pre-organized with your hire company when you book your; the company must have agreed that you can take the vehicle into Zimbabwe (very few do) and provide you with the appropriate documentation, including the registration document and letter of permission. As South Africa, Botswana, and Namibia are part of the same Southern African Development Community (SADC) customs agreement, you do not need cross-border permits to travel over borders between these countries; the Zimbabwe border is the first where this additional paperwork is required. It cannot be obtained at the border.

(see Sleeping, page 148) to the Rainbow Towers (page 67) in Harare Tue, Thu, Sat, Sun at 1400 and arrive about 1930. They also stop at Kadoma, Kwekwe and Gweru (see Midlands, page 91).

From Bulawayo to **Victoria Falls**, they depart at 1400 on Mon, Wed, Fri and Sat and arrive about 1930, but check at the Rainbow Hotels in advance. Costs are US$25 Harare–Bulawayo, US$50 Harare–Victoria Falls, and US$30 Bulawayo–Victoria Falls. **Pathfinder** (T09-61788, www.pathfinderlx.com) runs a daily service between Bulawayo and **Harare**, departing from each respectively at 0800 and 1400 and arriving at 1400 and 2000. They pick up and drop off at the Holiday Inns in each city. They may extend the service

soon to Bulawayo–Victoria Falls and Harare–Mutare so it's worth checking the website.

Citylink and **Pathfinder** operate new coaches with a/c, videos and refreshments. For getting to Bulawayo from South Africa, see Getting there, page 23).

Car

Driving in central Bulawayo is fairly straightforward; roads are clearly marked and most places are signposted. Watch out for commuter omnibuses as they can brake very suddenly to pick up passengers. For information about car hire rates, see Getting around, page 23.

Car hire Avis, airport T09-226 657/918, town office, corner Tenth Av and Robert

It's impossible to take a car hired in Zimbabwe across the border; for information on the necessary documentation for taking your own vehicle out of the country, see Essentials, page 23. If coming from Botswana, third-party insurance is available on the Zimbabwe side; there are also small road taxes and a carbon levy to pay in US dollars, Botswana pula or South African rand.

Public transport There are between five and seven buses daily between Bulawayo and Francistown, which should take about three hours, but up to six if the border is very busy. Buses are thoroughly searched at the border. There is also a thrice-weekly train service between Bulawayo and Francistown in Botswana. For information on this, see Getting there, page 22.

Sleeping For accommodation in Francistown, try the three-star **Peermont Metcourt Lodge** (D Blue Jacket St, T+267-2441100, www.metcourt.com), which has 53 modern a/c rooms with internet and satellite TV, and a **Golden Hills Spur** chain steak restaurant where breakfast is also taken. Overlanders can camp at the **Tati River Lodge** (D-F Old Gaborone Rd, T+267-2406000, www.trl.co.bw), which has 80 good standard rooms, a secure campsite with hot showers (US$6), a pool, restaurant and pub.

Moving on From Francistown, **Maun** (for the Okavango Delta) is 455 km to the west and Botswana's capital **Gaborone** is 440 km to the south. From Gaborone it's 73 km to the **Pioneer's Gate** border, and 50 km further south to the **Ramatlabama border**, both with South Africa.

If you are arriving from Botswana and heading to South Africa, it is a pretty uneventful 325-km drive on the A6 through remote and dry country to Beitbridge, the only direct border between Zimbabwe and South Africa. For details of crossing here, see page 127. The Bulawayo–Gaborone (Botswana) route makes a good alternative if you are heading both for the Cape and to Johannesburg, and it avoids the notoriously busy Beitbridge.

Mugabe St, www.avis.com. **Budget**, airport, T09-72543, www.budget.com. **Europcar**, airport T09-226185, town office, Ecological Safaris, Colshar House, Leopold Takawira Av, T09-67925, www.europcar.com.

Taxi
Taxis are plentiful and park up outside the City Hall on Eighth Av and on the streets around the Publicity Association (see page 138). **City Cab**, T09-56502.

Train
The railway station is on Lobengula St, T09-363111, www.nrz.co.zw. In theory, the **Harare** service departs Bulawayo Mon, Thu and Sat at 2100 and arrives the next

morning at 0650. In the opposite direction the train departs Harare Tue, Fri and Sun at 2100 and arrives in Bulawayo the next morning at 0835 (but they often run late). For more information including fares and classes, see Transport in Harare, page 81.

The overnight train from Bulawayo to **Victoria Falls** departs Bulawayo Tue, Thu, Fri, Sat and Sun at 2000 and arrives in Victoria Falls the following day at 0700. In the opposite direction it departs Victoria Falls Mon, Wed, Fri, Sat and Sun at 0730 and arrives in Bulawayo at 0700. However, the trains often run late, so expect to arrive in either destination nearer 0900. This is a wonderful rail experience, with part of the journey running through Hwange National

Park, though you won't see much in the dark. The coaches, though, some dating to the 1950s, are fairly dilapidated so check the lights, taps, etc are functioning and the door locks. Fares are around US$12 per person in Sleeper class, children under 12 half price, children under 3 free. Sleeper class has 2-berth rooms (known as coupés) and 4-berth rooms (known as compartments). For more on sleepers, see Essentials, page 25). The sleeping-cars are all British-built, the ones with wood-panelled interiors were built in Gloucester in 1952, the ones with the less attractive formica interiors in Birmingham in 1958. Although they now carry National Railways of Zimbabwe insignia, they are still painted in the original Rhodesia Railways colours, and windows and mirrors are etched with the 'RR' logo. There is also a thrice-weekly service between Bulawayo and **Francistown** in Botswana. For information on this, see Getting there, page 22.

❶ Directory

Bulawayo *p138, map p141*
Banks There are several banks in the centre of town, most with ATMs taking Visa and increasingly MasterCard. **Cultural centres** Alliance Française, 61 Heyman Rd, Suburbs, T09-250245. **British Council**, 2nd floor, West Zimdef House, 102 Fort St, T09-75815. **Immigration** Corner of Herbert Chitepo St and Eleventh Av, T09-65621. **Internet** Most hotels offer internet services or you can try the public library on the corner of Eight Av and Fort St, Mon-Fri 0830-1700, Sat 0830-1200. **Medical services** Bulawayo Central Hospital, St Luke's Rd, Woodlands, T09-252111. **Mater Dei Accident and Emergency Unit**, Cesterton Rd, Malindela, T09-240000-5. **Police** Corner Leopold Takawira Av and Fife St, T09-72515/68078. **Post** The principal branch is on the corner of Main St and Eighth Av, T09-62535, Mon-Fri 0830-1600, Sat 0830-1130, which also offers telephone and fax services. **Courier companies DHL**, corner of Ninth Av and Main St, T09-69747, www.dhl.co.zw.

Contents

Footprint features

Border crossings

At a glance

● **Getting around** Victoria Falls town is small and compact and everything is walkable. For activities and safaris in the outlying areas (including Hwange National Park and Chobe National Park in Botswana), transfers are included in organized trips.

● **Time required** At least of 3 days to see the falls and enjoy some of the activities, and at least 1 day for Chobe or Hwange National Park.

☼ **Weather** Most of the year there are moderate temperatures except before and during the rains, Nov-Apr, when it can be hot; the best time to see the falls is during high water, while the best time for whitewater rafting is during low water (see page 164).

✖ **When not to go** The rainy season is Nov-Apr when it can be hot and humid.

NAMIBIA

BOTSWANA

Lusulu

Kana

Gwelutshena

Eastnor

Bulawayo

Kamativi

Tshotsholo

Lupane

Kenmaur

Sawmills

Nyamandlovu

Msuna

Déka

Kennedy

Gwaai

Gamu

Tsholotsho

Livingstone

Hwange

Matetsi

Déte

Déka Safari Area

Sinamatella Camp

Hwange National Park

Pandamatenga

Robins Camp

Victoria Falls

Zambezi National Park

Kazuma Pan National Park

Zambezi

Gwayi

Déka

Matetsi

Gwai River

Gwabazabuya

Don't miss...

★ Viewing the Victoria Falls, page 167

1 Elephant-back safaris, pages 170 and 184

2 The Boma Place of Eating, page 175

3 Bungee jumping, page 179

4 Whitewater rafting, pages 180 and 182

5

40 km

40 miles

N

The Victoria Falls, where the mighty Zambezi River spills dramatically into the Batoka Gorge, are the principal attraction of Zimbabwe and Zambia. The energy and power of a body of water that is nearly 2 km wide crashing into the gorge 100 m below is a spectacular sight, and is best appreciated from the spray-drenched rainforest of the Victoria Falls National Park or the Mosi-oa-Tunya National Park on the Zambian side. Both Victoria Falls town in Zimbabwe and Livingstone in Zambia are unashamedly geared towards tourism, and while Victoria Falls has suffered from a dearth of tourists in recent years because of Zimbabwe's economic and political problems, Livingstone has flourished, as visitors have flocked to enjoy the Zambian side of the falls. Nevertheless, Victoria Falls town is on the up again and is undoubtedly Africa's adventure capital. Depending on how active you want to be, you'll need at least a few days to enjoy the region.

Victoria Falls and around

A World Heritage Site and one of the Seven Wonders of the World, the Victoria Falls are indeed one of the world's greatest geographical sights; the moment you arrive in the town and hear the roar and see the 'smoke that thunders' rise almost 500 m skywards, you'll be lured down the main street to the entrance of the Victoria Falls National Park. Here the smooth-flowing Zambezi River changes character and plunges into the Batoka Gorge in a profusion of whitewater. The falls are 1.7 km wide, and nearly 550 million litres of water cascade into the chasm below every minute during the Zambezi River's peak high-water flow. Victoria Falls is roughly three times the height of North America's Niagara Falls and well over twice the width of the Horseshoe Falls, also on the Niagara River. The only rivals in height and width are South America's Iguazú Falls.

Apart from the falls themselves there are few sights per se, but there are lots of activities below and above the falls and on the Zambezi River. Whitewater rafting and river boarding are the best ways to get wet and wild in the world-renowned Grade V rapids, while taking a 111-m-high bungee jump off the Victoria Falls Railway Bridge, abseiling into the gorge or soaring over it on a flying fox provide adrenalin highs.

It is just as enticing above the falls on the Upper Zambezi, with its palm-dotted islands and array of game. Sunset cruises and canoeing on the Upper Zambezi take you among hippos and crocodiles, or you can take an elephant ride, walking safari or horse trail in the surrounding national parks and wilderness. ▶▶ *For listings, see pages 172-186.*

Ins and outs → *For listings, see pages 172-186. Colour map 1, C1. Phone code: 013. Population 31,000.*

Getting there

Air **Victoria Falls International Airport** ① *21 km south of town on the Bulawayo Rd, T013-41575/6, www.caaz.co.zw,* serves domestic and regional flights from Harare and Johannesburg. However, preliminary work is underway to upgrade the terminal building and construct a 4-km runway that can accommodate larger wide-body aircraft for long-haul flights. Alternatively, there is the option of flying into Livingstone on the Zambian side of the border (see Livingstone Transport, page 201).

Until upgrading has been completed, the terminal building at Victoria Falls is very small, with just a couple of shops and no banks or ATMs. Visas are available on arrival if coming from Johannesburg. Some taxis meet flights at the airport; these should cost in the region of US$25-30, but the best way to get into town is by pre-arranging an airport pickup with your hotel or backpacker hostel, or with your tour operator; this should cost about US$10 per person, minimum of US$20. The car hire offices are in a row of sheds in the car park. ▶▶ *For further information, see Transport, page 184.*

Bus and train Victoria Falls is 440 km from Bulawayo on the A8. Local economy buses to and from Bulawayo arrive and depart from the terminal off **Pioneer Road** to the south of town near the hospital in the Chinotimba township. A better option are the private and quicker **City Link** or **Senator** buses (see Transport, page 184).

One of the most pleasurable (if long) ways of getting to Victoria Falls from Bulawayo is on the overnight train (see Getting around, page 25, for timetables and prices). It's at least a 12-hour journey, but at dawn (if heading towards Victoria Falls), there is the opportunity to spot game in the remote bush on the edge of Victoria Falls National Park from your sleeper car. The **Victoria Falls Station** is an attractive Edwardian building, with a historical avenue of trees leading to the entrance of the **Victoria Falls Hotel**. **Livingstone Way**, the town's main drag, is a short walk along the platform northwards, or exit the main entrance to the station on **Mallet Drive**, where there are taxis (if not, you'll find them in the car park of the **Kingdom Hotel** opposite).

Car The 440-km tarred road from Bulawayo is generally very good with the exception of a few slightly bumpy patches. It's very isolated though, so ensure you fill up with fuel in Bulawayo as there are no fuel stations until **Halfway House** (a petrol station, hotel and restaurant, see page 174), and the first 160 km or so out of Bulawayo is almost devoid of habitation. What is more, you can't rely on there being fuel at Halfway House, especially diesel. The road stretches north through attractive parkland terrain with tall mopane, acacia and teak trees. Motorists should look out for cows and goats feeding on the grass verges, and caution is needed. Night driving is not advisable. The turn-off to **Hwange Safari Lodge** and **Main Camp** is 265 km from Bulawayo; Hwange town is a further 70 km, and Victoria Falls another 102 km. On approaching Victoria Falls, you'll pass the airport on the left 21 km before the town; 6 km beyond here, as the woodland thins out and the road descends a low ridge, you should see the spray of Victoria Falls rising above the savannah.
▸▸ *For getting to Livingstone from Victoria Falls, see page 187.*

Getting around
Victoria Falls town is very small. Despite its former glory as a holiday resort and centre for adventure sports, it is not much more than the main street, **Livingstone Way**, which tails off downhill for about a kilometre to the Victoria Falls Bridge and the two border posts on either side. An offshoot, **Parkway**, leads to the rest camp and a faded row of shopping centres. The latter, a hive of activity, is where adventure activities, tours and safaris can be organized in a string of booking offices. To the northwest of this road junction is the town's main residential area, where some of the cheaper guesthouses and backpacker hostels are located. Everything is walkable but taxis (found outside the post office on Livingstone Way, along Parkway and at the border post) should cost no more than US$3-5 to get to the bridge (if it's too hot to walk up and down the slight hill) or to the lodges in the outlying areas of bush beyond the town's perimeter.

For all activities the operators will pick you up and drop you off from your place of accommodation, usually in air-conditioned minibuses, so there is no need to hire a car.

The other option is to hire a bike. **Shoestrings** and **Victoria Falls Backpackers** (see Sleeping, page 174) hire out bikes, as does an unnamed office run by **Shana Edison** ① *to the left (with your back to the shops) of the tourist office on Parkway, T031-42156, Mon-Sat 0800-1700.* For bike hire, expect to pay US$2 per hour and about US$15 per day. Mr Edison also hires out shoot-and-point digital cameras for US$10 per day. However, be aware that no more than 500 m from town you may well come across some unexpected hazards in addition to the usual potholes: elephants. These have been known to wander around the town's streets, into the rest camp, and can be seen regularly munching on the foliage on the Bulawayo road, especially in the dry season (when they also drink in the swimming pools of lodges and private homes). Baboons, too, are infamous for not giving drivers or cyclists the right of way around town. Nevertheless, hiring a bike is a good option for getting around town and going to the Victoria Falls National Park.

Best time to visit

There are different reasons for visiting the Victoria Falls, depending on the season and climate. The falls are at their most spectacular when rain has fallen upstream in Namibia, Zambia and in the river's tributaries in Angola. By contrast, the best whitewater rafting

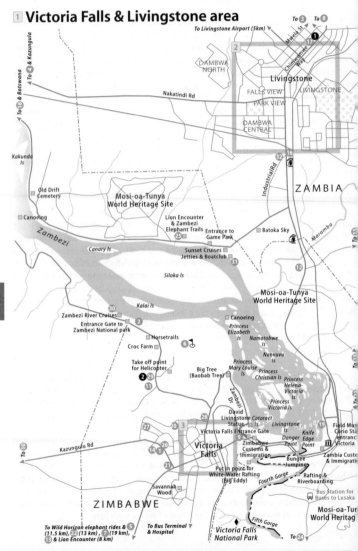

1 Victoria Falls & Livingstone area

To Livingstone Airport (5km)

Livingstone

DAMBWA NORTH

FALLS VIEW
PARK VIEW

DAMBWA CENTRAL

Nakatindi Rd

To 4 & Kazungula

To 18 & Botswana

Kakunda Is

Old Drift Cemetery

Canoeing

Mosi-oa-Tunya World Heritage Site

Zambezi

Canary Is

Siloka Is

Kalai Is

Lion Encounter & Zambezi Elephant Trails

Entrance to Game Park

Sunset Cruises Jetties & Boatclub

Batoka Sky

ZAMBIA

Industrial Rd

Maramba

Mosi-oa-Tunya World Heritage Site

Zambezi River Cruises

Entrance Gate to Zambezi National park

Horsetrails

Croc Farm

Take off point for Helicopter

Big Tree (Baobab Tree)

Canoeing

Princess Elizabeth Is

Namatobwe Is

Nanvuvu Is

Princess Mary Louise Is

Princess Christian Is

Princess Helena-Victoria Is

Princess Victoria Is

David Livingstone Statue

Cataract Is

Victoria Falls Entrance Gate

Zimbabwe Customs & Immigration

Livingstone Is

Danger Point

Knife Edge Point

Field Mus Curio Sta entranc Victoria

Zambia Custo & Immigrati

Bungee Jumping

Rafting & Riverboarding

Bus Station for Buses to Lusaka

Mosi-oa-Tun World Heritag

Zambezi Dr

Kazungulu Rd

Victoria Falls

Savannah Wood

Put in point for White-Water Rafting (Big Eddy)

Fourth Gorge

Fifth Gorge

ZIMBABWE

To Wild Horizon elephant rides & 5 (11.5 km), 22 (13 km), 7 (19 km), 13 & Lion Encounter (8 km)

To Bus Terminal & Hospital

Victoria Falls National Park

To 24

in the world occurs when the level of water in the Zambezi drops to expose the rapids. Effectively, it is a choice between seeing the Victoria Falls in all their powerful glory and rafting what are arguably the best rapids in the world. Game-viewing and birdwatching are also governed by the seasons, as is the prevalence of mosquitoes (possibly malaria-carrying). See box, page 164, for more information about the best times to visit. Temperatures in winter (May to mid-August) are mild and dry, with average high temperatures of 25-27°C, and average lows of 7-10°C. Summer (mid-August to end April) is generally hot and wet during the rainy season (mid-November to April), with average highs of 32-34°C and average lows of 15-19°C.

20 km
20 miles

Sleeping 🛏
Amadeus Garden **1**
A'Zambezi River Lodge **2**
Chapa Classic Lodge
   & Chanters Inn **3**
Chundukwa River Lodge **4**
Elephant Camp **5**
Elephant Hills Hotel
   & Golf Course **6**
Gorges Lodge **7**
Grotto **8**
Ilala Lodge **9**
Imbabala Zambezi Safari
   Lodge **10**
Lokuthula Lodges **11**
Maramba River Lodge **12**
Masuwi Safari Lodge **13**
Pamusha Lodge **14**
Prana Cottage
   & Tented Camp **15**
Protea Hotel Livingstone **16**
Rite Inn **17**
River Club **18**
Royal Livingstone
   & Zambezi Sun **19**
Savanna Lodge
   Backpackers **20**
Sprayview **21**
Stanley & Livingstone **22**
Stanley Safari Lodge **23**
Taita Falcon Lodge **24**
Thorntree River Lodge **25**
Tokkie Lodge **26**
Victoria Falls Backpackers **27**
Victoria Falls Rainbow Hotel **28**
Victoria Falls Safari Lodge **29**
Zambezi National Park
   Lodges **30**
Zambezi Waterfront **31**
Zig Zag **32**

Eating 🍴
Armadillo **1**
The Boma Place of Eating **2**

Tourist information

The friendly **Publicity Association** ① *412 Parkway, T013-44202, vfpa@mweb.co.zw, Mon-Sat 0800-1700*, has brochures to give away and maps of Victoria Falls and Zimbabwe for sale. It doesn't act as a booking office, but the staff can refer you to nearby adventure companies and tour operators. These include the **Backpackers Bazaar** ① *Shop 5 Old Vic Falls Centre, T013-45828, www.zimtravelagent.com, Mon-Fri 0800-1700, Sat-Sun 0900-1600*, just across the road, which is an independent booking agency and information service for all activities and safaris. Activities and services can also be booked at **Adventure Zone**, **Shearwater** and **Wild Horizons**, among others, on the opposite side of the street from the tourist office (see page 181 for a full list of tour operators). Effectively, you can arrive in Victoria Falls, walk into any of these offices and book all accommodation, activities, airport transfers and even restaurants in one hit in about 30 minutes. They act as agents for all the local businesses, and also run their own programmes. Despite Zimbabwe's economic woes, Victoria Falls retains its tourism ethos and it aims to please, whatever you want to do. Prices are generally pretty similar across the different companies, with businesses operating a sort of 'small-town' agreement. If you contact an operator in advance,

A year at Victoria Falls

January Height of the rainy season; hot and humid with thunderstorms and torrential downpours; can include several days of continuous rain. The falls become more intense with increased river flow; vegetation is thick and grass at its most nutritious, encouraging animals to disperse widely across the veld, and therefore not the best time for game-viewing. The rainforest above the falls is very damp and most rainforest flowers are in bloom; there's lots of bird activity, as many nestlings are raised. Whitewater rafting will normally change to the high-water season (see page 182) and possibly close altogether until about March.

February Days are hot and nights warm with plenty of rain, and 'the smoke that thunders' (the spray from the falls) rises high in the sky. This is a good time to do aerial activities as most of the rainforest is under constant shower and the river level rises significantly. Activities include 'high-water' whitewater rafting. There is dramatic bush growth because of the rains, African ebony trees come into fruit, and it is the waterbuck breeding season.

March Hot days and warm nights; the rainy season is coming to an end but river levels are still very high and the falls are pumping furiously. There are huge volumes of spray, making viewing of the falls from the ground difficult (raincoats, waterproof cameras, etc will be necessary) and aerial activities are the better option. Rafting often closes due to high water levels swallowing the rapids. Migrant birds start to depart; kudu and buffalo breeding peak; grasslands are in full seed; baobab trees start to fruit.

April End of the rainy season, but the water from the catchment area upstream in Zambia has arrived; the falls are at their highest flow with an average of 500 million litres of water falling per minute (the highest ever recorded was 700 million litres in 1958). Most animals are in peak condition at the end of the rainy season due to the volume of food available; impala, wildebeest and warthog are in their rutting season; final departure of migrant birds.

May This is the beginning of autumn; the days are warm to hot with a chill coming into the evening air. The Zambezi is flowing strongly despite the advent of the dry season; deciduous trees begin to lose their leaves. This is the best month for fishing in the Zambezi. White-backed vulture and wild dog breeding season.

June Autumn gives way to winter; warm to hot days, dry weather but chilly at night. The Zambezi River levels drop. Raptor courtship displays are more evident and game becomes more concentrated near water as the grass cover recedes.

July This is mid-winter and the height of the dry season, with no rain. Days are

organize an airport transfer at the same time. Another good source of information is the website www.gotovictoriafalls.com, a marketing initiative by a group of local businesses.

Safety

Despite its small size, Victoria Falls has a history of petty crime, such as snatch-and-grab incidents, late-night muggings, etc. The good news is that the reduction in tourism has caused crime to fall dramatically in the last decade or so. This is due mainly to the determination of residents employed in tourism (most of the town) to protect their industry and contain any hazards relating to visitor safety. Muggings are are now very rare, still warm, but cold spells occasionally creep in for a few days. Nights are very chilly, so bring something warm to wear. Elephants migrate to winter pastures; it's the raptor breeding season; and mopane leaves take on their distinctive winter hue of burnt orange.

August Dry, warm days and cool nights; sometimes windy, which signals a shift in the seasons. The Eastern Cataract on the Zambia side of the falls often becomes exposed due to the low water levels; the whitewater rafting 'low water' season begins (see page 182), lasting through to December. There's usually an increase in elephant population on the Zambian side of river, which is the winter feeding ground for elephant from northern Zimbabwe and Botswana.

September Spring brings a noticeable increase in temperatures; days are hot and nights are becoming warmer. There's excellent whitewater rafting as the water levels drop and the Grade III-V rapids are exposed. The first migrant birds arrive from Europe and elsewhere in Africa and weaver birds begin breeding; knob thorn acacia trees begin flowering.

October This is the hottest month of the year, sometimes called suicide month because of the heat, which is building up to the start of the rainy season; occasional storms take the edge off high temperatures. The Eastern Cataract of the falls in Zambia is usually dry, but

elsewhere the whitewater rafting is excellent. Breeding plumage appears in certain birds and there are heightened courtship displays; marula trees are in flower; and new mopane trees show leaf growth. This is probably the optimum time for sunsets, best seen on a river cruise.

November This is usually the start of the rainy season; days are very hot and nights are warm; the falls are at their lowest ahead of the upstream rainy season, and whitewater rafting is still excellent. The baobab trees are in flower, as are rainforest flowers such as blood lilies and white gardenia. Elephant begin to disperse from Zambia back to Zimbabwe and Chobe National Park in Botswana; it's impala calving season, and more migrant birds arrive. There's a dramatic increase in insect activity, including mosquitoes, which are prevalent throughout the rainy season until April.

December It is hot and humid as the rainy season works towards its peak, though it is cooler than October because of cloud cover. There can be several days of continuous rain. The falls are still quite low but levels are starting to rise with rains from the localized catchment area; the Eastern Cataract is still exposed, and whitewater rafting is still excellent. Dragonflies are at their most active in the rainforest and flame lily and other rainforest flowers are in bloom; it is the wildebeest breeding season.

as there is no longer very much nightlife in the town, and security at accommodation is top-notch. Nevertheless, the normal rules apply: don't flash your wealth or put temptation in the way of opportunist thieves, keep valuables concealed or in a hotel safe and don't wander around at night.

Throughout Zimbabwe's economic meltdown and the violent farm invasions of the 1990s Victoria Falls was viewed as its own entity and was largely spared from such trouble. It is also at the end of the long road from Bulawayo, and somewhat distant from the rest of Zimbabwe's problems.

There are many, many street vendors in the town, holding up one carved elephant or giraffe after another. Unfortunately for them, the dwindling number of tourists since Zimbabwe's collapse has drastically reduced the vendors' livelihoods and they are desperate to make a sale; they can be a bit of a nuisance, to the point of jumping out of the bush at unsuspecting tourists. The business community in Victoria Falls has set up and funded a task force of over 30 tourism police to keep the vendors in check and to assist with any other (rare) crime problem. They are affiliated to the regular police force but wear distinctive yellow bibs saying 'tourism police', are exceptionally friendly and will often walk with tourists. They work in pairs from 0900-1900.

Background

For a considerable distance above the Victoria Falls, the Zambezi River – the fourth-longest river in Africa at around 3540 km, and the largest river flowing into the Indian Ocean – flows over a level sheet of basalt rock in a shallow valley bounded by low and distant sandstone hills. The river's course is dotted with numerous tree-covered islands, which increase in number as the river approaches the falls. There are no mountains, escarpments, or deep valleys, which might be expected to create a great waterfall, and most visitors are surprised at seeing only a plateau extending hundreds of kilometres in all directions. However, Victoria Falls are one of the most spectacular waterfalls in the world. They dip dramatically and furiously from the flat savannah into the Batoka Gorge over 100 m below. This scenic tree-lined gorge is the floodgate to the seasonal river. The river then snakes its way along the gorge for about 120 km towards Lake Kariba on the border of Zimbabwe and Zambia. Just below the falls the river carries a torrent of whitewater over a series of rapids.

The first European to see the Victoria Falls was David Livingstone on 17 November 1855, during his 1852-1856 journey from the Upper Zambezi to the mouth of the river. The falls were well known to local tribes and the Matabele named them Mosi-au-Tunya, 'the smoke that thunders'. Early Arab slave traders and Voortrekkers from the south had reported them, but the Europeans were sceptical about these reports, perhaps because that the lack of mountains and valleys on the plateau made a large waterfall unlikely. Livingstone had been told about the falls before reaching them from upriver and being paddled across to a small island that now bears the name Livingstone Island. The explorer was very impressed and wrote of the falls, "No one can imagine the beauty of the view from anything witnessed in England. It had never been seen before by European eyes; but scenes so lovely must have been gazed upon by angels in their flight." He then renamed them in honour of Queen Victoria. Livingstone's fantastic stories about the falls attracted many European adventurers and travellers, and the town of Victoria Falls steadily expanded throughout the 20th century. The Victoria Falls Bridge (see box, page 167) was built in 1905.

Livingstone's discovery encouraged hunters, traders and missionaries, who were followed by prospectors for coal to Hwange in what is now northern Zimbabwe, and for copper into Northern Rhodesia (now Zambia), from about the 1890s. From the offset, the bridge attracted curio dealers selling locally crafted items to tourists. Percy Clark of Clark's Curios was allegedly the first entrepreneur in this field to set up shop when the bridge was built. Better accommodation, apart from the sleeping compartments on the train, was a priority, and work commenced in 1905 on a wood and corrugated-iron inn – now the celebrated and much-expanded, luxury **Victoria Falls Hotel**. Today the hotel retains

Victoria Falls Bridge

Before 1905, the Zambezi was crossed above the falls at the Old Drift by dugout canoe or a barge towed across with a steel cable. The bridge across the gorge was built in 1905 as part of Cecil Rhodes' ambitious but never realized Cape-to-Cairo railway (in fact, the railway ended up at the border with the Congo). At Victoria Falls, Rhodes insisted that the railway be built where spray from the falls would fall on passing trains, so the site at the Second Gorge was chosen. The Victoria Falls Bridge was designed by George Andrew Hobson, of the consultant engineering firm Sir Douglas Fox and Partners. A single-span steel arch was chosen as meeting all requirements for a double-track railway. The main arch of the bridge – 198 m long and 128 m high above the low-level water mark of the river – was joined on 1 April 1905 and officially opened on 12 September of that year. While the bridge had two railway lines it had no road in the early days; the few road vehicles that wanted to use it had to pay to be transported over the river by rail, or use the Old Drift upstream. In 1930 the bridge was widened to permit road traffic and one of the two rail tracks was removed. This modification involved widening the bridge by 4 m to carry the road and sidewalks. In 1975, during the Bush War, the bridge was the site of unsuccessful peace talks between the African National Congress and Ian Smith's Rhodesian government; the parties met in a train carriage poised above the gorge for 9½ hours. The centre of the bridge now marks the boundary between Zimbabwe and Zambia and is the site of the famous Victoria Falls bungee jump (see page 179).

its Edwardian architecture and atmosphere and has a decidedly colonial air; likewise the **Victoria Falls Railway Station**, built in 1904, with its pond and palm trees, still emits an air of bygone years.

Tourism boomed again in the 1960s, despite the political issues surrounding the Bush War. Further improvements were made to the town's infrastructure and Victoria Falls developed as a 'resort', with hotels and shopping centres sprouting up.

The falls

ⓘ *The main entrance to the falls is on Livingstone Way just a few metres before the immigration offices at the border, T013-42294, www.zimparks.com, US$20, children (6-12) US$10, children under 6 free, 0600-1800.*

The falls were formed during the Jurassic period some 150-200 million years ago, when lava erupted out of fissures in the earth and covered large parts of southern Africa. These dark basalt deposits are up to 300 m thick and formed the sides of the Bakota Gorge below the falls. As the lava cooled and solidified, cracks appeared in the basalt crust, mostly in an east-west direction, but these were joined by smaller north-south fissures. Reputedly, a lake formed over the area, and with time deposits of clay and lime filled the cracks in the basalt. Then the Zambezi, with its force of water, cut through the soft clay and lime, and formed a series of waterfalls.

The Victoria Falls comprises five separate falls. Four of these are in Zimbabwe (the Devil's Cataract, Main Falls, Rainbow Falls and Horseshoe Falls) and one, the Eastern Cataract, in Zambia. The **Devil's Cataract** is about 70 m deep and is derived from an adjacent island in the Zambezi River, a place said to have been the site of sacrificial ceremonies; with the arrival of missionaries, this practice was frowned upon and considered 'devilish', hence the name. **The Main Falls** are the most majestic part of the falls, with a wide curtain of water thundering 93 m into the gorge below; at peak high water levels the water flows at about 700,000 cu m per minute. This section throws out the spray that continually nourishes the evergreen rainforest around the area. **Horseshoe Falls** are named for their horseshoe shape and are around 95 m deep; they usually dry up at the height of the dry season between October and November. **Rainbow Falls**, named after a beautiful rainbow that can be seen from the viewpoint here, are 108 m high at this point, the deepest in the series; at full moon (when the park stays open late) a faint lunar rainbow can be seen. The **Eastern Cataract** falls are situated on the Zambian side but present a stunning spectacle from the Zimbabwean side. At 101 m deep they are the second-deepest falls of the series.

The area surrounding the falls is known as the rainforest, and is created by the perpetual spray. It's a beautiful forest of fig, mahogany and date palm trees; during the rainy season, the forest floor is coloured with scarlet lilies and wild yellow gladioli. The rainforest is home to more than 400 species of birds, including bulbuls, warblers, barbets and strikes; look out for the Livingstone's lourie, nectar-feeding sunbird and trumpeter

2 Victoria Falls

Victoria and Livingstone maps
1 Victoria Falls & Livingstone area, page 162
2 Livingstone, page 191
3 Victoria Falls, page 168

200 metres
200 yards

N

Sleeping
Kingdom at Victoria Falls 1
Shoestrings Backpackers 2
Victoria Falls 3
Victoria Falls Rest Camp & Lodges 4

Eating
Chicken Inn, Pizza Inn, Creamy Inn & Haefieis 1
Mama Africa 2

Bars & clubs
Hunter's Nite Club 3

hornbill. Butterflies are numerous too, floating through the mist and rainbows. Mammals in the forest include warthog, vervet monkey and baboon, also easily seen on the streets in town and even at the border post. Klipspringers and clawless otters can be glimpsed in the gorges, but these are mainly known for 35 species of raptor. The Taita falcon, black eagle, Peregrine falcon and Augur buzzard breed there. Above the falls, herons and fish eagles are common. The river is home to 39 species of fish below the falls and 89 species above it, mostly black cod and trout.

Paths, carefully blended with their surroundings, have been laid through the forest and lead to a total of 19 viewpoints poised at suitable intervals on the lip of the gorge. Collectively, they provide an uninterrupted collection of views of the falls from one end to the other. You'll need to have waterproof protection for cameras, etc; although you'll probably escape a soaking from the spray in the dry season, in the wet season bring a raincoat. The wettest viewpoints are those facing the Main Falls (see box, page 164, for details on the changing seasons).

From the park entrance the first viewpoint is over Devil's Cataract. Turn left from here, to the bronze **statue of David Livingstone**, beyond which the path leads off upstream. The inscription at the base of the statue quotes Livingstone's motto: 'Christianity, Commerce and Civilization'. To the right, the path leads through the rainforest to the viewpoints overlooking the other falls: Main, Horseshoe and Rainbow. Viewpoint No 7 provides the best view of the Main Falls, and from the right-hand corner of the viewing site it is possible to see the river at the bottom of the gorge. At the end of the walk is the dizzying **Danger Point**, the last part of the walk on the Zimbabwean side near the Victoria Falls Bridge, and so called because the viewpoint juts out on the cliff edge. From here, you can look across to the Eastern Cataract in Zambia and down the abyss at the **Boiling Pot** – a swirling eddy where two branches of the river collide. Reached via a steep footpath from the Zambian side, it is about 150 m across; while its surface is smooth at low water, at high water it is marked by enormous, slow swirls and heavy turbulence. From here, the river turns in a southeasterly direction and follows the Batoka Gorge on its switchback way over a series of rapids. In different eras the river has fallen into different chasms, which now form a series of sharply zig-zagging gorges downstream from the falls. To get a full perspective of the size and majesty of the falls, consider doing an aerial activity (see page 178), or the 'flight of angels', coined from David Livingstone's words.

Around the falls

The Big Tree
ⓘ *Follow either parkway or Zambezi Drive out of town for about 1 km.*

At 20 m high and 16 m in circumference, this baobab tree (*Adansonia digitata*) is thought to be about 1500-2000 years old and is simply known as The Big Tree. However, it is neither old nor big by baobab standards, and is only about one-third of its full size. It has some graffiti dating from the early 1900s. The baobab is capable of providing shelter, food and water for the animal and human inhabitants of the African savannah regions. The cork-like bark is fire-resistant and is used for textile and rope, and the leaves are used for condiments and medicines. The fruit, called 'monkey bread', is rich in vitamin C and eaten. Mature trees are often hollow, providing living space for animals and humans alike. Because of its root-like branches, a baobab is often referred to as the 'upside down' tree that the gods, in a frivolous mood, planted the wrong way up.

Victoria Falls Crocodile Park and Nature Reserve

ⓘ *3.6 km from town along Parkway towards the entrance to the Zambezi National Park, 0800-1700, feeding 1115 and 1545; US$5, children (under 12) US$2.50.*

This is a commercial crocodile farm that produces good-quality leather, as well as meat for the local restaurants. Visitors can walk around the attractive palm-lined enclosures on walkways and bridges to view the crocs in the various pools, and learn about them from the informative guides. You may even get the opportunity to hold a baby croc when the guides demonstrate how strong their jaws are, even at such a young age. In November and December you can organize trips to see the eggs hatching. Other animals present include monitor lizard, duiker and ostrich, and there is good birdlife in the trees. There's also a tea room and a very well-stocked shop selling croc leather products, including some well-designed and luxurious handbags and wallets. You can also visit the workshop and watch the items being made.

Zambezi National Park → *Colour map 1, C1.*

ⓘ *6 km along Parkway, T013-42294, www.zimparks.com, US$20, children (6-12) US$10, children under 6 free, 0600-1800.*

The Victoria Falls National Park and the Zambezi National Park are effectively two parks with two entrances, but they are jointly managed and together cover an area of 56,000 ha. The **Zambezi River Drive** starts at the Victoria Falls and ends 46 km upstream on the western boundary of the Zambezi National Park. This part of the park is formed by the Upper Zambezi River, which runs along the border between Zimbabwe and Zambia for much of its length. A wide variety of larger mammals may be found within the park, including the Big Five (elephant, lion, buffalo, leopard and white rhino), herds of sable antelope, eland, zebra, giraffe, kudu, waterbuck and impala, as well as many of the smaller species of game and in the river crocodile and hippo. The Zambezi is also home to a large variety of fish and is famous for its bream and fighting tigerfish. Zambezi River Drive has 25 picnic sites along the riverbank, with lovely shady riverine vegetation, where you can picnic or fish. There is some accommodation at the entrance to the park, but you will need a car to explore; an alternative way of seeing the park is to go on a river cruise (see page 180).

Elephant Park

ⓘ *9 km from town towards south Hwange and then 2.5 km from main road to the left (east), book through Wild Horizons (see page 184), pickups 0630 in summer, 0700 in winter, and 1530, elephant interaction only (including snacks) US90, elephant ride with breakfast US$110, and elephant ride with snacks in the evening US$150, no children under 10.*

Wild Horizons manages a concession area containing 20 elephant, including babies. Eighteen people can visit at any one time. Visitors arrive at the **Elephant's Wallow**, a restaurant and viewing deck overlooking a small dam and the place where the elephants are mounted. The excursion departs Victoria Falls in the early morning or late afternoon, as the elephants spend the middle of the day grazing in the bush. They are brought in from the bush by the handlers, and after a presentation detailing their habits and history guests can enjoy the opportunity to interact with them, before walking up the ramp and climbing aboard. The 1½- to two-hour ride (two people plus the handler on each elephant) goes to the gorge above Rapid 9, where you can dismount to enjoy the views of the gorge before the return ride. The whole excursion lasts about three hours before the transfer back to Victoria Falls.

Chobe National Park

A visit to Victoria Falls is almost always teamed with at least a day trip to the 10,566-sq-km Chobe National Park in the far corner of northwestern Botswana. It is just over the border and (including the border crossing) is only a little over an hour's drive from Victoria Falls. The park is divided into four distinctly different ecosystems: **Serondela** with its lush plains and dense forests on the Chobe River area in the extreme northeast; the **Savuti Marsh** in the west, about 50 km north of Mababe gate; the **Linyanti Swamps** in the northwest; and the hot dry hinterland in between. The normal drill on a day trip is to go to one of the lodges, usually the Chobe Safari Lodge, in Kasane, a springboard for the park, and from there enter the park on a morning game drive, followed by lunch, and then an afternoon river

cruise on the Chobe River, which joins the Zambezi just a short distance away at Kazungula. This area of the park is the Serondela section but is also known as the Chobe Riverfront and features dense teak forests and grassy plains. It is a prime region for game-watching, especially as the river attracts animals to drink. Like Hwange National Park (see page 204), Chobe is best known for its spectacular elephant population: the estimated 80,000 elephant, some of which migrate between Chobe and Hwange, are considered to be the largest concentration of elephant in Africa. Also present are giraffe, zebra, impala, tsessebe, roan, sable, wildebeest, kudu, buffalo, waterbuck, warthog and eland, and accompanying predators include lion, hyena, jackal, bat-eared fox, cheetah and wild dog.

The Lion Encounter

ⓘ *The booking office is on Livingstone Way, T013-40178, www.lionencounter.com, 0600-1900; the excursion operates in the Masuwe River Concession, a 10-min drive from Victoria Falls, departures from town are at 0630,1000,1345 and 1530, US$110, no children under the age of 15 or shorter than 1.5 m.*

The four juvenile lions here have come from Antelope Park (see page 86) near Gweru, where you can also walk with captive-bred lions. The lions that are used for the walk are generally around 14 to 17 months old, as at 18 months they are fully grown and, being too big and boisterous for the walk, are returned to Antelope Park. The three-hour excursion includes transfers from accommodation in Victoria Falls, plus a full English breakfast on the morning walk and snacks, soft drinks and beers in the afternoon. You need to wear long trousers as the lions rub up against visitors. A maximum of 10 people per two lions walk through the bush for about 1½ hours, presenting a great opportunity to get close up and watch them play with each other. Each lion is under the charge of a handler and the trips are lead by an armed guide, who also carries a first-aid kit and hand-held radio. The guide will provide information about the lions and the environment in general. On the way back to town, there is a stop at **Masuwe Lodge** where you can view, and buy if you wish, a DVD of your walk.

For Sleeping and Eating price codes and other relevant information, see pages 29-34.

● Sleeping

Victoria Falls *p160, maps p162 and p168*

Victoria Falls has accommodation to suit all budgets. At the top of the range is the historical **Victoria Falls Hotel** and the acclaimed **Victoria Falls Safari Lodge**, which are super luxurious in sublime settings. But there is also an excellent range of budget accommodation for the backpacker arriving off the train, and self-drive overlanders cannot go far wrong with the rest camp. Although it's always a good idea to book in advance, there should be no problem in finding accommodation to suit your budget on arrival.

L Elephant Camp, 9 km from Victoria Falls and then 2.5 km to the left from main road, book through Wild Horizons (see page 184), www.wildhorizons.com. This is a new camp with 9 very large 50-sq-m luxury tents set in the concession where Wild Horizons organize elephant riding, with views over the bush to the spray of the falls. Each tent has a private pool, outside shower, lavish bathroom, lounge, colonial decor, white drapery from the ceiling, and the central area is in a massive tent with deck, restaurant and bar, all looking down on the area where the elephants graze, so sightings are guaranteed.

L Imbabala Zambezi Safari Lodge, 72 km from Victoria Falls on the Kazungula road (to the Botswana border), in a private concession area on the Zambezi River; access by prearranged transfer, book through Wild Horizons (see page 184), www.wildhorizons.com. This 8-room luxury lodge is situated on a 14-km riverine fringe of the Zambezi shaded by ebony trees, on the spot where Zimbabwe, Botswana, Zambia and Namibia converge. Excellent wildlife-viewing including extensive herds

of elephant. Accommodation in well-appointed individually decorated thatched suites overlooking the river; pool, sundeck, restaurant and cocktail and pool bars, plus lounge with fireplace and wildlife reference library. Guided game activities by vehicle, on foot and by boat. No children under 12.

L Stanley & Livingstone, reservations through Rani Resorts, Johannesburg, T+27(0)83-6313888, www.stanleyand livingstone.com. This small, extravagant and exclusive hotel is in a private wildlife park about 13 km out of town, with 16 lavish suites in thatched buildings on landscaped gardens under large shady trees with ponds, lawns and a pool. There's a restaurant and bar with wine cellar; decor is in grand colonial style with antique furniture and rich upholstery.

A Masuwe Safari Lodge, 8 km from town off the Bulawayo road, T013-44510, www. safpar.com/masuwe. Set in a private 405-ha (1000-acre) concession adjacent to the Zambezi National Park. Run by Saf Par, with 10 large, en suite safari tents, which are elevated on wooden decks. The thatched main area houses a bar, dining and lounge areas and overlooks an active waterhole. There's also a pool. Rates are either B&B or full board.

A Victoria Falls Safari Lodge, off Parkway, 2.5 km from town, T013-43211-20, www. victoria-falls-safari-lodge.com. Impressive 5-star lodge in a superbly designed thatched structure that resembles an opulent open-plan tree house overlooking a busy waterhole. Quality African decor, mosaic-tiled walls and floors, stunning stone-rimmed pool and deck, excellent restaurants (see Eating), sumptuous rooms and all with tremendous views.

A-B The Victoria Falls Hotel, 2 Mallet Dr, reservations T031-44751, www.zimsun. co.zw. The grand old lady of the falls built in 1905 with 160 rooms including 5 honeymoon suites, a marble-floored reception, manicured gardens from where you can see the bridge and mist. Beautifully furnished in colonial style with antiques, old prints, sweeping drapes, 4-poster beds and Victorian bathtubs. Facilities include a/c, DSTV, restaurants, **Stanley's Bar**, pool, tennis courts and beauty spa.

B A'Zambezi River Lodge, 308 Parkway, 5 km from town next to the entrance to the Zambezi National Park, T031-44561, www. azambeziriverlodge.com. The only hotel with a river frontage, designed in a wide thatched arc. The majority of the 83 a/c rooms face the river or swimming pool, while the rest face the national park and all have DSTV and tea and coffee stations. Facilities include restaurants, bars and a boat for sunset cruises.

B Elephant Hills Hotel, 3 km from town off Parkway, T031-44793, www.africansun hotels.com. Some may argue that this massive 289-bedroomed 5-star hotel should never have been built in a prime piece of bush overlooking the Zambezi, but there's no arguing that the service and facilities are top-notch, with a championship golf course (see page 178), tennis courts, gym, spa, 3 restaurants, several bars, casino, 3-tiered pool and curio shops. Decor in the public areas has a pleasing African mosaic theme with floor-to-ceiling windows to take in the jaw-dropping views.

B Gorges Lodge, 9 km towards the airport and then 10 km down a signposted dirt road to the right, T09-245051, www.gorgeslodge. co.zw. Just 10 single- or double-storey stone and thatch chalets with wide verandas, fans and fridges. You can't beat the dramatic location of this lodge as it's perched right on the lip of the Batoka Gorge with incredible views (it may not be suitable for those with a fear of heights as the bar literally curls over the lip of the rock face), and there's a restaurant and pool. Ideal for birdwatchers, who can view the raptors riding on the thermals above the gorge. Complimentary shuttle service to and from town.

B Ilala Lodge, 411 Livingstone Way, T013-44737, www.ilalalodge.com.

A long-established quality hotel on the edge of the Victoria Falls National Park, this is an attractive whitewashed and thatched building with 34 spacious and elegant a/c rooms with all mod cons, patios or balconies looking out into the bush where elephant and other wildlife are regularly seen. It has a superb restaurant, **The Palms** (see Eating, page 175), cocktail bar, and attractive pool and sunbathing deck. It also runs its own game-watching/sundowner boat on the river.

B-C Lokuthula Lodges (pronounced 'Lock-oo-too-la'), off Parkway, 2.5 km from town, T013-44717, www.lokuthulalodges.com. This is a timeshare self-catering resort, so you'll need to book at least 3 months in advance. On the same property as the Victoria Falls Safari Lodge, it has 11 3-bed and 26 2-bed thatched self-catering units with fully equipped kitchens, bright decor with African touches, braais and pool. Breakfast is included. Good for groups as the units sleep up to 8 people. Handy for **The Boma Place of Eating** restaurant (see page 175).

C The Kingdom at Victoria Falls, 1 Mallet Drive, T013-44275, www.africansunhotels. com. This was built in the late 1980s as a full-blown African-theme hotel with a nod at the ancient kingdoms of Zimbabwe. There is impressive, if over-the-top, architecture of domes, pillars and bridges over many water features, and African tribal decor. The 294 a/c rooms have standard made-for-hotel furnishings but most have good views of the hotel's man-made lake and waterfalls. The central dome is dominated by a (now-deserted) casino, bar, a couple of chain restaurants (see Eating, page 176) and some gift shops.

C Sprayview Hotel, corner of Livingstone Way and Reynard Rd, T031-44344. An old-fashioned but inexpensive hotel with 64 motel-style rooms in single-storey blocks in extensive grounds, with fans and a/c, coffee-making facilities, large pool, restaurant with poolside tables, and 2 bars, which are popular with the expat community.

C Victoria Falls Rainbow Hotel, 278 Parkway, T013-44583, www.rtg.co.zw. Opened in 1972, this has 88 a/c rooms, but ask for a room in the new wing that opened in 2009, as they are superior, with king-sized beds, DSTV, Wi-Fi, tea and coffee stations, terracotta tiled floors, balconies or patios, and are a very good standard for a 3-star hotel. There is also a restaurant, bar and pool with swim-up bar, and if you climb on the roof there are great views of the spray over the falls and Livingstone beyond.

C-D Victoria Falls Rest Camp & Lodges, entrance on Parkway opposite West Drive, T013-40509, www.vicfallsrestcamp.com. A few years ago this was taken over from the municipality by Ilala Lodge and completely revamped and now is an excellent and secure budget option in the very centre of town. There are over 40 units ranging from double permanent tents and 2- to 3-bed chalets using shared bathrooms (from US$30-70), self-catering en suite units sleeping 2-6 (US$90-180), plus same-sex dorms (US$11) and camping (F/US$10). There's broadband internet at reception (or Wi-Fi vouchers can be bought), a pool, and the In-dabele Restaurant (see Eating, page 176). Rather delightfully the campsite dog is called Camp, and when it's hot, he walks across the road and lies in the doorway of the a/c Backpackers' Bazaar.

D Pamusha Lodge, 583 Manyika Rd, T013-41828, www.pamusha.com. Set in a peaceful suburb, this B&B has 17 a/c rooms, including good-sized triples and family rooms, with DSTV, fans and tiled floors, in an established garden full of teak trees. There's a pool and thatched open *lapa* (entertainment area) with braai. Evening meals on request. There's also has a 5-bed self-catering house to rent with maid, and a cook can be arranged.

D Zambezi National Park Lodges, 6 km along Parkway, close to entrance to the Zambezi National Park, T013-42294, www.zimparks.com. Typical park rest camp with 2-bed self-catering brick chalets with fridge and stove. There are also 3 exclusive fishing camps (F) in the park on the banks of the Zambezi, which have a flush toilet, cold shower, running water, cement table and braai. There are also 4 minimum development **camping sites (F)** available. Situated on the banks of the Zambezi, these areas are unfenced and equipped with a braai stand and bush toilet only. **Chundu 1** (25 km upstream from the reception office) and **Chundu 2** (26 km) are situated in an acacia forest close to the river's edge. **Chomuzi** (40 km) is sited near some rapids and **Siamunungu** (47 km) is located at the end of the Zambezi River Drive (the name of the main road through the park), on a particularly lovely stretch of the river. Each camp can accommodate a maximum of 12 people.

D-E Amadeus Garden, 538 Reynard Rd, T013-42261, www.amadeusgarden.com. Pleasant and friendly owner-run guest lodge with 11 en suite rooms, with fans and Wi-Fi, thatched gazebo in the tropical garden, and pool with sun loungers. Rates are for B&B and other light meals are available.

E Halfway House Hotel, 240 km from Bulawayo and 200 km before Victoria Falls, T089-355. Just about the only stop on the drive between Bulawayo and Victoria Falls. 21 simply furnished but adequate en suite rooms in thatched rondavels in manicured gardens. Has a bar with TV and restaurant that also caters to passing motorists. The BP petrol station next door is open 24 hrs.

E Victoria Falls Backpackers, T031-42209, www.victoriafallsbackpackers.com. A large number of beds in cramped dorms and small rooms with or without bathrooms, but set in lovely tropical gardens. Has a laid-back backpackers' atmosphere with a games room, TV lounge, giant outdoor chess set, beautician for massages, self-catering kitchen under thatch, pool, internet and friendly staff. Toast, tea and coffee included and all meals are available on request.

E-F Savanna Lodge Backpackers, 68 Courteney Selous Crescent, T013-40167, www.safpar.com/savanna. A well-run spot owned by Saf Par, with exceptionally cheerful staff in bright orange uniforms,

11 rooms with shared bathrooms, dorms and a big lawn for camping. Lively bar and restaurant on a wooden deck with big screen for watching rafting videos; tents in the garden sell curios or offer massages, and there's a pool.

E-F Shoestrings Backpackers,12 West Drive, T013-40167, 42207, www.zimtravel agent.com. A lively place with a bar and restaurant, with DSTV for watching sports, kitchen for self-catering, internet facilities and pool. Camping, dorms and en suite double/twins; pay a little more for a/c. Owner Mags, who also runs Backpackers' Bazaar, can arrange all activities. A good place to meet other travellers.

E-F Tokkie Lodge, 224 Reynard Way, T/F013-43306, reservations@tokkielodge. co.zw. Backpacker set-up in a quiet suburb, a 3-km walk or taxi ride from town, with 12 simple rooms and 2 dorms with bedding, towels and fans, camping (US$5), shared bathrooms, DSTV lounge, honesty bar, self-catering kitchen, and pool. Good place for overlanders as Rob is an ex-overland truck driver and can advise on permits, carnets and mechanics.

🍴 Eating

Victoria Falls *p160, maps p162 and p168*
Unfortunately there are few individual cafés and restaurants open anymore (even the Wimpy has closed down), so for quality eating the hotels are the best bet. For cheap eats, try the bakery counters at **Spar** and **TM** supermarkets which sell passable, though not very healthy, fried chicken, pies, sugary cakes and biscuits. **Chicken Inn**, **Pizza Inn**, **Creamy Inn** and **Haefieis**, a kind of Swiss bakery, are on Parkway.

🍴🍴🍴 **Amulonga**, the A'Zambezi River Lodge, see Sleeping, T031-44561, www.azambezi riverlodge.com, T0700-2200. Well-located restaurant on the banks of the Zambezi, with an atmospheric fire-pit, offering passable buffet dinners. Although the soups and salads are uninventive, the

crocodile tail and vegetables are well prepared and presented. The highlight is the local group of dancers and traditional singers who are energetic and very entertaining.

🍴🍴🍴 **The Boma Place of Eating**, the Victoria Falls Safari Lodge complex, see Sleeping, T013-43238, www.thebomarestaurant.com. Open 1900-2200. Unashamedly touristy but a must-do in Vic Falls, this impressive, partially open thatched boma has a great African atmosphere with dancing, singing and a fortune teller. It offers a superb nightly buffet of traditional Zimbabwean dishes such as fried kapenta fish and mopani worms, a variety of game meat and *potjies* (stews), though there's plenty for less adventurous tastes, including spit-roasts, stir-fries, various vegetarian dishes and decadent desserts. Go with an empty stomach and enjoy the delightful extras such as the enamel cup of traditional beer, dancing with the drummers, or the certificate if you manage to eat a worm.

🍴🍴🍴 **Makuwa-Kuwa**, at the **Victoria Falls Safari Lodge** (see Sleeping), T013-43211-20, www.victoria-falls-safari-lodge.com. Open 0700-2200. Expensive 5-star eating in a special location on a thatched terrace with African decor, serving gourmet breakfasts like haddock, spinach and poached eggs or pepper and salami frittata, deli platters or ostrich fillets for lunch, and sole with prawns or crocodile curry for dinner. There is also a small but thoughtful choice for vegetarians. Don't miss the Amarula and baobab fruit dessert. Its name means 'Royal Drum'. Booking is essential to get a table on the edge of the deck for unparalleled views of the **Victoria Safari Lodge**'s floodlit waterhole. A cappella performers entertain in the evening, and diners can retire to sofas in the bar for a nightcap.

🍴🍴🍴 **Palm Restaurant**, at the Ilala Lodge, see Sleeping, T013-44737-9, www.ilalalodge. com. Open 0700-2200. Pleasant candlelit terrace setting with bush views at this quality hotel, serving a light lunch menu of poultry and meat dishes, gourmet sandwiches and inventive salads, and more ambitious dishes for dinner such as Moroccan beef kebabs or warthog fillet. Excellent service and a comprehensive wine list.

¶¶¶ The Victoria Falls Hotel, see Sleeping, T031-44751, www.zimsun.co.zw. Open 0700-2200. There are a number of dining rooms at this historical hotel; the **Livingstone Room** is well known for its silverware, crystal and starched white linen, the **Jungle Junction** has a more African slant, while **Stanley's Terrace** is the place to go for afternoon tea (1500-1700) – think 3-tiered silver platters with cucumber sandwiches and fancy cakes, with a choice of tea and overlooking the spray of the falls (most definitely a Vic Falls must-do, and for a not unreasonable US$12).

¶¶ In-dabele (see Sleeping), **Victoria Falls Rest Camp & Lodges**, T013-42749. Open 0700-2130; the bar often stays open later. This popular restaurant is towards the bottom end of the Rest Camp overlooking the swimming pool, with a thatched open-air terrace, comfy wicker chairs with cushions, a pool table, and a good casual menu. They are best known for their tilapia fish and chips and crocodile nuggets but also do good breakfasts, home-made burgers, steak, egg and chips and vegetarian pasta.

¶¶ The Kingdom at Victoria Falls, see Sleeping, T013-44275, www.africansun hotels.com. Various opening hours but all open daily for lunch and dinner and the **Whitewaters** restaurant is additionally open for breakfast. There are 3 restaurants here: the **Whitewaters** is the regular hotel restaurant with a large open room and towering ceilings and domes surrounded by striking water features. The **Thundercloud Spur** and **Panarroti's** are South African franchise chain restaurants located on the edge of the hotel's casino; the first is a steak chain, the second an Italian chain. Menus are predictable but reliable, and it is inexpensive and child-friendly. Diners can choose from either menu regardless of which restaurant they are sitting in.

¶¶ Mama Africa, Landela Complex, Livingstone Way, T013-41725. Open 1000-2200. With a colourful African themed decor, and pleasant outside terrace, this offers traditional African meals such as ostrich steaks and crocodile tail, or meat and peanut stew, *sadza* and beef, or more conventional dishes like rump steak and pork chops. Specials are chalked up on the blackboard. Very friendly staff who can talk you through the menu.

Cafés

River Cafe, Landela Complex, Livingstone Way, T013-42994. Open 0800-1800. Simple café in the small shopping mall, serving instant coffee, toasted sandwiches, burgers and filled pancakes. There are also a few curio shops nearby and on occasion a wildlife artist sits nearby while he works.

⊕ Bars and clubs

Victoria Falls *p160, maps p162 and p168*
A few years ago nightlife in Victoria Falls was pumping. There were a number of lively spots and tourists, overlanders from the rest camp, and 'river gods' (rafting guides) would party hard. Sadly no more, as all closed in the recent economic lean years. The few choices that remain are limited to the restaurants and hotel bars, so don't expect much more than a quiet nightcap. The **Kingdom** at **Victoria** hotels offers a pretty much deserted casino with bar, while the **In-dabele** at **Victoria Falls Rest Camp & Lodges** stays open fairly late, has a well-stocked bar and pool table and still attracts campers and overlanders. Anyone wanting to party with other budget travellers should head to the bar at **Shoestrings Backpackers**, which can get fairly lively. For sharing a Black Label beer with the locals, you could try **Hunter's Nite Club** on Parkway, opposite the rest camp; but it's not a nightclub, just a pretty seedy bar, as attested to by the iron bars around the terrace.

⊕ Entertainment

Victoria Falls *p160, maps p162 and p168*
There used to be traditional dancing at
a venue in the Falls Craft Village, but this
is presently closed. An evening at **The
Boma Place of Eating**, see Eating, is now
the only place to see traditional dancing
and drumming.

⊙ Shopping

Victoria Falls *p160, maps p162 and p168*
Books
Vic Falls Bookshop, on Parkway next to the
Wild Horizon office. Mon-Sat 0800-1700.
This tiny shop is a pretty sad affair with just
a few shelves of curled up text books and
a rack of faded postcards. For coffee-table
books on Zimbabwe (they do exist and are
readily available in South Africa), try the
Shearwater office or the gift shops in the
upmarket hotels.

Crafts and curios
The **Falls Craft Village** is off Livingstone Way
behind the post office (0800-1800). There's
a line of curio shops here and an outdoor
market where many craftspeople exhibit
and sell their wooden carvings, soapstone
sculptures, baskets, crocheted items, batiks,
etc. Prices are mostly negotiable, especially
in the outside section. The most notable
shops include **Jairos Jiri**, which sells crafts
made by the disabled and blind (there's
another branch in Bulawayo), and **Sopers
Curios**, which rather astonishingly opened
in 1911. Also here is the **Elephant's Walk**
mall, with more upmarket curio shops
and a café, and to the right of Elephant's
Walk another outdoor craft market known
as **Sinathankawu Open Curio Market**,
established in 1999, which takes school
leavers and teaches them how to produce
curios. When buying these items, always
inspect them carefully for flaws – cracks
in a wooden carving, for example. **Fedex**
is in the Falls Craft Village, while **DHL** is in

Elephant's Walk for international shipping
(see Directory for details). Wrapping of items
can be done at **Impressions of Africa** next to
the post office (see Directory, below).
Ammonite, Elephant's Walk, T0912-369998.
Mon-Sat 0900-1800, Sun 0900-1700. The
most stylish luxury shop in Victoria Falls,
selling hand-chosen and one-off pieces by
local Zimbabwe designers, including hand-
crafted silver, crystal and gemstone jewellery,
porcelain, some clothes and sumptuous
leather bags. All beautifully presented.
Impressions of Southern Africa, next to
the post office on Livingstone Way, T013-
43567. Open 0800-1900. Small shop with
affable staff and quality Shona soapstone
sculptures. Offers a wrapping service for
other souvenirs to send from the post office
next door. They wrap them in cardboard,
string (as required by the post office),
plus a tape or string handle. Expect to pay
around US$5 for wrapping a wood carving
measuring about 50 cm, and US$15 for a
1-m wooden carving of a giraffe. See Post
office in Directory, below, for information
about posting these items.
Prime Art Gallery, Elephant's Walk
Shopping Village, T013-42783. Open
0900-1700. Top-quality gallery selling vivid
paintings and Shona stone sculptures by
acclaimed Zimbabwean artist Dominic
Benhura, who also exhibits internationally.
Can arrange air and sea shipping.
Savanna Wood, 452 Miles Rd, T013-40239,
www.savannawood.co.zw. Mon-Fri 0800-
1630. Hardly souvenirs to take home though
they do produce some excellent furniture
made from Zambezi teak and old teak
railway sleepers.

Supermarkets
There are 2 fairly large supermarkets in
town: the **Spar** is behind Parkway; follow
the arcade next to the Adventure Zone
office, and the **TM Supermarket** is towards
the industrial area behind the Landela
Complex. Both are fairly well stocked and are
open Mon-Fri 0830-1730 and Sat-Sun 0830-

1330. However, don't become complacent about prices: a packet of crisps or a local-brand beer may be inexpensive, but a can of imported tuna may be exorbitant.

▲▲ Activities and tours

Victoria Falls *p160, maps p162 and p168*
All activities and tours can be booked at any of the tour operators (see below); most include transfers. By booking combinations of activities you can get discounts of up to 30%. For example, a sunset cruise and 2 activities could cost in the region of US$225, or 3 main activities about US$275.

Bungee jumping
See box, page 179.

Canoeing
US$120, full day, US$95 half day, breakfast/sundowner US$60. This is a great way to get a handle on the Upper Zambezi and is a tranquil way to game-view and birdwatch around the islands above the falls. Inflatable 2-man canoes are used and the full-day trail begins about 25 km upstream with a continental breakfast. About 18 km is spent canoeing, with a stop on an island for a picnic lunch. There's also a shorter half-day trip (mornings only), also with breakfast, when you paddle for about 12 km, and a short 3-hr breakfast cruise (with breakfast) or sundowner cruise (with drinks and snacks), which use 3-man fibreglass canoes and take on an additional guide to paddle for you. Overnight and multi-day trips can also be arranged; these can be combined with walking safaris.

Golf
Elephant Hills Hotel, 3 km from town off Parkway, T031-44793, www.africansun hotels.com. An internationally recognized championship 18-hole, 6025-m, 72-par course, which was designed by Gary Player. Set in a truly natural environment, with regular sightings of warthog, impala and sable – all critically appraising your swing. The pro shop hires out clubs, and caddies (who know the course very well). A round for an international visitor will cost in the region of US$80 with a 25% discount for Elephant Hills guests, US$20 club hire, and about US$10 for a caddie. Fairly smart attire is expected. There is also a driving range.

Helicopter flights
12-13 mins US$120, 25 mins US$240 per person. There are daily flights over the Victoria Falls, and the helicopter seating is designed so that all passengers have a good view on the falls and the scenery below. It's a fantastic way to appreciate the majesty and power of the falls. Flights operate all day and have a capacity for 5 passengers.

Hire-wire adrenalin activities
Abseiling is descending backwards down the gorge and lowering yourself all the way to the bottom. With **rapp jumping** your harness is connected backwards so that you can run or walk down the cliff facing down into the gorge. The **flying fox** involves sliding 200 m across the gorge on a cable, while the **zip line** is similar but longer at 425 m and faster at up to 105 kph (it is considered to be the longest zip line in the world). The **gorge swing** drops 70 m into the gorge and is different from the bungee jump as it swings out rather than up and down like the bungee does.

Access to the site set up by **Wild Horizons** is just to the right before the border. There are a number or ropes and pullies strung across the gorge, offering exciting aerial activities, including a 120-m abseil/rapp jump (US$80), flying fox (US$30), zip line (also called a foofie slide, US$55), and 70-m gorge swing (US$70), tandem (US$105). They'll accept children from 8-10 but they need to be able to fit in the harnesses. From the site there are good views of the Victoria Falls Bridge and Victoria Falls Hotel.

5-4-3-2-1... Bungee!

Bungee jumping operates off the middle of the **Victoria Falls Bridge**. Book through Shearwater (page 183) or any of the operators or just turn up (0900-1700, Mar-Jun 1000-1700), US$115 single jump, US$155 tandem jump, DVDs US$35, photos US$15, minimum age 14 years, minimum weight 40 kg, maximum weight of 140 kg. Passports are required by jumpers and spectators to access the bridge; you must notify passport control at immigration that you are only going to the 'bungee' and they will give you a gate pass. This does not entitle you to enter the country on the opposite side of the falls.

Bungee jumping off the Victoria Falls Bridge has to be one of the most challenging, terrifying and crazy things to do, but to date over 50,000 people have done it and there is a 100% safety record. Some say that this is the best bungee in the world. At 111 m, it's not the highest anymore (that now goes to Bloukrans Bridge in South Africa, which is an incredible 233 m high), but the backdrop of the Victoria Falls – you can sometimes feel the spray – or maybe just the fact that you are free-falling down towards the mighty Zambezi make it a unique experience. Standing on the lip of the bungee platform, looking out into the gorge and the swirling rapids below, is a massive adrenalin rush.

Once on the bridge, the registration area is on the right, on the Zambian side of the river. Here, jumpers pay, or present their vouchers if they have pre-paid, sign an indemnity form, and are weighed, their weight and jumper number being recorded on their hands with a marker pen. The bungee operators adjust the bungee cords according to weight. At any point, the jumper can change his or her mind, even when on the bungee platform;

however, no money is refundable after registration. No special clothing is required, though jumpers are advised to remove jewellery and accessories and it is absolutely essential to take a friend with you to hold your passport.

After registration you go back to the bungee platform in the middle of the bridge where you get strapped up. There are two components to the ankle harness: padding to protect the ankles and webbing, which is bound around the padding to secure your feet firmly together. The knot in the webbing is a self-loading knot that cannot possibly come undone during the jump. Your feet are then attached to the bungee cord and you are hooked up to a waist harness, with a separate attachment to the bungee cord as a back-up; this is also used to pull the jumper back up to the bridge. After shuffling forward on the platform, it's 5-4-3-2-1... Bungee! The bridge falls away, the Zambezi rapids rush towards you, the walls of the gorge bounce around your peripheral vision, and for a few exhilarating seconds you are flying through nothing until the tug of the bungee cord signals your attachment with the bridge again. Then, the cord takes the jumper on a series of giant bounces around the Batoka Gorge and the bridge comes flying back at you. When it's over and the cord grows reasonably still, you are hanging upside down over the Zambezi (with perhaps an eye out for crocodiles) until someone comes down and winches you back up to the bridge.

Digital photos and DVDs are taken throughout the whole process and can be viewed within 10 minutes of your jump. You can buy a T-shirt to prove that you've been there and done it.

Whiterafting, river-boarding and kayaking

Running the rapids below the Batoka Gorge is said to be the wildest one-day whitewater experience in the world, and the Zambezi River is also recognized by rafting and kayaking enthusiasts as one of the top 10 paddling rivers on the planet. It has been classified by the British Canoe Union as Grade V – 'extremely difficult, long and violent rapids, steep gradients, big drops and pressure areas'. They were first run in 1981, and now some 50,000 people go down each year. This is a high-volume, pool-drop river with little exposed rock either in the rapids or in the pools below the rapids. River conditions are determined by seasonally predictable fluctuations in water levels (see box, page 182). Due to the steepness of the gorge, wildlife is not abundant, but an occasional baboon, vervet monkey or klipspringer may be spotted and there are crocodile in the river. This is not as alarming as it may sound, as they are only small, due to the unsuitability of the river as a habitat (and they don't live in the fast-flowing rapids themselves but along the long quiet pools between the rapids). The birdlife is far more impressive, especially raptors: Taita falcon, black eagle and angur buzzard can be seen on the cliffs.

You'll need to wear shorts (preferably waterproof), swimwear, T-shirt, and sturdy waterproof shoes such as velcro-fastening sandals or trainers (no flip-flops; remember there is a 750-m climb out of the gorge at the end), sunglasses with a strap, and hat or cap (but you may lose this if you fall out). Each raft carries a dry-bag for spare dry T-shirts and sunscreen.

There are various options on the river; the most popular are the one-day trips: (U$120; or shorter half-day trips for US$95), which you can book with one of the tour operators just a day beforehand. The longer trips need more notice. Which rapids the trips start at and finish from depend on the season (see box, page 182). The one-day trip includes transfers from your accommodation and a light breakfast at the top of the gorge and

Horse trails

Run by **Zambezi Horse Trails**, these operate at the top of the gorge and along the Zambezi. They are a good way to get close to the wildlife such as bushbuck and duiker and, on the longer rides, elephant and buffalo. There are a number of options including a 2-hr novice ride (US$65), a 4-hr experienced ride (US$90) and a 6-hr experienced ride (US$120). Well-schooled horses are chosen for both novices and experienced riders.

River cruises

A gentle way to explore the Upper Zambezi is on a river cruise. There are a number of pontoon-style boats on the river and the normal routine is to float around one or more of the islands and along the shore of the Zambezi National Park. There are excellent opportunities to see game as they come down to drink and even elephant have been seen swimming across the river. A guide on the boats points out animals and answers questions about them. The most popular is the 3-hr sunset cruise (US$35, including snacks and drinks), and although this is often referred to as the 'booze cruise' they don't all get rowdy. The breakfast and lunchtime cruises are US$45 and include drinks and more substantial meals.

Safaris

Chobe National Park The popular day trip over the border to Chobe National Park (see box, page 171) departs from Victoria Falls at around 0730, then crosses the border at Kazungula 73 km away to Kasane. It includes a safety briefing, before the very steep climb down the 100-m gorge to the inflatable rafts, and then lunch later in the day on one of the islands or small beaches. Most people go on a highsider raft, steered by an oarsman in the middle and enabling the rafters just to hang on to the side, shift their body weight when required and occasionally fall out, though there is also the option of a paddle raft where the rafters sit on the side and paddle while the guide steers from the back. The latter are less likely to flip than a highsider, as there are more paddlers, but there is a much higher chance of falling out as you are perched precariously on the edge. Digital photos, DVDs and, of course, T-shirts are available to buy after the excursion.

The overnight trip (US$190) involves the same kind of thing: clients on the high water one-day trip are pulled out at Rapid 23 but spend the night at the top of a gorge in a campsite before returning to Victoria Falls the next morning.

Rates include tents, bedrolls, sleeping bags, dinner, breakfast and soft drinks. Alcoholic drinks can be pre-organized prior to departure. The two-day/two-night trip (US$460; available during low water only) is similar but with another 56 km of rafting on the second day and a second night at a campsite at the top of the gorge.

River boarding (US$140) is combined with whitewater rafting on the one-day trip. Introduced on the river in 1996, it involves surfing the rapids on a body board, which you are attached to by a wrist band, with a guide; basic skills are taught at the beginning. Enthusiastic boarders can stop at play spots along the way to surf, ride whirlies and 'squirt' (best described as flying underwater). You'll need to be reasonably fit to do this. Kayaking (US$160) also runs with the one-day whitewater rafting trip; Topolino Duo Kayaks are used with a guide. For more information on any these activities, contact the operators on page 181.

a 2½-hr game drive in the morning, lunch at a lodge and a 2½-hr game cruise in the afternoon for US$170. Very few nationalities need visas for Botswana. However, remember if you don't have a double-entry visa back into Zimbabwe, you'll have to get another one on return. Trips usually arrive back in Victoria Falls at around 1700.
Hwange National Park Day trips to Hwange National Park (see page 204), US$150, depart Victoria Falls at 0630 and arrive back at around 1800, and include picnic breakfast and lunch, usually taken at one of the game-viewing platforms around the park. Overnight and multi-night trips can also be arranged from US$250. **Leon Varley Walking Safaris**, bookings through Backpackers Bazaar, Old Vic Falls Centre, T013-45828, 44611, www.walkafrica.com.

Personally guided walking safaris in Hwange and Chizarira National Parks, with renowned local guide Leon, who has been guiding for 25 years; his expertise and experience in the bush is unrivalled in Victoria Falls. On safari, you have a choice of either backpacking or a fully backed-up safari where you don't carry anything. Accommodation is in campsites with bush showers and toilets. Prices start from US$150 per day and are inclusive of transfers, parks fees, guide, food and drinks.

Tour operators
All the larger booking agents for activities and safaris are on and around Parkway and open daily 0800-1800. There are more around town and the hotels and backpacker hostels all offer a booking service for the same activities. Combos

The Zambezi's whitewater rapids

During low-water season, rapids Nos 1-18 are run for approximately 24 km. During high-water season, only rapids 11-23 are run, over approximately 28 km. For high adventure enthusiasts, whitewater rafting is most exciting when the Zambezi waters are low, generally from August to December. (Details of individual rapids have been provided by Safari Par Excellence/Adventure Zone, www.safpar. net, www.adventurezonevicfalls.com.)

Grade IV/V Against the Wall, No 1: The Boiling Pot, accessible only from the Zambian side, is the start of the low-water trip. From here the river hits a wall forming a wild cushion wave and eddy.

Grade III The Bridge, No 2: A wild mixture of waves best in the early part of the low-water season. Clearly visible to bungee jumpers and spectators on the Victoria Falls Bridge.

Grade IV Rapid No 3: A steep and radically fast wave with an easily avoidable hole. The second part of this rapid is best in the early part of the season, when it is a small wave train with an excellent pocket on the Zambian side.

Grade IV/V Morning Glory, No 4: The first major rapid offering varying lines with an almost river-wide hole at the top, followed by a few diagonals off the right-hand wall and finally a big hole at the bottom.

Grade V Stairway to Heaven, No 5: Best in the early part of the season, with an 8-m drop over 10 m; very steep and powerful with a heap of massive waves and holes. Although it isn't too technical, its size and volume make for an amazing spectacle and an even more amazing ride.

Grade IV Devil's Toilet Bowl, No 6: A short rapid with a deceptively steep and powerful hole on entry followed by some nasty boils and whirlpools.

Grade V Gulliver's Travels, No 7: A very respectful 700 m of high-volume whitewater at certain levels. This is the longest and most technical rapid on the one-day whitewater trip. The run consists of a main channel with smaller channels feeding into it. Includes the 'Temple of Doom', 'The Crease', 'Patella Gap' and 'Land of the Giants'.

Grade III/V Midnight Diner, No 8: This rapid has three runs. On the left is 'Star

for activities can be booked; these are often good value and may include a free sunset cruise on the river. There is little need to shop around, as rates are almost identical throughout the town; if one whitewater rafting company, for example, is offering the excursion for US$20 less than the competitors, it is worth asking where this saving has come from. It may be from insurance liability or poor wages for the staff, for instance. The Zimbabwe National Parks and Wildlife office (T013-422294/44566) is on Livingstone Way next to the police station, but it is erratically staffed and with inconsistent opening hours and telephone numbers. For accommodation in the chalets in the

Zambezi National Park, take a chance and go there direct.

There are a number of international tour operators (see page 46 for UK and South African contact details) which run tours of the region from Victoria Falls and Livingstone to Chobe and Hwange National Parks. These include **Acacia Africa** (Victoria Falls reservations T013-41164, www. acacia-africa.com), which run 5-day tours from Victoria Falls including transfers and accommodation: either a canoe safari or whitewater rafting and a day trip to Chobe (US$210 per day); or a 5-day package including a sunset cruise on the Zambezi and a day trip to Hwange and the Painted Dog Conservation Centre (US$115 per

Trek' with a hole of up to 5 m reserved for the brave. The 'Muncher Run' in the centre takes you through a window of 'Star Trek'. On the right is the 'Chicken Run' for the less brave.

Grade V/VI Commercial Suicide, No 9: The Zambezi's most infamous rapid. This is a river-wide pour-over with a very narrow slot of less than 1 m on the right. While the safety kayakers may attempt it, most of the rafts are carried around this.

Grade IV Gnashing Jaws of Death, No 10: An easy run before lunch...

Grade V Overland Truck Eater, No 11: A big barrel for about two weeks in the year during the transition between high and low water in mid-January and early July. Watch out for the hole, eddy line and whirlpool. This is the first rapid on the high-water run.

Grade III/IV Three Sisters, No 12A, B, and C: 12B is the famous Zambezi surfing wave for kayakers, where the surf is best between August and December with a massive green shoulder and a big eddy. Rafters prefer the term 'three little pigs'.

Grade IV/V The Mother, No 13: A massive wave train at its best, the first three waves are super fast.

Grade III Rapid, No 14: A big S-bend in the river, though the centre chute is avoided at lower water levels.

Grade V Washing Machine, No 15: Simple wave train but un-runnable in the middle because of a huge crashing hole. Rafts go left or right of the eddy.

Grade VI The Terminators I and II, No 16: A massive wave train at higher levels, but demanding during low water.

Grade V Double Trouble, No 17: A simple wave train but un-runnable because of two large holes – also known as 'The Bitch'.

Grade V Oblivion, No 18: 3 waves make up what is considered to be the best rapid on the Zambezi. The third crashing wave is responsible for more raft flips than any other in the world – only about one in four attempts succeed! This rapid marks the end of the 'low water' one-day run.

Grade II/III Rapids, No 19-No 25: Easy runs at the end of the day. Rapid No 23 is the last rapid on the high-water one-day run.

day); or a 4-day trip including the major activities in Livingstone (US$160 per day). **Africa Travel Co** and **Wildlife Adventures** (book through Wild Horizons locally, www. africatravelco.com) offer good-value 5-10-day trips with time for activities in Victoria Falls and Livingstone plus short overnight safaris to either Chobe or Hwange, and on the longer trips, the northern sections of the Okavango Delta in Botswana. Daily rates are similar to above.

Adventure Zone, Shop 4, Pumula Centre, T013-44424, 42051, www.adventurezone vicfalls.com. General booking office for all activities. Runs its own whitewater rafting, river boarding, canoeing, transfers, river cruises, Chobe day trip and the **Masuwe**

Safari Lodge and Savanna Backpackers Lodge (see Sleeping, pages 172 and 174).

Backpackers Bazaar, Shop 5 Old Vic Falls Centre, T013-45828, 44611, www.zimtravel agent.com. Friendly, helpful one-stop shop for all bookings, including renowned walking safaris with Leon Varley (see page 181). Also has a book exchange (including guide books) and is useful for picking up tourism fliers.

Frontiers Adrenalin Adventures, Landela Centre, T013-41092, www.frontiersadrealin. com. Runs its own whitewater rafting and river boarding, and books all activities.

Shearwater, Soper's Arcade, T013-44471, www.shearwateradventures.com. Again books all activities and transfers, and runs its own whitewater rafting, river boarding, and helicopter flights.

Shockwave Rafting, Old Vic Falls Centre, T013-43002, 42470, www.shockwaverafting.com. Specialise in rafting, tandem kayaking and river boarding.

Wild Horizons, there are 2 offices; one opposite the entrance to the rest camp, T013-42013 (0700-2000), and the other, in an old train carriage next to the bike hire place, T013-42014, (0700-1700), www.wildhorizons.com. Books all activities and transfers and runs its own Chobe day trip, high-wire activities on the Victoria Falls side of the falls (gorge swing, zip line, flying fox and abseiling, see page 178), elephant-back safaris, whitewater rafting, canoeing, and also runs the new Elephant Camp and Imbabala Safari Camp (see Sleeping, page 172). Also operates 2 boats on the Upper Zambezi for cruises. An excellent all-round operator for activities.

⊖ Transport

Victoria Falls *p160, maps p162 and p168*
Air
The airport is 21 km south of the town. **Air Zimbabwe** flies from **Johannesburg**'s OR Tambo International Airport on Tue, Thu and Sat, departing 0930 and arriving at Victoria Falls at 1115 and departing from Victoria Falls at 1230 and arriving back in Johannesburg at 1415. **British Airways** (BA) flies from Johannesburg to Victoria Falls daily, departing Johannesburg at 1125 and arriving at Victoria Falls at 1310, and then departing again at 1350 and arriving back in Johannesburg at 1530. **South African Airways** (SAA) flies from **Johannesburg** daily except Sun, departing from Johannesburg at 1055 and arriving at 1240, and departing again at 1330 and arriving back in Johannesburg at 1510. Expect to pay in the region of US$290 for a return trip. From **Harare** there are daily flights with **Air Zimbabwe**, which depart from Harare at 1200 and arrive at 1300, then depart again at

1530 and, after touching down in Bulawayo, at 1645 arrive back in Harare at 1830. Expect to pay around US$225 for a return trip between Harare and Victoria Falls and US$230 for a return trip between Victoria Falls and Bulawayo (again via Harare).

Very few taxis that meet the flights at the airport, but they should charge in the region of US$25-30. The best way to get into town is by pre-arranging an airport pick-up with your hotel or backpackers, or with your chosen tour/activity company, about US$10 per person, minimum of US$20.

Airline offices Air Zimbabwe, on Parkway next to the banks, T013-4318, 4417/41501, www.airzimbabwe.aero, Mon-Fri 0800-1630, Sat 0800-1130. There's also a desk at the airport. **British Airways**, at the airport, T013-42053, Johannesburg OR Tambo International Airport, T+27-11-387 9000, www.britishairways.com. **South African Airways**, Johannesburg OR Tambo International Airport, T+27-11-978 1111, www.flysaa.com.

Bus
Local economy buses to and from **Bulawayo** arrive and depart from the terminal off Pioneer Rd to the south of town near the hospital in the Chinotimba township in Bulawayo. These usually depart from both Victoria Falls and Bulawayo during the early morning from about 0600-0900. They can take 5 hrs or longer, as they stop along the way on the Victoria Falls–Bulawayo road. The better options are the **City Link** buses to and from the Rainbow hotels in **Bulawayo** and Victoria Falls which cost around US$30 and depart at 0700 in both directions; check at the Rainbow hotels in advance: **Bulawayo Rainbow** T09-9888968, and **Victoria Falls Rainbow** T013-44583. There is a long-distance bus service with the South African company **Intercape** from Cape Town to Livingstone in Zambia via Namibia (see Getting there, page 23 for more details).

Border crossings

Zimbabwe–Zambia: Victoria Falls Bridge

The Victoria Falls Bridge serves as no-man's land between Zimbabwe and Zambia, though you can get a gate pass to go (or watch) bungee jumping. UK, Canadian, Australian and New Zealand nationals need visas (US$50); Irish passport holders do not. If you are just visiting for the day and returning back to Victoria Falls across the bridge, then a day visa is S$20. The border is open 0600-2200. If you are taking a vehicle across, you'll be required to pay a small road toll and to take out a short-term policy of third-party insurance (available at the border). If you are travelling in a foreign vehicle, your carnet de passage will be stamped out of Zimbabwe and into Zambia. Just beyond the Zambian immigration offices is the entrance to the Mosi-oa-Tunya National Park for viewing the Victoria Falls from the Zambian side; Livingstone is 11 km further north.

Zimbabwe–Botswana: Kazungula

The Kazungula border, open 0600-1800, is 80 km west of Victoria Falls; the road to the border runs though the Zambezi National Park on the south side of the Zambezi River, which can be glimpsed from the road on occasion. Although the foliage is quite thick, game is frequently spotted (keep your speed down as an elephant may appear in the road rather suddenly). The border is straightforward and fairly quiet; you get stamped out of Zimbabwe and then stamped into Botswana after filling out a short immigration form. Visas are not required for Botswana. **Kasane** (for Chobe National Park) is a small town 6 km beyond the border, close to the point where four countries meet in the middle of the Zambezi – Zimbabwe, Botswana, Zambia and Namibia. It has a number of riverside lodges and campsites, a bank with ATM, fuel and some shops. The tour operators in Victoria Falls offer day trips across the border to Chobe (see page 171) or can organize transfers to Kasane for about US$50. Most hire companies won't let you take a vehicle out of Zimbabwe, and those in the neighbouring countries won't let you take a hired car into Zimbabwe, but if you are in your own vehicle and travelling on a carnet de passage, you will get this stamped on departure into the member countries of the Southern African Development Community (SADC), which include Botswana, Namibia and South Africa. In the opposite direction, from Botswana to Zimbabwe, drivers are required to take out a short-term policy of third-party insurance (available at the border). There is also a border crossing between Botswana and Zambia by ferry across the Zambezi (see below).

Zimbabwe–Namibia: Ngoma Bridge

From Kasane, there's a main road through the north of the Chobe National Park, 54 km from the Ngoma Gate border (0700-1800) between Botswana and Namibia. If you are only using this road to reach the border, you don't have to pay park fees, but keep your speed down as there are elephant on the road. The first major settlement in Namibia is **Katima Mulilo**, where there are a number of riverside and island lodges in the Zambezi. The drive between Katima Mulilo and Victoria Falls (217 km) should take no more than three hours, including the two border crossings. Very few nationalities require visas for Namibia.

Car hire

Avis airport, T013-43506, town office, at the Total Service Station, 251 Livingstone Way, Mallet Dr, T013-44532/3.

Taxi

Taxis gather at the border post, in the car park outside the Ilala Lodge, banks and post office and the big hotels. Distances are short so prices are reasonable and a few US dollars cash ride hardly needs to be negotiated. But transfers for all activities and large hotels can also be arranged through the tour operators and are usually free if you make bookings with them.

Train

One of the most pleasurable ways of getting to Victoria Falls from **Bulawayo** is on the overnight train (see page 160), as it passes on the edge of Victoria Falls National Park. The Victoria Falls Station is between the Kingdom and Victoria Falls hotels, off Livingstone Way.

❶ Directory

Victoria Falls *p160, maps p162 and p168*
Banks Barclay's, Standard Chartered and Zimbank are lined up next to each other on Livingstone Way between the post office and Ilala Lodge. Each has an ATM taking Visa, though by the time you read this MasterCard may be accepted too. If they are feeling generous and not too busy, they may break down larger US dollar cash bills for you for use for small purchases. Bank hours are Mon-Sat 0800-1500, Sat 0900-1130.
Internet Most accommodation options offer internet services including Wi-Fi, and there's an internet café next to the Spar supermarket beyond the Saf Par office,

0800-1800. **Medical services** Victoria Falls Hospital, Pioneer Rd, T013-44692, is the public hospital but standards are very poor so it's best avoided. **Victoria Falls Pharmacy**, next door to the Adventure Zone office in the arcade off Parkway, T013-44403, Mon-Fri 0800-1730, Sat 0830-1300. **Victoria Falls Surgery**, Dale Crescent, T031-44311/43356, Mon-Fri 0730-1600, is the best option for minor ailments. **Police** On Livingstone Way just north of Parkway, on the left, T013-44206 (see also Safety, page 164).
Post Livingstone Way, between the Falls Craft Market and the banks, Mon-Fri 0800-1600, Sat 0800-1130. This branch is used to dealing with sending packages of souvenirs from the nearby markets and shops. The post office itself also sells a small collection of souvenirs and postcards. Expect to pay in the region of US$14 per kg to Europe and about US$16 per kg to the rest of the world. Maximum weight is 20 kg. Surface mail from Zimbabwe at the time of writing had been suspended. There's a small souvenir shop next to the post office that runs a wrapping service (see Shopping, page 177). **Courier services:** DHL, Elephant's Walk, T013-43500, Mon-Fri 0800-1700, Sat 0800-1300. **Fedex** at the craft market, T013-42197, www.fedex.com/zw, Mon-Fri 0800-1700, Sat 1000-1500, Sun 1000-1300. Both of these provide a service for shipping large souvenirs home.
Telephone Cardphones (cards available at the post office) can be found along Parkway and at the rest camp, though whether they work or not is another matter. Cell phone reception is reasonable on roaming or with a local sim card, which are sometimes available at the airport, and by the time you read this, probably in other places such as post offices and supermarkets.

Livingstone and around

The Victoria Falls border Zambia, and there are more thriving tourist sites and activities based around the town of Livingstone on the other side of the falls. The Zambian side of the falls lie in the Mosi-oa-Tunya National Park, twin park to the Victoria Falls National Park on the Zimbabwean side. Mosi-oa-Tunya, 'the smoke that thunders', is a UNESCO World Heritage Site. Just 11 km north of the falls is the historical town of Livingstone, the capital of the Southern Province of Zambia. Between the falls and the town is a well-accessed river frontage, where there are hotels and launches for river cruises on the Zambezi. Apart from more opportunities to see the falls, the Zambian side offers the same menu of adventure activities as Victoria Falls. In fact, while staying on the Zimbabwe side of the falls, visitors sometimes find themselves being ferried across the Victoria Falls Bridge and the border to partake in adventures in Zambia. ▸▸ *For listings, see pages 194-202.*

Ins and outs → *Colour map 1, B1. Phone code: 0213. Population 97,000.*

Getting there

After passing through Zimbabwean immigration, cross the Victoria Falls Bridge (passing the bungee jump) to get to Zambian immigration on the other side. Single-entry visas cost US$50 and double-entry visas US$80, available at the border. (Multiple-entry visas cost US$160 but are only available from embassies). However, day-trippers need pay only US$20, so it's quite feasible to walk across to see the falls from the Mosi-ou-Tunya National Park; the entrance is just beyond the Zambian immigration offices. Livingstone is 11 km further north; taxis wait at the border and cost about ZMK30,000/US$6. The tour operators provide transfers across the border to the lodges and Livingstone Airport for around US$20, and transfers are included in the rates of the adventure activities operated on the Zambian side of the falls.

Livingstone Airport ⓘ *5 km to the west of town, T0213-321682, www.nacl.co.zm; follow Libala Drive past the post office and market.* There are flights between Livingstone and Lusaka (Zambia's capital), and international flights between Livingstone and Johannesburg. ▸▸ *See Transport, page 201.*

Getting around

Taxis run between the border and Livingstone town. Some of the hotels and backpacker hostels organize transfers to the border, or utilize transfers from Victoria Falls. Everything you need, including banks, restaurants, curio market and shops are located somewhere along Mosi oa Tunya Road, the town's main drag; this is walkable but you may want to get a taxi from one end to the other. Taxis won't cost more than a few dollars and can be found conveniently parked at most junctions, but you'll need to negotiate the fare before getting in.

Best time to visit

The climate on the Zambian side of the falls is similar to that on the Zimbabwean side (see box, page 164). Winter (May to mid-August) is mild and dry, with average high temperatures of 25-27°C, and average lows of 7-10°C. Summer (mid-August through April) is generally hot and it is very hot and wet during the rainy season (mid-November to April), with average highs of 32-34°C and average lows of 15-19°C.

Border crossings: Zimbabwe–Namibia

Sesheke–Katima Mulilo

The border with Namibia and Zambia, open 0600-1800, is at Sesheke and goes over the Katima Mulilo Bridge into Namibia, 84 km west of Livingstone on a new tar road. The bridge over the Zambezi opened in 2004, completing the 2100-km Trans-Caprivi Highway (named after the Caprivi Strip in Namibia; the finger of land that juts across the top of Botswana to Zambia and Zimbabwe), which now links Zambia's capital city, Lusaka, via Livingstone, with the port of Walvis Bay in Namibia.

Tourist information

Zambia Tourism ① *Mosi-oa-Tunya Rd just south of the National Museum, T0213-321404, www.zambiatourism.com, Mon-Fri 0800-1600.* All the hotels and backpackers provide booking services for activities and have a variety of leaflets available. Information can also be found on the **Livingstone Tourism Association**'s website www.livingstonetourism.com.

Safety

Petty theft is rare but can occur so try to avoid carrying anything valuable and don't leave anything on display in a vehicle. For the most part, however, Zambians are very friendly and helpful.

Background

Although a little neglected, Livingstone has a colonial character and easy-going African charm. It was named after the missionary and explorer David Livingstone, the first European to discover, name and tell the rest of world about the mighty waterfall. The town was founded on completion of the Victoria Falls Bridge (see box, page 167) which carried the railway over the river in 1905. Residents of an earlier riverside settlement called Old Drift, where there was a dugout canoe crossing of the Zambezi, moved to the new site beside the railway line 11 km upstream from the falls. The move was instigated by the high prevalence of malaria on the swampy, mosquito-infested banks of the Zambezi. For a while the town was the capital of what was known as North-Western Rhodesia and was a centre for trade from across the Zambezi and timber production from the forests to its northwest. The capital moved to Lusaka in 1935, a change designed to take commercial interests closer to the copperbelt in the northeastern part of the territory, where copper mining was fuelling the economy of the colony.

From the late 1960s, when the Rhodesian Bush War forced Zambia to close the border at Victoria Falls Bridge, Livingstone suffered an economic decline, as tourism fell and trade to the south dwindled. The timber industry had come to a natural end, as the forests were just about depleted, and prosperity was further affected by national economic woes brought on by low copper prices and the failure of the government of newly independent Zambia (1964) to manage the enconomy. When trade to the south restarted with Zimbabwean independence in 1980, Livingstone seemed stuck in a time warp, unable to afford new development or maintain the existing infrastructure. Although this meant that historic colonial buildings were not replaced by new development, it also meant the town could not afford to preserve those that it had. To this day, sections of Mosi-oa-Tunya Road are lined with classic, but decaying, colonial buildings, with wide verandas and corrugated-iron roofs, typical of British settler architecture.

However, in the last decade or so, with the decline of Zimbabwe as a tourist destination, Livingstone' tourism has flourished again, attracting hotel chains like **Sun International** and new modern shopping centres. Apart from tourism, Livingstone's economy has been bolstered by the development stimulated by the Walvis Bay Corridor (Walvis Bay is a port in Namibia) with the opening of the Katima Mulilo Bridge between Namibia and Sesheke in Zambia, 184 km west of Livingstone on a newly tarred road; this now funnels more trade through the town.

Mosi-oa-Tunya National Park

Ins and outs The main entrance to the falls is just north of the immigration offices at the border; the gate to the game park section is about 2 km west of the boat club, US$10, children (five to 12) US$5, under fives free. Open 0600-1800.

Sights

Mosi-oa-Tunya, 'the smoke that thunders', comes from the Kololo or Lozi language and the name is now used throughout Zambia, and in parts of Zimbabwe, to describe the Victoria Falls. The Mosi-oa-Tunya National Park covers 66 sq km and stretches from the falls in a northwest arc along some 20 km of the Zambezi riverbank. It has two main sections, with separate entrances: a game park at its northwestern end, and the land adjacent to the falls themselves in the southern section just over the border with Zimbabwe. From the falls, it extends downstream along the Batoka Gorge. The game park section has tall riverine forest with palms, miombo woodland and patches of grassland, and is home to giraffe, zebra, buffalo, baboon, vervet monkey and antelope, including sable, impala and eland. After a tragic incident in 2007, when the two white rhino in the park were attacked by poachers (they were both shot but only one survived), another five white rhino were introduced to the park in 2009. During the dry season elephant can sometimes be seen crossing the river from Zimbabwe. Crocodile and hippo live in the river.

In 2009, the **Lion Encounter** (see below) opened near the Thorntree Lodge within the park. It is a similar set up to the Lion Encounter at Victoria Falls (see page 171) in Zimbabwe. Within the game park section is the **Old Drift Cemetery** (a plaque marks the spot), at the point of the Old Drift, a ferry across the river before the Victoria Falls Bridge was built; some of the early settlers were buried here. The Victoria Falls section of the park in the south includes the rainforest on the cliff opposite the Eastern Cataract, a jungley area of mahogany, ebony and wild date palms watered by the spray of the falls; a network of paths leads to lookout points over the falls. There is also a new statue of David Livingstone in this section of the park, erected in 2005, when another plaque was also placed on **Livingstone Island**, marking the spot where the explorer first viewed the falls. The **Knife-Edge Bridge**, a footbridge, was constructed in the 1960s to enable access to the cliffs looking over the **Rainbow Falls** and the **First Gorge**'s exit to the Boiling Pot (see page 169) in the **Second Gorge**. A steep footpath also goes down to the Boiling Pot, with views of the Second Gorge and the **Victoria Falls Bridge**.

The Lion Encounter

ⓘ *Close to the Thorntree Lodge, Mosi-au-Tunya National Park, T0213-327122 www.lionencounter.com; 0630, 1030 and 1630, US$125, no children under 15 or under 1.5 m*

Livingstone Island

Livingstone Island is where David Livingstone got his first view of the falls in 1855. It is less than 1 m from the top of the Victoria Falls on the Zambian side. During the dry/low water season, from about August to December, a shallow rock pool, known as the Devil's Pool, appears just off the island, at the very top of the falls, where the water gushes over into the Boiling Pot some 100 m below, close enough for daredevils to peek over the torrent of water. It's reasonably current-free and you can swim here, as the natural wall of rock just below the surface prevents you from being swept away. Many of the hotels and hostels offer this activity, which includes a boat trip across to the island for about US$45, but remember this is obviously a dangerous activity and unregistered access to the island is illegal. Nevertheless, it's a totally unique and exciting experience.

tall; children's excursion US$75; night excursion 1645-2200, US$195, no children under 8; combination of 1630 lion walk and the night excursion US$295.

This is the sister operation to the Lion Encounter at Victoria Falls, featuring lions from the Antelope Park in Gweru (see page 86); its ultimate goal is to release the lions into the wild. Excursions can be booked through any of the tour operators in Livingstone or direct with the company itself, and rates include transfers from lodges to the reception boma in Mosi-oa-Tunya National Park. The excursion begins with a short film about the lion release programme and a safety briefing, followed by a 1½-hour walk with some juvenile lions. The morning excursion includes breakfast and the afternoon one provides snacks and drinks. Under-15s, who are not permitted on the lion walk, can go on a bush walk while their parents go with the lions; if there are cubs between three and five months old in residence, children over 10 can visit them in the cub enclosure. The newest activity is the night excursion, which departs at 1645 and gets back to Livingstone lodges at about 2200, and includes dinner. The trip involves tracking the older lions (18-30 months) by open 4WD vehicle as they practise their hunting techniques in the park. With the help of a red-filtered spotlight, it is sometimes possible to see them search for game, stalk, chase and perhaps even make a kill. Lion Encounter has recently been featured in a six-part television series on the UK's ITV network, drawing 4.8 million viewers for its first episode; a second 12-part series was filmed in 2010.

Zambezi Elephant Trails

ⓘ *Book through Safari par Excellence, T0213-321629, www.safpar.net, or any hotel or backpacker hostel, US$180, 0615-1030, 1015-1430, 1415-1830, no children under 10.*

Like the Lion Encounter (above), Zambezi Elephant Trails is located near Thorntree Lodge, approximately 10 km from Livingstone. It offers one-hour elephant riding, with a strong emphasis placed on an elephant experience rather than just a ride, and guests are encouraged to interact with the elephants. There are six elephants, each of which carry two people and the handler on walks through the Mosi-oa-Tunya National Park. There are also two calves; one born in 2004, and one born in 2007 (they are fully grown at about 10), which accompany their mothers on the walk, frolicking along with the herd. Rates include transfers and a full English breakfast on the early morning trip and snacks and drinks later in the day. DVDs of your elephant ride are available for an extra US$40.

Livingstone

Livingstone (National) Museum

ⓘ *Mosi-oa-Tunya Rd, T0213-323566, www.museums.co.zm, US$5, children (under 12) US$2, 0900-1630, craft shop and café.*

Devoted to archaeology, ethnography and history, the Livingstone Museum, also referred to as the National Museum, contains an interesting collection of memorabilia relating to David Livingstone. In front of the museum is a statue of him, as well as of Czech ethnographer Emil Holub, erected in 2005. (Holub was the first European explorer and ethnographer to produce a detailed map of Victoria Falls in 1895.) The museum has four galleries: prehistory (archaeology), ethnography and art, history, and natural history. The first effort to establish a museum in Livingstone was in 1930 when Mr Moffat Thomson, the Secretary of Native Affairs for Northern Rhodesia, convinced the colonial government

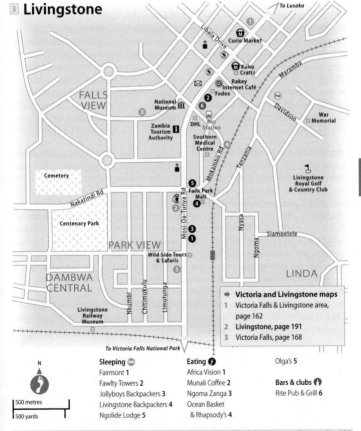

3 **Livingstone**

Sleeping 🛏
Fairmont **1**
Fawlty Towers **2**
Jollyboys Backpackers **3**
Livingstone Backpackers **4**
Ngolide Lodge **5**

Eating 🍴
Africa Vision **1**
Munali Coffee **2**
Ngoma Zanga **3**
Ocean Basket
 & Rhapsody's **4**

Olga's **5**

Bars & clubs 🍸
Rite Pub & Grill **6**

➡ **Victoria and Livingstone maps**
1 Victoria Falls & Livingstone area, page 162
2 Livingstone, page 191
3 Victoria Falls, page 168

David Livingstone (1813-1873)

David Livingstone was an explorer and Scottish missionary. He was born in Blantyre, South Lanarkshire just south of Glasgow, where there is now a museum to him in his former home on the banks of the River Clyde. He studied medicine and theology at Glasgow University, and later moved to London and became a minister, joining the London Missionary Society. During his explorations in Africa in the mid-1800s his purpose was to open trade routes whilst gathering useful information about the largely unknown continent. In 1855, he was the first European to see the magnificent waterfalls, which he renamed the Victoria Falls after Queen Victoria. His expeditions included an eight-year exploration of the Zambezi River (1858–1864), but when the river was found to be unnavigable beyond the Cahora Bassa rapids (now in Mozambique) the British government recalled the expedition. The press made a big deal of highlighting Livingstone's failures, and he returned home briefly before setting out again in March 1866 to find the highly debated 'Source of the Nile'. Deep in Africa, Livingstone lost contact with the outside world for six years. In 1871, Henry Morton Stanley was sent out to find him as a publicity stunt for *The New York Herald*, and eventually tracked him down at Ujiji on the shores of Lake Tanganyika (now in Tanzania), where he delivered the well-known line, "Dr Livingstone, I presume?" Together they explored the north of Tanganyika for a while until Stanley left the next year, urging Livingstone to return to Britain. Refusing to give up until his mission was completed, he worked on, eventually submitting to malaria and a bowel obstruction which caused internal bleeding. In 1873 he died in Chitambo, Barotseland (now Zambia).

of the need to collect material evidence of the culture of the various ethnic groups, before they died out. The collections were housed in colonial offices in Livingstone before 1934, at which point they were put on public display in the old Magistrate's Court building. The collection was extended to include items relating to David Livingstone, such as letters, photographs and personal possessions, obtained through donations and loans from individuals. In 1961 the collection was moved to this purpose-built museum, which was refurbished in 2003 with funding from the European Union. The main themes include Livingstone's early life, his missionary work at Kuruman (now in South Africa), his Zambezi expedition when he became the first European to see the falls, his meeting with Henry Stanley (see box, above), and ending with his death at Chitambo. The exhibition relates how his expedition team carried his body to the coast some 2000 km away and records his burial service in Westminster Abbey in London.

In addition to David Livingstone memorabilia and tribal artefacts, such as burial costumes and traditional medicine, there is a room dedicated to the political unrest that preceded the independence of Zambia in 1964.

Livingstone Railway Museum
ⓘ *Follow the road next to the railway line as it crosses Mosi-oa-Tunya Rd, US$3, 1000-1730.*
For many years Livingstone was the railway capital of a vast region, and much of its wealth came from the railways. The museum traces the history of the railway in Zambia, and is housed in the restored Zambezi Saw Mills loco-shed buildings. It contains lots of photos and items like brass signal lamps and morse code machines, and outside there are

steam locomotives and other rolling stock dating back a century or more, which you can clamber over. The **Mulobezi Railway** (once known as the Zambezi Saw Mills Railway) was constructed in 1905 after the completion of the Victoria Falls Bridge, and was used to carry timber from Mulobezi on the north bank of the Zambezi to the northwest of Livingstone, to the southern province of Northern Rhodesia (Zambia) and Southern Rhodesia (Zimbabwe). The timber was Rhodesian teak (now referred to as Zambezi teak), which is hard, strong and termite-resistant, and found a market in all the Rhodesian colonies for doors, window frames and parquet floors. It was also used to make railway sleepers. Today furniture made out of old teak railway sleepers is popular in Zambia and Zimbabwe; **Savanna Wood** (see page 177) has a factory in the industrial area in Victoria Falls and the furniture is also sold at **Doon Estate** in Harare (see page 77). By the 1920s, the Mulobezi forest was mostly depleted and wrought-iron sleepers were introduced on the railways of southern Africa. The **Mulobezi Railway** ceased working in the 1970s but two locomotives were restored – one is at the museum in Livingstone, while the other went to the UK, where it is now an exhibit at the National Railway Museum in York. In 1976, a documentary film of that journey called the *Last Train to Mulobezi* was broadcast by the BBC. Today the *Royal Livingstone Express* train (see page 199) runs on part of this line.

For Sleeping and Eating price codes and other relevant information, see pages 29-34.

☉ Sleeping

Livingstone *p187, maps p162 and p191*
Most accommodation in Livingstone will organize transfers from both the Zimbabwe border and airport. Make arrangements in advance. Apart from the upmarket lodges on the Zambezi River, cheaper accommodation in the town centre, in the way of guesthouses and B&Bs, can be found at the website of the **Livingstone Lodges and Guest Houses Association (LILOGHA)** (www.livingstonelodges.com). There are also a couple of highly recommended backpacker hostels (see below).
L The River Club, 18 km upstream on the Zambezi, www.theriverclubafrica.com, reservations through **Wilderness Safaris**, www.wilderness-safaris.com. Set in 13 ha of pristine bush, with 10 open-fronted, split-level chalets on the edge of the Zambezi. There's a dining room, bar, library in the main building (which used to be a farmhouse), pool, tennis courts, gym, jacuzzi, sauna and spa. This is an award-winning **Wilderness Safaris'** luxury lodge, which also helps fund programmes in the local village of Simonga, such as educational projects and sinking boreholes.
L Stanley Safari Lodge, 3 km to the east of the Mosi-oa-Tunya Rd, clearly signposted, T097-848615, www.stanleysafaris.com. Luxury lodge on the edge of the Mosi-oa-Tunya National Park with good views of the spray of the falls, even though it isn't on the river. Has 10 individually decorated suites with a colonial feel, some with private plunge pools and open-sides; the main building has a bar and restaurant serving 3-course meals. This is a popular honeymoon destination, and they can arrange boat trips to Livingstone Island.

L Taita Falcon Lodge, 11 km from the border, downstream from Victoria Falls, T0213-321850, www.taitafalcon.com. Perched high up above the Batoka Gorge, this has 7 brick-and-thatch suites enclosed by reed fencing to provide a private garden. African decor, pool, pleasant wooden deck for dining; rates include transfers, all meals, drinks, and guided bush and bird walk.
L Thorntree River Lodge, in the game park section of the Mosi-oa-Tunya National Park, 12 km from Livingstone, reservations through **Safari Par Excellence**, T0321-321629, www.thorntreelodge.net, or **Three Cities** hotel group, South Africa T+27-(0)31-3103333, www.threecities.co.za. Set in the park with broad river views, this lodge has 9 stone-and-thatched suites with wooden decks. Candlelit dining is around a long table with the other guests. Good-value 3-night packages include game drives and sunset cruises and rates include all meals, pool with a water-level bar, and thatched lounge. **Zambezi Elephant Trails** (page 170) is based here, and the **Lion Encounter** (page 171) is close by.
L-B The Royal Livingstone and Zambezi Sun Hotels, just beyond the border on Mosi-oa-Tunya Rd, T0321-323 1122, www.suninternational.com. Opulent twin hotels run by the South African chain **Sun International**, with direct access to the falls in the Mosi-au-Tunya National Park. Comprises the 5-star **Royal Livingstone** with 173 luxury rooms spread along the riverbank, with verandas and Victorian baths, and the 3-star **Zambezi Sun** with 212 rooms overlooking the bush or pool. Both have restaurants and bars and activity booking desks, and the **Royal Livingstone** has a spa.
A Chundukwa Lodge, 22 km off the Kazungula road from Livingstone, T0977-781215, www.chundkwariverlodge.com. Small lodge with 5 riverside units with reed walls and open frontage onto the river,

1 with 3 bedrooms for a family. Rates include a personal cook, pool, home-cooked food, full bar facilities; activities include visits to the local village and river cruises.

B Protea Hotel Livingstone, adjacent to the Falls Shopping Complex on Mosi-au-Tunya Rd, T0213-324630, www.proteahotels.com. A new and efficiently modern hotel run by the high-quality South African **Protea** group, with 80 a/c rooms with DSTV, Wi-Fi and smart decor in muted browns and creams. There's a pool and a restaurant serving buffet meals and a snack menu. Set across 6 double-storey brick buildings.

B-E Zambezi Waterfront, 4 km upstream from the Victoria Falls towards Livingstone and 1.5 km off the Mosi-oa-Tunya Rd towards the river, reservations through **Safari Par Excellence**, T0321-323 1122, www.safpar.net/waterfront. This is an excellent riverside set-up opposite Siloka Island in the Zambezi, popular with travellers across a broad range of budgets, with 23 thatched ensuite chalets (US$200 for a family room and US$160 for a standard double) to 30 permanent 9-sq-m dome tents (US$40), and a campsite (US$10 per person), both with good shared ablutions. The resort has a popular bar and restaurant with great views up and down the river, an adventure booking office (a one-stop shop), plunge pool, wooden game-viewing deck, and is the launch site for Saf Par's river cruises.

C Maramba River Lodge, 4 km from the border towards Livingstone off the Mosi-oa-Tunya Rd, T0213-324189, www.maramba-zambia.com. On the Maramba River, a narrow tributary to the Zambezi, this is a pleasant bush retreat, and game, including elephant, is often spotted, though in low water mosquitoes can be irritating. Accommodation comprises chalets and permanent tents with hand-crafted wrought-iron furniture, smaller 'budget' safari tents (from US$100 per night), and there's a restaurant and bar on a wooden deck with a fire pit during cooler months.

C Ngolide Lodge, 110 Mosi-oa-Tunya Rd, T0213-321091, www.ngolidelodge. com. Small but comfortable with 16 a/c rooms with flat-screen TVs and Wi-Fi in an attractive thatch-and-stone building centred on a tranquil courtyard with a comfy semi-open lounge area over a water feature. Best known for the excellent **Kamuza Restaurant**, which is popular with locals (see Eating, page 196).

C Prana Cottage & Tented Camp, 4 km on a dirt track off Mosi-oa-Tunya Rd; the turn-off is just south of the Maramba Village, T0213-332 7120, www.pranazambia. com. A pleasant quiet retreat in the bush with 1 large house with 3 a/c rooms and 3 bathrooms, kitchen for self-catering or a cook can be arranged, and pool. Ideal for families, but you can also book rooms individually. Nearby are 3 additional en suite safari tents; rates include breakfast and other meals on request. Owner Bev holds yoga classes, and beauty treatments are available.

D Chanters Inn, Lukulu Crescent, off Obote Av, T0213-323412, www.chanters-living stone.com. Simple but spacious with 12 a/c rooms with DSTV and Wi-Fi. A good budget option, spotlessly clean and run by affable host Richard Chanters, who is a fount of knowledge about the area. Has a pool, garden and restaurant serving continental and African dishes, including Zambezi bream and traditional Zambian meat and bean stews.

D Chapa Classic Lodge, 66 Nehru Way, T0213-332 2065, www.chapaclassiclodge. com. Fairly plain, but has 23 spacious rooms with bath and shower, giant flat-screen TVs on the wall with DSTV, in a quiet street away from the main drag of Mosi-oa-Tunya Rd. Spotless bathrooms, cool tiled floors, secure parking, pool, English breakfast and a short walk (taxi at night) to restaurants in town.

D New Fairmont Hotel, 441/2 Mosi-oa-Tunya Rd, T0213-332 0075, www.new fairmounthotel.com. An old-fashioned concrete block with dated furnishings that is primarily geared towards the local conference market, but reasonably comfortable with good service and value for money. Rooms have a/c, satellite TV, and tea and coffee facilities. The 2 restaurants offer Indian and Chinese dishes and often feature live music; there's a business centre and (noisy) nightclub at the weekends.

D Rite Inn, 301 Mose St, T0212-323264. A neat modern set up with 10 very large rooms with king-size beds, a/c, DSTV. Also here is the **Armadillo** restaurant (see Eating). The pool area is attractive, with a fountain and open-air bar. Good-value rates include breakfast.

D ZigZag, 693 Industrial Rd, T0213-3322814, www.zigzagzambia.com. Small but with 12 good-standard en suite rooms, including 1 family room, with motel-style parking, a/c, mosquito nets draped over 4-poster beds, set in a row in well-tended gardens. There's a good-sized swimming pool, children's playground and popular restaurant. See Eating, page 197.

E Fawlty Towers, T0213-323432. A rambling low building with 18 simple double/twins and several dorms, neat gardens with large pool, camping, bar, a beauty salon for massages. Can organize bike hire for US$10 for half a day or US$15 for a full day, ideal for cycling down to the falls. Helpful and friendly staff.

E Jollyboys Backpackers, 34 Kanyanta Rd, T0213-332 4229, www.backpackzambia. com. Centrally located behind the museum, this well-organized backpacker hostel has dorms, doubles in thatched huts, as well as camping, a funky chill-out area with cushions, internet café, lively bar and pool. A good place to hook up with other travellers.

F The Grotto, Maambo Way, T0213-322370. Pleasant old colonial house, with large pool, grassy gardens for camping, some basic rooms which share ablutions with campers, popular bar on the wooden terrace, witin walking distance of town. Can book activities, and runs its own whitewater

rafting company. A well-used spot by overlanders, with secure parking and basic vehicle workshop facilities.

F Livingstone Backpackers, 559 Mokambo Rd, T0213-332 3432, www.livingstoneback packers.com. A fairly youthful party spot which hosts many international volunteers on aid projects with a good-sized pool, thatched boma bar, climbing wall, 18 dorms with 4-8 bunks (US$5), or you can take a whole dorm (US$20), or camp (US$3). Free lifts to the falls and border pick-ups and free Wi-Fi access.

🍴 Eating

Livingstone p187, maps p162 and p191

🍴🍴🍴 **The Royal Livingstone and Zambezi Sun Hotels**, just beyond the border on Mosi-oa-Tunya Rd, T0321-3231122, www. suninternational.com. Open 0730-1000, 1100-2300. With good views of the falls from the wooden deck, the 5-star Royal Livingstone does an all-you-can-eat buffet breakfast with sushi, pastries and cheeses for US$25, afternoon tea between 1500-1700 on the lawns for US$20, and more expensive à la carte dinners in the grandly dressed restaurant. The 3-star Zambezi Sun has good-value buffet meals – breakfast (US$15) and dinner (US$35) – which will appeal to big eaters.

🍴🍴 **Armadillo**, 48 Mosi-oa-Tunya Rd, T0213-332 4781. Open 0800-2200. Part of the **Rite Inn**, this has a varied choice of food including good brunches, and international, halaal, Zambian and oriental dishes. Cosy black and white decor with fat armchairs and banquette seating, good service, well-stocked bar with locally made lights and paintings by local artists on the walls. Good choice for vegetarians on the Indian menu.

🍴🍴 **Kamuza**, at the Ngolide Lodge, 110 Mosi-oa-Tunya Rd, T0213-321091, www. ngolidelodge.com. Very popular with locals for the best Indian cuisine in Livingstone. The restaurant imports ingredients from

India; try the chicken tikka masala or the vegetarian paneer dishes; friendly service, separate bar, good wine list.

♥♥ Ngoma Zanga, just south of the Falls Park Mall, Mosi-oa-Tunya Rd, T0979-441441. Open 1200-1500, 1830-2300. Traditional African food in a colourfully decorated house with vivid textiles and beaded mats, terrace tables, good music from live musicians on drums and a glockenspiel made from gourds. Dishes like *kapenta* (fish), crocodile steak, chicken in peanut sauce, Mopani worms, *katapa* (cassava leaves), *chibwabwa* (pumpkin leaves and ground nuts), and a welcome drink of *munkoyo* (distilled roots, sugar and water). Great atmosphere, and impromptu dancing is a regular feature.

♥♥ Ocean Basket, in the Falls Park Mall, Mosi-oa-Tunya Rd, T0213-321274, www. oceanbasket.com. Open 1100-2200. Quality South African seafood chain offering anything from fish and chips to sizeable and good-value seafood platters. Offers a good choice of South African wines, modern decor and good service.

♥♥ Olga's, Nakatindi Rd, T0213-324160, www. olgasproject.com. Wed-Mon 0700-2200, closed Tue. Very authentic Italian restaurant with a pleasant outdoor garden. Popular with families at the weekend, for its generous wood-fired pizzas, home-made pasta and ice cream and freshly made Italian bread. Also sells packets of Parma ham and imported cheese. All profits from the food and gift shop go towards a skills-training project for disadvantaged young people in Livingstone.

♥♥ Rhapsody's, Falls Park Mall, Mosi-oa-Tunya Rd, T0213-332214, www.rhapsodys.co.za. Open 0830-2200. Smart modern restaurant with sophisticated decor, a neat outside bar, which closes at 2400, an hour after the restaurant closes. There are also branches of **Debonair's** (takeaway pizza) and **Subway** (sandwiches) in the Falls Park Mall.

♥ ZigZag, 693 Industrial Rd, T0213-3322814, www.zigzagzambia.com. Sun-Wed 0800-

2100, Thu-Sat 0800-2300. Café/bar at the hotel of the same name, serves the best cappuccino in Livingstone, plus an extensive breakfast menu, cooked to order in front of you in the open kitchen. Freshly prepared lunches and snacks, including daily specials chalked up on a blackboard, and a wide range of evening meals.

Cafés

African Vision, south of Ngoma Zanga, just south of the Falls Park Mall, Mosi-oa-Tunya Rd. Mon-Sat 0800-1700. Vegetarian-friendly café in an old colonial house with a tin roof and sprawling garden. Serves light meals such as sweet potato soup, good chocolate cake, and drinks such as cappuccino or mango smoothies. Also sells a few curios and books.

Munali Coffee, opposite the post office, Mosi-oa-Tunya Rd, T0213-324201. Mon-Sat 0800-2100, Sun 0800-2000. A bakery and coffee shop on the main drag in the middle of town, with counters selling takeaway fried chicken, pastries, bread, muffins and cakes, plus drinks. Also has a few formica-topped tables to eat at; popular with Livingstone's teenagers.

🎵 Bars and clubs

Livingstone *p187, maps p162 and p191*
Fez Bar, Nakitindi Rd. Open 0700-2400, closes at 0200 at the weekends. This local watering hole run by a New Zealander is popular with the expat community and rafting guides. It has a cavernous bar, beer garden, widescreen TV for watching sport, and serves light meals such as gourmet burgers, fish and chips and Mexican nachos. Has a live band on Wed and Sat.

Rite Pub and Grill, opposite the post office, Mosi-oa-Tunya Rd. Open 1100-late. A fairly rough and ready pub but the place to meet locals over a cold Mosi beer. In a double-storey terrace, with pool tables and TVs showing football.

○ Shopping

Livingstone *p187, maps p162 and p191*
The main **curio market** is in the centre of town along Mosi-oa-Tunya Rd and is open daily from 0800-1800. Vendors are accommodated in a row of brick stalls and it's easy enough to wander around. Items include wooden sculptures, batiks, beaded products, metal statues and baskets. There's another curio market outside the entrance to the falls just over the border from Zimbabwe. Livingstone's **main market** in the centre of town is a bustling colourful market with just about every type of business venture imaginable. There are rows and rows of stalls for second-hand clothes (some excellent deals can be found), women selling fresh vegetables and dried beans, stacks of *chitenge* (women's sarongs) and places to fix your bike, sew your backpack, buy a bed or get a toy made from copper wire and a couple of bottle tops. The fairly new **Falls Park Mall** on Mosi-oa-Tunya Rd near the junction with Nakatini Rd (the road to Kazungula) has a large branch of **Shoprite** supermarket (Mon-Sat 0800-2000, Sun 0800-1300), coffee shops, restaurants including **Ocean Basket** and **Rhapsody's** (see Eating) and a bank with ATM.
Bookworld, Falls Park Mall, T0213-321414. Mon-Fri 0900-1700, Sat 0900-1300. A reasonable choice of guidebooks, as well as bird, nature and history books for the region, plus novels, children's titles and cookery books.
Kubu Crafts, 133 Mosi-oa-Tunya Rd, T0213-332 0230, www.kubucrafts.com. Mon-Sat 0900-1730. A good-quality curio shop that also manufactures local art, furniture and accessories for the local lodges in the region, with strong African tribal themes. There are other branches at **Livingstone International Airport** and the **Sun International Resort**.
The River Gallery, Falls Park Mall, Mosi-oa-Tunya Rd, T0213-322452. Mon-Fri 0900-1700, Sat 0900-1300. Good selection of wildlife paintings by local artists, plus photographic prints, jewellery, gemstones, hand-painted candles, cushion covers and other textiles.

▲ Activities and tours

Livingstone *p187, maps p162 and p191*
All activities can be booked through the hotels and backpacker hostels, or alternatively through the **Livingstone Adventure Company**, T0213-320058, www.livingstonesadventure.com, which markets separate local companies, including the **Batoka Sky Adventures** for microlight and helicopter rides, and **Jet Extreme** for the jet-boats. The cable car built at Rapid 23 was set up by Jet Extreme; it also transfers rafters out of the gorge and the 8-min ride is included in rates for both jet-boating and rafting.

Abseiling
Abseil Zambia, at the top of the Batoka Gorge, 4 km from the Mosi-oa-Tunya Rd and the border, T0213-321188, www.thezambeziswing.com. Unlimited activities (full day US$85, half day US$75), or single activities, abseil US$25, gorge swing US$45 (or US$55 for a double/2-person swing), flying fox US$25 and zip line US$25. Similar set-up to the high-wire activities on the Zimbabwean side of the falls; a full day here includes lunch, soft drinks and beers, day visas for Zambia if coming from Zimbabwe and transfers. The abseil is 54 m and you can also go forward (a rapp jump). The flying fox and zip line go for 80 m across the gorge, while the gorge swing has a free fall of just over 50 m before the rope swings you at 120 kph across the gorge. Full-day clients can do this as often as they like and can try to break the record of a staggering 22 swings in one day.

Bike hire
Mrs Amina, T097-7545754 (mob), can deliver mountain bikes to all accommodation in Livingstone (or organize this through hotels and hostels), for US$15

Royal Livingstone Express

ⓘ *Pickups from hotels around 1700, and transfers to a siding near the Royal Livingstone Hotel, return at 2200, book at the Royal Livingstone Hotel, T0213-323232, www.royal-livingstone-express.com, US$150 per person.*

The Royal Livingstone Express is a vintage train, a unique dining experience, and a great way to watch the sunset in the Mosi-oa-Tunya National Park; the six-course dinners are prepared by the chefs at the Royal Livingstone Hotel. The train has five air-conditioned carriages – two dining cars, a kitchen car, lounge car and an observation car – and is pulled by either a 10th class No 156 or a 12th class No 204 steam locomotive. One of the dining cars, The Wembley, was built by the Birmingham Railway Carriage and Wagon Company, and went on display at the British Empire Exhibition in London in 1924. It was shipped to the Union of South Africa and entered service on 19 May 1926. The two wood-panelled dining cars have tables for two or four, with silver cutlery, crystal glassware and damask linen. The train follows part of the old Mulobezi line to the north of Livingstone (see Livingstone Railway Museum, page 192), which runs parallel to the Zambezi River and goes through the Mosi-oa-Tunya National Park, a journey of about 17 km. It then stops for dinner and to watch the sunset before turning around in a siding and bringing the carriages back to the Royal Livingstone Hotel.

per day. It takes about 25 mins to cycle from the centre of town to the Mosi-oa-Tunya National Park. **Fawlty Towers** (see Sleeping) also rents out bikes.

Golf

Livingstone Royal Golf and Country Club, in the centre of town to the east of Mosi-oa-Tunya Rd, T0213-320440, www.lrgcc.com. This is an 18-hole, 72-par course, established in 1908. In 1925 it hosted Prince Edward, England's then Prince of Wales – hence the 'Royal' in the title. It was fully renovated in 2006 and the clubhouse, a beautiful example of Cape Dutch architecture, has a long veranda with fans and rattan furniture. There's an excellent restaurant, historical bar, state-of-the-art gym and beauty spa. Club hire and caddies are available.

Horse riding

The Royal Livingstone and Zambezi Sun Hotels, just beyond the border on Mosi-oa-Tunya Rd, T0321-323 1122, www.suninternational.com. Has stables and can organize 1½-hr horse rides around the top of the gorge for about US$80. Departure times are 0700, 1030, 1430 and 1600. The 12 well-schooled horses are suitable for novices.

Jet-boating

Jet Extreme, T0213-321375. Open 0730-1030, 1230-1530. US$95, jet-boat and helicopter combo US$295, minimum age 7 and minimum weight 40 kg. This thrilling excursion in the rapids in the Batoka Gorge takes approximately 3 hrs, including transfers, rides in the cable car going down into the gorge (or a helicopter ride out over the falls), and a 30-min jet-boat ride that spins through the rapids. You are firmly strapped in and wear life jackets but expect to get wet. Pickups can also be arranged from Victoria Falls. The 22-seater boat is 700 horsepower, making it one of the largest and most powerful commercial jet-boats of its kind ever built. To walk out of the gorge takes an average person 40 mins, but with the cable car (which takes 25 passengers), only 8 mins. T-shirts and DVDs are available to buy, as are snacks and drinks at the launch site at the bottom of the gorge. The cable car also transfers rafters out of the gorge.

Microlight and helicopter flights

Batoka Sky, T0213-320058, www.batokasky. com. Mircolight US$120 for 15 mins, US$240 for 30 mins, minimum age 6, maximum weight 100 kg; helicopter 12-15 mins US$120, 30 mins US$240, no age or weight restrictions. In the microlight, the passenger sits in front of the pilot, in an open cockpit; the shorter flight goes over the falls, while the longer flight goes over the falls and Mosi-oa-Tunya National Park. You can't take a camera, as passengers are strapped in tightly, but the pilot will take photos from a camera strapped to the wing; a CD is an extra US$20. The helicopter takes the same route. You can also opt to take a helicopter out of the gorge from the landing pad at Rapid 23 where the jet-boat launch site is (see above).

United Air Charter, T0213-323095, www. uaczam.com. Helicopter US$130 for 12 mins, US$260 for 25 mins. The longer flight enters the gorge and skims the river, and they can also organize helicopter transfers from the airport for US$210 (minimum 4 people), and helicopter flights out of the Batoka Gorge for US$135 from the jet-boat or rafting.

River cruises

Taonga Safaris, T0213-322508, www. taongasafaris.com. US$45. Organizes the most popular 2½-hr sunset cruises on the Zambian side of the river, going around the Siloka Island for game-viewing and to watch the sunset. Includes transfers from hotels, an on-board barbecue and all you can drink. Saf Par (see below) also offers cruises.

Safaris

Walking safaris, around US$80, usually take around 3-4 hrs and are conducted by a guide and armed ranger. They often get close to rhino and antelope in the Mosi-oa-Tunya National Park and offer the opportunity for good birdwatching and to learn about the flora and fauna and how the local people use the habitat in their daily lives. Rates include transfers, and pickups are from 0630 to 0845 for morning trips and 1400 to 1500 for afternoon trips, depending on season.

Bwaato Safaris, T0213-332 4227, bwaato@ zamnet.zm. Rhino walks in Mosi-oa-Tunya National Park with lunch or snacks and soft drinks, can be combined with a canoeing trip on the Upper Zambezi.

Livingstone Walking Safaris, T0213-332 2267, gecko@zamnet.zm. 3-hr walking safari to see rhino and antelope in the Mosi-oa-Tunya National Park with excellent home-made snacks and refreshments (guide Mickey's wife is a chef).

Tour operators

Bundu Adventures, T0213-324407-8, www. bunduadventures.com. Whitewater rafting on the Zambian side of the falls is more or less the same as on the Zimbabwean side (page 201). There is the option, though, of taking the cable car out of the Bakota Gorge at Rapid 23. Offers full-day trips for US$145, half-day for US$130, from Rapids 1 and 23, and high-water season trips for US$130, from Rapids 10-25. They also offer half-day canoe trips for US$100, and full-day trips for US$110, on the Upper Zambezi, or a combined canoeing and game drive in the Mosi-oa-Tunya National Park for US$120.

Hemingways, T0213-320996, www. hemingwayszambia.com. Specialist company for organizing tailor-made holidays in and around Livingstone for disabled clients with a vehicle equipped for wheelchairs (with a lift); also rents out fully equipped 4WDs with camping/cooking equipment for self-drive.

Safari Par Excellence, office at the Zambezi Waterfront (see Sleeping), T0213-3324601, www.safpar.net. Books all activities and runs its own whitewater rafting and canoeing trips, plus cruises on the Upper Zambezi on the *Lady Livingstone*, a state-of-the-art boat with 3 levels and seating 144 people. Also organizes multi-day canoe trips on the Lower Zambezi, on the stretch of river opposite Zimbabwe's Mana Pools National Park (see page 222).

Wild Side Safaris, Mosi-oa-Tunya Rd, just south of the Falls Park Mall, T0213-323726, www.wildsidesafaris.com. General booking agent for activities in and around Livingstone. Can also arrange day trips to Chobe National park (see page 171).

Whitewater rafting

The low-water run is approximately Jul to Jan. Usually there are 3 possibilities: a full-day trip from Rapids 1-23, a morning half-day trip from Rapids 1-10 or an afternoon half-day trip from Rapids 10-23. The high-water run is from approximately Jan to Jul (stopping altogether if the river level becomes too high), which runs from Rapids 10-23. A cable-car lift out of the gorge at Rapid 23 is included in the price of rafting. At other points, clients will have to walk out of the gorge.

⊖ Transport

Livingstone *p187, maps p162 and p191*
Air

Livingstone Airport is 5 km to the north-west of town (see page 187). There are daily flights between Livingstone and Johannesburg in South Africa with **South African Airways** (SAA), **British Airways** (BA); operated by **Comair**) and South African budget airline **1-Time**. The 1-Time flights, which are easily the best value from about US$110 one-way, leave **Johannesburg** on Mon, Thu and Sun at 1010 and arrive at 1120, departing from Livingstone again at 1250 and arriving back in Johannesburg at 1435; on Fri they leave Johannesburg at 0935 and arrive in Livingstone at 1120, departing at 1210 and arriving back in Johannesburg at 1355. The SAA flight departs Johannesburg at 1040, arrives

in Livingstone at 1230, departs again at 1310 and arrives back in Johannesburg at 1510, and costs about US$120 one-way.
British Airways/Comair flies daily between Johannesburg and Livingstone, for about US$155 one-way, departing Johannesburg at 1145, arriving in Livingstone at 1245, departing again at 1330 and arriving back in Johannesburg at 1515.

Airline offices 1-Time, Livingstone Airport, T0213-322744, South Africa, T+263 (0)11-9288000, www.1time.aero.com. **British Airways/Comair**, Livingstone Airport, T0123-322867, South Africa T+27(0)11-4418600, www.britishairways.com. **South African Airways**, Livingstone Airport, T0213-323032/33, South Africa, T+27-(0)11-9781111, www.flysaa.com.

Bus

There are several economy buses a day between Livingstone and **Lusaka** in Zambia; times vary, but usually the first bus leaves around 0600 and the last one around 1400. Tickets should be booked and paid for the day before departure at the bus station in town on the corner of Mosi-oa-Tunya Rd and Mutelo St. Cost is around US$25 and they take about 6-7 hrs. The South African company **Intercape Mainliner** bus runs between Livingstone and **Windhoek** in Namibia on Mon and Wed at 1200, arriving in Windhoek the next day at 0525. From Windhoek to Livingstone, it departs from Windhoek on Wed and Sun at 1730 and arrives in Livingstone the next day at 1255. There is no contact detail in Zambia, but tickets can be purchased online using a credit card at www.intercape.co.za. The buses depart and arrive next to Barclay's Bank in the middle of town. If travellers are willing to spend a day in Windhoek, another Intercape bus goes from Windhoek to **Cape Town** in South Africa the following evening at 1830; this is a long bus journey but the buses are comfortable with reclining seats, toilets, a/c, and snacks and drinks are served.

ⓘ Directory

Livingstone *p187, maps p162 and p191*
Banks There are banks along the main Mosi-oa-Tunya Rd in the middle of town; **Barclay's**, **Standard Chartered** and **Zanaco**, which have ATMs and foreign-exchange counters. Visa is accepted but you'll have to go into the branches to withdraw from MasterCard. If you pay for hotels, activities, etc with credit/debit card in Zambia, there is a surcharge of about 5%. **Emergencies** 999. **Internet** Most hotels and backpacker hostels offer internet access, some with Wi-Fi; there is also **Rakey Internet Cafe**, opposite the banks on Mosi-oa-Tunya Rd, 0800-2000. **Medical services** Southern Medical Centre, Plot 1967 Mokambo Rd, T097-7777017. Dr Sanjay Shinde is recommended. **Link Pharmacy**, Falls Park Mall, T0213-324222, Mon-Fri 0800-1800, Sat 0800-1300. **Police** Livingstone Central Police Station, Maramba St, behind the market, T0213-323575, 320116, 991. **Post** The main branch is in the middle of town on Mosi-oa-Tunya Rd, Mon-Fri 0800-1700, Sat 0800-1300. **Courier services**: DHL, Mosi-oa-Tunya Building, Mosi-oa-Tunya Rd, www.dhl.com, Mon-Fri 0830-1700. **Fedex**, opposite the post office, T0977-806508, www.fedex.com, Mon-Fri 0830-1700.

Hwange National Park and around

Hwange is the largest national park in Zimbabwe and covers an area of 14,650 sq km – about the size of Belgium – and is larger than all of Zimbabwe's other national parks put together. It's less than two hours' drive southeast from Victoria Falls and makes a popular add-on safari to a visit to the falls. Travellers making their way from Bulawayo to Victoria Falls will pass the main turn-off to the gate. The park was the royal hunting grounds of the Ndebele warrior-king Mzilikazi in the early 19th century and was set aside as a national park in 1929. Hwange boasts a tremendous variety of wildlife with over 100 species of mammal and nearly 400 bird species recorded. The elephants of Hwange are famous and the park's elephant population, is one of the largest in the world, though they migrate to and from Chobe National Park in Botswana, depending on the season, and estimates of their numbers range from 20,000-75,000. The sight of the elephants coming to drink in the dry season at the Nyamandhlovu Pan in the north of the park is a wildlife extravaganza; there are invariably at least a dozen species of game in or near the water, or on the great plain that surrounds it. But when the elephants arrive in herds of 50 strong, the other animals scatter while the elephants wade, splash, throw mud on themselves, and drink their fill. There are also a couple of attractions around Hwange including the adjoining Kazuma Pan National Park and the Painted Dog Conservation Area.
▶▶ *For listings, see pages 208-210.*

South of Victoria Falls → *For listings, see pages 208-210.*

Kazuma Pan National Park → *Colour map 1, C1.*

ⓘ *T013-433526, www.zimparks.com. Take the Robins Camp/Pandamatenga turn-off from Victoria Falls–Bulawayo road (A8), 50 km from Victoria Falls, proceed for 25 km along this gravel road to the Parks and Wildlife offices in Matetsi where visitors are required to check in. Continue along the Pandamatenga road for a further 39 km to the Botswana border. These roads are gravel and can be rough. As access to Kazuma is along the Zimbabwe/Botswana border road, visitors are asked to check in with the Zimbabwe police at Pandamatenga. Kazuma Pan National Park is some 25 km further along, northwest of Pandamatenga. Access via Kazungula is strictly prohibited.*

This park lies on the Botswana border a short distance northwest of Hwange National Park. Some 313 sq km in area, it provides one of Zimbabwe's few areas of plains scenery, with good visibility and sparse but important mammal populations, including roan antelope, tsessebe, cheetah, rhino, buffalo and giraffe. A special species endemic to the Kazuma Depression is the oribi, a small antelope, not often seen in other parts of the country. The park includes a series of pan depressions, some of which are continuously pumped from boreholes in the dry season. As a result, large concentrations of game seasonally migrate between Botswana and Zimbabwe, especially from September through to the first rains of November or December. Much of the park consists of grassland, fringed by mopane and Kalahari sand woodlands, and a series of seasonally flooded pans in the southwest of the park attracts a wide variety of waterfowl, including storks, crowned cranes, stilts, cormorants, ducks and kingfishers. Kazuma Pan was proclaimed a national park in 1949, but this was revoked in 1964 as no development had taken place. It regained its national park status in 1975. A 4WD is essential at all times of the year; the park is closed to the public in January and February due to the wet conditions which make the roads impassable.

Hwange

Hwange was named after a local chief, and was known as Wankie until 1982. It was founded in 1899 when coal was discovered and a village grew up to accommodate the mine workers. Today, Hwange Colliery is the biggest coal mine in Zimbabwe, producing about 5 million tons of coal per year; a coal-fuelled power plant was built here in the late 1990s. Tragedy struck the village in 1972, when an underground explosion occurred in Wankie No 2 Colliery, and 426 miners lost their lives. The main A8 road doesn't go through Hwange itself, and it's a short detour to the left if coming from Bulawayo (take Coronation Drive, between two petrol stations, to get to the centre). There's little reason to stop however, though there is a branch of **TM Supermarket** for provisions.

Painted Dog Conservation Centre

ⓘ *8 km from the turn-off from the main A8 towards Hwange National Park, T018-710, www.painteddog.org, 0800-1800 (get there before 1500 to see the dogs), free but donations appreciated.*

Painted dogs, also known as African wild dogs, are unique to Africa and they are among the continent's most endangered species. It is estimated that a mere 3000 remain. The population in Zimbabwe is one of the last strongholds of the species, and this conservation charity, funded mostly by overseas donations, provides a refuge for rescued wild dogs, mostly pups that have lost their mothers to lions. They are also involved in anti-poaching in Hwange National Park where wild dog get caught and killed in wire snares, which have been put down by poachers to trap antelope. The centre has collected more than 12,000 wire snares from in and around the park since 2001, and some of these have been incorporated into the walls of the thatched visitor centre (built in 2007), a reminder of the damage these snares do. There are also some sculptures made out of the snare wire for sale. The visitor centre is mostly aimed at school groups, but there is nothing you can't learn about wild dog here. A series of giant book pages relates the story of Eyespot, a pup's journey from birth. It includes typical wild dog behaviour and development, such as being fed, learning to hunt and starting a pack. The excursion begins with a guided tour of the visitor centre followed by a walk along an elevated boardwalk over a large enclosure that is home to wild dog. Be warned though: while it is an impressive structure, it's 2.5 m above the ground and a fairly long walk (because of the single hand rail, it is not suitable for small children). Remember to take water. At the other end of the walk, another guide introduces visitors to the dogs at the centre, which is presently home to 10. Whenever possible they are returned to the wild. The wild population of these dogs in Hwange and around is thought to be about 700 today, almost double what it was in the early 1990s when the Painted Dog Conservation project was established.

Hwange National Park → *Colour map 1, C2. For listings, see pages 208-210.*

ⓘ *T018-371/372, www.zimparks.com, 0600-1800, US$20, children (6-12) US$10, under 6 free, car US$5.*

Established in 1929, Hwange National Park is Zimbabwe's biggest and oldest game reserve and was named after a local Nhanzwa chief, Hwange Rosumbani. During colonial times the British mispronounced and misspelt the name of the park, calling it and the nearby town by the unfortunate name of Wankie. It was declared by the Rhodesian government as one of the last retreats for game animals not threatened by human encroachment. Additionally, because of the presence of tsetse fly (which kills cows), the land couldn't be commercially farmed. The first warden was Ted Davison, who held the job for 33 years and developed the roads, camps and boreholes. In 2009 the park celebrated its 60th anniversary as a national park.

Ins and outs

Getting there and around Hwange National Park has three distinctive camps and administrative offices at Robins, Sinamatella and the largest one at Main Camp. The turn-off to the main gate of the park is off the A8, 172 km (a two-hour drive) southeast of Victoria Falls and 265 km (three-hour drive) northwest of Bulawayo. From Victoria Falls,

Hwange National Park

Sleeping 🛏
The Hide **1**
Hwange Safari Lodge **2**
Ivory Lodge **3**
Main Camp **4**

Makololo Plains Camp
 & Little Makololo **5**
Miombo Lodge **6**
Robins Camp **7**
Sikumi Tree Lodge **8**

Sinamatella Camp **9**
Somalisa Camp **10**

the A8 first passes the access road to Robins Camp and the little-visited Kazuma Pan National Park and the small town of **Hwange**, at 70 km from Victoria Falls, before the turn-off to the park's main gate. The 21 km to the main gate is tarred. From the well-signposted junction to the gate it is 11 km to **Hwange Safari Lodge** and 23 km to **Main Camp** just beyond the park gates.

To get to **Robins Camp**, turn off on to a gravel road off the A8, 48 km south of Victoria Falls. From the junction it is approximately 70 km to Robins Camp: en route there is a turn-off to the headquarters of the Matetsi Safari Area (a predominantly hunting concession so therefore not listed) and to Pandamatenga, which then leads to the Kazuma Pan National Park. Robins Camp can also be reached by road through the park from Main Camp during the dry season, but this will take the best part of a day. Accessed by a gravel road about 4 km southeast of Hwange, **Sinamatella Camp** is about 45 km further on, on the border with the Deka Safari Area. The camp can also be reached from Main Camp (again taking most of a day but with game-viewing all the way). Although Hwange borders on northern Botswana, there is no border crossing open to the public.

There is a network of 480 km of gravel roads within the park, but not all the roads are in good condition, especially after the rains. The most popular game-watching area is around **Main Camp** during peak season (July/August), as this is easily accessible by self-drive visitors and the roads are the better ones in the park and regularly graded. Elsewhere the roads require at least high clearance and mostly 4WD in the wet. A number of hides at man-made dams allow visitors to get out of their cars. Accommodation ranges from hotel-type lodges to basic national park chalets at Robins, Sinamatella and Main Camp to luxury privately owned lodges on surrounding private concessions. If you are not in your own vehicle, safaris operate from Victoria Falls (see page 209).

Best time to visit The dry season is from July to September. It is hot during the day but can drop to below freezing on particularly cold winter nights. During these dry months the animals are concentrated around the man-made waterholes, without which they would die as there are few sources of water and Hwange has experienced some long periods of drought in recent years. This is the peak season for game-viewing as the animals are readily seen at the waterholes. Game-viewing is at its very best between September and November when the waterholes lure daunting volumes of wildlife, including roan and sable antelope from across the border in Botswana. During the rainy season, from late November or December until the end of March or early April, big fluffy clouds release the summer rains and the vegetation bursts into life. Daytime temperatures are on average 18–28°C.

Sights

Hwange resembles what much of the interior of Africa was like more than 150 years ago, with plentiful game and unspoiled bush. The landscape comprises grasslands, granite outcrops, savannah, scrubland and scattered woodland. The most remarkable physical aspects of the park are the shallow pans, and the number of natural salt licks (sodium and lime-flavoured water) that attract a large number of game animals from the adjoining Kalahari Desert. Most of the pans are about 20-30 m in diameter and when full of water are about 1 m deep.

All Zimbabwe's protected animals are to be found in Hwange, and the park hosts 105 mammal species, including elephant, buffalo, lion, leopard, white and black rhino, cheetah, giraffe, sable, kudu, eland, waterbuck, wildebeest, impala, zebra, baboon, jackal, bat-eared fox, warthog and many other smaller species. It is the only protected area where gemsbok

Friends of Hwange Trust

Hwange National Park has no perennial rivers and very little natural surface water. The Friends of Hwange Trust was formed in 2005 on the back of an extreme drought in 2004 that severely affected the park. The National Parks and Wildlife Management Authority of Zimbabwe, plagued by lack of funding and a decrease in tourist arrivals, did not have the funding to keep enough borehole pumps going. As a result, only a handful of waterholes had water, and countless animals died of thirst. The trust was formed to offer a long-term solution to water-supply problems in Hwange. Since its inception, it has been responsible for 10 waterholes in the north of Hwange. This has involved raising funds to purchase diesel as well as repairing and maintaining the diesel

engines, boreholes and troughs. Owing to the expense of diesel (a single borehole engine uses around 500 litres a month) alternative methods of pumping have been explored. Since 2007, windmills have been established at five of the boreholes; while the windmills are robust and affordable, their pumping capacities are limited. However, their function is to provide a head start for the waterholes so that they are at least as full as possible by the start of the long dry season, thereby reducing diesel requirements during drier months. Future plans include the installation solar pumps at the waterholes. The trust completely relies on charitable donations from both Zimbabwe and overseas. For more information visit www.friendsofhwange.org.

and brown hyena occur in reasonable numbers, and the population of African wild dog to be found in Hwange is thought to be one of the largest surviving groups in Africa. Birdlife is prolific with some 400 species, including 50 species of raptor.

Elephant have been enormously successful in Hwange, possibly to do with the fact that, compared to elephants in other parts of Africa, they have particularly large tusks, which has gone some way to protecting them against ivory hunters. Today, the estimated population of between 20,000 and 75,000 has increased so much that it cannot be naturally supported by such an area. As a result, some 50 or so man-made waterholes are operated in the park; the first ones were established by sinking boreholes in 1939. However, recent consecutive years of drought in the Hwange region have put a lot of strain on the resources of the park, and has become harder and harder to maintain the water facilities, although the Friends of Hwange (see box, above) perform an incredible job keeping many of the pumps in working order, with the help of privately donated funds.

The park is not fenced and surrounding the park are private concessions (used for game ranching and in some cases hunting), which act as buffer zones for the migratory movement of animals, which are mostly attracted by the availability of water. Elephant, for example, move northwestwards, in and out of Chobe National Park in Botswana. Most of the safari lodges lie just outside the park, in the concession areas where there is still plentiful game.

In the park, the best area to spot game is around **Main Camp** in the north, where the vegetation becomes sparser and the natural pans (fed by the waterholes) make for great game-viewing during the dry season. There are viewing platforms and hides at some of the waterholes, allowing visitors to get out of their vehicles. The **Ten-Mile Drive** from Main Camp to the **Nyamandlovu Pan** showcases all the park's major mammals, and many can be seen from the camp itself.

For Sleeping and Eating price codes and other relevant information, see pages 29-34.

◉ Sleeping

Kazuma Pan National Park *p203*
See page 203, T013-433526, www.zim
parks.com. There are no facilities or
accommodation in the park but camping is
permitted. There are 2 campsites available
and only 2 groups of 10 visitors are allowed
to camp at each site at any one time. The
campsites each have bush toilets, braais
and water.

Hwange National Park *p204, map p205*
Apart from the 3 camps in the park run
by the **Zimbabwe Parks and Wildlife
Management Authority**, the private safari
lodges are on private concession areas.
All the accommodation options offer
game drives into the park, and some offer
additional night drives and walking safaris
within their own areas. Transfers from
Victoria Falls can be arranged with the
private lodges.
L The Hide, next to the Kennedy Gate of
the park, 38 km from the A8, the turn-off is
17 km beyond the turn-off to Main Camp,
towards Bulawayo, reservations Harare, T04-
498835, www.thehide.com. In a peaceful
location overlooking a waterhole, with
8 spacious well-furnished tents under
elaborate thatched roofs, with wooden
decks and outside showers. The honeymoon
suite has a delightful partially open
bathroom with freestanding bathtub. The
central feature is the thatched double-storey
A-frame building with lounge bar (all drinks
are included), where meals are taken around
a large table with the other guests and the
hosts. Pool.
**L Makalolo Plains Camp and Little
Makalolo**, in the east of the park on
the Makololo Pan; reservations through
Wilderness Safaris, www.wilderness-safaris.

com. These are exclusive luxury camps in
a private concession area within the park's
boundaries; Wilderness Safaris provide all
transfers. **Makalolo Plains Camp** is built on
raised teak decks with boardwalks, with 10
large tented rooms, lounge, bar, dining room
and plunge pool, while **Little Makalolo** has
6 spacious rooms, each with private plunge
pool, fireplace and outdoor shower, and an
open-sided lounge and dining boma.
L Somalisa Camp, to the east of the park
in a private concession area, reservations
Harare, T04-234307, www.africanbush
camps.com. Remote camp in the savannah
region on the estern side of the park with
6 elegant en suite tents furnished in colonial
style with outside showers, and special
touches such as hot-water bottles on chilly
evenings or fresh muffins on the game drives.
Very good gourmet food, swimming pool,
which can only be used if elephant aren't
drinking from it (which they do regularly).
B Ivory Lodge, the turn-off is on the
right of the A8, 2 km past the turn-off to
Main Camp if going towards Bulawayo,
reservations, T09-243954 (Bulawayo), www.
ivorysafarilodge.com. Just 6 en suite rooms
set on elevated platforms among the trees,
overlooking a waterhole which is floodlit at
night. You can watch from around an open
fire. Also has a hide, central dining area, bar
and library, set around a pool.
C Hwange Safari Lodge, 11 km from
the A8 on the access road to the Main
Gate, reservations T04-736645 (Harare),
www.africansunhotels.com. Overlooking
a pan, this is a large somewhat dated
lodge with over 100 a/c rooms, some with
TV, in double-storey blocks with patios and
balconies, in extensive grounds. Has a large
pool, cocktail bar, 2 restaurants and a curio
shop. African and continental buffets are
served for dinner, which is accompanied
by traditional dancing. A reasonably
comfortable option but a bit too
impersonal for some.

C Sikumi Tree Lodge, off the A8 3 km beyond the turn-off to Main Camp towards Bulawayo, reservations through **Rainbow Hotels**, T04-772588 (Harare), www. sikumitreehotel.com. Comfortable en suite accommodation in 13 thatched chalets on stilts (not tree houses), partially open-sided with curtains. Pool, central boma with restaurant and bar, buffet meals, curio shop, a fire is lit in the evening, and there are electric blankets for chilly nights.

C-D Main Camp, just beyond the main gate, T018-371/2, www.zimparks.com. This is a large rest camp, where the main office is located. There are also a grocery shop for basic provisions (though no fresh food), restaurant which serves breakfast and the likes of steak and chips and a vegetarian dish for lunch or dinner, bar, curio shop and fuel station (though don't rely on fuel supplies). Accommodation is in a variety of mostly thatched units, including 1- or 2-bed fully equipped self-catering lodges with fridge, stove and all utensils; 1- or 2-bed cottages sharing a central open cooking and dining area with hot plates and fridges but no utensils; 1- or 2-bed chalets with fridge and braai and shared ablutions in a communal block; and a campsite (**F**) with a braai, a tap at each pitch and an ablution block.

C-D Miombo Lodge, 17 km along the access road to Main Camp, then turn left for 10 km, T018-446, www.miombolodge. com. Nestled in the bush overlooking a waterhole, this has 3 en suite tree houses on stilts and under thatch, with fans and balconies, 4 simple rooms with outside shower, and a spacious sandy campsite (**F**) with hot showers, communal cooking area, and a bonfire at night. There's a restaurant, bar and pool, and night drives and walks can be organized.

C-D Robins Camp, T018-371/2, www. zimparks.com. One of the 3 national park camps, this is close to the western boundary of Hwange, approximately 60 km from Sinamatella (see below) and 140 km from Main Camp (see above); traffic between

Main Camp and Robins (and the other way round) must leave by 1200. It can also be reached independently from the A8 (see page 205 for details about access). This camp was bequeathed to the government in 1939 by a local farmer, Harold Robins, hence the name. It has lodges, chalets and camping sites as described in Main Camp, plus a restaurant, bar, shop and fuel station.

C-D Sinamatella, T018-371/2, www. zimparks.com. Established in 1966, this part of the park was a former cattle ranch and the camp is located near the northern boundary of the park on a 55-m-high outcrop overlooking a distant riverbed and grassy plain. The camp is approximately 120 km from Main Camp (see above), though vehicles are not allowed to travel between the 2 camps after 1400. It can also be reached independently from the A8 (see page 205 for details about access). Again accommodation and facilities are the same as Main Camp.

▲ Activities and tours

Hwange National Park *p204, map p205*
Main Camp can organize short 2-km game walks with an armed ranger to a hide at **Sedina Pan** where you can sit for a while and watch. For US$6 per person they also do night drives at full moon only. Early morning and late afternoon game drives into the park are offered by all the private lodges and are usually included in the rates. Day trips to Hwange National Park from Victoria Falls are organized by the tour operators there (see page 181), for around US$150, departing Victoria Falls at 0630 and arriving back at around 1800; they include picnic breakfast and lunch, usually taken at one of the game-viewing platforms around the park. Overnight and multi-night trips can also be arranged from US$250.
Leon Varley Walking Safaris, bookings through **Backpackers Bazaar**, Old Vic Falls Centre, T013-45828, 44611, www.walkafrica. com. Leon (see page 181) runs a 5-day

walking safari in the Sinamatella area of Hwange using mobile camps. Prices start at US$150 per day and are inclusive of transfers from Victoria Falls, parks fees, guide, food and drinks.

Varden Safaris, reservations, T04-861766 (Harare), www.ridinginhwange.com. James and Janine can organize 7-night/8-day horse-riding safaris in Hwange for about US$2900 per person. These start with a night at Ivory Lodge followed by 5 nights in mobile camps in the park, in basic tents. (The horses are kept in a canvas shelter surrounded by a portable electric fence.) The safari ends at Somalisa Camp (see Sleeping) on the last night. Transfers are arranged from Victoria Falls.

⊖ Transport

Hwange National Park *p204, map p205*
Air
There is an airstrip south of Hwange Safari Lodge but no commercial flights operate anymore.

Bus
Economy buses and the **City Link** service travel along the A8 en route between **Victoria Falls** and **Bulawayo**. However, only the economy buses will stop at the junction for Main Camp. It may be possible to hitch the 11 km to the Hwange Safari Lodge or the 23 km to Main Camp, but this is not to be relied upon. The best option is to organize a transfer from Victoria Falls with one of the tour operators – try **Wild Horizons** (page 184), which charges around US$60 per person for a transfer to Hwange Safari, or book a safari from Victoria Falls. The private lodges around Hwange also organize transfers for their guests.

Contents

Zambezi Valley

At a glance

⊖ **Getting around** Local economy
buses or car hire from Harare to
Kariba town. A ferry runs the length
of Lake Kariba.
◐ **Time required** 1 day in Kariba
to see the dam, 3 nights on a
houseboat, 3 days in Mana Pools
National Park.
◑ **Weather** Hot and dry Sep-Nov,
hot and wet late Nov-Mar, cool and
dry May-Aug.
✕ **When not to go** Although
game-viewing is best Sep-Nov,
temperatures can be 40°C.

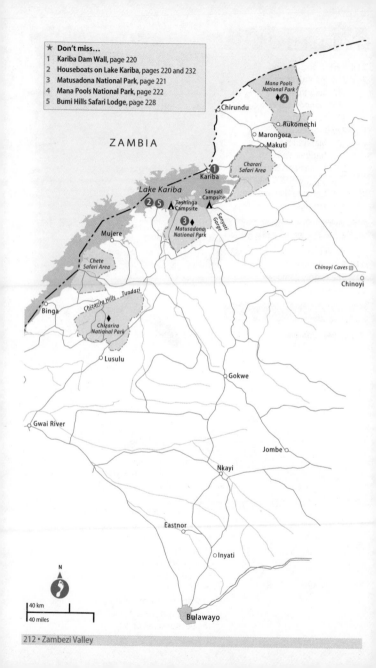

★ Don't miss...
1 Kariba Dam Wall, page 220
2 Houseboats on Lake Kariba, pages 220 and 232
3 Matusadona National Park, page 221
4 Mana Pools National Park, page 222
5 Bumi Hills Safari Lodge, page 228

ZAMBIA

Mana Pools
National Park

Chirundu

Rukomechi

Marongora

Makuti

Lake Kariba

Kariba

Charari
Safari Area

Sanyati
Campsite

Tashinga
Campsite

Sanyati
Gorge

Matusadona
National Park

Mujere

Chinoyi Caves

Chinoyi

Chete
Safari Area

Chizarira Hills   Tundazi

Binga

Chizarira
National Park

Lusulu

Gokwe

Gwai River

Jombe

Nkayi

Eastnor

Inyati

N

40 km
40 miles

Bulawayo

At 226 km long and 40 km wide in some places, and with a surface area of over 5000 sq km, Lake Kariba is Africa's largest man-made dam, and by volume is the largest artificial lake and reservoir in the world. It dams the Zambezi River about 1300 km upstream from the Indian Ocean, about halfway between the river's source and its mouth. It was filled between 1958 and 1963 and is considered to be one of the greatest engineering feats in Africa. It also sparked one of the largest animal relocations that's ever happened, when thousands of animals were rescued from the rising floodwaters in Operation Noah. Today, the lake provides considerable electric power to both Zambia and Zimbabwe and supports a thriving commercial fishing industry. The creation of the lake has also provided a spectacular shoreline which attracts big game, endless views, stunning sunsets, and opportunities for great fishing and boating.

The town of Kariba, born as a place to house the dam's construction workers, has evolved into a springboard for a number of lakeshore lodges and has a harbour full of houseboats to take visitors on leisurely cruises. It also offers access to the national parks on the Lower Zambezi, including the remote Matusadona and more accessible Mana Pools.

Kariba and around

Kariba town is on the lakeshore but it's little more than a sprawling village that acts as a service centre for the local lodges and houseboats on Lake Kariba. It is also the nearest settlement to the dam wall from where there are viewpoints. The drive from Harare to Kariba is very pleasant, especially as it approaches the Zambezi Escarpment, 500-600 m over the lake itself, and then sinks down into the Zambezi Valley, though there are few worthwhile stops except for the Chinhoyi Caves. The highlight of this region is the magnificent Mana Pools National Park with its attractive Zambezi riverfront which attracts numerous species of game. ▸▸ *For listings, see pages 228-233.*

Ins and outs → *Phone code 061. Population 20,000.*

Getting there and around

Air Kariba has an **airport** to the east of town. **Air Zimbabwe** has ceased flying there but **Federal Air** has been running a shuttle service between Harare and Kariba (see Transport, page 233). The company can also organize charter flights to the various lodges that have airstrips.

Car Kariba is 366 km northwest of Harare via **Chinoyi** along the A1, part of the Great North Road, which continues on into Zambia and all the way through to Tanzania and Kenya. About 41 km from Harare it passes over **Zimbabwe's Great Dyke**. This is a shallow trough, estimated to be about 500 km long, which is rich in mineral wealth; mining activities can be seen along the length of the ridge. About 92 km from Harare the road passes through the small agricultural and mining town of **Banket**, and then 20 km beyond reaches Chinoyi, the location for the unusual Chinoyi Caves (see below). From here, it continues northwest for another 176 km to **Makuti** where there is a turn-off to the left for Kariba, a spectacular 79-km drive that descends the Zambezi Valley. Elephant are often spotted on this road, and the engineers who built the road when the dam was constructed followed the course of a well-worn elephant path, as the animals clearly knew the easiest way was to descend the valley to the Zambezi. The A1 continues northwest to the border with Zambia and Chirundu (see Border crossing, page 226), another 64 km, climbing the Zambezi Escarpment before dropping down to the border. Access to the southern end of the lake is via **Binga** from the A8, the Bulawayo–Victoria Falls road (see page 226). Economy buses run from Harare to Kariba to the Mahombe Kombe Township near the post office and shops.

Ferry The **Kariba Ferry** ⓘ *www.karibaferries.com*, was suspended for several years but has been operational again since 2009. It travels along the whole of Lake Kariba from Kariba town to Mlibizi, which is 80 km north of the A8 Bulawayo–Victoria Falls road and the junction is 16 km east of Hwange National Park's main gate, 172 km southeast of Victoria Falls. This is a passenger and car ferry (see Transport, page 233 for contact details and prices). It carries up to 70 people and 15 vehicles, and departs from both Kariba and Mlibizi at 0900 and arrives at both at 0700 the following day, taking 22 hours in either direction. Booking is essential. Sleeping is in reclining chairs or on mattresses on deck (a pillow and blanket are supplied), there are toilets and hot showers, and rates include three meals a day and tea and coffee; there's also a cash bar. With a vehicle, this service is a means of getting from one end of the lake to the other, and even without a vehicle a two-way

Nyaminyami

The name Kariba is corrupted from a local BaTonga name, *kariwa*, meaning trap, and refers to a rock which once thrust out of the swirling waters of the Zambezi. Close to the dam wall, it is now buried more than 30 m below the surface of the water. In BaTonga legend, this rock was regarded as the home of the river god Nyaminyami, who was revered as the god of water, on which the BaTonga people relied. The god is believed to be a serpent-like creature, with the head of a fish, and about 3 m wide (reputedly nobody dared guess its length). The BaTonga believed that Nyaminyami was married, and the building of the dam wall on Lake Kariba would separate him from his wife. The construction of the dam would therefore anger him and cause him to threaten the dam project, thus representing the vengeance of the BaTonga people, who were themselves angry about losing their homes.

It seems they were right. The colonialists mocked the stories of Nyaminyami, but when construction started they became apprehensive. On the night of 15 February 1950 a cyclone from the Indian Ocean swept up the valley, something that had never been known in this landlocked territory, and

the river rose 7 m that night. Then a survey team perished in a landslide. On Christmas Eve 1955, with work on the dam well underway, an unprecedented flood stormed down the gorge and washed away the foundations of the coffer dam and the recently constructed pontoon bridge. The flood peaked, receded and then peaked again, also unprecedented. Nyaminami struck again in 1956 when the river rose almost 6 m in a 24-hour period and surged over the coffer dam, and a flood in 1957 destroyed equipment and access roads; 18 workers died when they fell into wet concrete. An even larger flood in 1958 carried a staggering 16 million litres of water per second, destroying the access bridge, the coffer dam and parts of the main wall. Nyaminyami had made good his threat – he had recaptured the gorge.

Although man eventually won the battle and the dam finally opened in 1960, there was a whole new respect for the power of the river god. The BaTonga still live around Lake Kariba, and many believe that one day Nyaminyami will fulfil his promise and destroy the dam, allowing them to return to their homes on the banks of the river.

trip is an excellent way to see the lake on what could be described as a 'Karibean Cruise'. Accommodation in Mlibizi is restricted to a small lakeside resort (self-catering chalets and a campsite) next to the ferry terminal (see Sleeping, page 231).

Best time to visit

The climate on and around Lake Kariba is generally tropical with three reasonably defined seasons: a hot rainy season from late November to March, when there can often be high humidity and violent afternoon thunderstorms, a cool dry season from May to August, and a very hot dry season from September to November. Annual rainfall ranges from 400 mm in the Zambezi Valley to about 700 mm on the Zambezi Escarpment. Daytime winter temperatures rarely go below 13°C in the cooler months and hover at about 40°C in the hotter months. Game-watching along the lakeshore is better in the dry seasons as there is no long grass to restrict viewing, but these are also the hottest times and too uncomfortable for many people. Mosquitoes are a problem all year in the Zambezi Valley,

Kariba & Kariba East

ZAMBIA

Zambezi

Kariba Dam

Kariba

Nyyamhunga Township

Sampakaruma Island

Rhino Island

Redcliff Island

Long Island

Antelope Island

Fothergill Island

Changachirere

Spurwing Island

Bed Island

Tstetse Island

To Tiger Bay, Tashinga Campsite

Matusadona National Park

Sanyati

Dandawa Sampakaruma

Game Fence

ZAMBIA

Kariba Dam

Border Post

Shops

Spar Supermarket

Andora Harbour

Commercial Fishing Harbour

Kariba Yacht Club

Kariba Heights

Kariba Country Club

Church of Santa Barbara

so precautions must be taken (see Health, page 40).

Tourist information

There is no tourist information office in Kariba but **Wild Zambezi** ⓘ *www.wildzambezi.com*, is a private enterprise offering listings of local operators and lodges in the Zambezi Valley. It is the most up-to-date resource in the region.

Background

Lake Kariba is over 226 km long, up to 40 km wide and 29 m deep. It covers an area of 5580 sq km and its storage capacity is an immense 185 cu km. The dam was an initiative of the Federation of Rhodesia and Nyasaland, formed by British-ruled Northern and Southern Rhodesia (now Zambia and Zimbabwe) and Nyasaland (Malawi), with the aim of producing a hydroelectric power station for the region. Despite the fact that damming the great Zambezi flood plain would result in vast areas of forest and scrub being inundated, thousands of wild animals losing their habitats and local villages being relocated, analysis of the economic advantages convinced the authorities that the benefits of building a dam would outweigh the loss of wildlife and disturbance to people's lives. Building the dam wall began in the late 1950s, with the French engineer Andre Coyne, a specialist in 'arch dams', who had designed 55 dams around the world, taking the helm. Well over a million cubic metres of concrete was poured into the 36.6-m-high wall to obtain a thickness of over 24 m, sufficient to sustain the pressure of nearly 10 million litres of water passing through the spillway each second. At the end of 1958, the sluice gates were closed and by 1963 the lake was full.

The land on which the dam was built was home to more than 50,000 people, mostly of the BaTonga tribe (see page 251), many of whom were vehemently against being

To Makuti Airport & Mana Pools National Park

Charara

Zebra Island

Charara Point

Game Fence

Charara Safari Area

Nyaodza Point

Nematombo

Mudzema

Namunga

⑥

Sleeping 🛏
Bumi Hills **1**
Caribbea Bay Hotel & Casino **2**
Chura Bushcamp **3**
Cutty Sark Hotel **4**
Fothergill Safari Lodge **5**
Gache Gache Lodge **6**
Lomagundi Lakeside
  Association **7**
Rhino Safari Camp **8**
Spurwing Island **9**
Warthogs Bushcamp **10**

Eating 🍴
Polly's **1**

N

4 km
4 miles

displaced. Although land was set aside for them further up the valley, they were reluctant to leave their tribal lands and feared displeasing their god Nyaminyami (see box, page 215). It took many months of reasoning and coaxing to convince the people that the dam would provide power – a luxury they had no knowledge of – for the whole country. Eventually, however, when the trucks moved in to relocate them, they conceded, having little choice. Schools and clinics were built in some of the new areas, and wells installed. Some of the new villages that were relocated close to the water's edge have prospered through fishing. The introduction from Lake Tanganiyika of kapenta (see page 252), a tiny sardine-like fish, was very successful and has become a high-protein staple food for those living around the lake. But many BaTonga people mourned the loss of the rich alluvial river soil of their former home and battled to produce crops in the higher sandier areas. For the most part, the move was a severe disruption of their way of life and compensation was minimal.

Operation Noah

As the dam began to fill, it became evident that thousands of animals were being stranded on what were effectively man-made islands, with little or no hope of getting off, or even of survival. The small islands formed by the rising water could not possibly feed all the game trapped on them. Appeals were made and money raised to buy boats and equipment for their rescue and relocation, and over 60 game wardens from both Southern and Northern Rhodesia were recruited. The project took place between 1958 and 1964 and became known as Operation Noah. It was a mammoth task and beset by numerous hazards: submerged trees and stumps threatened the hulls of the boats and huge concentrations of snakes, including the deadly black mamba, infested the islands. Numerous ways of capturing the animals were employed. The rhino, for example, were darted, loaded onto rafts buoyed up by petrol drums, and towed to the mainland; an astonishing 44 rhino were rescued in this way. The rescuers also discovered that many of the animals could swim, in which case they were herded through the water and on to dry land. Those that could not swim were driven to shallow water where the animals were easily captured and transported to shore.

Word of the operation spread, and in February 1959 the British newspapers published details of the rescue. Quickly it caught the world's imagination, and within days, reporters, feature writers and film crews were on their way to Kariba. Soon, there were more media people than rescuers, and their presence frequently hampered operations. But they captured in words and in pictures some of the most dramatic and heart-warming sights of the rescued animals, which would have otherwise gone unrecorded and unseen. The story triggered public support overseas and put pressure on governments to help the rescue project. Better equipment arrived on the ground, particularly from Britain and the United States.

In all, some 6000 animals were saved during Operation Noah, including elephant, antelope, rhino, lion, leopard, zebra, warthog, small birds and even snakes. But there were many sad stories too – monkeys starving on treetops, unable to swim to shore, and countless smaller animals, reptiles and insects that simply drowned. Nevertheless, the project is still considered one of the world's most successful and remarkable rescue stories. The operation was led by senior game warden Rupert Fothergill, after which Fothergill Island in the lake is now named.

The mighty Zambezi

The Zambezi River rises in northwestern Zambia and its catchment area covers 1,352,000 sq km. It is 3540 km long and runs through six countries: Zambia, Angola, Namibia, Botswana, Zimbabwe and Mozambique, where it enters the Indian Ocean at Quelimane. It is the fourth-largest river in Africa after the Nile, Zaire and Niger rivers, and the largest to flow into the Indian Ocean. The population of the Zambezi River Valley is estimated to be about 32 million and it supports one of Africa's greatest concentrations of animals. It bubbles up very close to the border where Zambia, Angola and the DRC meet, and then enters Angola for about 230 km, where it accumulates the bulk of its headwater drainage, re-entering Zambia again at Cholwezi rapids, flowing due south but substantially enlarged by the entry of various tributaries. As it turns to an easterly direction, it forms the border between Zambia and Namibia and eventually joins up with the Chobe River in the Caprivi Swamps, briefly forming a border with Botswana. For the next 500 km it serves as the border between Zambia and Zimbabwe, thundering over the Victoria Falls and through the narrow, steadily deepening Batoka Gorge, which flattens out at the broad Gwembe Valley. From here, it flows into Lake Kariba for 265 km and is then joined by two large tributaries, the Kafue and Luangwa from Zambia. Over the border of Mozambique it flows into the 270-km-long Lake Cahora Bassa, and after another 650 km fans out into a delta and enters the Indian Ocean, augmented by the Shire River, which joins the Zambezi 160 km before the sea, bringing waters from Lake Malawi. The resources of the Zambezi are harnessed at various points along the way including the Kariba and Cahora Bassa dams, which have both formed great lakes. Kariba provides electricity for Zimbabwe and Zambia, while Cahora Bassa provides electricity for Mozambique and South Africa.

Chinhoyi Caves → For listings, see pages 228-233. Colour map 1, B6.

ⓘ 8 km northwest of Chinhoyi off the A1; sunrise-sunset; US$10, children (under 12) US$5.

The town of Chinhoyi lies 115 km northwest of Harare on the A1 en route to Chirundu and Kariba. Oddly for the region, it was established by Italian settlers in 1906. The area around Chinhoyi is full of limestone and dolomite sinkholes, once used by the local Shona tribes for storing grain and as a refuge from invading tribes. The largest are the Chinhoyi Caves, named after a local chief who used them as a refuge from Ndebele raiders. The first European to see them was the explorer Fredrick Selous in 1887. This system of caverns and tunnels is dying (in geological time spans), in that they are slowly collapsing. The **Wonder Hole**, the main feature of the caves, has a collapsed roof; hence its name. The 46-m descent in the Wonder Hole, with its pool of cobalt-blue water, is very impressive. The daylight from above and the high concentrations of limestone give the crystal-clear non-flowing water a translucent aquamarine colour. It is known as the Sleeping Pool or Chirorodzira ('Pool of the Fallen'), as in the early 19th century locals were often thrown into the pool by invading tribes. Exploration by divers has revealed several underwater passages, but all those so far explored lead back to the Sleeping Pool.

The temperature in the pool never varies from 22°C and the diving is worth a dip (see page 232). With local negotiation and properly equipped, you could camp here.

Getting around

Although Kariba is very small, its layout is a little confusing, as it spreads out over about 12 km of lakeshore and some big hills. Local commuter omnibuses link the various townships and the Kariba Heights suburb (the original village, where the Zimbabwean whites later had their holiday homes). There's a small supermarket here, a bank, and the Kariba Country Club, with good views of the dam from a higher elevation. Nyamhunga Township, on the flat lakeshore out towards the airport, is probably considered to be the centre of Kariba, where the council offices, a **Spar** supermarket, a bank, fresh produce market and small shopping centre with basic shops, are located. Mahombe Kombe Township at the harbour also has a **Spar** supermarket, petrol station and post office. The other petrol station is on the main road coming into Kariba, about 1.5 km after the turn-off to the Cutty Sark Hotel, where there's also a takeaway.

The dam wall

Anytime spent in Kariba should include a visit to the dam wall, if nothing else to witness its sheer size. A display at the entrance of the bridge across the top describes the building of the wall and the statistics involved. To go on to the wall itself, you'll need to show your passport at the police checkpoint. You can also scramble up the hill to **Observation Point** to see the dam wall in its entirety. The contrasting views – of the vast lake stretching to infinity on the one side and the sheer drop to the gorge on the other – is very impressive. When the land was flooded, the tops of many trees in the lake remained above water. The mopane and leadwood trees (among the world's hardest woods) lost their foliage and died, but did not rot immediately. Without their leaves, and because of the hardiness of their wood, they appear to have fossilized. Today, these stark sentinels are home to a rich bird population.

Church of Santa Barbara

Built by the Italian construction company that worked on the dam wall, the Church of Santa Barbara is in Kariba Heights. A curved semi-open structure reminiscent of the dam's shape, it is dedicated to those who built the wall, and particularly to 87 workers who died during its construction. They died through accidents, malaria and heatstroke, and there's a plaque with their names.

Houseboats

Easily the best way to explore Lake Kariba is on a houseboat, which cruise around the islands and creeks and along the shore of the Matusadona National Park. They are very comfortable, the experience is very relaxing, and there are excellent opportunities for spotting game as the animals come down to the water to drink. For those who are interested you can catch tigerfish and bream from a tender boat. When the vessels are in the middle of the lake, you can swim – there's no danger of hippo and crocodiles in the deeper water – and some of the boats have a 'swimming cage' which is dropped into the lake. There are dozens of houseboats in Kariba's harbour of varying sizes but most are pontoons with large boxey double-storey structures on top. Most are well equipped, with en suite bedrooms, air conditioning, a lounge and bar area, and some have a plunge pool, large deck with sun loungers and wrap-around balconies. They can accommodate 6-12 people and are ideal for a group of friends or two families travelling together, with three nights being the average length of a trip. Nights are spent parked up in a remote bay on the lake; if you have a mosquito net, you can sleep on deck. It's blissfully quiet except for the occasional roar of a lion. You can opt for catered trips, or self-catering, in which case you'll need to take your own food and drinks, though the crew will cook for you and stock the bar with your beverages (all these can be bought from the Spar supermarket in the Mahombe Kombe Township). Costs depend on which option you choose and the size of the boat, from US$300 to US$800 per night to charter the whole boat. Most houseboats are individually operated and owned, so the best way to book is through an agent (see Activities and tours, page 232). Alternatively, if you have the time to organize a trip yourself, make your way to the harbour and ask around.

Matusadona National Park → For listings, see pages 228-233. Colour map 1, B4.

Matusadona became a game reserve in 1963 and, in 1975, a national park. The principal lakeside location of rescued animals during Operation Noah in the 1950s and 1960s (see page 218). It comprises 1400 sq km of rugged lakeside and mountainous wilderness with limited access. Its name is a corruption of the local name of *Matuzviadonha* meaning 'falling dung', which may be a reference to the sight of elephants dropping dung balls as they struggled up the hills. Operation Noah contributed greatly to the increase of large mammal populations in the area, especially elephant, rhino and buffalo, and the grass on the shoreline needs only fluctuating lake levels to replenish its nutrients. With this ready food source, waterbuck, zebra and impala have thrived, and with them the predators, including a large number of lion. There are very few tracks in the park and most people visit the park's shoreline from the deck of a houseboat or from one of the private lodges. In any case, this is where you'll see most of the game, as the animals come down to drink.

Ins and outs

ⓘ *The national park is approximately 30 km across the lake from Kariba by boat; open sunrise-sunset; US$15, children (under 12) US$7.50, car US$5.*

There is a small, 800-m landing strip at Tashinga Camp (see Sleeping, page 229) that can take small charter aircraft, but this must be prearranged with **Zimbabwe Parks and Wildlife Management Authority** first (see page 32). Houseboats (see above) often come across the lake from Kariba (about 30 km) and moor overnight on the park's shoreline; entry to the park is included in the cost of the houseboat charter, although passengers aren't allowed to get off the boat unless it can arrange an armed ranger for a walking safari (discuss this when booking). By road, the park is normally reached via Karoi on the A1, the Harare–Chirundu/Kariba road. From Karoi, the turn-off is 8 km north of town (turn left through the Hurungwe communal land, and then after 115 km cross the Sanyati River, continue on the Binga Road for a further 62 km and then turn right and continue for 82 km to Tashinga Camp, the headquarters of the park). Except for a short distance of narrow tar, when you leave the Harare–Chirundu road, the roads are either gravel or dirt. The last 82 km are particularly rough and 4WD is mandatory, as there are several river crossings. Game-viewing roads within the park are closed during the rainy season. **Note** There is no fuel available outside the main centres on either the A1 or A8 so carry extra jerry cans. If you don't have a 4WD and aren't on a houseboat trip, the most practical way to visit the park is to book into one of the lodges on the periphery of the park (see Sleeping, page 228), which organize light aircraft or speedboat transfers.

Sights

Matusadona has three distinct ecological areas: the lake and shoreline grassland with its rich and fertile flood plains; the Zambezi Valley floor, a mass of thick jesse and mopane woodland; and the 700-m escarpment area of munondo and mountain acacia woodlands, with a rising wall of mountains serving as a majestic backdrop. Animal species that are found in abundance include elephant and buffalo. The latter are especially prominent and herds up to 1000-strong often congregate along the shoreline in the dry season. Other common species include honey badger, civet cat, small spotted genet, mongoose, spotted hyena, wild cat, lion, black rhino, zebra, warthog, common duiker, grysbok, klipspringer, waterbuck, bushbuck, vervet monkey, baboon, side-striped jackal, hippo, roan antelope and kudu, and smaller mammals like dassie (rock hyrax), porcupine and bush squirrel. Some of the more elusive species include reedbuck, sable, eland, bush pig, wild dog and cheetah. There are over 240 species of bird present, including waders, herons, plovers, storks and cormorants. African fish eagles are a common sight on the lake, where they perch on the remains of the half-submerged trees jutting out of the water. Another birdwatching highlight is seeing the saddlebill stork – Africa's largest stork – in the marshy areas of the lakeshore.

Mana Pools National Park → *For listings, see pages 228-233. Colour map 1, A5.*

Easily one of Zimbabwe's highlights, the 2196-sq-km Mana Pools National Park is a wildlife conservation area and a UNESCO World Heritage Site located along the shores of the Zambezi in the extreme north of Zimbabwe, on the border with Zambia. It's often overlooked by foreign visitors who favour Hwange National Park because of its proximity to Victoria Falls, but the adventurous will find Mana Pools the most scenic and wildest park in Zimbabwe. The region actually covers three different areas: the Mana Pools National Park, and the Sapi and Chewore safari areas, which in total cover an area of over 10,000 sq km, where the animals roam freely. On the riverine strip, large groups of animals congregate on the flood plains during the dry season when water elsewhere is scarce. The park is home to over 6500 elephants, 11,000 buffalo, as well as healthy populations of black rhino, lion, hippo, crocodile, leopard and cheetah, numerous species of antelope and 350 species of bird. The mountains of the escarpment across the border in Zambia form a beautiful backdrop to the park, and the shady acacia and mahogany trees make it an ideal environment for rewarding walking safaris.

Ins and outs

① *Open sunrise-sunset, US$15, children (under 12) US$7.50, car US$5; the park may be closed for some months during the rainy season, check with the Zimbabwe Parks and Wildlife Management Authority, Harare, T04-706077-8, or Bulawayo, T09-65592, www.zimparks.com.* During the dry season (May to November), the main tracks in Mana Pools are accessible to 2WD vehicles with a high ground clearance, but a 4WD is preferable, even in the dry season, as this allows you to drive on the less used tracks in the park. Access to the park is from the A1, the Harare–Chirundu tarred road. The Zimbabwe Parks and Wildlife Management Office is on the main road at the top of the Zambezi Escarpment, at Marongora, 16 km northwest of Makuti, the turn-off to Kariba and the last fuel stop, and 315 km northwest of Harare. You must stop at the office (before 1530) to pay and get permits. From the office, continue for 6 km to the bottom of the escarpment and the turn-off to the park, which is 25 km northwest of Makuti and 39 km before the Chirundu border post. Just before the junction there is a tsetse-fly barrier where a vet will inspect your vehicle. Immediately after turning off the main road there is a boom where a warden will sign the permit that you picked up at Marongora. From here, all roads are unsealed and tough with sharp stones; it's 80 km to the main camp at Nyamepi, which should take about two hours depending on the state of the road. About 30 km after the first boom gate, there is a second one at Nyakasikana Gate, where permits are checked again. This boom is on a T-junction, and to get to Nyamepi you need to turn left. You should have seen game by now, especially elephant. It is now 47 km to Nyamepi, on a better stretch of road. As you enter the clearer area of the flood plain the game becomes more abundant. On arriving at Nyamepi, you must register at the office.

There is a formal campsite at Nyamepi, but there are also several places for wilderness camping in the park; for example, from Nyamepi, you can backtrack for about 3 km, follow

Mana Pools National Park

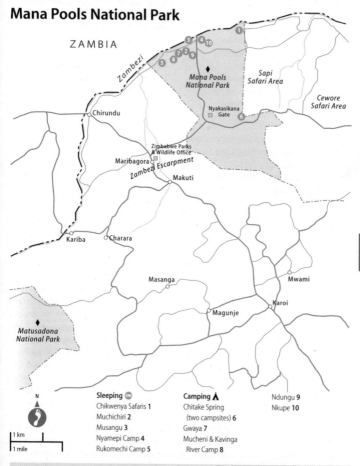

ZAMBIA

Zambezi

Chirundu

Mana Pools
National Park

Sapi
Safari Area

Cewore
Safari Area

Nyakasikana
Gate

Zimbabwe Parks
& Wildlife Office

Maribagora

Zambezi Escarpment

Makuti

Kariba   Charara

Masanga

Mwami

Magunje   Karoi

Matusadona
National Park

N

1 km
1 mile

Sleeping
Chikwenya Safaris **1**
Muchichiri **2**
Musangu **3**
Nyamepi Camp **4**
Rukomechi Camp **5**

Camping
Chitake Spring
(two campsites) **6**
Gwaya **7**
Mucheni & Kavinga
River Camp **8**

Ndungu **9**
Nkupe **10**

Walking in the wild

A traveller's guide to walking safely in the African bush: caution and common sense will help, paranoia will not. If you are likely to be nervous, take an armed guide with you. The following tips are provided by www.wildzambezi.com:

- Respect the fact that the animals are wild and may behave unpredictably, especially if they are frightened, wounded or have young.
- Don't walk alone or at night.
- Walk at times of the day when predators are less active, such as morning to mid-afternoon.
- Walk quietly so that all your senses can be fully alert and be aware of what's around you at all times.

- Avoid long grass or thick bush.
- Avoid the temptation to get too close to animals in order to get that ultimate photo opportunity. Instead use binoculars and a telephoto lens.
- If you are taking photographs, make sure that somebody else keeps an eye on the surroundings and can warn you if anything approaches.
- If you come unexpectedly close to an animal or a snake, stop, try to remain calm and then back off very slowly, or stay still until it moves off. Do not run or shout.
- Never swim in rivers or pools and stay back from the water where banks are shallow; crocodile and hippo are some of Africa's most dangerous predators to humans.

the tracks to the Zambezi and camp under any tree (see Sleeping, page 230). There are no compounds or fences in these areas, so your visitors will be elephant, hyena, honey badger and the like. It is pretty safe to leave camping equipment strewn around but secure all food stocks. It is forbidden to bring fruit into the park, as the smell attracts monkeys, baboons and hyenas, among other animals. If leaving your tent at night, shine a torch around too, as hyenas are likely to be sniffing around your campsite and have little fear of humans. Also be aware that malaria precautions are absolutely essential and temperatures can reach a suffocating 45°C in the middle of summer. If driving, it is also essential to bring extra jerry cans of fuel and drinking water.

Walking safaris

There are a number of game-viewing roads running along the Zambezi and further inland. The name 'Mana' means four in Shona, and this applies to the four large pools inland from the Zambezi River. These pools are the remnant ox-bow lakes that the Zambezi carved out thousands of years ago as it changed course northwards. They are home to hippo and crocodile, and attract a wide variety of aquatic birds as well as large herds of elephant, which come out of the thickly vegetated areas to drink. Compared to other parks, which have few places where you are permitted to get out of a vehicle, the beauty of Mana Pools is that you are allowed to get out of your car and walk – anytime, anywhere. That said, this is not necessarily advisable and those uninitiated in bush-lore would do better to hire an armed ranger from the offices at Nyamepi Camp or book an organized tour (see Activities and tours, page 232). Visitors can walk cautiously in the open woodland of mahogany, wild figs, ebonies and baobabs, around the pools and along the river, which is wide and lazy here, dotted with sandbanks and grassy islands. Visibility is good, and elephant, eland, buffalo, impala, waterbuck, baboon, monkey, zebra, warthog and hippo are some of the larger herbivores to be seen regularly. Lion, leopard, spotted hyena and cheetah are present in the area, but their secretive nature makes them more difficult to see. Despite this, it is not often that the visitor leaves Mana Pools without seeing at least one of these large carnivores.

Mana Pools is also a very special place for birds. Fish eagles and many species of stork, heron and other water-based fowl are common, scarlet carmine bee-eaters visit in the dry months to nest in colonies in the river banks, and rare treats include the elusive Pels fishing owl and the African skimmer, which nests on sandbanks in the middle of the river. Also look out for crested guinea fowl, the less common species of the guinea fowl family.

Inland from the Zambezi, the Chitake River rises in the Zambezi escarpment and weaves its way through the majestic hills down to the flat valley below, flowing into the Ruckomeche River and then finally into the Zambezi itself. The river is seasonal, flowing sporadically during the rainy season from December to March. During the dry months, the river consists of long lengths of sand with intermittent waterholes. One of these, the **Chitake Spring** seeps up through the sand of the Chitake River and runs for about 1.3 km, depending on the season, and then disappears again into the sand. Although the depth of the spring is shallow, usually only a few inches, the constant flow enables large herds of buffalo, elephant and impala plus groups of kudu, eland and numerous other species of game and birds to get their fill. With these large concentrations of game at the water, it is, of course, also home to a large pride of lion.

Canoe safaris The other option to walking in Mana Pools is to go on a guided canoe safari on the river. Most run from the Zambian border at Chirundu over three to nine days and can be arranged in Zimbabwe or Zambia (see Activities and tours for a list of operators and agents, page 232). This is an extraordinary way to watch game; the canoe paddles lap gently through the ever-changing coloured water, the surroundings are completely tranquil, and the only dramas are dodging pods of hippos, or a lumbering bull elephant as he splashes through the shallows, and perhaps the thud of a crocodile as it slithers into the water from the bank. In the evening, sunsets are drop-dead gorgeous. To some, this may sound like a dangerous activity, but the safety record in relation to the danger of wild animals on the river has been exemplary for many years. In reality, except for curious gazes from some animals, they have no interest in the plastic canoes with their human occupants. Canoes are two-man and the paddling is not too strenuous, as they move with the current and there are frequent stops. Nonetheless, be prepared for a wilderness experience and come prepared with hat, sunglasses, plenty of sunscreen, something to cover up during the day to protect again the sun and something to prevent mosquito bites in the evening. Although arrangements vary with the different operators, there are effectively two canoe safari programmes. **Full-participation trips** are camping trips where clients pitch their two-man dome tents, usually on a sandbank on the edge of the river, or sleep under a mosquito net tied to a tree (canoe paddles are also useful for this). The guide prepares meals but the participants help with camp chores such as cleaning up and fetching water from the river. Going to the toilet involves digging a hole in the ground and burning toilet paper. The alternative is a **back-up safari**, with walk-in tents and en suite ablution facilities – normally a 'bladder' shower (a canvas bag filled with hot water with a shower head on it) and long-drop toilets – and chef and waiter service for meals. Both can be combined with walking safaris into the park with an armed guide.

Either way, the itineraries usually start with an early wake-up with coffee/tea and buiscuits at about 0630, followed by canoeing, and then a one-hour stop for breakfast at 0900; it's then back on the river again until a lunchtime break of about two hours at about 1200. After that, it's back on the river, arriving at camp at about 1730.

Border crossings: Zimbabwe–Zambia

Chirundu

The Chirundu border is 63 km north of Makuti and the turn-off to Kariba, 322 km northwest of Harare and 142 km south of Zambia's capital, Lusaka. UK, Canadian, Australian and New Zealand citizens need visas (US$50), Irish passport holders do not. The border is open 0600-1800. If you are taking a vehicle across, you'll be required to pay a small road toll and must take out a short-term policy of third-party insurance (available at the border). If you are travelling in a foreign vehicle, your carnet de passage will be stamped out of Zimbabwe and into Zambia (see Essentials, page 23, for further information on crossing borders with vehicles). There are two road bridges side by side over the 400-m-wide expanse of the Zambezi, carrying the Great North Road into Zambia and eventually all the way up to Kenya. This border is very busy with trucks – it processes some 250 per day – though this doesn't deter elephants in the region from wandering through the border post sniffing out grain and fresh produce on the vehicles.

Southwestern Lake Kariba → *For listings, see pages 228-233. Colour map 1, B3.*

The southwest of Lake Kariba is far less developed than the eastern side, with a few remote scattered villages linked by very poor dirt roads. However, the big draw is the rarely visited Chizarira National Park – Zimbabwe's third largest park (see below). The only other places of mild interest to visitors are the sleepy lakeside kapenta fishing villages of **Binga** and **Mlibizi**, the latter being the terminus for the Kariba Ferry. However, this is an impoverished part of Zimbabwe, and despite the lakeshore settings and views of the kapenta boats bobbing around on the water, they are both scruffy and unappealing.

The only way to get to this region is by sturdy 4WD; the roads are steep and winding in places and are only tarred as far as Binga if coming from the south, and even then are severely potholed. There are two routes to Binga on the lakeshore and for Chizarira National Park further inland (see below). Mlibizi (for the Kariba Ferry) is 80 km north of the A8 Bulawayo–Victoria Falls road, with the junction 16 km east of Hwange National Park's main gate, 172 km southeast of Victoria Falls. Binga is 66 km further north.

Another route goes from Kwekwe (see page 84) on the A5, which crosses 280 km to the Chizarira National Park and then on to Binga, roughly another 120 km; this is a much longer and more remote journey.

Chizarira National Park → *For listings, see pages 228-233. Colour map 1, B3.*

South of Matusadona National Park is the rarely visited Chizarira National Park, which covers 192,000 sq km and is Zimbabwe's third largest national park. It was proclaimed a national park in 1958 and, like Matusadona, was a venue for the relocation of animals during Operation Noah (see page 218). Bordering the park are the Chete and Chirisa safari areas, which are not listed, as they are hunting areas (especially for elephant). Chizarira is a remote and wild park, and features magnificent gorges, plateaux and flood plains. Chizarira takes its name from the word *sijalila*, meaning 'great barrier' in the local BaTonga language; it refers to the range of mountains forming part of the 500-m-high Zambezi Escarpment on the park's western border.

Ins and outs

① Open sunrise-sunset, US$10, children (under 12) US$5, car US$5.

Chizarira is strictly 4WD; the access roads are difficult and within the park there are only challenging faint tracks, which are often impassable in the wet, with deep ruts and steep rocky sections. The best time to visit is during the dry season from June to September. There are two main routes by road to the park. From Victoria Falls, take the Bulawayo road, the A8, and turn left towards Kamativi and Binga. From Kamativi follow the Binga road and turn right along the Siabuwa road after 133 km. Follow this dirt road and then turn right after 47 km at a sign indicating Chizarira National Park. This road then leads up the escarpment for 20 km to the park office. If you need fuel or provisions, you'll have to make a short detour into Binga on the way. The other route is the 300-km or so road via Kwekwe on the A5 (see above); again you turn up to the park office 47 km beyond Siabuwa towards Binga. There is one private camp on the edge of the park and very basic campsites within the park, for which you need to be completely self-sufficient and carry extra jerry cans of fuel and water.

Sights

The scenic diversity of Chizarira National Park is quite spectacular. Its northern boundary, the top of the Zambezi Escarpment, is blanketed in Brachystegia woodland and dotted with crystal-clear springs, from where there are endless views of Lake Kariba, 40 km to the north. It quickly drops to acacia bushveld and the sandy Busi River. Most of the plains game is present in Chizarira National Park, including kudu, impala, tsessebe, sable and roan, along with bigger species such as elephant, lion, leopard and buffalo. Unfortunately, because of the remoteness of the park, rhino have been poached out, and because of the hunting activities on the neighbouring safari areas, elephant are very wary of humans and vehicles, and as at Gonarezhou National Park, are known for their aggressiveness. There are also many species of smaller animals, including the klipspringer, famous for its ability to inhabit rocky outcrops. Birdwatching is good too, with highlights including the African broadbill, Livingstone's flycatcher, yellow-spotted nicator, emerald cuckoo and the rare and elusive Angola pitta. Chizarira is also home to the Taita falcon, which nests on the cliffs within the park.

For Sleeping and Eating price codes and other relevant information, see Essentials pages 29-34.

◉ Sleeping

Chinoyi Caves *p219*

F Chinoyi Caves. You can negotiate to camp on a grassy site at the top of the caves, and there are ablution blocks (hot water in the showers is not guaranteed).

Kariba *p220, map p216*

B Caribbea Bay Hotel and Casino, 425 Impala Dr, T061-2452, www.africansun hotels.com. Large lakeside resort with 83 well-appointed rooms with balconies, a/c, cool tiled floors, some with extra bunk beds for children. There are also some disabled rooms. Facilities include 2 large pools, 1 with slide, playground, fully functioning casino, indoor and poolside restaurants, 4 bars and room service. All game activities can be organized, including a popular sunset cruise. This is a good all-round family resort. Odd for Africa, but far from unattractive, the design of the buildings have a Mediterranean-style.

B-C Gache Gache Lodge, on the opposite side of the lake from Kariba town, transfers by road or boat can be arranged, or you can drive (4WD only), reservations T04-852362 (Harare), www.gachegache.com. Set on the Gache Gache River with great lake views are 10 comfortable rustic-style thatched chalets with verandas. The main building has a dining room, bar and upstairs sun deck; game activities on offer include day and night drives, walks, sunset cruises on the lake and fishing for tigerfish.

C-D Cutty Sark Hotel, Nzou Dr, 2.5 km from the main road, reservations T04-494017 (Harare), www.cuttysark.co.zw. Excellent lakeside position with 56 a/c en suite rooms, most lake-facing. There are some cheaper budget rooms from US$85 for a double, breakfast extra. There's a restaurant, pool, tennis court, children's playground with trampoline. Activities can be arranged, and it has its own boat with a bar for sunset cruises.

D-F Lomagundi Lakeside Association, from the airport turn left at the Cutty Sark Hotel turn-off, then turn left again off the tar road and follow the dirt road and the power lines for 3 km, where you will see a signpost for **Warthogs Bushcamp**, go past that and just up ahead you will see the sign for **Lomagundi Lakeside Association**, T061-3037, kiarahammond@iwayafrica.com. 12 simple chalets in large grounds with lake views and a swimming pool. Self-catering with cooking and eating equipment, some with their own kitchens with electric plates, others with outside shared braais. Some are en suite while others have shared ablutions, which can be used by campers, who also have access to electricity points. The chalets have linen and mosquito nets but no towels.

F Warthogs Bushcamp, near the Cutty Sark, 2.5 km from the main road, reservations, T04-860978 (Harare), www.warthogs. co.zw. A secluded camp with 9 thatched double open-sided A-frames raised off the ground, with mattresses, bedding and mosquito nets, including 1 with 4 beds for families. Also a campsite with shared ablutions (hot showers) and central braai area. Limited crockery and pans available, small swimming pool, volleyball pitch. The pub, which is popular with locals, sells braai packs, and there's a raised viewing deck over the lake, ideal for watching the sunset.

Matusadona National Park *p221*

L Bumi Hills Safari Lodge, situated on top of a hill on the edge of the park 55 km southwest of Kariba from where access is by boat, reservations T04-885200 (Harare), www.africaalbidatourism.com. This stone lodge was built in the 1970s, then closed for much of the 1990s before reopening after an expensive refurbishment in 2009. Has 20 stylish a/c rooms with solid silver tea trays, balconies or verandas with commanding lake views. Public areas are decorated with African decor and include a lounge, snooker room, bar, dining room serving beautifully presented gourmet food, rim-flow pool and spa. Rates are full-board including drinks. All game-viewing activities are on offer, plus flights over the Kariba Dam wall in the small plane they use for transfers from Victoria Falls. Sundowners on the beach of the lake in the evening. No children under 12.

L Musango Safari Camp, the mouth of the Ume River at the west of the park, reservations, T013-43358 (Victoria Falls), www.musangosafaricamp.com. Run by renowned guide Steve Edwards, who has over 35 years' experience in the region, this has 6 luxury safari tents under thatch with verandas and en suite bathrooms built of natural stone, 2 of which are secluded honeymoon suites with private plunge pools. The central building has an elevated viewing deck, bar and pool, and dining is outside on a terrace overlooking the lake. Rates are inclusive of all meals and game activities.

L Rhino Safari Camp, Elephant Point on the mainland, reservations T04-753901 (Harare), www.rhinosafaricamp.com. A traditional bush camp with a good level of service, 7 thatched rooms on stilts with both open and reed walls, thatched roofs, outside showers, lake views, central dining and bar boma and bonfire. Lit with paraffin lamps in the evening. Good guides for game activities, including rhino tracking. Can arrange air or boat transfers from Kariba.

B Fothergill Safari Lodge, Fothergill Island, boat transfers from Kariba, T061-2452, www.africansunhotels.com. Popular with fishermen, this lodge blends well into the acacia trees and has 14 A-framed en suite units (1 with 2 bedrooms for a family) with open sides, fans and outside showers. Central dining room (all meals included), pool, upstairs bar on a viewing deck, guides available for walks, drives and cruises, and all-day fishing trips.

B Spurwing Island, Spurwing Island, boat transfers are arranged from Kariba, T061-2466, www.spurwingisland.com. Situated on one of Kariba's tranquil islands with spectacular views of the Matusadona Mountains. Accommodation is in 11 en suite tents, enclosed under thatch, 6 cabins and 3 larger chalets suitable for families, all set in an attractive grove of shady acacia woodland with scenic views of the lake. All meals are inclusive of the rates and are served in a centrally located dining area with open sides. Also a bar, and a swimming pool right on the edge of the lake. Game activities include cruises, walks, game drives and fishing.

B Tiger Bay, the Ume River to the west of the park, boat transfers arranged from Kariba, reservations South Africa, T+27-(0) 21-683-6576, www.club52.co.za. Set in a shady forest overlooking the Matusadona Mountains, with 12 thatched 2- or 4-bed en suite, comfortably furnished A-frame chalets overlooking the river. There's a spacious entertainment and dining area with an upstairs bar and lounge with an impressive thatched roof that reaches the ground, and a pool. Rates are fully inclusive of meals, drinks and 2 activities a day, including game drives, cruises, fishing, guided walks and a bush dinner. Fishing rods, tackle and binoculars are available at no charge for guests.

D Chura Bushcamp, part of Tiger Bay, same contact details. A few hundred metres downriver from Tiger Bay, this is a self-catering option, though you can also eat at Tiger Bay. 6 double tent-under-thatch rooms with en suite hot showers, a dining room/lounge/bar with a viewing platform, pool, braais, and fridge and freezer (powered by generator). Activities can be organized at Tiger Bay. Again boat transfers from Kariba, but if you are self-catering you need to bring everything with you, so check how much the boat will let you carry.

F Zimbabwe Parks and Wildlife Management Authority campsites, for access see page 221, bookings through

Zimbabwe Parks and Wildlife Management Authority office in Harare, T04-706077-8, or Bulawayo, T09-65592, www.zimparks. com. There are 2 basic campsites in the park: **Tashinga** on the lake shore, which has an ablution block with hot and cold water, braais (firewood is available), and sleeping shelters on some of the pitches; and **Sanyati Camp** on the Sanyati Gorge, again with an ablution block with hot and cold water, braais and a laundry trough. There are other undeveloped campsites in the park but these are rarely used and are accessible only by 4WD in the dry season or by boat.

Mana Pools *p222, map p223*

L Chikwenya Camp, on the Zambezi on the northeast side of the park, accessed by road or air transfers, reservations T04-499165 (Harare), www.chikwenyasafaris.com. Good river views from 8 luxury a/c lodges with outside showers and claw-foot baths, built on teak platforms with private decks. The honeymoon suite has a spa bath, central thatched lounge and dining room; the pool, bar and fire pit are set right on the river; activities offered are game drives, walks, fishing and canoeing.

L Ruckomechi Camp, accessed by air charter, www.wilderness-safaris.com. This is a luxury **Wilderness Safaris** camp on the banks of the Zambezi southwest of the park's accommodation at Nyamepi. They do not take direct reservations but they will recommend a local agent if you contact them through the website. There are 10 very spacious en suite tents all overlooking the river, with indoor and outdoor showers and baths, central dining, bar and library areas, and deck with infinity pool. Activities include game-viewing on foot, 4WDs, canoe or cruises.

A Kavinga Bush Camp and Kavinga River Camp, access by self-drive or air charter, reservations T04-308498 (Harare), www. kavingasafaris.com. This safari company runs 2 dry season (May-Nov) bushcamps in Mana Pools, set up for about 3 nights, with

1 near the river about 12 km upstream from Nyamepi, and 1 near the Chitake Spring, using dome tents with stretcher beds, hot 'bladder' showers, and a temporary toilet set up in a canvas tent. All meals included. The emphasis is on game-viewing walks with an armed guard.

C Zimbabwe Parks and Wildlife Management Authority accommodation, reservations through Zimbabwe Parks and Wildlife Management Authority office in Harare, T04-706077 or Bulawayo, T09-65592, www.zimparks.com. Along the riverfront to the northeast and southwest of the park HQ office at Nyamepi are a number of campsites and 2 park lodges. The latter are **Musangu** and **Muchichiri**, just upstream from Nyamepi, which each have 1 2-bed lodge sleeping 8, with 2 bathrooms with hot showers, plus 3 4-bed en suite lodges under thatch. Each has a kitchen with stove, deep-freeze, utensils for eating and cooking, bedding and towels, and there's an outside braai.

E-F Camping, reservations as above. The Nyamepi Camp campsite is located near the office and has 30 sites plus ablutions with hot water, braais and laundry troughs. There are a number of exclusive campsites situated along the river. These are for visitors seeking solitude who want to experience the wilderness and challenges of the bush. Each site has a braai stand and rudimentary long-drop toilet. Water is collected from the river or the reception office. The camps allow only 2 vehicles and 12 people per night. Camping is US$20 per person but US$25 per person at the exclusive camps. **Mucheni** is 8 km west of Nyamepi and has 4 secluded campsites; **Nkupe** is 1 km east of Nyamepi and has 1 campsite; **Ndungu** is just east of the car park area at Nyamepi and has 2 campsites; **Gwaya** is a short distance upstream from the lodges and has 1 campsite, with cold-water shower, flush toilet and basin and a braai stand. There are 2 completely wild camping sites located in the southern sector of the park – close to Chitake Spring near the foothills of the

Zambezi Escarpment. The check-in point for these 2 camps is at Nyakasikana Gate. Both campsites are without any facilities and are accessible with 4WD drive vehicles all year: **Chitake Camp 1 (Nzou)**, located 150 m downstream from the Chitake River crossing under a large Natal mahogany tree near the river, and **Chitake Camp 2 (Shumba)**, on top of a small hill near a number of baobab trees and with a magnificent view south to the escarpment, north to the distant Zambezi, east to Mangangai and west to the Rukomechi River. The camp is about 1 km from the Chitake Spring.

Southwestern Lake Kariba *p226*
D-F Mlibizi Zambezi Resort, next to the Kariba Ferry terminus, Mlibizi, reservations T09-245051 (Bulawayo), cozim@coz.co.zw. This has a variety of fully equipped, 2- to 6-bed self-catering chalets with fans, gas stove, fridge and braais, set in pleasant gardens, a campsite with ablution block, braais and very basic camper's shelters with mattresses and fan but no linen or equipment. Pontoon boats for hire for game cruises or fishing, though there's no equipment or bait available. The entrance is next to a supermarket and bottle store.

Chizarira National Park *p226*
A Chizarira Lodge, roughly 5 km before the entrance to the Chizarira National Park office, reservations T04-884226 (Harare), www.chizlodge.com. Great location perched on a cliff face with extensive bush and lake views, built of stone and thatch, with 8 double en suite A-frame chalets, with balconies and partially open sides. Pool, nightly campfire, bar and dining with the hosts at a long table. The food is surprisingly good for such a remote area. Activities include game drives and walks, and they will also set up a mobile camp within the park. Air charters are organized from Harare or Victoria Falls.

E Zimbabwe Parks and Wildlife Management Authority accommodation, reservations through Zimbabwe Parks and Wildlife Management Authority office in Harare, T04-706077, or Bulawayo, T09-65592, www.zimparks.com. The park has 7 basic campsites, each of which has a limit of 12 people, with basic thatch-and-reed sleeping shelter, long-drop toilet and braai. Most are within the radius of the park office. Everything needs to be brought with you including water; ask at the park office for firewood. **Mucheni View Camp** and **Mucheni Gorge Camp** are located on the edge of the Zambezi Escarpment and offer spectacular views of the Zambezi Valley floor. **The Platform** has a game-viewing platform on stilts (where you can sleep) overlooking a favourite watering place for elephant and buffalo, while **Busi Camp**, 40 km south of the park office, is surrounded by untamed wilderness on the scenic Busi River. Road access to this camp is very rough. **Kaswiswi I Camp** and **Kaswiswi II Camp** are situated on the upper reaches of the Rwizilukulu River, in an area known for its good birdlife. **Mabola Camp** is on the banks of a small but perennial river, the Mucheni, and below the Manzituba Spring.

Eating

Kariba *p220, map p216*
The hotels are best bet for eating. In fact, there's really no other choice, although **Polly's** at the petrol station on the main road 1.5 km from the turn-off to the Cutty Sark Hotel towards the harbour sells pies, ice cream and other snacks. Self-caterers should go to the 2 **Spar** supermarkets; 1 in Mahombe Kombe Township and 1 in Nyamhunga Township. For houseboat trips, you can either go to the supermarkets yourself, or pre-organize catered trips with the companies.

▲Activities and tours

Chinoyi p219
Tour operators
Scuba World, Harare T04-304001, www.scubaworld.co.zw. Perhaps a little unlikely for a landlocked, country, Craig runs PADI Open Water courses and single dives in the pool at the Chinhoyi Caves. The caves don't have much fish life but it's a deep dive and visibility is excellent to see the underwater rock formations. Water temperatures are a steady 22°C.

Kariba p220, map p216
Fishing
Fishing can be organized at hotels or through the houseboat companies. The main catches are tigerfish and bream.

Houseboats
The following are agents for houseboats on Lake Kariba:
Afrizim, South Africa, T+27(0)31-762 2424, www.afrizim.com.
Kariba Houseboats, Kariba, T061-2404, www.karibahouseboats.com.
Marineland, T061-3114, www.marineland.co.zw.
Rhino Rendezvous, Harare, T04-291 7900, rhinoren@zimbomail.com.
Sail Safaris, Harare, T04-335668, www.africansailsafaris.com.
Venues for Africa, South Africa, T+27-(0)21-683 6444, www.venues4africa.com.

Mana Pools p222, map p223
Canoe safaris and game walks
African Bush Camps, T09-234307, www.africanbushcamps.com. Canoeing and game drives in Mana Pools. Staff go ahead of clients to set up mobile camps. Also runs mobile camps in Botswana.
Classic Africa Safaris, T04-884226 (Harare), www.classic.co.zw. Can organize custom-made multi-day combined driving, walking and canoeing safaris in Mana Pools from Apr-Nov, using mobile camps with large

walk-in tents, en suite bathrooms and flush toilets. Can be combined with safaris in Hwange and Matusadona national parks, with transfers to/from Victoria Falls and Harare. The camps are used for only 3 weeks before being moved to another area of the Zambezi riverfront.
Goliath Safaris, T04-739836 (Harare), www.goliathsafaris.com. Walking and canoeing. Operates seasonal camps on the river in Mana Pools from Apr-Oct.
Natureways Safaris, T04-745458 (Harare), www.natureways.com. Operates mobile camps in Mana Pools Apr-Nov to complement their walking and canoe safaris. A bit more upmarket with large walk-in tents, en suite toilets and showers. Rates include bottled water and alcoholic drinks.
River Horse Safaris, T061-3332, www.riverhorsesafaris.com. 4- to 6-day canoe trips.
Safari par Excellence, T0213-321629, www.safpar.com. Runs 3- to 9-day canoe safaris using mobile camps in the Lower Zambezi National Park in Zambia, opposite Mana Pools.
Sengwa Safaris, T061-3215, www.sengwa.com. Organizes multi-day canoe trips on the river using mobile camps, plus fishing trips, and is an agent for houseboats.
Sun Path Safaris, T04-304043 (Harare), www.sunpathsafaris.com. Canoeing safaris, and can also arrange houseboats and 3- to 4-day sailing trips on Lake Kariba in a catamaran.

Chizarira National Park p226
Leon Varley Walking Safaris, bookings through Backpackers Bazaar, Old Vic Falls Centre, Victoria Falls, T013-45828, www.walkafrica.com. Personally guided 6-day walking safaris in Chizarira National Park, with renowned local guide Leon, who has been guiding for 25 years. His expertise and experience in the bush is unrivalled in Zimbabwe. On safari, you have a choice of either backpacking or a fully backed-up safari on which you don't carry anything. Accommodation is in campsites with bush

showers and toilets. Prices start at US$190 per day and are inclusive of transfers, parks fees, guide, food and drinks. Leon also operates in Hwange National Park (see page 203).

⊖ Transport

Kariba *p220, map p216*
Air
Kariba has an airport to the east of town. **Federal Air** (T0712-395 9000, www.fedair. com) runs a 10-seater shuttle service on Tue, Thu and Sun between **Harare** and Kariba, departing Harare at 0900, arriving in Kariba at 1010, and departing Kariba at 1100 and arriving back in Harare 1210. Costs about US$120 one way. Can also organize charter flights to the lodges that have airstrips.

Bus
Local economy buses run from **Harare** to the Mahombe Kombe Township near the post office and shops.

Ferry
The **Kariba Ferry** (reservations Harare, T04-614162-7, www.karibaferries.com), runs between Kariba town and Mlibizi, which is on the banks of the Lower Zambezi (see page 214). This is a passenger and car ferry which runs on selected dates, and not every month. Booking is essential. It departs from both Kariba and Mlibizi at 0900 and arrives at at 0700 the following day, taking 22 hrs in either direction. Sleeping is communal in reclining chairs or on mattresses on deck (a pillow and blanket are supplied), there are toilets and hot showers, and rates include 3 meals a day and tea and coffee and there's a cash bar. Adults US$100, children (under 12) US$50, (under 2) free, sedan car US$100, 4WD US$140.

❶ Directory

Kariba *p220, map p216*
Banks There is a bank in Kariba Heights with an ATM and another in Nyamhunga Township out towards the airport.

Contents

Background

History

Earliest times

Little is known of Zimbabwe's early history, but archaeologists believe it has been inhabited for at least 100,000 years, and Stone Age tools have been found. It is thought that the San people, now living mostly in the Kalahari Desert, are the descendants of Zimbabwe's original inhabitants, but with the arrival of the Bantu-speaking Shona from the north between the 10th and 11th centuries AD, the San were driven out or killed. The ruins of ancient stone buildings provide evidence of early civilization; most notably the remains of Great Zimbabwe (see page121) near Masvingo, after which the country is named. This elaborate city was thought to be built by the Shona, who established a loose form of feudalism in the region. It dates from the 11th century, though building continued for 300 years. The buildings are evidence of great labour and technical ability. Massive stone walls enclose a palace complex with a great conical tower, while impressive dry-stone granite masonry is used in a fortress or acropolis at the top of a nearby hill. A Shona word, Zimbabwe means 'stone houses'.

By the 1440s, Great Zimbabwe had developed into the Mwene Mutapa (or Monomotapas) empire, which stretched between the Limpopo and Zambezi rivers in modern-day Zimbabwe and Mozambique. The wealth of this empire was based on small-scale industries such as iron-smelting, textiles, gold and copper, along with agriculture, and trade was conducted with Arab and Swahili merchants on the coast.

In the early 16th century the Portuguese arrived and began a series of wars which left the empire so weakened that it entered the 17th century in serious decline, and Great Zimbabwe was abandoned. While the Portuguese stayed on the coast to control the trade routes, the interior lay virtually untouched by Europeans until the arrival of explorers, missionaries, ivory hunters, and traders some 300 years later. Meanwhile, mass migrations of indigenous Africans took place. Successive waves of more highly developed Bantu peoples supplanted the original inhabitants. They are the ancestors of the region's Africans today. Most notable among them were the Ndebele people, who were driven north out of the Transvaal region of South Africa and across the Limpopo River by the Boers in the 1830s. With their aggressive Zulu-like warrior tradition, and powerful king, Mzilikazi, they conquered and settled the western half of the region, which became Matebeleland and effectively enslaved the indigenous Shona people until the end of the 19th century.

European expansion

David Livingstone, a Scottish missionary and explorer (see page 192), was chiefly responsible for opening the whole region to European penetration. His explorations in the 1850s focused public attention on Central Africa, and his reports on the slave trade stimulated missionary activity. In 1855, he was the first European to see the Victoria Falls, and in 1858 Robert Moffat, Livingstone's father-in-law, established Inyati Mission at a site 60 km northeast of present-day Bulawayo, the first permanent European settlement in what is now Zimbabwe.

In the last quarter of the 19th century, British colonial expansion advanced north of the Limpopo River, when Cecil Rhodes (see page 146) formed the British South Africa Company (BSAC). Established with a royal charter, its intention was to extend British rule into central Africa and to exploit the region's mineral wealth. Rhodes had already made his fortune in South Africa, in diamonds in Kimberley and gold on the Transvaal. Although he was initially met with resistance, and there were skirmishes between his soldiers and both the Ndebele and the Shona between 1893 and 1897, in 1888 he signed a treaty with Lobengula, the son of Mzilikazi, and the leader of the Ndebele people. This granted Rhodes the gold-mining rights in part of Lobengula's territory in exchange for 1000 rifles, an armed steamship for use on the Zambezi and a monthly rent of £100.

The first party of colonists crossed the Limpopo in 1890 and began prospecting for gold. They settled on the site that became the town of Salisbury (today Harare). The government declared the area a British protectorate in 1891 and by 1892 there were 1500 European settlers throughout the region, with more joining them. Rhodes named the territory up to the Zambezi River Southern Rhodesia after himself; Northern Rhodesia – present day Zambia – was proclaimed in 1890. Rhodes' railway from South Africa's Cape (see page 142) reached Bulawayo in 1896 and Victoria Falls by 1904.

The colonial period

By the turn of the 20th century, the growing population of white settlers insisted on having a voice in the colony's legislative assembly, which by 1903 consisted of seven officials of the British South Africa Company (BSAC) and seven elected settlers. Following the abrogation of the BSAC charter in 1923, Southern Rhodesia's white settlers were given the choice of being incorporated into the Union of South Africa or becoming a separate entity within the British Empire. After a referendum, the settlers chose the latter, and Southern Rhodesia was formally annexed by the British later that year as a self-governing colony with its own legislature, civil service, armed forces, and police. Its African inhabitants thereby became British subjects and the colony received its basic constitution. At the time of the referendum, the European population was 34,000, which rose to 222,000 within 30 years.

After the introduction of self-government, the major issue in Rhodesia was the relationship between the European settlers and the African population. After 1923, the settlers concentrated further on Rhodesia's rich mineral resources and agricultural potential. To do this they needed land, and in 1930 an act was passed which excluded Africans from the ownership of land. Under this measure, about half the total land area (including the best farmland, the mining and industrial regions and the areas served by railroads or roads) was reserved for Europeans. The rest was designated as Tribal Trust Land, native purchase land, or unassigned land. The labour law, passed in 1934, prohibited Africans from entering skilled trades and professions, and as a result Africans were forced to work for subsistence wages on white farms, mines and factories. Later acts firmly entrenched the policy of dividing the country's economic fortunes on a racial basis.

By the 1950s the political future of all the African colonies was under intense discussion. In 1953, the Central African Federation was formed, consisting of the three British territories of Northern Rhodesia (now Zambia), Nyasaland (now Malawi), and Southern Rhodesia, with each territory retaining its original constitutional status. The intention was to derive the greatest economic benefit from the larger region by pooling resources and markets. It was a self-governing colony, with its own assembly and prime minister. The first prime minister was Lord Malvern, and from 1956 Roy Welensky. In the early years the colony was economically prosperous, thanks mostly to the rise of copper prices on the global market, for Northern Rhodesia had plentiful supplies of copper. However, since the formation of the federation, Africans were permitted to join the legislative councils, and pressure grew to break up the federation. In March 1963, by which time all three colonies were demanding independence, the British government finally conceded, and the federation was formally dissolved.

When Britain gave independence to Zambia and Malawi in 1963, political agitation in Rhodesia increased. However, while African nationalists were demanding African majority rule, it was the white-settler government that clamoured for independence.

Ian Smith's government

Ian Smith had founded a new party in 1962, the Rhodesian Front, which was committed to white supremacist policies and offered the promise of an independent Rhodesia governed by the European minority. In elections of that year the new party won a surprise victory, and in 1964 Ian Smith became Prime Minister of Rhodesia; he started pressing for independence from Britain on the basis of white majority rule. The British maintained that before they would grant independence, there must be a greater equality for blacks. Since Smith knew the whites would never agree to their conditions, he took matters into his own hands, and in November 1965 made a Unilateral Declaration of Independence (UDI), informing British Prime Minister Harold Wilson of this by telegram. The British government, and later the UN, deemed this illegal. Further attempts at a negotiated settlement, including two meetings between Wilson and Smith on warships off Gibraltar, ended in failure. In 1966, the UN Security Council imposed mandatory economic sanctions on a state for the first time in history, and in 1968 unanimously voted to broaden the sanctions by imposing an almost total embargo on all trade with Rhodesia, investments in the country, and transfers of funds there. It also imposed restrictions on air transport to the territory. Despite this, in a referendum held in 1969, the Rhodesian electorate – 92% of which were white – approved the establishment of the Republic of Rhodesia, which was declared in early 1970. Again, the UK and the UN deemed this unconstitutional and illegal, and Britain cut all ties with Rhodesia.

Meanwhile, Africans themselves objected to white majority rule and a number of nationalist groups were formed. The first leader to emerge was Joshua Nkomo, who in 1957 was elected president of the local branch of the African National Congress (ANC), renamed the Zimbabwe African People's Union (ZAPU) in 1961. His colleagues included Ndabaningi Sithole and Robert Mugabe, both of whom split from ZAPU in 1963 to form the Zimbabwe African National Union (ZANU). However, after the collapse of the federation in 1963, both ZAPU and ZANU were banned, and the majority of their leaders were imprisoned. One of Smith's first acts in office as prime minister was to order the arrest of Nkomo and Mugabe (Sithole joined them in 1965), and they remained in detention until 1974. Nevertheless, ZAPU and ZANU took up arms, and from 1965 engaged in guerrilla warfare and sabotage against the regime, resulting in bloody clashes with the Rhodesian security forces, which after 1967 were backed by South African forces. This spread to all-out war in 1972, later known as the Rhodesia Bush War. After they were released from prison in 1974, and after unsuccessful appeals to Britain and the US for military assistance, Mugabe, based in Mozambique, procured arms from China, while Nkomo, based in Zambia, was supported by the Soviet Union. Initially, it seemed unlikely that the white Rhodesians would stand a chance against the African nationalists (in 1977 there were 270,000 Rhodesians of European descent and more than six million of African descent in Rhodesia), but they did have some early victories. The situation changed dramatically with the end of Portuguese colonial rule in Mozambique in 1975. Rhodesia now found itself almost entirely surrounded by hostile states (the exception being South Africa), which permitted guerrilla bases to be set up in their territories.

A combination of the pressures of a bloody war and embargo-related economic hardships forced Smith to concede. He agreed to a meeting in Geneva with the British government and black nationalist leaders to seek an end to the conflict. By 1977 a detailed plan was put forward with proposals for majority rule, neutrally administered with pre-independence elections, a democratic constitution and the formation of an integrated army. Reactions were mixed, but no party rejected them. In return for guarantees securing white political and economic interests, Smith agreed to multi-racial elections in 1979. These put Bishop Abel Muzorewa of the United African National Council (UANC) as the first black prime minister and the country was renamed Zimbabwe-Rhodesia. Despite all parties meeting in Geneva, the UANC was the only one that was permitted to participate in the elections, as it denounced violence. The Patriotic Front, still involved in a guerrilla campaign that had by now claimed more than 20,000 lives since 1972, was banned.

Meanwhile, the British government had begun new consultations on the conflict, and in August 1979, at the Commonwealth of Nations Conference in Lusaka, Zambia, committed to seeking a settlement. The British government, under the newly elected Margaret Thatcher, invited all parties for negotiations at Lancaster House in London the following month. They were attended by Smith, Nkomo, Mugabe, and Muzorewa, among others, and resulted in an agreement in December, on a new, democratic constitution, democratic elections, and Independence. The Zimbabwe-Rhodesian parliament was dissolved and the country reverted to formal colonial status during the transition period before Independence. Sanctions were lifted and a ceasefire declared.

Elections took place in February 1980, supervised by the British government and hundreds of observers. Nine political parties campaigned. The ZANU-PF won an absolute majority and Mugabe became prime minister (later president) of a coalition government.

The new State of Zimbabwe became legally independent in April 1980. The United States opened an embassy in Salisbury on that very day, the first nation to do so. The government held Independence celebrations in Rufaro Stadium in Sailsbury, attended by Prince Charles and many African and world leaders, and singer Bob Marley sang 'Zimbabwe', a song he had penned for the occasion.

Meanwhile, Mugabe convinced Smith that whites could, and should, stay in the new Zimbabwe. Perhaps surprisingly, Smith was one of those who did stay, and he eventually retired on the family farm. Nevertheless, in the decade that followed Independence, 60% of whites emigrated, mostly to South Africa.

Post Independence

Initially, Mugabe indicated that he was committed to a process of national reconciliation and reconstruction as well as moderate socio-economic change. His priorities were to integrate the various armed forces, re-establish social services and education in rural areas, and resettle the estimated one million refugees and displaced persons. Mugabe also announced that his government would begin investigating ways of reversing past discriminatory policies in land distribution, education, employment and wages. Britain agreed to provide funds to purchase the land of British farmers willing to sell, for a much-needed land distribution programme. Mugabe's government changed the capital's name from Salisbury to Harare in April 1982 in celebration of the second anniversary of Independence.

Following Independence, Zimbabwe initially made significant economic and social progress and Mugabe ruled in a conciliatory manner. But internal wrangling and the long-simmering rivalry between Mugabe's dominant ZANU-PF, which represented most of the Shona people, and Nkomo's ZAPU, which had the support of the Ndebele, increased. A major point of contention was Mugabe's intention to make Zimbabwe a one-party state.

Meanwhile, Mugabe sacked Nkomo from the Cabinet in 1982, after just two years, and ethnic tensions worsened, especially in Matabeleland, where Nkomo supporters resorted to terrorism. This prompted a state of emergency and the deployment in 1983 and 1984 of thousands of government troops into the area. These were the Fifth Brigade, a highly trained unit loyal to Mugabe, subsequently accused of atrocities towards civilians. The situation evolved into a low-level civil war, and an estimated 20,000 people lost their lives. In 1987, there was a round of particularly brutal killings – men, women, and children. Consequently, to improve the situation, Mugabe and Nkomo eventually signed a unity agreement late in 1987 and the parties merged in 1988 under the banner of ZANU-PF, with Nkomo rejoining the Cabinet and becoming one of the two vice-presidents.

Modern Zimbabwe

The 1990s

Elections in early 1990 resulted in another overwhelming victory for Mugabe and ZANU-PF, but the 1990s also featured a number of strikes by government workers over pay. In 1994, and again in 1996, widespread industrial unrest weakened the economy, and in December 1997 a national strike all but paralyzed the country. Sensing an erosion of political support, Mugabe restricted human and political rights, weakened the Bill of Rights, placed checks on the judiciary, and tampered with voters' rolls and opposition party financing. Mugabe was also panicked by demonstrations by war veterans, who had been the heart of incursions 20 years earlier in the war for Independence, and he agreed to pay them pensions, a foolish and unbudgeted financial commitment. New taxes to finance these pensions caused more strikes and demonstrations, and riots over steep food hikes broke out in Harare and other cities in January 1998, with over 800 people being arrested.

In an attempt to retain power and control, the government unveiled the land reform programme (see box, page 242). This had been a promise since Independence, but there had been only a modest resettlement of land; even in the 1990s some 4000 white farmers owned over two-thirds of the land. Although the controversial Land Acquisition Act was passed in 1992, allowing the government to purchase commercial farms at below-market prices to redistribute to black rural Zimbabweans, not much had happened. But in November 1997 a list of more than 1000 targeted farms was published, and in 1998 the government began seizing white-owned farms, compensating owners only for improvements made to the land, such as houses, but not for the land itself. Many landowners refused to move, resulting in some cases of homeowners being forcibly removed by war vets (see box, page 242), a tactical move by Mugabe, who instructed the police and military not to stop the farm invasions. Unease among whites grew, and the 'white flight' from the country began.

Meanwhile, from 1997, opposition to the government was forming within the trade union movement, spurring the formation of the Movement for Democratic Change (MDC) in 1999. The official launch of the MDC at Rufaro Stadium on 11 September 1999 was followed by the first Congress at which Morgan Tsvangirai (see box, page 244) was elected president, and Gibson Sibanda his deputy. From the beginning, the MDC showed signs of being able to mount a very serious challenge to ZANU-PF in forthcoming elections.

A spiralling crisis

The MDC's first test came in February 2000, at a national referendum for constitutional changes. These were strongly pro-regime and would have made Mugabe's government and military officials immune from prosecution for any illegal acts committed while in office, and allow the government to confiscate white-owned land without compensation. Voters soundly rejected the proposals much to the chagrin of the ruling party, and the results catapulted Morgan Tsvangirai and the MDC into a leading position as they headed into the June parliamentary elections. Officially, but without the sanction of international observers, ZANU-PF claimed 62 of 120 elective seats in the House of Assembly, with the MDC taking 57 seats. This was Mugabe's biggest challenge to date.

In 2001, Finance Minister Simba Makoni publicly acknowledged that Zimbabwe was in economic crisis, saying that foreign reserves had run out and warned of serious food shortages. Most Western donors, including the World Bank and the International Monetary

Zimbabwe's land reforms

When the Lancaster House agreement was signed in 1979, leading to Independence in 1980, one of the issues was land reform: to redistribute land from the minority whites to the disenfranchised landless blacks. There was a clause in the agreement, to last for 10 years until 1990, that white farmers could sell their farms to the Zimbabwe government on a 'willing seller, willing buyer' principle. Initially, Britain provided a £44 million resettlement grant to fund this, but Mugabe's government had spent this by 1988. The 1985 Land Acquisition Act gave the government the first right to purchase land for redistribution, but it had limited impact, both because the government did not have the money to compensate landowners, and also because of vigorous opposition by white farmers who didn't want to sell. The second Land Acquisition Act, which was passed in 1992, removed the willing seller, willing buyer clause, and allowed the government to buy land compulsorily. In 1997, the government published a list of 1471 farms it intended to buy. Mugabe claimed the UK should pay the compensations, but the British government pointed out that they had already paid compensation for land reform and since the Lancaster House agreement had expired, it was no longer their responsibility.

What happened next was that hundreds of farms were taken, but instead of ending up in the hands of rural Zimbabweans, many were given to cabinet ministers, government officials and wealthy businessmen (Mugabe himself owns three farms), most of whom didn't have the necessary infrastructure or farming knowledge to work the large commercial plots. In the 1990s, 1 million ha were acquired by the government, but fewer than 20,000 families were resettled. In 1999, the government tried to change the land reform clauses in the constitution with ones that would allow the government to acquire farms without paying

Fund, had cut lending to Zimbabwe because of Mugabe's land reform programme. Then in 2002, a state of disaster was declared as worsening food shortages threatened famine. While the government blamed drought, the UN's World Food Programme claimed disruption to agriculture was a contributing factor.

In the 2002 presidential elections, Mugabe officially claimed to get 53.8% of the vote compared to 40.2% for Tsvangirai and 6% for others. But the elections were widely considered fraudulent. Mindful that Tsvangirai's main support was in urban areas while Mugabe's was in rural Zimbabwe, the government made it impossible for some voters in urban districts to register and reduced the number of polling stations there, while increasing polling stations in rural areas. Intimidation of opposition voters was widespread, resulting in some 30 being killed and over 300 being tortured (mostly by war vets). In addition, preceding the elections, the government had passed legislation that curtailed free speech, free press, and rights of assembly. International election observers claimed the elections were far from free and fair, and Mugabe's government received worldwide condemnation. Zimbabwe was suspended from the Commonwealth, the EU imposed travel restrictions against senior Zimbabwean officials, and the USA and EU froze the financial assets of selected ruling party officials.

By 2003 Zimbabwe was in a deep political, social and economic crisis. Thanks to the negative impact of the land reforms, hundreds of thousands of people had lost their jobs compensation, but they were defeated in a referendum. However, on 6 April 2000, parliament pushed through an amendment, taken word for word from the draft constitution that had been rejected by voters, allowing the seizure of white-owned farmland without due reimbursement. Soon after this, the pro-Mugabe Zimbabwe National Liberation War Veterans Association (ZNLWVA), organized groups (not necessarily war vets as many were too young to have played a part in the war against Ian Smith's government) to march on white-owned farms. The war vets began forcibly seizing farms, often violently, and the majority of white landowners fled the country. At the end of 2002, Agriculture Minister, Joseph Made, announced that the land-grab was over and more than 14 million ha of former white-owned farmland had been taken and redistributed. Today about 300 of the original farmers remain on more than 4000 commercial farms. In 2005,

a constitutional amendment was passed to deprive original landowners of the right to challenge the expropriation of land in court.

The results of the post-2000 land reform have been disastrous for Zimbabwe's economy and have contributed to food shortages, which in the mid-2000s were arguably at famine level. The large commercial farms, which were once financed and managed well, and worked with modern agricultural methods and machinery, are now in the hands of small-scale subsistence farmers using basic tools. Much of the land stands idle, is overgrown with weeds, has reverted to bush or has been reduced to small plots of maize. The new farmers have little experience of commercial farming, and with no collateral or official land titles cannot borrow money from banks to finance large-scale farming. In short, a country once so rich in agricultural produce has become one that struggles to feed its own population.

on farms, there was a 90% loss in productivity in large-scale farming compared to the 1990s, and almost half the 11.5 million population needed food aid. Additionally, there was a lack of fuel and commodities, and because of the lack of preventative healthcare more than 30% of Zimbabweans were living with HIV/AIDS. Zimbabwe also suffered from a crippling inflation rate. The Reserve Bank of Zimbabwe had a routine policy of printing money to satisfy government debts, which introduces excessive currency into the economic system. This policy caused the inflation rate to soar from 32% in 1998 (already considered to be extremely high by most economic standards) to 228% in 2003, and then to an astonishing 11.2 million% by 2007. With a growing list of human rights abuses by the government, the Commonwealth decided to continue with Zimbabwe's suspension; Mugabe retorted by withdrawing Zimbabwe from the Commonwealth altogether.

2005 elections Divisions within the opposition MDC began to fester early in the decade, after Tsvangirai was arrested and accused of treason in 2002. (He'd been lured into a government sting operation, in which he was videotaped talking about Mugabe's removal from power, but was later acquitted in 2004.) Nevertheless, this crippled his management of party affairs and raised questions about his competency as leader. It precipitated a major split within the party, with the opposing faction being led by Arthur Mutambara. This division severely weakened the opposition, and as parliamentary and presidential

Morgan Tsvangirai

Morgan Tsvangirai was sworn in as the prime minister of Zimbabwe in February 2009. He had long been advocating democracy and economic reform through the MDC, pitting himself directly at odds with President Mugabe. For this, he has suffered over a decade of harassment and intimidation since establishing the Movement for Democratic Change (MDC) in 1999.

Born in 1952, Tsvangirai began his career as a foreman in a nickel mine, before rising to vice president of the Mine Workers Union in 1985, and then the Secretary General of the Zimbabwe Congress of Trade Unions in 1988. He lost the 2002 presidential election to Mugabe under allegations of massive voting irregularities. In the 2008 presidential elections he received more votes than Mugabe but didn't get enough (officially) to cross the 50% threshold needed to avoid a run-off. Tsvangirai initially planned to run in a second round against Mugabe, but withdrew shortly before it was held, arguing that the election would not be free and fair due to widespread violence and intimidation by government supporters.

Tsvangirai, by his count, has survived four assassination attempts, including a 1997 attempt to toss him out of a 10-storey window, and a reported assassination plot delayed Tsvangirai's return to Zimbabwe in 2008 for the election run-off. He has been arrested numerous times, including on a charge of treason for an alleged plot to assassinate Mugabe after the 2000 elections (for which he was acquitted in 2004), and was badly beaten in custody in 2007, after being arrested for proceeding with a banned protest. Also in 2007, his bodyguard since he formed the MDC in 1999 was beaten to death.

He also suffered personal tragedy on 6 March 2009, when he was injured and his wife Susan killed in a car accident near Harare (see page 88); the driver of the lorry with which Tsvangirai's car had collided was allegedly asleep at the wheel. Then a few days after Tsvangirai returned to work after his wife's death, his grandson drowned in a swimming pool in their house in Harare.

elections approached, Tsvangirai announced that his part of the MDC was going to boycott the elections, further weakening the opposition. Again, the 2005 elections in which ZANU-PF won a two-thirds majority were deemed flawed by international observers. Although the campaign period and election day were largely non-violent, the election process was marred by repressive legislation that limited freedom of speech and assembly. In addition, millions of expatriate Zimbabweans were not permitted to vote (by this point an estimated three million economic migrants were in South Africa), the government used food distributions to influence an increasingly hungry population, and discrepancies in officially announced results led to questions about fraud.

2006 to 2007 The Zimbabwe crisis continued to spiral out of control. In August 2006 runaway inflation of 1000% forced the government to replace its existing currency with a revalued one, but this didn't ease economic problems for long. By 2008 the Zimbabwe dollar was practically worthless. In September 2006, riot police disrupted a planned demonstration against the government's handling of the economic crisis, and union leaders were taken into custody and later hospitalized, allegedly after being tortured. After years of frequent water cuts, in 2006 Harare's drinking water was deemed unfit to drink and dysentery and cholera swept through the city. Tsvangirai was badly beaten in March 2007 after being arrested for attending a rally and held in a Harare police station. The incident provoked an international outcry, and the US issued further international travel restrictions on the Zimbabwe government. Unemployment in formal jobs was running at a record 80%, food shortages continued, and after a poor wheat harvest the country's bakeries shut down in October 2007 and supermarkets warned that they would have no bread for the foreseeable future. Also in 2007, Mozambique vastly reduced its electricity supply to Zimbabwe, as the country was sitting on a US$35 million debt; power cuts were up to 20 hours a day. On 8 December 2007, Mugabe attended an EU-Africa summit in Lisbon, where he was widely criticized over human rights issues; British Prime Minister Gordon Brown boycotted the summit on account of Mugabe's presence.

The government of national unity

Both the parliamentary and presidential elections were held on 29 March 2008. In the parliamentary contest, Tsvangirai's MDC defeated ZANU-PF with 99 seats to 97 in the assembly. Despite well-documented cases of vote tampering and ballot-stuffing by Mugabe's supporters, polls suggested that Tsvangirai had also defeated Mugabe in the presidential election, but Mugabe refused to release the results for more than a month and merely said that he would contest a second round, scheduled for 27 June. When the results did come out, the Zimbabwe Electoral Commission announced that Tsvangirai had won 47.9% and Mugabe 43.2%. But again Tsvangirai didn't get more than 50%, thus necessitating a run-off or second round. However, Tsvangirai withdrew from the second round a week before it was scheduled to take place, citing violence against his party's supporters and saying that his supporters risked being killed if they voted for him. Nevertheless, the second round went ahead, despite widespread criticism, and the lack of opposition naturally led to victory for Mugabe. He was sworn in again as president for his sixth term on 29 June. Nevertheless, MDC chairman Lovemore Moyo was elected as speaker of parliament, the first opposition MP to hold the post since the country's Independence in 1980.

When the African Union (AU) called for a 'government of national unity' in January 2009, Tsvangirai announced that he would do as the leaders across Africa had insisted and join a coalition government with Mugabe. Official negotiations between both parties began on 10 July, and on 22 July the leaders met for the first time in Harare to settle disputes arising out of the presidential and parliamentary elections. The talks were mediated by South African President Thabo Mbeki. On September 2008, the leaders of the 14-member Southern African Development Community (SADC) witnessed the signing of the power-sharing agreement deal, with Mugabe remaining president and Tsvangirai prime minister. The prime minister position was created specifically for Tsvangirai as a result of the accord, but the powers granted to the role were initially somewhat nebulous. After several rounds of talks over the formation of a government, the two sides remained deadlocked for months over the distribution of ministries between Zanu-PF and the two branches of the MDC. With millions of people dependent on food handouts and an outbreak of cholera in Harare, aid agencies warned that the political impasse was creating a humanitarian crisis. South Africa said it would withhold US$28m of agricultural aid until a representative government was put in place. Eventually, cabinet posts were decided and Tsvangirai was officially sworn-in as prime minister in January 2009, and by July the unity government began talks on framing a new constitution. Also in July, the BBC was allowed to resume reporting from Zimbabwe after their ban in 2001.

Operation Murambatsvina

From May to July 2005, the government began Operation Murambatsvina. In Shona, the word roughly translates as 'drive out rubbish' but officially in English it was also known as Operation Restore Order. It was designed to get rid of illegal structures, illegal businesses and criminal activities in urban areas (effectively slums), and was also proclaimed as a move to curb infectious diseases. It targeted informal communities, most notably Mbare in Harare. Families and traders were often given no notice before police destroyed their homes and businesses; others were able to salvage some possessions and building materials but had nowhere to go, as they no longer had a base in the countryside. Estimates after the operation put the number of displaced people at around 320,000. According to the UN, it was a campaign against the urban poor, who comprise much of Mugabe's opposition. It has also been suggested that the swelling slum population in Zimbabwe was creating a fertile ground for a mass uprising, and by moving people from urban to rural areas, they were easier to control. The government campaign of forced evictions continued in 2006, albeit on a lesser scale, but they also built houses.

The future

The programme to write a new constitution has been plagued by delays, bickering between coalition partners and shortages of cash to deploy lawmakers and officials. Finally in June 2010, nearly a year after initial talks on forming a new constitution, the unity government started a process to consult Zimbabweans about formulating a new constitution. Hundreds of monitors, selected by the three political parties, were sent out to over 2500 meeting centres to find out what people wanted included. (One thing that had alredy been agreed was that presidents would be limited to two five-year terms.) The outreach programme will be followed by negotiations between the three parties, and if the parties agree on the new constitution, which will reflect all their issues, it will then be put to voters in a referendum. After that, in theory, Zimbabwe's unity government will end, as new (foreign-regulated) elections will be held in 2011.

Economy

Since the 1960s, major growth industries in the economy have included steel and steel products, tobacco, asbestos, textiles, agriculture and food processing. The Rhodesian economy experienced a modest boom in the early 1970s, when real per capita earnings for blacks and whites reached record highs. Nevertheless the disparity of incomes meant that blacks earned only about one-tenth as much as whites. After 1975, however, Rhodesia's economy was undermined by the effects of the Rhodesian Bush War, which began in 1972, and foreign sanctions, declined earnings from commodity exports, and increased public spending on the defence budget all took their toll. There was also an increasing emigration of white managers and owners in the agriculture and manufacturing sectors. When Mozambique severed economic ties, including access to the port at Beira, the Ian Smith government was forced to depend on South Africa for importing commodities into landlocked Rhodesia.

Following Independence in 1980 and the lifting of sanctions, Zimbabwe enjoyed a brisk economic recovery, and real growth for 1980-1981 exceeded 20%. However, depressed foreign demand for the country's mineral exports, the onset of a drought affecting agriculture, and the fact that some members of the government exploited their new-found positions to siphon off government funds through corruption, cut sharply into the growth and by the end of the 1980s the growth rate was zero. This was coupled with Zimbabwe's decision in 1998-2002 to send troops to help rebel leader Laurent Kabila in the Democratic Republic of Congo (DRC) take over that country. Mugabe's reputed intent was to tap into the wealth (diamonds, gold, copper and other minerals) of the former colony of Zaire, then Congo, in return for military assistance. Whatever the payback was, and wherever it went, Zimbabwe's domestic economy went from bad to worse, as the operation cost a huge amount of money.

Some market reforms were attempted in the 1990s, including a 40% devaluation of the Zimbabwe dollar. However, inflation did not improve, the deficit remained well above target, and many industrial firms, notably in textiles and footwear, closed in response to increased competition and high interest rates. The incidence of poverty in the country increased during this time. Meanwhile, the Zimbabwe National Liberation War Veterans Association (ZNLWVA), a 50,000-strong force, began a series of often violent demonstrations, fuelled by their anger that those in government, which also took part in the struggle for independence, were getting rich from the pickings of corruption while they were sinking into poverty. Although the national budget could hardly afford it, Mugabe agreed to pay them pensions, simply to appease what was a large and potentially dangerous threat to the government. New taxes to finance the pensions provoked strikes and demonstrations, and riots broke out in Harare and other cities.

The economy of Zimbabwe shrank significantly from 2000 onwards, due to gross economic mismanagement by the government, and horrendously bad press over the farm invasions (see box, page 242), which all but stopped foreign investment. The previously large exports of tobacco, cotton, soya and horticultural produce fell. At this point, there was widespread poverty, especially in the rural areas, and unemployment had risen to 80%. Between 2000 and December 2007, the economy contracted by as much as 40%, inflation vaulted to over 66,000%, GDP per capita dropped by 40%, agricultural output dropped by 51% and industrial production dropped by 47%. Without foreign currency earned from exports, Zimbabwe couldn't import commodities, and there were persistent shortages of currency, medicine, fuel and food. Additionally, there wasn't enough money in the government coffers to maintain infrastructure and services (Harare City Council went bankrupt) and water, electricity and telephone supplies were hit hard. Blackouts were common, people resorted to sinking boreholes in their gardens, and telephone lines fell into disrepair. Because of the violent farm invasions, the International Monetary Fund (IMF) cut off funds to Zimbabwe in 2001 (the country was then suspended from the IMF in 2004), financial institutions began withdrawing support, and the EU and USA imposed sanctions. The terms of the sanctions insisted that all economic assistance would be structured in support of democratization, respect for human rights and the rule of law.

The Zimbabwe dollar crashed, and hyperinflation became an everyday word.

Zimbabwe began experiencing severe foreign exchange shortages, exacerbated by the difference between the official rate and the black market in 2000. In 2004 a system of auctioning scarce foreign currency for importers was introduced, which temporarily led to a slight reduction in the foreign currency crisis, but by mid-2005 foreign currency shortages were once again chronic. The official Zimbabwe dollar exchange rate had been frozen by the Reserve Bank of Zimbabwe at Z$101,196 to US$1 since early 2006, but by mid-2006 the black market rate had reached Z$550,000 to US$1. By comparison, 10 years earlier, the rate of exchange was only Z$9.13 to US$1.

Despite the government devaluing the Zimbabwean dollar in 2006 by Z$1000 to Z$1 dollar, chronic and rapid inflation continued. By April 2007, the black market was asking for Z$30,000 to US$1, and by the end of the year this had dropped to Z$2,000,000 to US$1. In January 2008, the Reserve Bank of Zimbabwe began to issue higher denomination Z$ bearer cheques (a banknote with an expiry date), including Z$10 million bearer cheques – each of which was worth less than US$1.35 on the black market at the time of first issue. On 4 April 2008 the Reserve Bank of Zimbabwe introduced new $25 million and $50 million bearer cheques. At the time of first issue they were worth US$0.70 and US$1.40 on the parallel market respectively. Throughout 2008, even higher denomination cheques were issued – Z$250 million (US$1.30), Z$5 billion (US$19.30), Z$25 billion (US$96.50) and Z$50 billion (US$193). However, in August 2008, the Reserve Bank of Zimbabwe redenominated cash and cheques by removing 10 zeroes, so Z$10 billion became Z$1 dollar. As well as cheques, higher denomination bank notes were issued too; from Z$10,000 in 2008 to a staggering Z$100 trillion in January 2009. To put this in perspective, one egg cost Z$50 billion and a loaf of bread Z$100 billion.

In February 2009, a final redenomination cut a further 12 zeroes. After that the Zimbabwe dollar was officially abandoned on 12 April 2009 and the US dollar was introduced as hard currency. By then, it was widely in circulation in any case as the de facto currency because of the worthless Zimbabwean dollar and the shortage of notes. This move made normal forms of business possible again and in 2009 Zimbabwe recorded the first signs of economic growth in a decade: about 4%. It also meant that with US dollars, commodities like food and fuel could be imported again, and while the majority of the population is still impoverished and unemployment is high, supermarkets are now fully stocked and petrol shortages are less common.

Social conditions

Population estimates were around 13 million in 2000, but in the last decade the population of Zimbabwe has been very difficult to ascertain. It is 'guestimated' to be about 8 million at the time of writing. The farm invasions from 2000 resulted in a considerable 'white flight' from the country, and the economic crisis spurred a 'black flight' of an estimated three to four million Zimbabweans heading into South Africa and other bordering countries (see Africa's Rio Grande, page 129).

Probably the most detrimental effect on Zimbabwe's dwindling population has been the prevalence of HIV/AIDS. With around one in seven adults living with HIV (some estimates have put it as high as a quarter of the population), Zimbabwe is experiencing one of the harshest HIV/AIDS epidemics in the world. In a country with such a tense political and social climate, it has been difficult to respond to the crisis. When HIV/AIDS first emerged in Zimbabwe, in around 1985, the government was slow to acknowledge the problem. Despite the introduction of the National HIV/AIDS Coordination Programme (NACP) in 1987, which implemented short-term and medium-term HIV/AIDS programmes, discussion of the virus was minimal and Mugabe's government rarely addressed the subject. The reality is that infant mortality has doubled since 1990 (about 62 per 1000 births), and the average life expectancy for women, who are particularly affected by Zimbabwe's HIV/AIDS epidemic, is 34 – the lowest in the world. Officials from the World Health Organisation (WHO) have admitted that since this figure is based on data collected a few years ago, the real figure may be as low as 30. Men average about 37 years. Zimbabwe has a higher number of orphans, in proportion to its population, than any other country in the world, according to UNICEF, which estimates that as many as one in four children in Zimbabwe are orphaned as a result of parents dying from HIV/AIDS. Nevertheless, there is recent evidence of positive changes in sexual behaviour: condom use has increased, a higher number of young people are delaying first-time sex, and many people have reduced their number of sexual partners – perhaps more because of direct experience of HIV/AIDS in families or communities rather than the the effect of education or health and government support.

Culture

People

The vast majority of Zimbabwe's people stem from the great family of Bantu-speaking migrants who first ventured east and south across Africa some 2000 years ago. Iron-makers and agriculturists, they settled on the highveld, middleveld and around the eastern highlands of Zimbabwe.

The Africans in Zimbabwe are divided into two major language groups, which are subdivided into several ethnic groups. The Mashona (Shona speakers) constitute about 75% of the population, have lived in the area the longest and are the majority language group. Between the 11th and 15th centuries, the Shona are believed to have built the ruins of Great Zimbabwe (see page 121), some of the oldest and largest structures in southern Africa. The Ndebele (Sindebele speakers) represent about 20% of the population and are concentrated in the southwest around Bulawayo. More than half of the whites, primarily of English origin, arrived in Zimbabwe after the First World War. Afrikaners from South Africa and other European minorities, including Portuguese from Mozambique, are also present. Between the mid-1970s and the mid-1990s there were about 1000 white immigrants a year.

Shona

Shona is the collective name for several groups of people in Zimbabwe and southern Mozambique who speak a range of related dialects, the standardized form of which is also known as Shona. Bantu-speaking farmers, either Khoisan settlers or Iron Age migrants from the north, were the first inhabitants of the region (AD 500-1000). Some foundations and stonework at Great Zimbabwe date from the 11th century, and the settlement is generally regarded as the birthplace of Shona civilization. However, the term Shona is only as recent as the 1920s, when it was introduced to identify people who had previously called themselves Karanga. The Karanga had created empires and states on the Zimbabwe plateau, including Great Zimbabwe, the Torwa and Munhumutapa states, which succeeded Great Zimbabwe, as well as the Rozvi state which succeeded Torwa. These states were based on kingships, with chiefs, sub-chiefs and headmen. When the British colonized the territory, all kingships were banned. The Shona were traditionally agricultural, growing beans, peanuts, maize, pumpkins and sweet potatoes, as many rural people do today. Dialect groups have never been important in the Shona language, as there are many similarities among the dialects. They are even more irrelevant now because 'standard' Shona is spoken throughout Zimbabwe; dialects help only to identify which town or village a person is from.

Ndebele

The Ndebele (also known as Matabele, a British spelling) are a branch of the Zulus on the north coast of present-day South Africa, who split from King Shaka in the early 1820s under the leadership of Mzilikazi, a former general in Shaka's army. Mzilikazi and his followers, initially numbering about 500 people, moved west towards the area near the present-day city of Pretoria, where they founded a settlement called Mhlahlandlela (a name which lives on in the modern-day Bulawayo suburb of Malindela). Here they came into violent contact with the Twasana people, who are credited with giving this band of Zulus the name Matabele – *tebela* meaning to chase away. They then clashed with the Boers and moved northwards over the Limpopo River in 1838 where they carved out what is now

Matabeleland in the west of Zimbabwe. In 1868, Cecil Rhodes negotiated a territorial treaty with the Ndebele, permitting British mining and colonization of Matabeleland. Between 1870 and 1881 the kraal at Bulawayo served as the kingdom's political centre; their economy depended on livestock, predominantly cattle, which it still does today. The Ndebele language is a corruption of the Zulu language.

Whites

A small number of people of European ethnic origin first came as settlers in the second half of the 19th century, when a self-governing colony was established by the British. Numbers increased steadily at end of the First World War, and as happened elsewhere in Africa's colonies white immigrants took a privileged position. Extensive areas of prime farmland and senior positions in the civil service were reserved for white people only. After the country's independence in 1980, white people had to adjust to being an ethnic minority in a country with an African government. Many white people emigrated in the early 1980s, being uncertain about their future, but others remained. Political unrest and the illegal seizure of farms from 2000 (when a dozen white farmers and in excess of 100 black farm workers were killed) resulted in a further exodus of whites. The 2002 census recorded 46,743 white people remaining in Zimbabwe; more than 10,000 were elderly and fewer than 9000 were under the age of 15. By 2008, some estimates put the white population at less than 30,000. However, these last figures may be misleading since there is a large community of white Zimbabweans who work overseas, while still having a home in the country. Since the farm invasions, whites in Zimbabwe have suffered further isolated incidents of harassment. In 2006, for example, several residents of the Harare suburb of Borrowdale were evicted from their homes because of their proximity to Mugabe's new house. Nevertheless, there has been success in the political arena; in the 2008 election three white candidates were elected to the House of Assembly on the MDC ticket.

In February 2009, the UK's *Times* newspaper reported on the difficulties the white community faces today. They cited the struggle to afford food and the high price of private healthcare, and the fact that most whites resident in Zimbabwe were financially dependent on relatives living abroad. In the same month, the British government confirmed that it would assist elderly British citizens living in the country to resettle in the UK. The repatriation plan focuses on Britons over 70 living in residential or nursing homes in Zimbabwe.

BaTonga

The BaTonga people (also known as Tonga and Batonka) have lived in the Zambezi River Valley for many centuries, and like the Shona were among the first Bantu migrants from the north from around AD 500-1000. Fishermen and farmers, they adhered to a lifestyle that had barely changed in centuries. But when the Kariba Dam was built in the mid-1950s things were never quite the same again. Before the entrapped waters of the Zambezi rose, the BaTonga had to be relocated to higher ground upstream. Apart from the physical stress of being forced to move from their traditional riverbank huts to the far less suitable and arid lands in the Binga region, 57,000 of these spiritual people had to leave behind their ancestral burial grounds, soon to be swallowed by the new lake. The world was told about Operation Noah (see page 218), the rescue of animals trapped on the vanishing hilltops as the waters rose, but the plight of the BaTonga people received scant coverage. Before Kariba, the BaTonga lived a very primitive existence, isolated and cut-off from the rest of the world. No more than 60 years ago they were scantily clad and sported reed 'bones' through their noses. David Livingstone, who encountered the BaTonga en route

Kapenta

Kapenta (*Limnothrissa miodon*) fishing is an important commercial enterprise on Lake Kariba from both Zimbabwe and Zambia, providing a living to a significant number of people. They are very small (about 6 cm long) silvery fish that swim in large shoals. Also known as the Tanganyika sardine, they were introduced to Lake Kariba in the 1960s from Lake Tanganyika in what is now Tanzania. When fried (usually with onions and tomatoes), they are not unlike whitebait. As early as 1860 on Tanganyika, the explorer Richard Burton described how circular nets were lowered from a canoe to catch fish attracted by the light of an *mbaula* (wood-fired brazier). Today, kapenta rigs have enormous lights, which they lower into the water, and are fitted with the same circular nets, albeit on a much larger scale. Commercial fishing of kapenta started on the Zimbabwean side of Lake Kariba in 1976 and on the Zambian side in 1980. At night, you can see the flickering lights of the rigs across the dark waters. Once landed, the fish is salted and dried in the sun. It has become a hugely important staple food, providing refrigeration-free protein to many people in Africa.

The possibility of introducing kapenta into Lake Kariba was considered as early as 1956, but the first experimental attempts began in 1962. Under the supervision of Dr George Coulter, Senior Fisheries Officer in Northern Rhodesia, 350 fry were caught in Tanganyika and flown to Kariba. Some 45% of the fry survived the flight and half of these were placed immediately in a lakeside storage dam; most died within a few minutes, possibly because of a difference in the water temperatures. The next day only 14 of the original 350 fish were still alive. These were placed in a net in the lake, where they lived and grew for more than three months until a storm wrecked the net and the fry escaped into the lake. The first introduction of sardines to Lake Kariba had taken place. In 1967, a further 250,000 were released into Lake Kariba from Lake Tanganyika, a scheme involving 26 airlifts. They have since flourished.

to discovering the Victoria Falls, was startled by the traditional greeting they reserved for eminent visitors at that time. Facing away from the missionary, they knelt and wiggled their bare buttocks in his direction. Tourism and the commercial fishing industry on the lake have brought the BaTonga into contact with the outside world, and now most make a living from kapenta fishing today (see box, above).

Art

Having first emerged in the 1940s, Shona sculpture is world renowned, and you will find it selling for extremely high prices in many galleries around the world. Most are carved from soapstone, but harder rocks such as serpentine and the rare verdite stones are also used. These are carved in animal forms, human faces or abstract designs, in essence a fusion of African folklore and European influences. Meanwhile the Ndebele are renowned for their woodcarvings, produced using the many hardwood species of tree that exist in Matabeleland, including Rhodesian teak (*Baikiaea plurijuga*). Artists have developed a unique talent for carving them into animal or abstract designs. Art is not restricted to carving though, as the Zimbabwe people are highly talented in pottery, basketware, beadwork, textiles, jewellery and many more crafts. Items are available to buy in the various curio markets. The National Galleries in both Harare (page 59) and Bulawayo (page 140) are well worth a visit to see some of the finest examples of Zimbabwe's indigenous art.

Religion

About 50% of Zimbabweans attend Christian denominations. Protestants represent about 33%, with the largest churches being Anglican, Seventh-day Adventist and Methodist. Roughly 7% of the population are Roman Catholics and the country contains two archdioceses in Harare and Bulawayo. As in much of the rest of sub-Saharan Africa, US-style evangelical denominations, primarily Pentecostal churches and Apostolic groups, have been the fastest-growing religious groups since 2000. One of the original ideals of these groups is to worship in the 'wilderness', and white-robed practitioners are commonly seen in obscure spots in Zimbabwe, perhaps on the side of a remote road or in the middle of a ploughed field. No firm figures are available, but it's estimated that around one million Zimbabweans are part of the Apostolic movement. Christianity in Zimbabwe is often mixed with indigenous beliefs, including ancestor worship and traditional healing. Islam accounts for 1% of the population, mostly south Asian immigrants from India and Pakistan, and there are a number of mosques in Harare and Bulawayo. Other faiths present in the country include Greek Orthodoxy, Judaism, Hinduism and Buddhism.

Land and environment

Geography

Landlocked Zimbabwe is bounded by Zambia, Mozambique, South Africa, and Botswana and covers 390,580 sq km. It is the 59th-largest country in the world and a below-average size for Africa. It lies on an extensive inland plateau 900 m or more above sea level, which drops into the Zambezi Valley in the north on the border with Zambia and the Limpopo River Valley in the south on the South African border. The mountains in the Eastern Highlands rise to roughly 2600 m above sea level, where Mount Nyangani at 2592 m is Zimbabwe's highest point. The Zambezi frames the country's northern edge for 715 km along the border with Zambia and encompasses the magnificent Victoria Falls, Lake Kariba and the Mana Pools National Park. The main towns and cities are located on a fertile ridge in the middle of the country, as are many of the farms.

Climate

The climate is tropical, although markedly moderated by altitude. There is a dry season, including a short cold season from May to September when the whole country has very little rain. The rainy season is typically a time of heavy rainfall from November to March. Nevertheless there can also be prolonged periods of drought in some years. The climate is moderate on the plateaus, with temperatures rarely exceeding 32°C, while the river valleys are hot and humid, with temperatures above 38°C.

Vegetation

The land is mainly covered with low scrubby bush and savannah grasslands with occasional forests. Common species of tree include the mohobohobo, msasa, acacia and Rhodesian teak, a beautiful wood often used for furniture and carvings, which can be found on the savannah regions. Baobab, acacia and mopane trees, which look similar to mohobohobo trees, are common in the Zambezi and Limpopo valleys. The Australian eucalyptus and Australian wattle are widespread on farms where they are used as windbreaks, fuel, and, in the case of the wattle, for tannin. Tall grasslands are present throughout much of the country, and over 5000 species of flowering plants can be found, many of which are still used medicinally. The beautiful flame lily is Zimbabwe's national flower. The mountains in the Easter Highlands are characterized sub-montane evergreen forest in the deeper ravines, with shrubs such as proteas, aloes and strelitzia.

Wildlife

The Big Nine

It is a reasonable assumption that anyone interested enough in wildlife to be travelling on safari in Africa is also able to identify the better-known and more spectacular African animals. Fortunately many of the large animals are also fairly common, so you will have a very good chance of seeing them on even a fairly short safari. They are often known as the Big Five, a term originally coined by hunters who wanted to take home trophies of their safari. Unfortunately, no one agrees on quite which species constitute the Big Five. In hunting parlance, the Big Five were elephant, rhino, buffalo, lion and leopard. Nowadays the hippopotamus is usually considered one of the major attractions for those who shoot with their cameras, whereas the buffalo is far less of a 'trophy'. Equally photogenic and worthy of inclusion are the zebra, giraffe and cheetah. But whether these are the Big Five or the Big Nine, they are the animals that most people come to Zimbabwe to see. With the possible exception of the leopard, and the white rhino, you have an excellent chance of seeing all of these animals in Zimbabwe's national parks.

The **lion** (*Panthera leo*), which weighs around 250 kg for a male, is the second-largest cat in the world after the tiger. They are unusual compared with other cats as they live in large prides consisting of related females and offspring and a small number of adult males. Groups of female lions typically hunt together for their pride; they are smaller, swifter and more agile than the males, and unencumbered by the heavy and conspicuous mane, which causes overheating during exertion. They act as a coordinated group in order to stalk and bring down the prey successfully. Total carnivores, they prey mostly on large antelope or buffalo. Visually, coloration varies from light buff to yellowish, reddish, or dark brown, and the underparts are generally lighter and the tail tuft is black. Lion is found in all of Zimbabwe's parks with healthy populations in Hwange, Mana Pools Matusadona, Gonarezhou and Chizarira national parks.

Of the better-known animals the only two that could possibly be confused are the leopard and the cheetah. The **leopard** (*Panthera pardus*) is less likely to be seen as it is more nocturnal and secretive in its habits than the cheetah. It frequently rests during the heat of the day on the lower branches of trees. The best chance for viewing leopard is in the Matobo National Park.

The **cheetah** (*Acinonyx jubatus*) is well known for its speed. In short bursts it can reach 90 kph. But it is not as successful at hunting as you might expect with such a speed advantage. The cheetah has a very specialized build that is long and thin with a deep chest, long legs and a small head. But the forelimbs are restricted to a forward and backward motion, making it very difficult for the cheetah to turn suddenly when in hot pursuit of a small antelope. They are often seen in family groups walking across the plains or resting in the shade. The black 'tear' mark on the face is usually obvious through binoculars. They used to be widespread in Zimbabwe but are now considered threatened due to loss of habitat. The only realistic chance of seeing one is in the Hwange National Park.

By contrast there are no shortage of **elephant** (*Loxodonta africana*) in Zimbabwe, and the population has been put at around 88,000, with 50,000 in Hwange National Park alone, many of which migrate seasonally to Chobe National Park in Botswana. Other sizeable populations are in the Zambezi Valley and Gonarezhou National Park. In fact, elephants can even be seen wandering around the streets in the towns of Victoria Falls and Kariba and think nothing of drinking out of people's swimming pools! They are awe-inspiring by their very size, and it is wonderful to watch a herd at a waterhole; you will not be disappointed by the sight of them. There are two opportunities to go on elephant-back rides on semi-tame elephants; on the Zimbabwe side (page 86) and on the Livingstone side (page 191) of the Victoria Falls.

Rhinoceros in Zimbabwe has suffered severely from poaching in the last half of the 20th century, for their horns, and were virtually wiped out in Zimbabwe 20 years ago. Both species of rhino are on the verge of extinction, and indeed if there had been no moves to save them they probably would have gone from the wild by now. The **white rhino** (*Ceratotherium simum*) and the **black rhino** (*Diceros bicornis*) occurred naturally in Zimbabwe once upon a time; now you will find them in the parks, where they have been reintroduced – mostly from breeding programmes in South Africa. The parks are Matobos, Hwange and Matusadona. Their names have no bearing on the colour of the animals as they are both a rather nondescript dark grey. The name white rhino is derived from the Dutch word 'weit' which means wide and refers to the shape of the animal's mouth. The white rhino has a large square muzzle and this reflects the fact that it is a grazer and feeds by cropping grass. The black rhino, on the other hand, is a browser, usually feeding on shrubs and bushes. It achieves this by using its long, prehensile upper lip, which is well adapted to the purpose.

The horn of the rhino is not a true horn, but is made of a material called keratin, which is essentially the same as hair. If you are fortunate enough to see rhino with their young you will notice that the white rhino tends to herd its young in front of it, whereas the black rhino usually leads its young from the front. The white rhino is a more sociable animal, and they are likely to be seen in family groups of five or more. Their preferred habitat is grasslands and open savannah with mixed scrub vegetation. The black rhino lives in drier bush country and usually alone. They will forage on twigs, leaves and tree bark.

The **buffalo** (*Syncerus caffer*) was once revered by the hunter as the greatest challenge for a trophy. But more hunters have lost their lives to this animal than to any other. This is an immensely strong animal with particularly acute senses. Left alone as a herd they pose no more of a threat than a herd of domestic cattle. The danger lies in the unpredictable behaviour of the lone bull. These animals, cut off from the herd, become bad tempered and easily provoked. While you are more likely to see them on open plains they are equally at home in dense forest. To see a large herd peacefully grazing is a great privilege and one to remember.

The most conspicuous animal in water is the **hippopotamus** (*Hippopotamus amphibius*). A large beast with short stubby legs, but nevertheless quite agile on land, it can weigh up to four tonnes. During the day it rests in the water, rising every few minutes to snort and blow at the surface. At night they leave the water to graze. A single adult animal needs up to 60 kg of grass every day, and to manage this it obviously has to forage far. They do not eat aquatic vegetation. The nearby banks of a river or waterhole with a resident hippo population will be very bare and denuded of grass. Should you meet a hippo on land by day or night keep well away. If you get between it and its escape route to the water, it may well attack. They are restricted to water because their skin would dry up if not kept damp and because their body temperature needs to be regulated.

The **giraffe** (*Giraffa camelopardalis*) may not be as magnificent as a full-grown lion, nor as awe-inspiring as an elephant, but its elegance as a small party of giraffe stroll across the plains is unsurpassed. Both male and female animals have horns, though in the female they may be smaller. A mature male can be over 5 m high to the top of its head. The lolloping gait of the giraffe is very distinctive and it produces this effect by the way it moves its legs at the gallop. While a horse moves its diagonally opposite legs together when galloping, a giraffe moves both hind legs together and both forelegs together. It achieves this by swinging both hind legs forward and outside the forelegs. They have excellent sight and acute hearing. They are browsers, and can eat the leaves and twigs of a large variety of tall trees, with thorns presenting no problem. Their only natural threat is lion, which will attack young animals when they are drinking. Giraffe can be seen in Hwange, Gonarezhou and Zambezi national parks, but not Mana Pools or the Lower Zambezi area, as the steep Zambezi Escarpment hampered any migration to this region.

The zebra is the last of the easily recognized animals. **Burchell's zebra** (*Equus burchelli*) will often be seen in large herds, sometimes with antelope. Zebras have stocky horse-like bodies, but their manes are made of short, erect hair, their tails are tufted at the tip and their coats are black and white striped. Its coat pattern can vary greatly in number and width of stripes. These stripes are a form of camouflage which breaks up the outline of the body. At dawn or in the evening, when their predators are most active, zebras look indistinct and may confuse predators by distorting distance.

The larger antelope

The first animals that you will see on safari will almost certainly be antelope. These occur on the open plains. Although there are many different species, it is not difficult to distinguish between them. For presentation purposes they have been divided into the larger antelopes, which stand about 120 cm or more at the shoulder, and the smaller ones, about 90 cm or less. They are all ruminant plains animals, herbivores like giraffe and zebra, but their keratin-covered horns make them members of the family *Bovidae*. They vary greatly in appearance, from the small dik-diks to the large eland, and once you have learnt to recognize the different sets of horns, identification of species should not be too difficult.

The largest of all the antelopes is the **eland** (*Taurotragus oryx*) which stands 175-183 cm at the shoulder. It is cow-like in appearance, with a noticeable dewlap and shortish spiral horns, present in both sexes. The general colour varies from greyish to fawn, sometimes with a reddish-brown tinge, with narrow white stripes on the sides of the body. It occurs in herds of up to 30 in a wide variety of grassy and mountainous habitats. Even during the driest periods of the year the animals appear in excellent condition. Research has shown that they travel large distances in search of food and that they will eat all sorts of tough woody bushes and thorny plants.

Not quite as big, but still reaching 140-153 cm at the shoulder, is the **greater kudu** (*Tragelaphus strepsiceros*) which prefers fairly thick bush, sometimes in quite dry areas. They are present in most of the parks, though you have just as much chance of seeing one at dusk by the side of the road outside of the protected areas. Although nearly as tall as the eland it is a much slender and more elegant animal. Its general colour also varies from greyish to fawn and it has several white stripes running down the sides of the body. Only the male carries horns, which are very long and spreading, with only two or three twists along the length of the horn. A noticeable and distinctive feature is a thick fringe of hair that runs from the chin down the neck. Greater kudu usually live in family groups of not more than half a dozen individuals, but occasionally larger herds up to about 30 can be seen.

The **roan antelope** (*Hippotragus equinus*) and **sable antelope** (*Hippotragus niger*) are similar in general shape, though the roan is somewhat bigger, being 140-145 cm at the shoulder, compared to the 127-137 cm of the sable. In both species, both sexes carry ringed horns that curve backwards; these are particularly long in the sable. Both animals have a horse-like mane. The sable is usually glossy black with white markings on the face and a white belly. The female is often a reddish-brown colour. The roan can vary from dark rufous to a reddish fawn and also has white markings on the face. The black males of the sable are easily identified, but the brownish individuals can be mistaken for the roan. Look for the tufts of hair at the tips of the rather long ears of the roan (absent in the sable). The roan is generally found in open grassland. Both the roan and the sable live in herds.

The **blue wildebeest** or **gnu** (*Connochaetes taurinus*) is a large animal about 132 cm high at the shoulder, looking rather like an American bison in the distance. The impression is strengthened by its buffalo-like horns (in both sexes) and humped appearance. The general colour is blue-grey with a few darker stripes down the side. It has a noticeable beard and long mane. They are often found grazing with herds of zebra. Blue wildebeest migrate during the summer months in search of fresh grasslands between Zimbabwe and Botswana, though their numbers have been greatly reduced by the construction of fences and attacks from predators around artificial water points in recent years.

The common waterbuck (*Kobus ellipsiprymnus*) stands at about 122-137 cm at the shoulder and has a shaggy grey-brown skin that is very distinctive. The males have long, gently curving horns that are heavily ringed. They can be distinguished by the white mark on their buttocks, which is a clear half-ring on the rump and round the tail, their rounded ears and white patches above the eyes and around the throat. Despite its name, the waterbuck is not an aquatic animal; it does, however, take refuge in water to escape predators, and has a shaggy brown-grey coat that emits a smelly, oily secretion thought to be for waterproofing. They are found in large numbers in the Gonarezhou National Park and in the Zambezi Valley.

The **red hartebeest** (*Alcephalus caama*) stands about 127-132 cm at the shoulder. It has an overall rufous appearance with a conspicuous broad light patch on the lower rump. The back of the neck, chin, and limbs have traces of black. The hartebeest has the habit of posting sentinels, which are solitary animals who stand on the top of termite mounds keeping a watch for predators. If you see an animal on its 'knees' digging the earth with its horns then it is marking its territory – they are very territorial in behaviour. Their odd appearance is caused by their sloping withers and very long face. They have short horns that differ from any other animal in that they are situated on a bony pedicel, a backward extension of the skull which forms a base.

With similarities to the size and appearance of the red hartebeest, the **Tsessebe** (*Damaliscus lunatus*) stands about 120-125 cm at the shoulder and have coats of a rusty red colour with black legs, chest and a black strip running from forehead to the tip of the nose. The horns are lyre-shaped and are conspicuously ringed and can reach 70 cm in both sexes. Males hold territories for their females and calves, and males fight over these by lunging on to their knees while whacking each other with their horns. Tsessebe can reach 70 kph when frightened and will sometimes jump over each other to get away from a threat. They have the reputation of being the fastest of all antelopes.

Another antelope with a black and white face is the **gemsbok** (*Oryx gazella*), which stands 122 cm at the shoulder. They are large creatures with a striking black line down the spine and a black stripe between the coloured body and the white underparts. The head is white with further black markings. This is not an animal you would confuse with another. Their horns are long, straight and sweep back behind their ears – from face-on they look V-shaped. The female also has horns but overall the animal is of a slightly lighter build. They are not common in Zimbabwe as they favour the Kalahari savannah to the south, but they sometimes stray into Hwange National Park from Botswana.

The chances of spotting the **sitatunga** (*Tragelaphus sekei*) are rare since this species of antelope favours swampy areas where there are thick reed beds to hide in. It is the largest of the aquatic antelope standing at 115 cm at the shoulder. If you catch only a glimpse of the animal you can be sure it was a sitatunga if the hindquarters were higher than the forequarters. Their coat is long and shaggy with a grey-brown colour, and they have thin white stripes similar to those of the bushbuck. The horns are long, twisted and swept back. They have long hooves that are highly adapted to soft, marshy soils. When frightened they will enter the water and submerge entirely, with just their snout breaking the surface. This is a very shy antelope that few visitors will see, but if you spend some time at a quiet location by the Zambezi River you may be rewarded with a sighting as they quietly move through the reedbeds.

The **nyala** (*Tragelaphus angasi*) stands about 110 cm at the shoulder. Although large in appearance, it is slender and has a narrow frame. This is disguised, in part, by its long shaggy coat, which is dark-brown in colour, with a mauve tinge. The lower legs are light sandy-brown. When fully grown the horns have a single open curve sweeping backwards. Look out for a conspicuous white streak of hair along the back. Another feature which helps identification is a white chevron between the eyes and a couple of white spots on the cheek. The female is very different: she is significantly smaller and does not have horns. Her coat is more orange than brown in colour and the white stripes on the body are very clear. Although rare in Zimbabwe, they may be spotted in Gonarezhou and Mana Pools national parks.

The smaller antelopes

The remaining common antelopes are a good deal smaller than those described above. The largest and most frequently seen of these is the **impala** (*Aepyceros melampus*) which stands 92-107 cm at the shoulder and is bright rufous in colour with a white abdomen. Only the male carries the long lyre-shaped horns. Just above the heels of the hind legs is a tuft of thick black bristles, which are surprisingly easy to see as the animal runs. This is unique to the impala. Also easy to see is the black mark on the side of the abdomen in front of the back leg. The impala are noted for their graceful leaps which they make as they are running after being startled. You are most likely to see them in herds in the grasslands but they also live in light woodlands. They are the most numerous of the smaller antelope and no matter what the state of the veld they always appear to be in immaculate condition. During the breeding season the males fight to protect, or gather, their own harem. It is great fun to come across such a herd and pause to watch the male trying to keep an eye on all the animals in the group. Young males may be seen in small groups until they are able to form their own harem.

The **common reedbuck** (*Redunca arundinum*), stands 70-85 cm at the shoulder. The males have rigid horns that are sharply hooked forwards at the tip. Its general colour is grey-brown with white underparts, black forelegs and a short bushy tail. It lives in pairs or small family groups and, during the hottest time of day, will seek out shelter in reed beds or long grasses, never far from water. Reedbuck are monogamous and live in pairs, though sometimes will gather in a herd if they feel threatened.

Another tiny antelope is the **oribi** (*Ourebia ourebi*), which stands around 60 cm, and is slender and delicate-looking. Its colour tends to be sandy to brownish fawn, its ears are oval-shaped and its horns are short and straight with a few rings at the base. The oribi live in small groups or as a pair. As the daytime temperatures rise, it seeks out its 'hide' in long grass or the bush. Like the reedbuck it never likes to venture far from water.

The **klipspringer** (*Oreotragus oreotragus*) stands at about 58 cm at the shoulder and the name in Afrikaans means 'rock jumper'. It is a very agile antelope and is most likely to be seen on and around Zimbabwe's balancing rocks; most notably those in Matobo National Park. The males have delicate little horns, though its ears are actually longer than its horns. Its coat is thick, dense and hard, with a speckled salt and pepper pattern of an almost olive shade, which camouflages it against the background of rocks, and it touches the ground with only the very tips of its vertically rising hooves. The Klipspringer is known for its remarkable jumping ability and is able to leap to a staggering 15 times its own height.

The last two of the common smaller antelopes are the bushbuck and the duiker. The **bushbuck** (*Tragelaphus scriptus*) is about 76-92 cm at the shoulder. The coat has a shaggy appearance and a variable pattern of white spots and stripes on the side and back, with two white crescent-shaped marks on the front of the neck. The horns, present in the male only, are short, almost straight and slightly spiral. The animal has a curious high rump that gives it a characteristic crouching appearance. The white underside of the tail is noticeable when it is running. The bushbuck tends to occur in areas of thick bush especially near water. It lies up during the day in thickets, but is often seen bounding away when disturbed. Bushbuck are usually seen either in pairs or singly.

The **common duiker** (*Cephalophus natalensis*) is a tiny, shy antelope that stands at about 50 cm at the shoulder with only the males having short horns. They have the ability to take off at high speed in a series of diving jumps when alarmed. The colour of the upper parts varies from a greyish to a reddish-yellow and considerable colour variation within populations has been observed in some areas. The underparts are usually white. Most have a black band on the lower part of the face near the nostrils.

Other mammals

Although antelopes are undoubtedly the most numerous animals to be seen on the plains, there are others worth keeping an eye open for. Some of these are scavengers that thrive on the kills of other animals. They include dog-like jackals, two species of which you are likely to come across. The **side-striped jackal** (*Canis adustus*) is greyish fawn and has a rather variable and sometimes ill-defined stripe along the side. The **black-backed jackal** (*Canis mesomelas*) is more common and will often be seen near a lion kill. It is foxy reddish-fawn in colour with a noticeable black area on its back. This black part is sprinkled with a silvery white which can make the back look silver in some lights. They are timid creatures which can be seen by day or night, though both species are more active at dawn and dusk. They can be seen in the national parks, but are also common on farmland.

The other well-known plains scavenger is the **spotted hyena** (*Crocuta crocuta*), a fairly large animal about 69-91 cm at the shoulder. Its high shoulders and low back give it a characteristic appearance. Brownish, with dark spots and a large head, it usually occurs singly or in pairs, but occasionally in small packs. Few people talk of the hyena in complimentary terms. This is as much to do with their gait as their scavenging habits. When hungry they are aggressive creatures; they have been known to attack live animals and will occasionally try to steal a kill from lions. They always look dirty because of their habit of lying in muddy pools, which may be to keep cool or alleviate the irritation of parasites. If camping, be very wary of hyena in unfenced campsites; they have little inherent fear of humans and will think of nothing of sniffing out and stealing food. Bear in mind they have bone-crushing teeth. Less likely to be seen is the similar but smaller **brown hyena** (*Parahyena brunnea*), which is present in Hwange National Park and along the border with Botswana. Their coats are shaggier and all brown (without spots) but their behaviour is the same.

Another aggressive scavenger is the **African wild dog** or **painted dog** (*Lycaon pictus*). These creatures are easy to identify since they have all the features of a large mongrel dog, and stand about 75 cm at the shoulder. They have a large head and a slender body. Their coat is a mixed pattern of dark shapes and white and yellow patches, and no two dogs are quite alike. The question is not what they look like, but whether you will be fortunate enough to see one, as they are seriously threatened by extinction (see box, opposite). The dogs live and hunt in packs. They are particularly vicious when hunting

The painted dog

The African wild dog is a medium-sized carnivore canine found on savannahs and other lightly wooded areas. It is also called the painted dog because of its distinctive spotted black and brown coats. The scientific name *Lycaon pictus* is derived from the Greek for 'wolf' and the Latin for 'painted'. There were once approximately 500,000 African wild dogs in 39 African countries, and packs of 100 or more were not uncommon. Now there are only about a pitiful 3000-5500 in fewer than 14 countries in eastern and southern Africa.

Throughout its range, the wild dog has suffered due to habitat loss and persecution. In many areas it still has an ill-deserved reputation as a ruthless killer – wild dogs hunt only to eat, and their killing methods are generally quicker than those of lion. They have suffered from trigger-happy farmers with shotguns (wary about attacks on their livestock), road accidents (as the dogs migrate between areas), and because of the large competition with larger carnivores such

as lion that rely on the same prey, which will often kill wild dogs (but do not eat them). Wild dog packs are now severely isolated with little opportunity to meet and thus breed successfully. In reality, they are incredibly social and non-aggressive animals, with all of the pack helping to raise pups and care for any sick or injured members. They will also bring food back to those that stayed back to watch the pups in the den while the pack were on a hunt.

The Painted Dog Conservation Centre (see page 203) is a conservation initiative on the edge of Hwange National Park. It works with local communities to create new strategies for conserving the wild dog and its habitat. It also provides a sanctuary for wild dogs, mostly orphans rescued from parents that have suffered lion attacks or been run over on the Bulawayo–Victoria Falls road. The information centre about wild dogs is fascinating and highlights the plight of this rare animal.

their prey and will chase an animal until it is exhausted, then start taking bites out of it while it is still alive. Their favourites are reedbuck and impala. In Zimbabwe, they are found in Hwange National Park, and along the northwest reaches of the Bulawayo-Victoria Falls road (the A8).

A favourite and common plains animal is the comical **warthog** (*Phacochoerus aethiopicus*). It is unmistakeable, being almost hairless and grey in general colour with a very large head, tusks and wart-like growths on the face. These are thought to protect the eyes as it makes sweeps sideways into the earth with its tusks, digging up roots and tubers. Warthogs often kneel on their forelegs when eating. They frequently occur in family parties. When startled the adults will run at speed with their tails held straight up in the air and followed by their young. Look out for them around the edges of waterholes as they love to cake themselves in the thick mud. This helps to keep them both cool and free of ticks and flies.

In rocky areas, such as the Matobo Hills, look out for an animal that looks a bit like a large grey-brown guinea pig. This is the **dassie** or **rock hyrax** (*Heterohyrax brucei*), an engaging and fairly common animal. During the morning and afternoon you will see them sunning themselves on the rocks. They have the habit of always defecating in the same place, and where the urine runs down the rock face the rock can have a glazed appearance. Perhaps their strangest characteristic is their place in the evolution of mammals. Ancestors of the hyraxes have been found in the deposits of Upper Egypt of about 50 million years ago. The structure of the ear is similar to that found in whales, their molar teeth look like those of a rhinoceros, two pouches in the stomach resemble a condition found in birds, and the arrangement of the bones of the forelimb are like those of the elephant. In spite of all these features it is regarded as being allied to the elephant!

You are likely to see three types of primates in Zimbabwe – the vervet monkey, the samango monkey and the Chacma baboon – and you are just as likely to see them outside a national park than in one. The **vervet monkey** (*Cercopithecus pygerythrus*) is of slim build and light in colour. Its feet are conspicuously black, so too is the tip of the tail. It lives in savannah and woodlands but has proved to be highly adaptable. On your first sighting you might think the vervet monkey cute. It is not, it is vermin and in many places treated as such. It can do widespread damage to orchards and other crops, and if given the chance will make off with your whole picnic, including the beers, in a matter of seconds.

The **Samango monkey** (*Cercopithecus mitis*) is much rarer than the vervet monkey and is only found in the moist evergreen forests of the Eastern Highlands, particularly around Vumba. The head and shoulders are dark grey, while the face, feet, hands and lower limbs are black, and the belly and throat are creamy white. They are not always easy to spot as they spend most of their lives in the tree canopy, but if you look up you may see a troop crashing through the branches.

The adult male **Chacma baboon** (*Papio ursinus*) is slender and can weigh up to 40 kg. Its general colour is a dark olive green, with lighter undersides. It never roams far from a safe refuge, usually a tree, but rocks can provide sufficient protection from predators. The Chacma baboons occur in large family groups, known as troops, and have a reputation for being aggressive where they have become used to human presence.

Reptiles

Found in all the rivers and dams in low-lying Zimbabwe, the **Nile crocodile** (*Crocodylus niloticus*) can reach lengths of 5 m and weights of 1000 kg for adult males. They have a scaly dark bronze hide, with black spots on the back and a dirty purple on the belly. The flanks, which are a yellowish green, have dark patches arranged in oblique stripes. Like all crocodiles, they are quadrupeds with four short, splayed legs, plus long powerful tails, and wide jaws which are capable of snatching prey from the riverbanks. The nostrils, eyes and ears are situated on the tops of their head, so the rest of the body can remain concealed underwater.

Although very rarely seen, the **African rock python** (*Python sebae*) is widespread in Zimbabwe and prefers savannah bush, usually near water where it can submerge for long periods. With lengths of up to 5 m, it is the largest snake in Africa. It is very bulky and has a dark arrowhead shape on its head, and brown blotches outlined by black on a tan background on its body. All pythons kill by constricting their prey. The African rock python can live for up to a year without food if the animal it eats is big enough to sustain it. Starch ligaments hold the jaw together, which stretches out like a rubber band allowing it to eat prey as big as an antelope.

Birds

Zimbabwe has a confirmed bird list of over 660 species of bird and new vagrants continue to be spotted. The best time to visit is October to March as most of the Palaearctic and intra-African migrants are present. However, the cooler and drier months of May to August will enable the keen spotter to concentrate on local species. There are many areas of interest for the visiting birdwatcher: the evergreen forests of the Eastern Highlands; the woodlands on the central plateau and Hwange National Park; the granite domes of Matobo; and the Zambezi River.

In the Eastern Highlands the evergreen forests attract around 400 species of bird. Look out for birds like the African black duck, thick-billed weaver, red-chested flufftail, Levaillant's cisticola, East African swee, blue swallow, singing cisticola, grassbird, broad-tailed warbler, common quail, Barratt's warbler, augur buzzard and long-crested eagle.

Over 400 bird species have been recorded around Harare. In the wet season, the ponds and marshes in places like the Mukuvisi Woodlands (see page 62) and the National Herbarium and Botanic Gardens (see page 61) attract exciting birds like streaky-breasted flufftail, several species of crake and black coucal and yellow-backed widow. In some areas all three species of long-claw (orange-throated long-claw, yellow-throated long-claw and pink-throated long-claw) can be found. Near Harare, over 275 bird species have been found at Ewanrigg Botanical Gardens (see page 63), which is best known for its collection of aloes and cycads that attract large numbers of nectar-eating birds, particularly sunbirds, and especially in June, July and August when the aloes are in flower. Species of sunbird to look for include the white-bellied, variable, scarlet-chested, amethyst and miombo double-collared, which are all common. Other birds include the grey-rumped swallow, cattle egret and Abdim's stork, and in the miombo woodland, Whyte's barbet and miombo and greater blue-eared starling.

About 420 bird species occur in Hwange National Park, including huge populations of raptors and others like crimson-breasted shrike, glossy starling, pied babbler, a number of waxbills, Meyer's parrot, long-tailed shrike, white-crowned shrike, red-billed francolin and lilac-breasted roller. Bradfield's hornbill is a species that is restricted to the teak woodland in this part of the country.

There are over 350 species of birds in the Matobo region, which is one of the best places to view raptors in Zimbabwe. These include African hawk eagle, African crowned eagle, Angur buzzard, Martial eagle, Pereguin falcon, brown snake eagle and black-chested snake eagle. Other species include yellow wagtail, common and wood sandpiper, grassveld pipit, buffy pipit and red-capped lark.

Close to 375 bird species can be seen around Lake Kariba. The safari islands, including Spurwing Island and Fothergill Island, have rewarding birdwatching. The nearby Matusadona National Park supports over 240 bird species. These include grey-headed gull and white-winged tern as well as plentiful raptors like African hawk eagle, Ayre's eagle, crowned eagle, peregrine falcon, rock pratincole and African fish eagle. In Mana Pools some 400 species have been identified. From April to December, African skimmers breed on the exposed sand banks, and in September, huge flocks of carmine bee-eaters are joined by flocks of white-fronted bee-eaters. Other species to look for along the river include mottled spine-tail and Bohm's spine-tail, white-browed coucal, blue-cheeked bee-eater, western banded snake eagle, white-crowned plover, long-toed plover, red-winged pratincole, green sandpiper, ringed plover, grey plover, Caspian plover, common redshank and bar-tailed godwit.

Books

Non-fiction

Barclay P *Zimbabwe: Years of Hope and Despair* (2010). Written by a former employee of the British Embassy in Harare and documenting his experiences of the country during his three years there, including a first-hand account of the disputed 2008 elections.

Buckle C *Innocent Victims: Rescuing the Stranded Animals of Zimbabwe's Farm Invasions* (2009). Covers the rescue by Meryl Harrison and her team of the many farm animals that were abandoned when the white farmers were evicted from their farms. They were also responsible for rounding up the many abandoned pet dogs which found themselves wandering around the streets of Harare and elsewhere. Buckle also wrote *African Tears* (2001) and *Beyond Tears* (2004) about her own farm being invaded by war vets.

Godwin P *The Fear: The Last Days of Robert Mugabe* (2010). Focuses on the period from the 2008 election and follows on from Godwin's compelling and moving memoirs, *Mukiwa; A White Boy in Africa* (2004), which covers his childhood in Rhodesia in the 1960-80s, and *When a Crocodile Eats the Sun* (2008), which tackles the story of his father's death set against the collapsing of Zimbabwe in the late 1990s. This is a personal journey through the country Peter Godwin grew up in and knows so well.

Holland H *Dinner with Mugabe: The Untold Story of a Freedom Fighter Who Became a Tyrant* (2009). Tracks down the key figures in Mugabe's life and probes the mystery of Africa's loyalty to one of its worst dictators. It begins with an account of the author having dinner with Mugabe some 30 years ago when he was a freedom fighter.

Lamb C *House of Stone: The True Story of a Family Divided in War-Torn Zimbabwe* (2009). Journalist Lamb's riveting account of Zimbabwe's brutal civil war in the 1970s, the elation of becoming the last British colony in Africa to win independence, and then the descent into madness. She alternates chapters from the perspectives of Aqui Shamvi, a poor black woman, and Nigel Hough, a wealthy white man.

Meldrum A *Where We Have Hope: A Memoir of Zimbabwe* (2006). A memoir by a journalist who was in Rhodesia to cover its 1980 Independence for the UK's *Guardian* newspaper, and who has subsequently written articles exposing various facets of the Mugabe's regime, which resulted in him being expelled from the country in 2003.

Meredith M *Mugabe: Power and Plunder in Zimbabwe* (2007). Covers Mugabe's early life and is a welcome alternative to the current one-dimensional portrayals of the president as an 'evil monster', reminding the reader that in his earlier days Mugabe was a much more considered political radical.

Norman A *Mugabe: Teacher, Revolutionary, Tyrant* (2008). Examines Mugabe's life prior to 1980 and his years in power. His words and deeds are scrutinized closely, and an entirely new theory as to the reasons for his behaviour is proposed (by a doctor of medicine) – that he has syphilis.

Rogers D *The Last Resort* (2010). Tells the eye-opening, harrowing and, at times, surprisingly funny story of the author's parents' struggle for survival in Zimbabwe, when Drifters, their once-famous game farm and backpacker lodge in the Eastern Highlands, was attacked by war vets.

Smith I *Bitter Harvest: The Great Betrayal by Ian Smith* (2008). The memoirs of the former prime minister of Rhodesia, published just 6 months after his death in November 2007. He tells the remarkable story behind the signing of the Unilateral Declaration of Independence, as well as the excesses of power that Mugabe has used to create the virtual dictatorship which exists in Zimbabwe today.

Fiction

Gappah P *An Elegy for Easterly* (2009). This is about life in Zimbabwe in the late 2000s through the eyes of a number of characters; it describes the resilience and inventiveness of the people who struggle to live under Mugabe's regime whilst also battling issues common to all people everywhere.

Wallace J *Out of the Shadows* (2010). A story of a young white schoolboy and his friends and how their lives change in the 1980s when Mugabe wins independence.

Contents

Footnotes

Glossary

Braai Outside barbeque, usually a metal grill where you light your own fire underneath with wood or coals.

Boma Thatched shelter, usually without walls, for entertaining, especially when braaiing.

Kraal Traditional African hut for living in, usually thatched with mud or stone walls.

Kopjie A hill or outcrop of rocks, which are usually balanced on top of each other and a common feature on wide open plains.

Potjiekos Three-legged cast-iron pots used for cooking over coals.

Bakkie A pickup car.

Biltong Dried meat to chew on as a snack, similar to beef jerky, often spiced.

Boerwors Spicy beef or game sausage popular for braaiing.

Chibuku A potent beer made from maize meal porridge, with a consistency that is a bit like cottage cheese, and is served in 1 litre cartons.

Highveld Refers to the higher regions of Zimbabwe, roughly above 1,300 m above sea level, while the lowveld refers to the lower areas below 500 m. In between is commonly referred to as the bushveld.

Mealies Maize corn; roasted over coals and eaten as a snack, or ground into maize meal flour to make sadza. The latter being a stiff porridge.

Nyama Meat; usually cooked in a stew to go with sadza.

Rondavel Usually circular with a thatched roof, these huts are used as accommodation rooms in many parks and camps.

Shamwari Generally word for friend, mate or pal in Shona.

Shona phrases

Hello *Mhoro*

How are you? *Makadini?*

I am fine *Ndiripo*

Good morning *Mangawani*

Good afternoon *Masikati*

Good evening *Manheru*

What is your name? *Munonzani?*

My name is… *Ndinonzi…*

Go well *Fambai zvakanaka*

Stay well *Sarai zvakanaka*

Please *Ndapot*

Thank you *Tatenda*

Index → *Entries in bold refer to maps*

Credits

Footprint credits

Project editor: Felicity Laughton
Text editor: Dorothy Stannard
Layout and production: Emma Bryers
Colour section: Pepi Bluck
Maps: Kevin Feeney
Cover design: Rob Lunn, Pepi Bluck

Managing Director: Andy Riddle
Commercial Director: Patrick Dawson
Publisher: Alan Murphy
Publishing Managers: Felicity Laughton,
Nicola Gibbs, Jo Williams
Digital Editor: Jen Haddington
Marketing and PR: Liz Harper
Sales: Diane McEntee
Advertising: Renu Sibal
Finance and administration:
Elizabeth Taylor

Photography credits

Front cover: Victoria Falls at sunset: Dmitry Pichugin /
Shutterstock
Back cover: Mana Pools National Park, a lioness: Christophe
Lepetit / hemis.fr
Page 1: David Paynter / www.agefotostock.com
Pages 2-3: D Allen Photography / photolibrary.com
Page 6: John Downer / photolibrary.com; Naomi Peck /
Robert Harding World Imagery; AfriPics.com / Alamy; John
Warburton-Lee / AWL Images Ltd; Stéphane Frances /
hemis.fr
Page 7: Nick Greaves / Alamy; Berndt Fischer -
www.agefotostock.com; Chris Kober / Robert Harding
World Imagery; John Fairclough / photolibrary.com.
Page 8: Jim Zuckerman / photolibrary.com
Wildlife section: NATUREPL (Karl Ammann, Ingo Arndt,
Peter Blackwell, Nigel Bean, John Cancalosi, Philippe Clement,
Richard Du Toit, Laurent Geslin, Tony Heald, Eliot Lyons, Pete
Oxford, Andrew Parkinson, Constantinos Petrinos, T J Rich,
Jose B Ruiz, Francois Savigny, Anup Shah, Mike Wilkes)

Manufactured in India by Nutech Print
Services.
Pulp from sustainable forests.

Publishing information

Footprint Zimbabwe
1st edition
© Footprint Handbooks Ltd
November 2010

ISBN: 978 1 907263 21 7
CIP DATA: A catalogue record for this book is
available from the British Library

® Footprint Handbooks and the Footprint
mark are a registered trademark of
Footprint Handbooks Ltd

Published by Footprint
6 Riverside Court
Lower Bristol Road
Bath BA2 3DZ, UK
T +44 (0)1225 469141
F +44 (0)1225 469461
footprinttravelguides.com

Distributed in the USA by Globe Pequot
Press, Guilford, Connecticut

Every effort has been made to ensure that
the facts in this guidebook are accurate.
However, travellers should still obtain advice
from consulates, airlines, etc about travel
and visa requirements before travelling.
The authors and publishers cannot
accept responsibility for any loss, injury
or inconvenience however caused.

Footprint Mini Atlas
Zimbabwe

① ②

ZAMBIA

MOZAMBIQUE

Zambezi

◆ Mana Pools
National Park

○ Makuti

Zambezi Escarpment

○ Muzarabani

*Lake
Kariba*

○ Kariba

◆ Matusadona
National Park

○ Madadzi

○ Chinhoyi

*Zambezi
National
Park*

Livingstone

○ Chete

HARARE

◆ Victoria Falls

○ Binga

Zambezi

◆ *Chizarira
National Park*

○ Gadzema

*Lake
Chivero*

○ Chitungwisa

*Nyanga
National
Park*

○ Juliasdale

◆ *Kazuma Pan
National Park*

○ Hwange

Gwayi
River

Golden
Valley

○ Kadoma

○ Ngwema

◆ *Hwange
National Park*

○ Kweke

○ Mutare

○ Gweru

*Chimanimani
National Park* ◆

○ Bulawayo

○ Mashava

Birchenough
Bridge

○ Zvishavane

◆ *Lake Mutirikwi
National Park*

Plumtree

◆ *Matobo
National Park*

○ Gwanda

○ West Nicholson

Buffalo
Range

BOTSWANA

○ St Josephs

Shashe

*Tuli
Safari
Area*

○ Mazunga

*Gonarezhou
National Park* ◆

Beitbridge

○ Sango

Limpopo

SOUTH AFRICA

③ ④

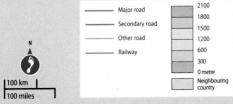

	Major road	2100
	Secondary road	1800
	Other road	1500
	Railway	1200
		600
N		300
		0 metre
100 km		Neighbouring
100 miles		country

Map 1

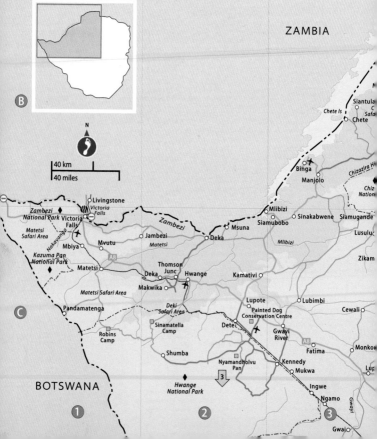

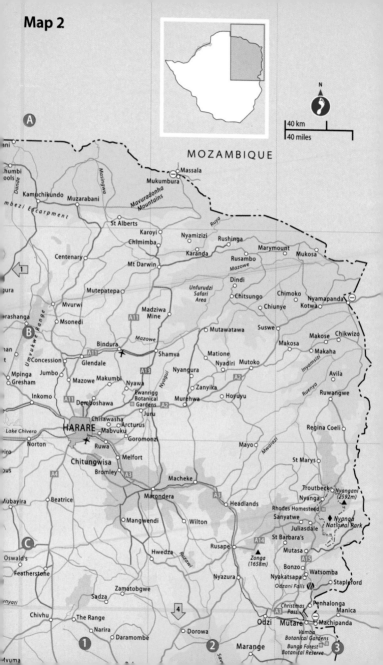

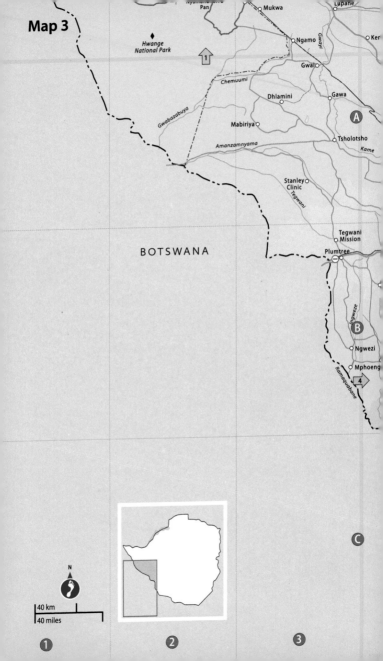

Map symbols

□	Capital city	▦	Building
○	Other city, town	■	Sight
⌇	International border	♰♰	Cathedral, church
⌇	Regional border	🛆	Chinese temple
⊖	Customs	🛕	Hindu temple
⬯	Contours (approx)	⚲	Meru
▲	Mountain, volcano	⌂	Mosque
⌐	Mountain pass	⚱	Stupa
⊥⊥⊥	Escarpment	✡	Synagogue
⌒	Glacier	🅷	Tourist office
⬚	Salt flat	🏛	Museum
⬮	Rocks	✉	Post office
✹	Seasonal marshland	Ⓟ	Police
⬚	Beach, sandbank	Ⓢ	Bank
⚐	Waterfall	@	Internet
⌒	Reef	♪	Telephone
═══	Motorway	🛍	Market
───	Main road	✚	Medical services
───	Minor road	Ⓟ	Parking
⌗⌗⌗	Track	🅵	Petrol
⋯⋯	Footpath	⚑	Golf
───	Railway	⸪	Archaeological site
⊢▪▪	Railway with station	♦	National park,
✈	Airport		wildlife reserve
🚌	Bus station	✲	Viewing point
Ⓜ	Metro station	Λ	Campsite
----	Cable car	⌂	Refuge, lodge
⊬⊬⊬	Funicular	🏰	Castle, fort
⛴	Ferry	⚓	Diving
⬛⬛	Pedestrianized street	♣♠♣	Deciduous, coniferous,
Ξ Ξ	Tunnel		palm trees
→	One way-street	✿	Mangrove
⠿⠿	Steps	⌂	Hide
⟩	Bridge	♠	Vineyard, winery
▬▬▬	Fortified wall	▲	Distillery
▦	Park, garden, stadium	⚓	Shipwreck
●	Sleeping	✕	Historic battlefield
●	Eating	➱	Related map
●	Bars & clubs		

Lizzie Williams

Originally from London, Lizzie has worked and lived in Africa for 16 years. Starting out on trips across the continent as a tour leader on overland trucks, she has sat with a gorilla, slept amongst elephants, fed a giraffe and swum with a hippo and is now something of an expert on border crossings and African beer. She lived in Harare for two years, working for a travel agency and running tours from Zimbabwe to Mozambique. For Footprint she is author of *South Africa*, *Namibia*, *Kenya*, *Tanzania* and *Cape Town Winelands & Garden Route*; has written the only country guide to Nigeria and the first city guide to Johannesburg for Bradt; is author of the AA *Key Guide to South Africa*, AA *Spiral Guide to South Africa* and *Africa Overland*, a glossy look at the overland route from Nairobi to Cape Town, is co-author of the DK *Eyewitness to Kenya* and Frommer's *Kenya* and *Tanzania*, and has contributed to Turkey and Egypt for Rough Guides. When not on the road, Lizzie lives in Cape Town.

Acknowledgements

Lizzie would like to thank many good friends in Zimbabwe including Helen Patchett (aka Patch) and Murry Black (aka Muzza) from Linde Safaris and Exodus in Harare for their excellent advice; special thanks goes to Patch for taking me to all the coffee shops in Harare and help me find a pair of genuine Jimmy Choo shoes in a second-hand shop (how they got to Zimbabwe is a mystery); and to Muzza for the wheels and clearing up last loose ends. Thanks also to Kerry Butler of Mozaic Travel in Maputo, and David Kimber from Sailaway in Vilankulo in Mozambique, for the road trip from Mozambique to Harare via the Gonarezhou National Park and research in the Eastern Highlands. In Bulawayo, Val Bell and her staff at the Bulawayo Publicity Association were extremely helpful. Thanks to the gang at Victoria Falls including Mags Varley and staff at Backpackers Bazaar, Brent Williamson at Adventure Zone, the staff at the Victoria Falls Publicity Bureau, Garth and Trish Pritchard from Africa Travel Co, Angus Pumpe from Acacia Africa, and Gary and Rene Archer from Wild Horizons. And thanks to Andrew Conolly and Sarah Brown from the Antelope Park and Lion Encounter. A special thanks goes to all the ordinary Zimbabweans I encountered who as always couldn't have been more friendly and helpful. Finally thanks to the Footprint team, including Felicity Laughton for putting it all together, and for giving me the opportunity to write this book on Zimbabwe, which is a country I dearly love and have great pleasure in promoting it to become a superb tourist destination once again.